COMPUTER LITERACY

Programming • Applications • Awareness

COMPUTER LITERACY

Programming • Applications • Awareness

Francis G. French

Staff Director, Office of Instructional Computing
Department of Education, City of Baltimore
Baltimore, Maryland

Zeney P. Jacobs

Mathematics and Computer Science Teacher
Boys Latin and Middle School
Baltimore, Maryland

William J. Moulds

Supervisor of Mathematics
Howard County Board of Education
Ellicott City, Maryland

Jacob G. Schuchman

Research Specialist
Howard County Board of Education
Ellicott City, Maryland

ALLYN AND BACON, INC., Newton, Massachusetts

Rockleigh, NJ   Atlanta   Warrensburg, MO   Dallas   Rancho Cordova, CA
London   Sydney   Toronto

The following teachers have reviewed this Program before publication:

L. Dale Braithwaite
Computer Science Teacher
Mountain View High School
Orem, Utah

Jan Bybee
Computer Science Resource Specialist
Jefferson County Public Schools
Lakewood, Colorado

ViAnn Olson
Chairperson, Dept. of Math and Computer Science
Cathedral High School
St. Cloud, Minnesota

Credits

Editorial Development Lois B. Arnold, Andrew P. Mastronardi
Preparation Services Martha E. Ballentine
Book Design Jonathan B. Pollard, L. Christopher Valente, George McLean
Book Manufacturing Annie Puciloski
Cover Design John Martucci, L. Christopher Valente
Cover Photo Naoki Okamoto
Photo Research Laurel Anderson
Editorial Services Elizabeth A. Jordan
Illustrations ANCO/Boston, Chartex/Boston, Robert R. Jackson

The authors wish to thank Dolores E. Hague for her valuable contribution
to this title.

A previous edition was published under the title *Beginning Computer Programming: Basic,* © Copyright 1984 by
Allyn and Bacon, Inc.

Hardbound Edition: ISBN 0-205-08491-5   Softbound Edition: ISBN 0-205-08539-3

Printed in the United States of America

1 2 3 4 5 6 7 8 9   90 89 88 87 86 85

CONTENTS

1 | Computers in Your World 1
Introduction

1.1 Libraries and Schools *2,*
1.2 Medicine *5,* **1.3** Business and
Industry *7,* **1.4** Sports and
Entertainment *12,* **1.5** Government *14*
1.6 Computers on the Job *16*

Computer Awareness: It All Began with
Counting *19*

2 | Meet Your Computer 21
Hardware and Keyboarding

Computer Awareness: People Who Made
It Happen *33*

3 | Watch the Monitor 37
The PRINT Statement

3.1 Numbers on Display *38,* **3.2** A, B,
C's on the Screen *42,* **3.3** Strings and
Things You Can See *45*

Computer Awareness: The Family
Tree *50*

4 | Put the Memory to Work 53
Line Numbers, Stored Programs, and Editing

4.1 Instructions, Waiting to RUN *54,*
4.2 Editing a Program *57*

Computer Awareness: Disks and
DOS *65*

5 | Memory and Mathematics 69
Values and Variables

5.1 Storage Space for Numbers *70,*
5.2 Calculation by Computer *73,*
5.3 Memory Locations for Letters—and
More *77*

Computer Awareness: What Is a
Computer? *86*

6 | Out of Order 89
GOTO and FOR-NEXT Loops

6.1 Program Jumps—From Line to Line *90,*
6.2 Again . . . and Again . . . and
Again . . . *94,* **6.3** More About
Loops *98*

Computer Awareness: From Mainframes
to Micros *108*

7 | Timers and Counters 111
More about Loops

7.1 S L O W E R Computing *112,*
7.2 Nested Loops—a Loop Inside a Loop
Inside . . . *115*

Computer Awareness: Computer
Components *126*

8 | Coming INPUT—Going Output 129
Numeric and Alphabetic Values

8.1 Data From the Keyboard *130,*
8.2 More Input about INPUT *137*

Computer Awareness: Getting Data in
and Out *143*

9 | Where the Information Goes 145
READ-DATA Statements

9.1 Values into Variables *140,* **9.2** More
Information about Data *150*

Computer Awareness: A Closer Look at
the Inside *159*

10 | Questions and Answers 161
IF-THEN Statements

10.1 What Comes Next? *162,* **10.2** And
Then He Said . . . *166,* **10.3** More
Decisions *172*

Computer Awareness: Planning
Programs *184*

11 | Charting the Course 187
Flowcharts and Branching

11.1 Pathways through Programs *188*, **11.2** Go with the Flow *196*

Computer Awareness: Electronic Files *205*

12 | Programming Top to Bottom 207
Good Programming Practices

12.1 Before BASIC *208*, **12.2** Keep the User Informed *212*, **12.3** Make Friends with a Computer *215*, **12.4** Best Face Forward *219*, **12.5** Read it Again *225*, **12.6** Data on Demand *229*

Computer Awareness: Sights and Sounds *238*

13 | For Use and Reuse 241
Subroutines

13.1 Reusable Routines *242*, **13.2** Errors to Avoid *250*

Computer Awareness: Role Playing and Reality *257*

14 | Computer Delights 259
BASIC Functions

14.1 Move it Over *260*, **14.2** Chop and Round *266*, **14.3** Pick a Number . . . *271*, **14.1** Bits of Strings *276*

Computer Awareness: Society's Servant *287*

15 | Summing it Up 289
Accumulating Values

15.1 Totals to Average *290*, **15.2** Count on Your Computer *295*

Computer Awareness: Rights and Responsibilities *304*

16 | Keeping it Together 307
Subscripted Variables

16.1 Lots of Lists *308*, **16.2** Playing with Arrays *314*, **16.3** Sets of Strings *320*

Computer Awareness: Computers of the Future *333*

17 | Making it RUN 335
Debugging and Editing

17.1 Trapping Bugs *336*, **17.2** Preparing for the Worst—Programs that Flop *340*

Computer Awareness: Careers and You *350*

18 | Software Applications 353
Evaluating and Using Software

18.1 Working with Words *354*, **18.2** Working with Data *360*, **18.3** Working with Numbers and Formulas *365*, **18.4** Working with Integrated Software *372*, **18.5** Looking at Software *376*

Computer Awareness: Before and after BASIC *385*

Appendix 388

Graphics for the Apple II *388*
Graphics for the TRS-80 *390*
Graphics for the Commodore 64 *392*
BASIC Language Statements and Features for Major Microcomputer Systems *394*
BASIC Statements and Commands for Major Microcomputer Systems *396*

Glossary 398

Index 405

Photo Credits 410

CHAPTER 1

COMPUTERS IN YOUR WORLD

Introduction

Welcome to the world of computers! Today's computers can do wonderful things. What sorts of things would you want to do with a computer? This chapter should give you some ideas.

Libraries and Schools

Alison and her friends were excited as they entered their homeroom. This was their first day in a brand new school.

Mr. Pierce, their homeroom teacher, welcomed the students. "Your new school has a few surprises for you," he told them. "We will begin our day with a tour of the building so that you can see what is really new here."

The first stop on the tour was the library. Alison loved to read and immediately began to look at the colorful displays of books. The first thing she noticed was the white and black label on each book. "Why do all the books have these labels?" she asked Mrs. Lopat, the librarian.

"Our library is computerized," replied Mrs. Lopat. "Each label is a coded number that identifies the book. The code is called a **bar code.** When you want to check out a book, the desk clerk types your name and homeroom number on a keyboard connected to our computer. Then she uses a special tool called a **bar code reader.** The reader is also connected to our computer. It sends the book's coded number to the computer. The computer matches the number with the title and author stored in its memory. Then it checks the book out to you.

Alison had another question. "Why do you need a computer to check out books?" she asked. "In our old school, we just signed a card."

"The computer does other useful things in the library," Mrs. Lopat told the students. "When you check out a book, the computer can search its memory to see how many other books you have already borrowed. It can find out if any of

A librarian entering a new book into a computerized catalog.

your books are overdue. We use the computer's printer to prepare overdue notices."

"The computer works very quickly and accurately," Mrs. Lopat continued. "If you need a book that you cannot find, the computer can tell us if someone else has borrowed that book. It can reserve the book for you and print out a notice for you when the book is returned."

"Come over here," Mrs. Lopat invited. "Mr. Pierce can demonstrate a **computer terminal,** this equipment that looks like a keyboard and TV screen. The terminal is connected to our computer. In your old school, you used a card catalog to find books. Here, the computer holds our card catalog in its memory. Mr. Pierce can enter a subject and all our books with information about that subject will be listed on the screen. He can make a **printout** of the list, using the printer connected to the terminal. You will all be able to use the terminal when you need to find information."

Alison began to understand that the computer could make the library much easier to use. She was eager to see more of the new school.

Memory Bank

*Devices attached to a computer, such as a printer or bar code reader, are called **peripherals**.*

Mr. Pierce took the students through several classrooms. Then he led them into a room that contained rows of microcomputers. "This is the Computer Center," he told the students.

"Who will use these computers?" one of Alison's friends asked Mr. Pierce.

"Everyone will," Mr. Pierce assured the class. "Each of you will come here to learn how to use the computer. As you know, computers cannot do a thing unless a human tells them what to do. The set of directions that tell the computer what to do is called a **program.** As you learn to write programs, you will learn a lot about how computers work. Learning how computers work, what they can do, and how to use them is an important new subject in your school schedule. It is called computer literacy."

Mr. Pierce introduced Miss O'Leary, the teacher in charge of the Computer Center. She told the students, "We have a library of our own right here—a library of computer programs, or **software.** Your teachers will use computer programs to help you learn and to let you practice things you have already learned. This use of computers is called **Computer Assisted Instruction (CAI).** It is a good way to learn and to practice because you can work at your own speed. Most of the programs will give you help if you need it. They will allow you to change incorrect answers or to try again if you make a mistake. Many of the programs also provide a printed record of your work for your teacher."

Alison and her friends did not want to leave the Computer Center. "Do you have a program that we could try?" she asked Miss O'Leary.

"Yes, the computers are ready for you. The program you will try is a **simulation.** A simulation puts you in a special situation and lets you make decisions that control what happens. In this simulation, you will be the owner of a small company. The computer will ask you questions about the supplies you want to order, the advertising you want to do, and the price of the product you make. You will have to make some good decisions if you want to make a profit. I am sure you will enjoy the program—and I hope you make a lot of money!"

Students in a Computer Center.

Exercises

1. What are three things that a computer can do in a library?
2. What topics are included in computer literacy?
3. What kinds of activities are done using CAI?
4. What kind of computer program puts someone in a particular situation?

1.2

Medicine

Mr. Alvarez had an appointment with a doctor at the local hospital. The nurse took his name and began typing, using a terminal connected to the hospital's computer. Mr. Alvarez answered many questions about his medical history and current symptoms. When the nurse read from the screen DO YOU HAVE ANY PAIN? Mr. Alvarez replied, "Yes, I do."

The computer asked a few more questions about the pain and then displayed a picture of a human body on its screen. Mr. Alvarez used a device called a **light pen** to point to the part of his body where he felt pain. The light pen enabled the computer to calculate the exact location of the spot Mr. Alvarez meant. The computer recorded this information and added it to Mr. Alvarez's medical record.

By the time the doctor saw Mr. Alvarez, a printout of the patient's history and a detailed description of his symptoms were ready. The doctor examined Mr. Alvarez and then entered some information into his own computer terminal. This information was also added to Mr. Alvarez's record.

Next the doctor directed the computer to compare Mr. Alvarez's symtoms to those of hundreds of illnesses and diseases stored in its memory. After a few seconds, the doctor read the results of the comparison on the screen. The computer suggested further tests. The doctor agreed and sent Mr. Alvarez to the hospital laboratory.

Many of the laboratory's tasks were controlled by computers. A computer connected to the instruments provided continuous checks of the

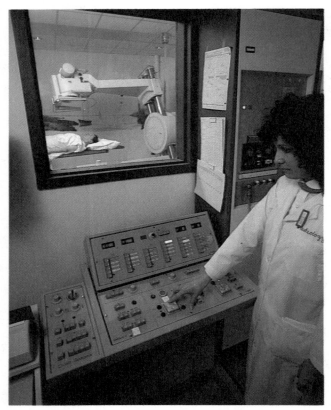

This patient's treatment is being planned and monitored by a computer.

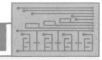

Memory Bank

A computer monitors a patient's condition by using sensors to record temperature, heart rate, blood pressure and other body functions.

quality of the work they did. Technicians were informed immediately if an error occurred. A computer made all of the calculations the laboratory tests needed and printed accurate reports. Because doctors make critical decisions based on the information they receive from laboratories, the high quality and accuracy that the computer helps provide is very important.

The results of Mr. Alvarez's tests were quickly ready for his doctor. The doctor prescribed treatment that soon had Mr. Alvarez feeling much better. Mr. Alvarez was fortunate not to have a serious illness. If he had, he might have seen many additional uses of computers.

A heart attack victim is usually sent directly to a special coronary care unit. There, advanced electronic equipment, including a computer, helps the medical staff diagnose and treat the patient. For example, a special camera connected to a computer can show doctors a picture of the heart, using the computer's **graphics.** The computer picture indicates which areas are healthy and which are diseased.

A patient recovering from a heart attack is watched carefully, not only by doctors and nurses but also by a computer. Special devices called **sensors** are attached to the patient's body. The sensors record the patient's heartbeat, temperature, and blood pressure continuously. They send reports to the computer. The computer compares the patient's records with normal readings stored in its memory. If the patient's readings are very different from the normal ones, the computer alerts the nurse. A printout of the sensor readings is available for the doctor, who can use this information to help decide what further treatment the patient needs.

Exercises

1. How did Mr. Alvarez tell the computer where he was feeling pain?

2. What are three things a computer does in a medical laboratory?

3. What are two ways a computer can be used to help a heart attack victim?

1.3

Business and Industry

Mrs. West looked carefully through the large selection of blouses in the department store. She chose one and took it to the cashier. Attached to the computerized cash register was a **wand,** a device that looked like a large, thick pen. The cashier passed the wand over the special tag on the blouse. Information from the tag was sent to the computer. The price of the blouse appeared on the small screen of the cash register. The tax and the total price were automatically calculated.

Mrs. West had decided to use her charge account. The cashier entered her account number and the computer found her credit record. It added the new charge to her account. The cashier gave Mrs. West the bag containing the blouse and her receipt, printed by the cash register.

Store managers like computerized cash registers because the information from the tags of items sold is stored in the computer's memory. The computer uses this information to prepare reports for the manager. The manager can easily learn which items are selling well, which departments have the most sales, and which items need to be re-ordered. The store's inventory, or record of items it has to sell, is kept by the computer. The inventory is changed as items are sold.

The computer is also used for other jobs, such as keeping records of the store's employees, bookkeeping, and billing.

Supermarkets also use computerized cash registers. Their system is not the same as that of retail stores. Products in supermarkets are

A scanner being used in a supermarket.

marked with a code called the **Universal Product Code (UPC).** The UPC contains information such as the name of the product and its manufacturer.

The UPC is passed over a **scanner,** or code reading device, connected to the cash register. Tone signals tell the clerk whether the UPC information has been sent to the computer or not. The computer's memory contains prices for each product. If the computer has received the UPC, the price of the item appears on the cash register's display screen. The computer totals the purchase and calculates any taxes. When the customer pays, the computer subtracts the total from the amount entered and displays the amount of change due. Then it prints a detailed receipt for the customer.

Supermarket computers keep a very accurate inventory of available products, just as retail stores' computers do.

While stores and supermarkets rely on people to use their computers as tools, some industries are using computers to replace human workers. These computers are **industrial robots.** They do not resemble the humanlike C3-PO of *Star Wars* or even his tin-can-like companion R2-D2. Most robots used in manufacturing are no more than arms with mechanical claws. Although they do not look human, they perform some kinds of jobs better than humans can.

The automobile industry is using ever-increasing numbers of robots in its production lines. Robots can do some difficult, dangerous and boring jobs faster and with more precision than human workers can. Robots can do welding without any discomfort from the extreme heat and without any fear of sparks. A robot performs exactly the same way each time it does a weld, so the work is done with consistently high quality. Robots are very reliable and have fewer absentee days than human workers do. They are tireless and can work many hours without a rest.

Besides welding, robots are used for such work as painting automobiles, dipping hot metal sheets into acid baths, and loading hot, heavy pieces of metal into stamping machines that shape the automobile parts. A robot must be directed to do these jobs by having a set of instructions placed in its memory. One way to do this is called a "walk through." A human operator guides the robot through the motions it must perform. The set of motions, in order, is recorded by the computer. When the robot is started, it will perform the same set of motions over and over, until it is turned off.

Robots are economical workers. Often a single robot can do the jobs of as many as a dozen human workers. Because robot work is always the same high quality, fewer products are rejected. This also saves money. Human workers replaced by robots have to find new jobs. Industry and government are searching for ways to help these workers.

While robots can do certain jobs with amazing skill, they are very limited in the kinds of work they can do. The claws of robots are not as sensitive to the things they touch as human hands are. They are more limited in the kinds of movements they can make.

Researchers are constantly trying to improve robots. A new Japanese robot has been "taught" to sort fish. The robot not only can sort the fish according to their size but also can sort different kinds of fish into different containers.

One of the goals of robot research is to make machines that have more than one sense, that is, robots that can "see" as well as "feel." Another goal is to make a robot that can "learn" and can make changes in its actions to match new conditions, as humans do. Experimenting with robots is one activity in the study of **artificial intelligence,** which is part of **computer science,** the study of computers.

Robots are not the only use that industry has for computers. Engineers use computer calculation and graphics to design and test new products. In the past, automobile engineers designed cars on paper and then had test models built. When changes in the design had to be made, new models had to be built and tested. This was an expensive, time-consuming process.

A robot working on an automobile assembly line.

Today, new cars can be designed, or changes made in current models, using computers. An engineer working on a design for a new bumper, for example, can add information about the bumper to a description of the car already in the computer's memory. The engineer can see a graphic display of the car with the new bumper on the computer's screen. The computer can test the fit of the bumper. It can calculate the bumper's strength under various crash conditions. With a light pen, the engineer can make changes in the screen image that will be recorded by the computer.

Computer-aided design has many advantages for industry. Computers make it much easier for engineers to experiment with different designs and to change existing designs. A computer's memory can hold all the information needed for a complicated design such as a car or an airplane. Seated at a computer terminal, an engineer can quickly and easily get whatever information is needed for the task.

Communication is also made easier by using a computer. Engineers working on different parts of a project can share their knowledge. Managers and customers can use a computer to examine new products. Graphics printers can give engineers precise copies of drawings or tables of information.

When a new product has been designed, **simulators** can be used to test it, or to train people to use it.

A new car must be tested in many ways to be certain that it will be safe and reliable. Automobile engineers use computer simulations of crashes to test individual car parts to find ways to make cars safer. Such details as the placement of seat belt anchors, the fabric used for the straps, and the length and width of the belts are the subjects of hundreds of simulations. Using a computer, engineers can make small changes and try new tests without the expense of actually crashing a real car. Engineers can study various car parts by simulating the kinds of stress that occur in different kinds of accidents. They can make changes that will result in greater protection for passengers.

This airplane flight simulator is being used for pilot training.

Simulators are also used to eliminate danger and reduce expense in training pilots. Flight simulators give pilots an experience that closely resembles real flight. The simulator includes a cockpit identical to one in an airplane. The windows of the training cockpit show views of an airport, its runway, and the surrounding buildings and field. The pilot may see a foggy evening or a bright, sunlit day. The computer image changes thirty times a second as the pilot takes off. The simulator can hold information about many different airports so the pilot can practice taking off and landing all over the world, without leaving the training site.

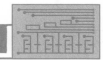

Memory Bank

Simulations, programs that use the computer to imitate a particular situation, are used in industry to test products and to train workers.

The use of simulators is much safer than learning in real flight. A variety of conditions can be faced in the simulator. Pilots can practice responding to all kinds of emergencies. They can spend hours in a simulator without using an expensive aircraft. Both civilian and military pilots are trained with flight simulators.

Exercises

1. How does a retail store clerk use a wand when a customer makes a purchase?
2. What are some advantages of using computers in supermarket check-outs?
3. What are some of the jobs done by industrial robots?
4. What does computer-aided design mean?
5. How do simulations make cars safer?
6. What are some of the advantages of using flight simulators to train pilots?

1.4

Sports and Entertainment

Arie Selinger, coach of the U.S. women's volleyball team for the 1984 Summer Olympics, has faith in computers. He knew that his team would need every edge to be successful against their highly trained Olympic competition. He used computers in several ways to be sure that their training was as effective as possible.

One technique used by the coach is called **digitization.** For this process, pictures of players in action are taken by high-speed cameras, from many different positions. A computer translates the photographs into **digital data,** numbers representing every part of the pictures. The data are used to produce graphics of the volleyball players. Coach Selinger used the computer images to study the timing and the style of his players. He created individual training programs to help each player perfect her skills.

He also studied graphic displays of certain plays, such as the *spike* used by a player near the net to smash the ball over to the opponents' side. Using the computer information, the players worked to refine and sharpen these plays.

Other computerized devices were used by the Olympic athletes to be sure that they got maximum benefit from their training programs. A *force platform* is a device that measures the force and the direction of body movement. It can help athletes by letting them know what kinds of motion produce the most effective performance. The athletes used the force platform to prepare for the Olympics.

Cyclists had help from computerized pedals that measured the force applied by the rider.

This Olympic cyclist received training help from a computer.

The computer helped the cyclists judge whether the force used by both legs was the same and whether the pedaling motion was smooth and efficient.

The success of the American athletes in 1984 will probably mean increased use of computers in the training programs in the future.

The first film animation, featuring drawings that seemed to move, appeared in the 1920s in Walt Disney's *Alice in Cartoonland*. Today, animation is entering a new era with the use of computer graphics. One of the first films to make extensive use of computer animation was another Disney production, *TRON*. This film used a combination of animation and live actors to create a world of the future.

Computer animators, the artists and technicians, work to make a solid object come alive on a flat screen. Animators working to design the light cycles, the bikes of the future in *TRON*, used a set of solid shapes stored in the computer's memory. This allowed the designers to experiment with many shapes. They could look at the cycles from every angle until they had the effect they wanted. The animators put the light cycles through fast-paced, intricate moves to create exciting effects on the movie screen.

Computer images are built from tiny points of light on the computer screen. The more points of light the screen can show, the sharper and more realistic the picture. An ordinary color television screen can show about 300,000 points. A frame of *TRON* may have as many as four million. This gave great clarity and sharpness of motion to the movie's animated sequences.

E x e r c i s e s

1. How did the coach of the U.S. women's volleyball team use a computer and a high-speed camera to help the team?
2. How did cyclists use a computer to help their performance?
3. How did animators for the movie *TRON* use computers?

1.5

Government

Most agencies of the federal government make extensive use of computers. The United States Bureau of the Census could not do its job without them. Every ten years, the Census Bureau collects information about every man, woman, and child in the country. Each household is sent a form with many questions. The person who completes the form fills in small circles for the answers for that household. In 1980, these little circles provided the answers to 3.3 billion questions. Without computers, it would have taken thousands of clerks more than ten years to tally the replies and to compute the totals of the answers to each question. Using high-speed computers, the Census Bureau completed the job in less than one year.

The marked census forms that arrive at the Bureau are first photographed on microfilm. They fill about five thousand miles of film! To translate the information on the film into computer language, a **FOSDIC** (Film Optical Sensory Device for Input to the Computer) is used. The FOSDIC stores all the information on magnetic tape, similar to the tape in music cassettes.

The computers that use the FOSDIC tapes count people in every part of the country and record important information about them. This information is used for many purposes, not only by the government but also by many individuals and businesses. Census data determines to what Congressional districts counties, cities, and towns belong and how many Representatives each state will have. It also helps determine how much federal aid an area will receive.

The 1980 census showed that many more Americans are living longer. This fact is very important to government agencies responsible for programs for the elderly. Businesses looking at the census data saw that not only could an American today expect a longer life but also that families were having fewer babies. Construction companies, after studying the census, could plan to build fewer schools and more retirement homes.

The government is always finding new ways to use computers. Research by the National Oceanic and Atmospheric Administration is improving the prediction of severe weather conditions by using computers. In a research laboratory in Colorado, NOAA is using computers to collect and put together weather information from many sources. Automated weather stations are a major part of the system. They provide a constant stream of facts about meteorological, or weather, conditions. Their information is combined with data from weather satellites and radar stations. The data are translated into color graphics that can show a vivid and accurate picture of local conditions. This gives weather forecasters a valuable tool to help them keep track of fast-moving storm systems within a small area.

The computerized weather system called **PROFS** (Program for Regional Observing and Forecasting Services) is in operation in the Denver area. Color pictures that are constantly being revised to show new conditions give forecasters a clear picture of weather in that area. The computer can put images of cloud formation on top of the area picture to show forecasters how strong storms are and in what direction they are moving. Because PROFS can collect more information and use it faster than previous systems, it helps forecasters give advance warnings about dangerous conditions such as tornados or flash floods. It can save lives and property when sudden, severe storms strike.

A meteorologist using the PROFS computerized weather system.

E x e r c i s e s

1. What does FOSDIC do for the U.S. Census Bureau?
2. What are some of the uses of census data?
3. What are some advantages of the PROFS system?

Computers on the Job

Like the telephone or typewriter, the computer is a tool that people in very different occupations and activities find useful. Often, a computer is essential for a particular task. Some people value computers chiefly for their ability to remember, to organize, to make decisions based on, and to report vast quantities of information. These activities are called **information processing.** Libraries, hospitals, stores and supermarkets, and the Census Bureau are among those who make use of information processing.

Police departments use the information processing ability of computers to help them fight crime. A new computer system stores records about missing children so police all over the country can get the description of a child quickly.

Other people depend more on the computer's ability to perform calculations rapidly and accurately. A high-speed computer can do more calculations in an hour than a person with a calculator could do in a lifetime. Engineers and research scientists find they can do much more work when they use a computer's ability to handle complicated calculations with speed and ease.

A computer is also a tool with many other uses. Banks keep records of all their customers' deposits and withdrawals with computers. New banking services such as automated teller machines are possible only with computers. Newspapers and magazines use computer programs, called **word processors,** to type, edit, and revise their stories. They use computers to set the type to print the publications. Government uses computers for all kinds of jobs, from keeping track of votes in Congress to sending probes to outer space.

The computer age is just beginning. New uses for this versatile tool are being discovered every day. More and more careers are appearing in computer-related fields. For students today, learning about computers is an essential part of education.

E x e r c i s e s

1. What are two abilities of the computer that make it a useful tool?
2. How do banks use computers?

C H A P T E R   S U M M A R Y

1. In libraries, bar codes on books and bar code readers are part of a computerized check-out system. The card catalog is stored in a computer's memory. Schools use computers to teach computer literacy. They offer computer-aided instruction and simulations to help students improve skills in many areas.
2. Hospitals and doctors use computers to keep records and to assist in the diagnosis of illnesses. Some computerized devices can show images of organs to reveal disease. Other devices monitor patients after surgery.
3. Stores and supermarkets use computerized devices to record sales and keep track of inventory. Manufacturers such as the automobile industry use robots to perform tasks that are difficult, dangerous, or boring for people. Industry also uses computers to design products and to train workers, using simulators.
4. The training of athletes is improving through the use of computer analysis of performance. Devices such as force platforms measure body movement. The film technique of animation is also receiving a new look as computer animators design futuristic scenes for the movies.
5. The government deals with vast amounts of data. Agencies like the Bureau of the Census use computers to work with these quantities of information. The FOSDIC system reads census forms

and prepares data for high-speed computers. Weather researchers are using computers to improve forecasting of local weather conditions.

6. New ways to use computers are being found daily and many new computer careers are developing.

PROBLEM SET   1

1. A device used to read a bar code is called a _____.
2. CAI means _____.
3. A record of what items a store has in stock is called an _____.
4. Devices that resemble mechanical arms and do dangerous work in factories are _____.
5. Computer-aided design makes use of the _____ capabilities of a computer.
6. When a computer creates a particular situation that is like a real-life situation, this is called a _____.
7. FOSDIC stands for _____.
8. Forecasters rely on data from automated _____.

Answer each question with a complete sentence.

9. This chapter described some ways schools use computers. In what other ways could computers be used by schools?
10. Computers are sometimes expensive. What reasons would you give someone for spending money on computers for schools?
11. The use of computers by doctors raises a number of ethical questions. Who is to blame if the doctor follows a computer's advice on a case and the computer is wrong? Who is to blame if the doctor ignores the computer's advice and the doctor is wrong?
12. Robots are replacing workers in many industries. Who would be responsible for finding new jobs or paying for retraining of these workers? Why?
13. The use of computers can give athletes a training edge. Would it be fair for two schools to compete in sports if one had computers to help with training programs and the other did not? Why or why not?
14. The Census Bureau tries to ensure privacy by eliminating names before census forms are processed. Is privacy important? Why? What other computer records about a person should be kept private?

COMPUTER AWARENESS

It All Began with Counting

The abacus was the first portable "calculator."

Since long before recorded history, people have tried to keep records and make predictions. Bones with strange markings have been found in ancient caves. They seem to be records of the changing faces of the moon over periods of time. On the walls of other caves are what appear to be pictures of the planets and their positions in the sky at different times. The bones and pictures suggest that the people who used these caves were recording the changes of the seasons.

In various parts of the world there are prehistoric stone constructions built so that the sun's rays hit certain spots only on particular days or so that certain stars can be seen through particular holes or spaces between stones only at certain times of the year. Scientists think that these constructions were, again, ways of knowing the seasons or of predicting eclipses.

If the scientists are correct, these bones, pictures, and constructions are all ancestors of the computer. All of them were used to record past events and, on the basis of these records, to predict the future.

They were not used for counting, however. Counting is an important function of the computer (the word count comes from the same Latin root as the word computer).

At first people probably used their fingers for counting. To keep records, these people used tally marks, bundles of sticks, piles of pebbles and even knots in cords.

When people began to trade, they needed to be able to add and subtract. The piles of pebbles began to be arranged in neat rows on the ground or in grooves in the sand. They could be moved to show increases or decreases. People could **calculate** (from the Latin word calculus meaning pebble or stone) with them.

When the pebbles were placed in stone grooves or strung, as beads, on cords, wires, or rods, the **abacus** was born. It is still used today, especially in China (where it is called the suan pan), and in Japan (where it is known as the soroban).

No one knows when the abacus first appeared. It is recorded in Egypt as early as 450 B.C. and in the Far East at least 150 years earlier. In some form, it may be as many as 5000 years old!

The next important aid in calculating is nowhere near that old. It was invented in 1617 by a Scotsman named Robert Napier, and it was a device to make multiplication easier. **Napier's rods** (or bones) were marked with numerals. By arranging the rods in certain ways, one could read the product of a multiplication, providing one could add one and two digit numbers and knew how to regroup or "carry" from one place value to another. What one did not have to know was the multiplication tables! Napier's rods could multiply a large number of digits by a single digit. If there were several digits in the multiplier, one did each multiplication separately and then added them together exactly as if one were doing the problem in the usual way.

Napier's rods were the first step (after the abacus and some paper-and-pencil adaptations of it) to make computation easier. Other steps came soon after. Devices of one kind or another, ancestors of the computer, had been keeping records for thousands of years. Now they were about to begin calculating.

What Do You Know?

1. For what were the prehistoric ancestors of the computer used? What kinds of information did they record?

2. What is a suan pan? A soroban?

3. Why is the abacus not a real calculator?

4. What marks were on Napier's rods?

5. What were the rods used for?

What Can You Find Out?

1. What is the difference between the Chinese and the Japanese abacus?

2. How is an abacus used?

What Do You Think?

1. How long have calculating devices been used?

2. What is one important difference between Napier's rods and the abacus?

3. What kinds of records do modern computers keep? What kinds of predictions can they make?

CHAPTER 3

MEET YOUR COMPUTER

Hardware and Keyboardin

You've looked at some of the things computers can d
Before you can learn to tell your computer how to c
what YOU want it to do, you need to learn about th
computer you will be using.

MEET CHIP CIRCUITRY

The invention of this tiny chip made small, efficient computers possible.

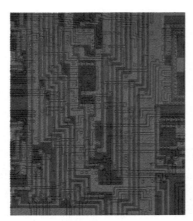

The first computers were made of vacuum tubes, electrical switches, and lots and lots of wires. Computers were so big that they filled very large rooms. Modern advances, particularly the invention of the integrated circuit **chip**, made it possible to build smaller, less expensive computers, able to do much more. The **chip** is so small that it can fit through the eye of a needle. The **chip** may be small in size but it has many **circuits** on its surface that can only be seen under a microscope. Meet the computer character *CHIP CIRCUITRY*. Chip will help you as you use this book while learning to communicate with the computer. Read and pay attention to what *CHIP SAYS*!

Boards hold the chips inside your computer.

LOOKING OVER YOUR COMPUTER

Your computer may look like the one below or like the photo on the left.

Mainframe computers often have no video screen. A printer shows their work.

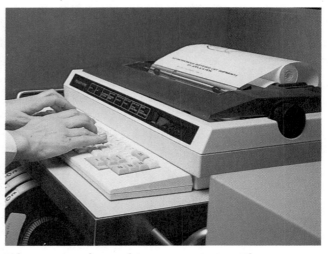

Teletypes may be used to communicate with some computers.

More likely it looks like this:

Both the video screen and the keyboard are in the same cabinet of this microcomputer.

Your computer has many parts. The two most helpful to you are the **keyboard**, shown on the left, and the **video screen**, below.

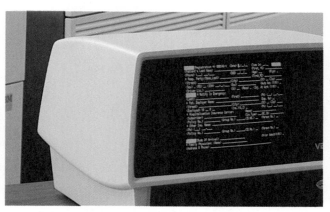

Some computer video screens are called monitors. They only work with computers.

Keyboards may have many keys not found on a typewriter. They do special computer jobs.

The keyboard lets you type numbers, letters, and other characters and send them into the computer. The video screen is like a TV screen that allows you to see what you have typed and can display the computer's work.

Memory Bank

Anything entered through the keyboard is called *INPUT*.

Anything that is displayed on the screen is called *OUTPUT*.

SWITCHING ON YOUR COMPUTER

Computers that have the keyboard and monitor in separate cabinets may have more than one power switch. These switches must be turned on before you can use the computer. (Most owner's manuals suggest that the computer user turn on the monitor *before* turning on the keyboard.)

Monitor switches are located in many different places. An Apple monitor, for instance, may have its power switch on the top of the case. Monitors also have controls for adjusting brightness and contrast, just as a television set does. These are usually clearly marked.

A single switch turns on the monitor and keyboard of the TRS-80. The switch is located under the right side of the keyboard, about three inches from the front of the keyboard. The Apple on/off switch is on the left side of the back panel of the keyboard. The Commodore 64 power switch is on the right side panel of the keyboard.

If you are not planning to use a disk, you may have to do more than simply turn the keyboard on. If you are using an Apple, hold the (CONTROL) (or (CTRL)) key down and press the (RESET) key. A square bracket (]), called a **prompt**, appears on the screen. The computer is ready for you to begin typing. If you are using a TRS-80, hold the (BREAK) key down and press the orange (RESET) button, the only colored key on the keyboard. Then press one of the white keys two times. The TRS-80's prompt is a greater-than symbol (>).

GETTING TO KNOW THE SCREEN

Your screen probably shows a small (perhaps blinking) square of light somewhere on its left side. This is called the **cursor** and it tells you where you are on the screen. Touch some of the keys (letters) on the keyboard and see what happens to the screen. As you press a key, that letter appears on the screen and the cursor moves across the screen. Continue pressing letters to see what happens when you go past the end of the line.

GETTING TO KNOW THE KEYBOARD

All of the letters you typed appeared on the screen, but the computer (the *real* computer, inside) does not *know* they are there yet. The letters must now be sent inside to the computer.

Look on your keyboard for a key that looks like:

> **ENTER**   or like: **RETURN**

Your computer should have one or the other. Now go ahead and press that key.

These things should have happened on your screen:

a. The cursor jumped down to the beginning of the next line. This is called a **carriage return**.

b. The computer printed a message telling you that you made an error or mistake. Do not worry about the error or the message. No harm was done.

c. If b. happened, another carriage return was made and the computer is waiting for your next entry.

Look a little more closely at the keyboard. The letters are <u>not</u> in alphabetical order, but are arranged as they are on a typewriter. In addition to letters and numbers, there are many other characters on the keys. Some of the keys have more than one character.

For example, this key: or this one:

> **#**   **+**
> **3**   **;**

and, of course, many others. The character on the top of the key is called an **upper character**. The character on the bottom of the key is called a **lower character**.

If you press any of these keys, the lower character will appear on the screen. To get the upper character, first find and press this key:

> **SHIFT**

Hold the ⌐SHIFT⌐ key down while you press the other key. After the upper character appears, release both keys.

Most microcomputers display only capital letters when they are turned on.

For the Apple IIe, press the ⌐SHIFT LOCK⌐ key and release it. When it pops up, you can type small letters.

For the Commodore 64, hold the Commodore logo key down and press one of the shift keys. Release the two keys to type small letters.

For the TRS-80, press a shift key and type ▯. Release the shift key for small letters.

When you are using small letters, hold the shift key down to make any letter you type a capital letter.

A CLOSER LOOK AT THE KEYBOARD

On most keyboards there is a long, unmarked key that looks like this:

This is called the **spacebar** and allows you to type in a blank space. Try it and see for yourself.

You can do all kinds of things with a computer, using only one or two fingers and hunting for each key as you need it. This can be a great waste of time, however. You will find it easier and more efficient if you master some keyboarding skills.

When you are using a computer, sit up straight, directly in front of the keyboard. Never slouch or slump in your chair. Your hips should be against the back of the chair, your feet flat on the floor, and your knees apart. You should be relaxed and comfortable, to avoid getting tired.

You will learn where all the keys are located as you practice using them. Typists use a standard hand position, resting their fingertips lightly on the **home keys**, as shown in the diagram on the next page.

Using correct posture will help keep you from getting tired.

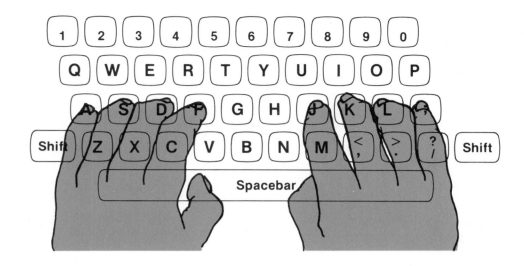

It is very important that you keep your touch light and quick! Many computers repeat keystrokes if a key is held down. Curve your fingers slightly and hold them as close to the keys as you can without depressing the keys. Use either your right or left thumb to depress the spacebar. Good keyboarding skills can only be developed through practice.

PRACTICE SKILL DEVELOPMENT

Sit comfortably in front of your computer and put your fingers in the home key position. Type the following lines, using the home keys. Be sure you use the indicated finger of the left or right hand. Space once between each group of letters in each line. Practice until you can type each line without a single mistake. (When you press the `RETURN` or `ENTER` key at the end of each line, ignore the error message that appears on the monitor.)

FIRST FINGER

```
JJJJ FFFF JJJJ FFFF JJJJ FFFF
FFFF JJJJ FFFF JJJJ FFFF JJJJ
```

SECOND FINGER

```
DDDD KKKK DDDD KKKK DDDD KKKK
KKKK DDDD KKKK DDDD KKKK DDDD
```

THIRD FINGER

```
LLLL SSSS LLLL SSSS LLLL SSSS
SSSS LLLL SSSS LLLL SSSS LLLL
```

FOURTH FINGER

```
AAAA ;;;; AAAA ;;;; AAAA ;;;;
;;;; AAAA ;;;; AAAA ;;;; AAAA
```

A finger on each hand is identified by its home key position. For example:

First finger, left hand, is the F-finger.
First finger, right hand, is the J-finger.
Second finger, left hand, is the D-finger.
Second finger, right hand, is the K-finger.

The diagram below shows what fingers are used for each of the other keys.

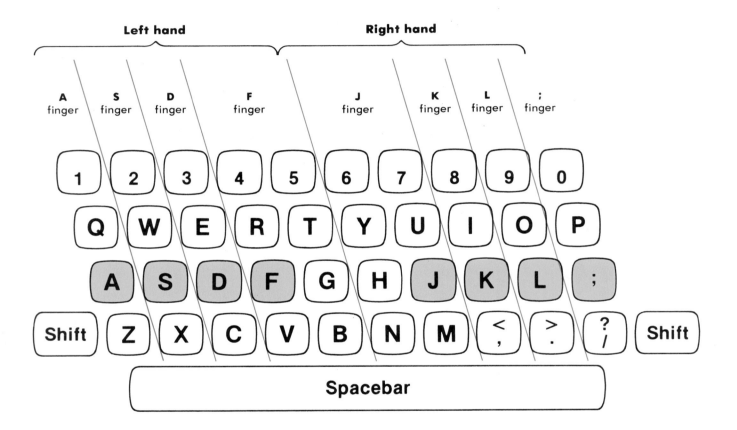

BOOST YOUR KEYBOARDING SKILLS

Using the correct finger-key assignment, type each of the following lines three times. Practice until you can type the lines without making a mistake. (Remember, use the shift key to type capital letters.)

1. PRACTICE MAKES PERFECT.
2. THE COW JUMPED OVER THE MOON.
3. GAIL LOVES HORSES AND HORSES LOVE HER.
4. 4 SCORE AND 7 YEARS AGO
5. MY FATHER IS 45 YEARS OLD TODAY.
6. MAX AMAZED BETH WHEN HE DOVE IN THE SEA.
7. 2395 BALTIMORE, MD 24738 ZIP CODE

E x e r c i s e s

Using your computer or a typewriter, type the following exercises to develop your keyboarding skills. Remember to use the correct finger-key assignment.

1. WASH WASH WASH WASH WASH WASH WASH WASH   S, A, J
2. P53K P53K P53K P53K P53K P53K P53K   F, ;, D, K
3. BASIC BASIC BASIC BASIC BASIC BASIC   F, A, S, K, D
4. LIFE LOVE LIFE LOVE LIFE LOVE LIFE LOVE   L, K, F, D
5. SPACEBAR SPACEBAR SPACEBAR SPACEBAR   S, ;, A, D, F

Identify the correct finger-key assignment for each of the following letters.

6. Q   7. V   8. 0 (zero)   9. M
10. R   11. 4   12. 9   13. X
14. 2   15. C   16. Y   17. 0

Type each of these sentences three times, without making a mistake.

18. NOW IS THE TIME FOR ALL GOOD PEOPLE TO COME TO THE AID OF THEIR COUNTRY.
19. 235 STUDENTS FAILED TO OBTAIN A PASSING GRADE OF 70.
20. THE MEMBERS OF THE COMMITTEE WILL MEET ON OCTOBER 15.
21. JOHN'S TUTOR WILL SEE HIM ON WEDNESDAY AT 3:45 P.M.

Chip's Challenges

22. Type the following letter without making a mistake. (Ignore error messages.) If you do make a mistake, start again at the beginning.

DEAR GRACE,

THIS IS MY FIRST TYPED NOTE. I HAVE LEARNED WHICH FINGERS TO USE FOR EACH KEY. (MY FINGERS SEEM TO "REMEMBER" WHERE THE KEYS ARE.) I AM BABY-SITTING TONIGHT TO EARN SOME MONEY. I AM SAVING ALL OF THE MONEY I EARN FOR MY OWN COMPUTER. I ALREADY HAVE $46!

LOVE,
ADA

CLEARING YOUR SCREEN

In this book you will often see the instruction **Clearscreen**. This is not really a command for the computer because each computer has its own special command for clearing the screen. Find out the correct command for your computer and use it each time the instruction Clearscreen is shown. Some of the correct commands used by microcomputers are listed below.

For Radio Shack TRS-80,	type CLS
For the Apple,	type HOME
For the Atari,	type GR.0
For the PET,	type PRINT"♡"

Finally, press the (RETURN) or (ENTER) key and type the word NEW.

Again, press (RETURN) or (ENTER) You have just given your computer the first message that it "understands." The word, NEW, tells the computer to clear out, or empty, everything, and permits you to begin again.

Chip's Bits

The BASIC words in this book are printed using a special typeface called Universal **OCR**. **OCR** characters were designed to be read by a special device which can enter information into computers. Each character is distinct and unique. It cannot be confused with another character. Some typewriters can use **OCR** type.

A WORD OF CAUTION

The letter O (oh) and the number 0 (zero) may look very much alike to you. To your computer, however, they are quite different. Most computers display the zero with a line through it like this:

0

Be very careful when typing these and other characters which look alike. Do not type one when you mean to type the other.

BASIC — A LANGUAGE OF THE COMPUTER

CHIP SAYS: BASIC IS AN EASY COMPUTER LANGUAGE TO LEARN.

Why do you think the computer printed error messages when you practiced on the keyboard? That is right. The computer did not understand what was typed. In order to communicate with the computer, it is necessary to learn a language that the computer will understand. The computer language you will learn in this book is called BASIC.

BASIC stands for, and is made up of, the first letter in each of the words Beginner's All-purpose Symbolic Instruction Code. It is the most popular conversational computer language.

CHAPTER SUMMARY

1. The computer can do wonderful things for you but only if you tell it what to do and how to do it.
2. You are introduced to the computer by looking at the keyboard and the video screen.
3. The cursor lets you know where the computer will place the next character on the screen.
4. Most of the keys on the keyboard are like those on a typewriter. They are not in alphabetical order.
5. Anything entered through the keyboard is called INPUT.
6. Anything displayed on the video screen is called OUTPUT.

PROBLEM SET   2

In Exercises 1 through 10, fill in the blanks with the word that completes the sentence correctly.

1. Two parts of the computer are very important for the beginner to understand. They are the _____ and the _____ _____.
2. The computer keyboard is very much like that of a _____.
3. The _____ tells you where the computer will place the next character on the screen.
4. Anything entered through the keyboard is called _____.
5. Anything that the computer displays on the screen is called _____.
6. Everything you type can be entered into the computer by pressing the _____ key or the _____ key.
7. When the computer begins a new line and goes to the beginning of that line, it has made a _____ return.
8. If a key has more than one character on it, you can produce the upper character by holding down the _____ key while pressing that key.
9. If you wish to place a blank space in what you type, you must press the _____ bar.
10. A computer language that you will use in this book is called the _____ language.

11. Find each of the characters below on your keyboard. If you must hold down the ⌈ SHIFT ⌋ key to produce that character, write the letter S in the space beside it. If you can type that character without holding the ⌈ SHIFT ⌋ key, write a zero in the space beside it. Do not write in this book.

a. * _____   b. + _____   c. A _____
d. W _____   e.) _____   f. 0 _____
g. < _____   h. ≑ _____   i. ￢ _____
j. - _____

The following exercises may be done on a typewriter or on the keyboard of a computer. If you use a computer, every once in a while you must press the ⌈ RETURN ⌋ or ⌈ ENTER ⌋ key. When you do this, the computer will print an error message. Just ignore all error messages. Type each of the following:

12. All of the letters of the alphabet, in alphabetical order.
13. Your name, address, and ZIP code.
14. Your phone number.
15. All of the numbers 0 through 9.
16. The sentence: MY DOG HAS FLEAS.
17. The sentence: THE QUICK BROWN FOX JUMPS OVER THE LAZY DOG.
    (This sentence contains every letter of the alphabet.)
18. Each of the characters:
    ? + = *) (' & % ≑ # " ! : ; ￢ . /
19. The tongue twisters below:
    a. SHE SELLS SEA SHELLS BY THE SEA SHORE.
    b. RUBBER BABY BUGGY BUMPERS.
    c. THE SINKING STEAMER SUNK.
    d. THE SIXTH SICK SHEIK'S SIXTH SHEEP.

COMPUTER AWARENESS

A model of Babbage's analytical engine.

People Who Made It Happen

During the fifteenth and sixteenth centuries, many scientists began to study the earth and the universe. They needed to complete long and difficult calculations. More than five hundred years ago, the Moslem mathematician Al-Kashi invented several tools to help astronomers and astrologers. These tools helped them compute the locations of planets and calculate the dates of eclipses.

Late in the sixteenth century, Francois Vieta, an Italian mathematician, began using letters to stand for unknown quantities. Today these letters are called variables. They are like the labels computers use for memory locations. With variables, scientists could write equations.

In 1623 a German mathematics professor, Wilhelm Schickard, designed and built a machine to do arithmetic automatically. This was probably the world's first mechanical calculator. Unfortunately, both the machine and its design were destroyed by fire, and Schickard died before he could design and build another. Only reports of his wonderful invention exist today.

Historians say that Blaise Pascal, a young Frenchman, began the calculator age. In 1642, when he was only nineteen, he built a mechanical adding machine that used gears to count as it added. The machine could carry values from one place column to another. It worked the way a bicycle or automobile odometer does when it "turns over" from 9 to 10 or from 999.9 to 1000.0.

Thirty years later, the German mathematician Gottfried Leibnitz invented a multiplier based on Pascal's ideas. Leibnitz's machine could not only multiply, it could also divide and find roots of numbers. It used a special device called the Leibnitz wheel to do the calculating. This wheel is the real ancestor of modern calculators. The machine itself had two separate parts. The first was used for addition and subtraction. The second was used for multiplication and division.

No other innovative ideas appeared in the history of computing until the beginning of the nineteenth century. Then a French weaver named Joseph M. Jacquard made an important contribution to computers. He invented a mechanical loom controlled by punched cards. Pins went through each card where there were holes and raised or lowered some of the warp, or foundation, threads. The position of the threads made the designs woven into the cloth. The cards made it possible to produce the same pattern over and over again. (In Jacquard's day, the holes were punched in the cards by hand. This was a slow process. Today, computers direct the hole-punching task quickly and accurately.)

In England, a banker named Charles Babbage designed and built a small "Difference Engine" to solve certain equations. (Most machines of that time were called engines.) Babbage's engine was powered by steam, the only energy source available at the time. A friend of his, Lady Ada Lovelace, wrote instructions for the machine and helped Babbage explain its operation. The British government gave Babbage money to work on a larger machine, but it was never built. Manufacturers in the early nineteenth century could not work with the precision and accuracy necessary to make the parts that this wonderful "Analytical Engine" would need. The larger machine would have had two parts. Babbage planned a Store, where variables and results of operations would be kept, and a Mill, where arithmetic operations would be performed. The operation of the machine, Lovelace suggested, could be directed by punched cards, as Jacquard's loom was. Because the cards could be changed, the machine would be able to work with many kinds of equations and be a general-purpose engine.

Babbage's models show that his planned engine would have provided for calculation, for storing information, and for its input and output. The machine's operation would have been directed by stored instructions, similar to today's programs. These are all characteristics of modern computers.

Pehr Georg Scheutz, a Swedish lawyer and printer, heard of Babbage's ideas. He taught himself the mathematics and the mechanical skills needed to build a Difference Engine. This Engine is now owned by the Smithsonian Institution.

At the same time that Babbage was designing his engines, another Englishman, George Boole, was using the ideas of algebra to solve problems in logic. Boolean Algebra is a way of comparing information and it is used by computers today. Boole used two mathematical symbols, 1 and 0, in his algebra. In his algebra, 1 symbolizes true and 0 symbolizes false.

Although the early calculating machines could compute, they could not make a permanent record of their results. The first practical machines to do this were invented by D. E. Felt and William S. Burroughs at the end of the nineteenth century. The familiar adding machine with its printed tape is a direct descendant of their machines.

During this same period Herman Hollerith designed a machine that could "read" information from punched cards. His ideas were based on the operation of the Jacquard loom. His machine sorted the cards.

Electricity passed through the holes and opened bins, where certain cards could be stored. Where there were no holes, no electricity could get through and no bins were opened. The machine needed a human operator to put the cards in the correct bins. Still, it was much faster than completely human card-sorting. Hollerith's machine was first used on a large scale in the 1890 census. The results of that census were made available in record time.

As the twentieth century progressed, practical know-how began to catch up with the dreams of computer designers. Machinery was now available to make the most accurate parts a computer builder could need, and electricity was ready to supply power.

In 1939, Howard Aiken of Harvard University and George R. Stibitz of the Bell Telephone Laboratories began work on an electromechanical computer. This machine, the Automatic Sequence Controlled Calculator, is called the MARK I today. MARK I had four major improvements over punched card machines. It could work with both positive and negative numbers, it could use mathematical functions, it was fully automatic, and it could calculate. The machine used electrically operated switches, or **relays,** to control and direct electric current. These relays were like those the telephone company used to direct calls. MARK I could add two numbers in one third of a second, and could multiply two 23-digit numbers in less than five seconds.

MARK I was the first real computer. It took five years to build, and it started a revolution in **data processing,** or information handling. Fifteen years after it was built, MARK I—and its descendants MARK II, MARK III, and MARK IV—was out of date, replaced by faster machines.

The man who led the way into the modern computer age was John von Neumann, a mathematician born in Hungary. During World War II, von Neumann worked for the United States government. He believed that mechanical computers would always be too slow and unreliable and thought they should be completely electronic. He thought that the number system based on ten fingers, the system you use, was too complicated. He said that computers should use a number system with only two digits, 1 representing electricity on and 0 representing electricity off. He wanted a computer to have a built-in memory that would hold incomplete results as the computer calculated. He believed the memory should also store a set of instructions—a program—to direct the computer and that this set of instructions should be easy to change.

A British mathematician and logician named A. M. Turing had proved that if a machine could do simple arithmetic and algebra it could do any complicated calculation. Von Neumann said that future computers should be universal Turing machines, able to do any computation their users wished.

The stage was set for the opening act of the computer age.

What Do You Know?
1. Who invented the first mechanical adding machine?
2. Who invented the multiplier?
3. What did Joseph Jacquard invent?
4. Who worked with Charles Babbage?
5. What ideas from the Analytical Engine are used in computers today?
6. What ideas of John von Neumann are used today?

What Can You Find Out?
1. What is Boolean Algebra?
2. What do the holes on Hollerith cards stand for?
3. Where are Hollerith cards used today?

What Do You Think?
1. Why was Jacquard's invention so important?
2. Why was MARK I slower than computers built today?

WATCH THE MONITOR

The PRINT Statement

The PRINT instruction makes a computer show numbers, answers to arithmetic computation, words, and symbols. Punctuation is used to arrange the information on the screen.

3.1

Numbers on Display

DISCOVER FOR YOURSELF

For each **PRINT** instruction, guess the computer's output. Write your guess on a sheet of paper. Check your answers by doing the exercises on your computer. Do not forget to press the RETURN or ENTER key after typing each line.

STEP

COMPUTER DISPLAYS

1. PRINT 5
2. PRINT 9+16
3. PRINT 17-8
4. PRINT 3+4,10
5. PRINT 7*12
6. PRINT 24/6
7. PRINT 9-5,11+4,2*8
8. PRINT 8,3,5
9. PRINT 8;3;5

WHAT DID YOU LEARN?

Unlike the typing experiments you performed in Chapter 2, these exercises made the computer do something. The computer completed an action because it was given a BASIC instruction that it *understood*. The word **PRINT** is a BASIC instruction that tells the computer to display (or print) information on the screen. The computer also printed numbers which were the results of **computations**. (Computer people like to call "numbers" **numeric constants**.)

See what happened in the *Discover for Yourself* exercise on the next page.

Step 2

```
PRINT 9+16
25
```

The **sum**, 25, was displayed instead of the example 9+16.

── Symbol for addition.

── Numeric constant.

Step 3

```
PRINT 17-8
9
```

The **difference**, 9, was displayed instead of the example 17-8.

── Symbol for subtraction.

── Numeric constant.

Step 5

```
PRINT 7*12
84
```

The **product**, 84, was displayed instead of the example 7*12.

── Symbol for multiplication.

── Numeric constant.

Step 6

```
PRINT 24/6
4
```

The **quotient**, 4, was displayed instead of the example 24/6.

── Symbol for division.

── Numeric constant.

Chip's Bits

If automobile design had advanced as fast as computer design has, a Rolls Royce would cost less than $3.00 and would travel three million miles on a gallon of gas!

Memory Bank

+ . . . *addition*
− . . . *subtraction*
* . . . *multiplication*
/ . . . *division*

Did you notice that several numeric constants (numbers) can be printed at the same time on the same line? Commas and semicolons in **PRINT** statements tell the computer to display more than one number on a line. For example:

Commas in a PRINT statement tell the computer to display numeric constants (numbers) evenly spaced across the screen. The areas on the screen where the numbers are printed are called **fields**.

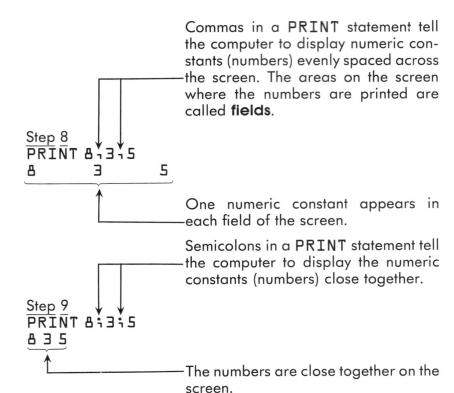

Step 8
PRINT 8,3,5
8   3   5

One numeric constant appears in each field of the screen.

Semicolons in a PRINT statement tell the computer to display the numeric constants (numbers) close together.

Step 9
PRINT 8;3;5
8 3 5

The numbers are close together on the screen.

Not all computers have the same number of fields across their screens. Some computers display three fields across while others display four.

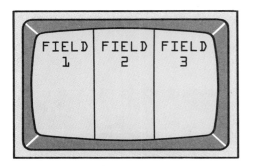

FIELD 1 | FIELD 2 | FIELD 3

CHIP SAYS: EXPERIMENT WITH YOUR COMPUTER USING COMMAS AND SEMICOLONS.

Type the following statements:

Commas	Semicolons
PRINT 1	PRINT 1
PRINT 1,2	PRINT 1;2
PRINT 1,2,3	PRINT 1;2;3
PRINT 1,2,3,4	PRINT 1;2;3;4
PRINT 1,2,3,4,5	PRINT 1;2;3;4;5
PRINT 1,2,3,4,5,6	PRINT 1;2;3;4;5;6

USE WHAT YOU HAVE LEARNED | Study the following PRINT instructions and the resulting computer responses.

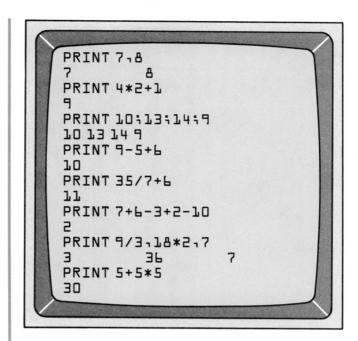

CHIP WONDERS: DO YOU AGREE WITH THE RESULTS COMPUTED AND DISPLAYED?

```
PRINT 7,8
7          8
PRINT 4*2+1
9
PRINT 10;13;14;9
10 13 14 9
PRINT 9-5+6
10
PRINT 35/7+6
11
PRINT 7+6-3+2-10
2
PRINT 9/3,18*2,7
3          36          7
PRINT 5+5*5
30
```

E x e r c i s e s

Write the BASIC instruction that will make the computer display each of the following numeric constants (numbers):

1. 13 and 26

2. Sum of 13 and 26

3. Odd numbers between 8 and 16

4. Difference between 18 and 12

5. Quotient of 112 divided by 7

6. Even numbers between 5 and 15

7. Year Columbus discovered America

8. Product of 83 and 52

9. Product of 9 and 3, decreased by 11

10. Year the Declaration of Independence was signed, divided by 16

Type the following BASIC instructions. Guess what the computer will display before you press (**RETURN**) or (**ENTER**).

11. `PRINT 1,4,7,8`

12. `PRINT 16-14+32`

13. `PRINT 16*2+64/16`

14. `PRINT 8/4*6-10`

Chip's Challenges

Type the following BASIC instructions. Guess what the computer will display before you press (**RETURN**) or (**ENTER**).

15. `PRINT 16-8/2`

16. `PRINT 3*8+4`

17. `PRINT 17*2+3*(9-5)`

18. `PRINT 3*(8+4)`

19. `PRINT (14+13)/9`

20. `PRINT (8+2)*(14-3)`

3.2

A, B, C's on the Screen

DISCOVER FOR YOURSELF

For each **PRINT** instruction, guess the computer's output. Write your guess on a sheet of paper. Check your answers by doing the exercise on your computer. Do not forget to press the RETURN or ENTER key after typing each line.

STEP

1. PRINT 5
2. PRINT 5+4
3. PRINT 3+6,7+5
4. PRINT 9+7;5+12
5. PRINT 5+6
6. PRINT "5+6"

COMPUTER DISPLAYS

?
?
?
?
?
?

WHAT DID YOU LEARN?

Did you get these results for Steps 5 and 6?

Step 5

PRINT 5+6 ◄——————What you typed.
11 ◄——————What the computer displayed.

Step 6

PRINT "5+6" ◄——————What you typed.
5+6 ◄——————What the computer displayed.

Did you notice that the **PRINT** instruction with quotation marks (**"**) in it made the computer display what was inside the marks? The computer did not display the sum of 5 and 6. In fact, you may put anything you want between the quotation marks and the computer will display it. Anything inside quotation marks is called a **string constant** or **string**.

USE WHAT YOU HAVE LEARNED

1. You enter: PRINT "2+3="
    The computer displays: 2+3=
    The computer prints everything within the quotation marks.

2. You enter: PRINT "JOHN";"DOE"
    The computer displays: JOHNDOE.
    Remember, a semicolon in a **PRINT** statement tells the computer to display items close together.

3. You enter: PRINT "JOHN ";"DOE"
    The computer displays: JOHN DOE
    A space inside the quotation marks often makes the computer output look better.

4. You enter: PRINT "4+5=",9
    The computer displays: 4+5=   9
    Remember, a comma in a **PRINT** statement tells the computer to display items in zones or fields.

Memory Bank

Strings

The computer displays anything within quotation marks in a **PRINT** statement. The item within quotes is called a **string constant** or **string**.

E x e r c i s e s

Each statement below has an error. Find the error and write the statement correctly.

1. PRINT YESTERDAY'S TEMPERATURE"
2. PIRNT "2+3=5"
3. PRINT MY NAME IS CHIP

Write a **PRINT** statement that will make the computer display each of the following strings:

4. 6+7=13
5. BOILING POINT OF WATER IS 100
6. ROSES ARE RED, VIOLETS ARE BLUE
7. 12=6+6

Chip's Challenges

8. Enter the following:

```
PRINT, 1/9
PRINT, 11/9
PRINT, 111/9
PRINT, 1111/9
PRINT, 11111/9
PRINT, 111111/9
PRINT, 1111111/9
PRINT, 11111111/9
```

a. Write down the results.
b. What does the comma immediately after PRINT do to the display?
c. What patterns can you find in the answers?

"Silicon Valley" is the name given to a small section of California about 45 miles south of San Francisco. It got the name because of the large number of microprocessor chips produced there. More than 3,000 electronics firms are located in the area, which is in Santa Clara County.

3.3

Strings and Things You Can See

For each PRINT instruction, guess the computer's output. Write your guess on a sheet of paper. Check your answers by doing the exercises on your computer. Do not forget to press the (RETURN) or (ENTER) key after typing each line.

STEP

COMPUTER DISPLAYS

1. PRINT 5
2. PRINT 5,4
3. PRINT "FIVE"
4. PRINT 6+2,6*2,6/2,6-2
5. PRINT "FIVE","FOUR"
6. PRINT 1,4,"THE MONEY"

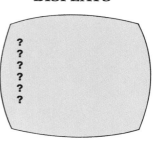

WHAT DID YOU LEARN?

Did you notice that numbers and letters appeared in the same PRINT statement in Step 6? The computer displayed:

```
1          4              THE MONEY
```

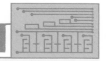

Memory Bank

Any combination of numbers and letters can appear in a PRINT statement.

By mixing numbers and strings within a PRINT statement, you can have the computer display timely messages.

45

Chip's Bits

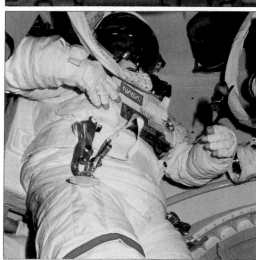

Pocket computers went into space in the November, 1982, flight of the space shuttle *Columbia*. Each astronaut carried a hand-held computer made by Hewlett-Packard. NASA said the pocket computers alone could have given the astronauts enough information to land the shuttle safely.

USE WHAT YOU HAVE LEARNED

1. **COSMIC COUNTDOWN**
   You enter:

   `PRINT 10;9;8;7;6;5;4;3;2;1; "BLASTOFF"`

   The computer displays:

   `10 9 8 7 6 5 4 3 2 1 BLASTOFF`

   Remember, a semicolon between constants in a **PRINT** statement makes the computer display them close together.

2. **HAMLET'S LAMENT**
   You enter:

   `PRINT 2;"B OR NOT ";2;" B"`

   The computer displays: `2 B OR NOT 2 B`

3. **ADDITION PROBLEMS**
   You enter: `PRINT "5+4= ";9`
   The computer displays: `5+4= 9`

   You enter:

   `PRINT 5;" + ";4;" = ";5+4`

   The computer displays: `5 + 4 = 9`

   There is no need to know the answer beforehand. The computer can compute it in a **PRINT** statement.

4. **SUBTRACTION PROBLEM**
   You enter: `PRINT "12-6= ";9`

   The computer displays: `12-6= 9`

   The computer prints everything between quotation marks. You can have it display statements that are obviously incorrect.

5. **NEW DEFINITIONS**
   You enter: `PRINT "TEN= ";30/2`

   The computer displays: `TEN= 15`

1. Use the **PRINT** statement to complete the following chart:

Feet	Inches
7	_____
3.5	_____
2.34	_____

   Remember, to change from feet to inches, multiply the number of feet by 12.

   Look at the solution on the next page.

   You enter:

```
PRINT 7;" FEET= ";7*12;" INCHES"
PRINT 3.5;" FEET= ";3.5*12;" INCHES"
PRINT 2.34;" FEET= ";2.34*12;" INCHES"
```

The computer displays:

```
7 FEET= 84 INCHES
3.5 FEET= 42 INCHES
2.34 FEET= 28.08 INCHES
```

2. Use the **PRINT** statement to find Ms Jones'
   Mystery Numbers:
   Number 1: 373*4
   Number 2: 250 times 6 minus 8
   Number 3: 4476 divided by 3
   Solution:
   You enter:

```
PRINT "NUMBER 1 ";373*4
PRINT "NUMBER 2 ";250*6-8
PRINT "NUMBER 3 ";4476/3
```

The computer displays: NUMBER 1 1492
                        NUMBER 2 1492
                        NUMBER 3 1492

E x e r c i s e s

Write the BASIC instruction to have the computer display the
following:

1. HI HO HI HO
2. TIPPECANOE AND TYLER, TOO
3. 2 4 6 8 WHO DO WE APPRECI 8

What will the computer display if the following statements are
entered?

4. PRINT "WORLD WAR I BEGAN IN ";638*3
5. PRINT "17+3*4= ";17+3*4
6. PRINT "TWELVE= ";45/3

 ## Chip's Challenges

Write **PRINT** statements to complete the following tables:

7. Sq Ft	Sq Yd
18	_____
35	_____
81.2	_____
42	_____
9 sq ft = 1 sq yd	

8. Scoops	Cones
_____	10
_____	72
_____	15
_____	30
1 cone = 2 scoops	

CHAPTER SUMMARY

1. The BASIC instruction—**PRINT**—makes the computer display information.
2. BASIC arithmetic symbols are:
    + for addition
    − for subtraction
    * for multiplication
    / for division.
3. Commas and semicolons are used to space information.
4. Computer professionals call numbers numeric constants.
5. Any collection of letters, numbers, symbols, or blank spaces enclosed in quotation marks is called a string constant or string.
6. You can mix any number of string and numeric constants in a **PRINT** statement. Make sure you use the correct punctuation.

PROBLEM SET   3

Write the BASIC instruction that will make the computer display each of the following numeric constants.

1. 134, 17, and 19
2. The difference between 1039 and 997
3. The whole numbers less than 7
4. The odd numbers between 64 and 76
5. The product of 61 and 22 increased by 107
6. The number of runs scoring when a grand slam home run is hit, multiplied by the number of points scored on a touchdown
7. The whole numbers greater than 15 but less than 27
8. The even numbers between 33 and 45
9. The year of the battle of the Alamo
10. Two hundred fifty thousand six hundred twelve

Type the following BASIC instructions. Guess what the computer will display before pressing the (RETURN) or (ENTER) key.

```
11.  PRINT 1776,1492,1860
12.  PRINT 82-60+22-40
13.  PRINT 19-3*4,84/4,16+18/2
14.  PRINT 43+31;92*4,36-23,224/16
15.  PRINT 3*4+17-25/5+18
16.  PRINT 12;" IS A FACTOR OF ";24
17.  PRINT "3+5= ";3+5
```

18. PRINT 1412;" E. BAYWOOD ST."
19. PRINT "WON 10 LOST 5 AVERAGE= ";10/15
20. PRINT "AMOUNT DUE ";25;" DOLLARS"

Use PRINT statements to complete the following tables:

21. Calculate the number of wirbuls.

Ridgets	Wirbuls	
5	?	
17	?	2 Wirbuls = 1 Ridget
43	?	

22. Calculate the number of miles shown on a map.

Inches	Miles	
6	?	MAP SCALE:
10	?	1 inch = 7 miles
2.5	?	

Chip's Challenges

23. Write PRINT statements to have the computer display:

a. The perimeter of the triangle.

3 in.   5 in.

4 in.

b. The perimeter of the rectangle.

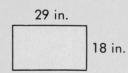

7 in.

6 in.

c. The area of the rectangle.

29 in.

18 in.

24. Write a PRINT statement to have the computer display your school's name.

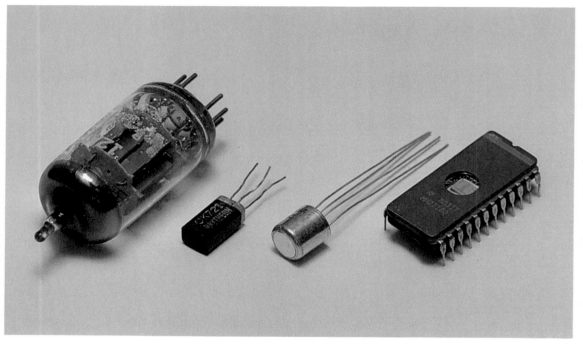

The four generations of computers: (from left) vacuum tubes, transistors, integrated circuits, and chips.

The Family Tree

During World War II, the governments of many nations invested in computer research. They believed that computers could help them in their war efforts. Professors and students at universities all over the world studied ideas of the past. MARK I was one result of the research at Harvard University. A computer called Whirlwind was built at the Massachusetts Institute of Technology. And, near the end of the war, something remarkable happened at the University of Pennsylvania.

When Thomas A. Edison invented the first practical electric light bulb in the late 1870s, he discovered that the heated wire of the bulb (the filament) gave off electrons. These electrons stayed near the filament. They formed an electron cloud or charge. Whatever work the electrons could do besides heat the wire was wasted in the bulb. The **vacuum tube** put the electrons to work.

A vacuum tube looks a little like a light bulb. Like a light bulb, it has a filament. It also has a metal plate inside the glass to catch electrons given off by the wire. The filament is heated by electricity coming into the tube. The tube controls the amount of electricity that is sent out. Like a relay, it acts as a switch. (A vacuum tube can do the switching in one millionth of a second!)

Vacuum tubes were the heart of the first **electronic** computer, called **ENIAC**, built in 1946. The name is an <u>acronym</u>, made from the initials of its official title, the <u>E</u>lectronic <u>Nu</u>merical <u>I</u>ntegrator <u>and</u> <u>C</u>alculator.

ENIAC was designed by J. Presper Eckert and John M. Mauchly. It used 18 000 vacuum tubes (a typical radio of that time had about six tubes). ENIAC used 11 000 electronic switches, all attached to panels that weighed more than thirty tons. It was much faster than MARK I. It could add five thousand numbers every second. Unfortunately, its vacuum tubes produced heat that could make them burn out, the way bulbs do. Then the computer had to be shut down while repairs were made.

In England, the Manchester University MARK I began operating in 1948. It was directed by a stored program of instructions. (Some people think this storage of instructions makes England's MARK I the first real computer.) The Ferrante MARK I, based on the English computer, was produced for sale in Europe in 1950.

Eckert and Mauchly also built **UNIVAC I,** which began operating in 1951. It was used for the United States Census until 1963. Its invention is usually thought of as beginning the **first generation** of computers. UNIVAC was the first computer to be mass-produced. (Fewer than 50 were actually sold.)

In 1953, International Business Machines—IBM—began producing computers. IBM is a descendant of the Tabulating Machine Company founded by Herman Hollerith in 1896!

Many first generation computers were programmed by magnetic tapes, which were prepared by other, non-computing machines. Other computers read programs from punched or marked cards, similar to Jacquard's cards. They produced their results on other cards.

The **second generation** began in the early 1960s. **Transistors** replaced vacuum tubes. Transistors were invented by scientists at the Bell Telephone Laboratories shortly after the end of World War II. Transistors do the same things that vacuum tubes do but they are much smaller, do not get as hot as vacuum tubes do, and use much less power. Tiny bits of nonmetallic material are printed with **electrodes,** which do the work of the wires and plates in vacuum tubes. The transistor is sealed in a small container about the size of a pea. It is connected to other parts of electronic devices by fine wires instead of pins, as vacuum tubes are.

Second generation computers, using transistors, were much smaller and lighter than first generation computers. Still, they were very cumbersome and very expensive. Instead of being purchased by their users, most of these early computers were rented or leased.

Early in the 1960s, Texas Instruments began to make **integrated circuits.** An IC is a very small chip of silicon that has been engraved with many electrical parts. (Silicon is one of the most common elements found on Earth. Grains of sand are mostly silicon. In a way, people are still using stones to compute!) Each IC can replace many wires, tubes, and transistors. The IC's invention began the **third computer generation.**

Dr. An Wang used ICs to build the first desk-size electronic calculators in 1964. Pocket calculators appeared in 1966. (The first pocket calculator cost almost $400!) The first true minicomputer was built about the same time. It was the size of a filing cabinet and it cost nearly $20 000.

Some third generation computers are still in use. Two models, built by Digital Equipment Corporation, are found in many schools. The first of these is the PDP-8 and the second is its faster relative, the PDP-11.

Scientists and engineers kept working to make computers smaller, faster, and more reliable. They designed **monolithic integrated circuits,** which are combinations of many ICs. Some of these are called **microprocessors.** They are really whole computers on a single chip of silicon.

Microprocessors are usually connected to **printed circuit boards.** PC boards are made of plastic coated with metal. Some of the metal is removed following an engineer's design. The remaining metal replaces some of the wires the earlier computers needed.

With microprocessors, it was possible to build the microcomputer, and the **fourth generation** of computers began.

The first true microcomputer went on sale in 1975. It was programmed by turning switches on and off. Its results were read from blinking lights on the front of the computer.

Computers were no longer only in offices and laboratories. They were in washing machines, watches, cars, and games. It seemed they were everywhere! Computers had come home to stay.

What Do You Know?
1   What was the major disadvantage of the first electronic computer?
2.   Who were UNIVAC's inventors?
3.   What is an IC?
4.   What is a microprocessor?

What Can You Find Out?
1.   What were the names of some other early computers?
2.   Who were some of the other important people in the hisotry of computers?
3.   Are any microprocessors in use in your home?
4.   If you have a microprocessor, what does it do?

What Do You Think?

1.   Is your computer faster than UNIVAC I?
2.   Is your computer more reliable than first generation computers?

PUT THE MEMORY TO WORK

Line Numbers, Stored Programs, and Editing

Line numbers direct a computer to store instructions as a single program. The number also instructs the computer to complete the program instructions in a particular order, when the program is RUN.

Instructions, Waiting to RUN

DISCOVER FOR YOURSELF

For each **PRINT** statement, guess the computer's output. Write your guess on a sheet of paper. Check your answers by doing the exercise on your computer. Do not forget to press the [RETURN] or [ENTER] key after each line.

STEP

1. PRINT 6 + 4
2. 5 PRINT 8 + 36
3. RUN
4. 8 PRINT 15 − 6
5. RUN
6. LIST

COMPUTER DISPLAYS

WHAT DID YOU LEARN?

Were you surprised that you did not get an answer when you entered the second step? Of course you were happy to see the answer when you entered the third step, were you not?

Compare the first and second steps. How are they different? To the computer, the big difference is the number 5 entered in front of the word **PRINT** in step 2. This number is called a **line number**. It tells the computer to store, or save, this instruction in its memory.

In step 4 you made the computer store a second instruction. How did you know that both lines were saved? You had two ways of knowing. First, when you entered **RUN** in step 5, you got two answers. Next, when you entered **LIST** in step 6, the computer displayed both lines.

Any set of instructions stored in the computer's memory is called a computer **program**. It is

Memory Bank

Line Numbers

An instruction with a line number is stored but not carried out by the computer.

An instruction without a line number is carried out but not stored by the computer.

Chip's Bits

A robot called BOB, for Brains on Board, has devices called ultrasonic sensors that warn it of objects it might run into. Other sensors recognize heat-giving objects. Since living things give off heat, BOB can tell the difference between people and furniture.

USE WHAT YOU HAVE LEARNED

```
MARY
HAD A
LITTLE LAMB.
```

only necessary that the number of the second line be greater than that of the first line (and so on for all lines). Many people who write programs count by tens when numbering lines. You will see why in the next section.

Every (well, almost every) program line has this form:

```
10       PRINT     5*4 + 2
```

Line   BASIC   Assorted numbers,
Number.   Keyword. letters, and other
                          symbols.

Once a program is stored, you must tell the computer what to do with it. There are some special instructions called **system commands** which do this. System commands should not have line numbers.

RUN   makes the computer complete or execute the program currently stored in memory. It begins with the statement having the smallest line number and takes each statement in order.

LIST   directs the computer to display the stored program lines. They are listed in order of line number.

NEW   instructs the computer to erase an entire stored program. This command should be entered any time you want to begin a new program.

Be sure to enter the command **NEW** before entering the following.

```
NEW
10  PRINT "MARY "
20  PRINT "HAD A "
30  PRINT "LITTLE LAMB."
RUN
```

Your screen may look like the one at the left.

CHIP WONDERS:
DID THESE COMMAS
DO THAT TO THE
OUTPUT?

Now try this one:

```
NEW
10  PRINT "MARY ",
20  PRINT "HAD A",
30  PRINT "LITTLE LAMB."
```

Did your screen look like this?

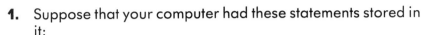

MARY   HAD A   LITTLE LAMB.

E x e r c i s e s

1. Suppose that your computer had these statements stored in it:
   ```
   10  PRINT 9 + 8
   20  PRINT 26 - 16
   ```
   a. What would your computer do if you entered LIST?
   b. What would your computer do if you entered RUN?
   c. What would your computer do if you entered NEW?
   Enter this exercise and try it.

2. Suppose that your computer had these statements stored in it:
   ```
   10  PRINT "16 + 4"
   20  PRINT 16 + 4
   ```
   a. What would your computer do if you entered LIST?
   b. What would your computer do if you entered RUN?
   c. What would your computer do if you entered NEW?
   Enter this exercise and try it.

3. Enter the program steps that will show the output to the left when you enter RUN: (Do not forget NEW and Clear-screen.)

4. Enter the program steps that will give the output to the left when you enter RUN:

Chip's Challenges

5. Enter the program steps that will give the following output when you enter RUN:

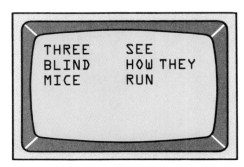

Editing A Program

Penny Dill ran her program on the computer and saw this on the screen:

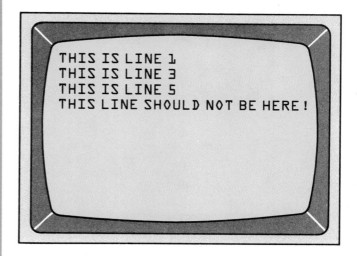

```
THIS IS LINE 1
THIS IS LINE 3
THIS IS LINE 5
THIS LINE SHOULD NOT BE HERE!
```

DISCOVER FOR YOURSELF

Study the output above and see if you can answer the questions below:

1. What program statement can you write to produce the first line of output above?
2. What program statement can you write to produce the second line of output above?
3. What program statements can you write to produce the third and fourth lines of output above?
4. Does the output make much sense to you? What output do you think would make more sense?

WHAT DID YOU LEARN?

Penny was saddened by the output. It did not say what she wanted it to say at all. She typed LIST and saw the program below. Compare it with the program statements you wrote for the *Discover for Yourself* Activity.

```
5  Clearscreen
10  PRINT "THIS IS LINE 1"
20  PRINT "THIS IS LINE 3"
30  PRINT "THIS IS LINE 5"
40  PRINT "THIS LINE SHOULD NOT BE HERE!"
```

A device called an Electro Gyrocator can show a motorist exactly where he or she is on a map. A gyroscope senses changes in direction and sends signals to a CPU. Other sensors send information about speed. The car's location is pinpointed on a transparent map mounted over a small video screen near the dashboard.

Here are some of the ways she wanted the output changed:

a. Get rid of the last line (The class rascal, Whitney, had typed it in when she was not looking.)
b. Place the statement, THIS IS LINE 2, between the first and the second lines.
c. Change line three to read THIS IS LINE 4.

Penny knew that she could have entered NEW and typed the whole program over, but she also knew an easier way to make the changes.

Enter the program (do not forget to type NEW first) and make the changes with Penny.

To erase line 40, Penny simply typed the line number 40 and pressed (RETURN) or (ENTER). When she typed LIST again, she saw that line 40 was no longer part of the program.

Much encouraged, she went on. She entered the following line:

```
15  PRINT "THIS IS LINE 2"
```

She typed LIST and saw this program appear on the screen:

```
5  Clearscreen
10  PRINT "THIS IS LINE 1"
15  PRINT "THIS IS LINE 2"
20  PRINT "THIS IS LINE 3"
30  PRINT "THIS IS LINE 5"
```

She knew that she could have used any number between 10 and 20 as the line number of the new line. The computer will accept the new line and put it in its proper place in the program.

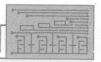

Memory Bank

Computer programmers *(people who write programs) must often put new lines in a program. Because they usually count by tens when numbering lines, they may put as many as nine lines between each two lines of the program.*

To make the last change in her program, Penny simply entered line 30 again. It looked like this:

```
30  PRINT "THIS IS LINE 4"
```

She typed LIST and saw this:

```
5   Clearscreen
10  PRINT "THIS IS LINE 1"
15  PRINT "THIS IS LINE 2"
20  PRINT "THIS IS LINE 3"
30  PRINT "THIS IS LINE 4"
```

Finally she entered RUN. This time she was pleased. Her output was exactly what she expected. If you followed Penny's steps, your output should also look like that shown on the left.

Adding a line, dropping a line, or making changes to a line of a program is called **editing** the program.

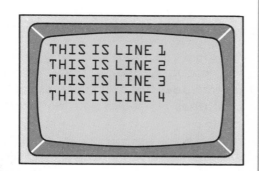

```
THIS IS LINE 1
THIS IS LINE 2
THIS IS LINE 3
THIS IS LINE 4
```

Memory Bank

Editing tips

To erase a line, type the line number and press RETURN *or* ENTER*.*

To change a line, retype the line, giving the new line the same number as the old line.

To insert a new line between two lines, give the new line a number between those of the original lines.

USE WHAT YOU HAVE LEARNED

CHIP WONDERS: DID THEY REALLY MEAN TO DO THIS?

Enter the following (incorrect) program and **RUN** it.

```
NEW
5  Clearscreen
10  PRIMT "THE SUM OF 5 PLUS 4 IS "
20  PRINT 5 + 4
RUN
```

If you typed the program exactly the way it is shown here, your computer gave you a message that you had made an error.

This kind of error is called a **syntax error** (SIN-tax), which means that a spelling, punctuation, or other language error, such as word order or missing word, was made. In this case, **PRINT** is spelled incorrectly. The computer did not have the slightest idea what was meant by **PRIMT**.

You can correct this error by typing a new line 10, spelling **PRINT** correctly this time.

```
10  PRINT "THE SUM OF 5 PLUS 4 IS"
```

Now **RUN** the program. Your screen should look like this:

```
THE SUM OF 5 PLUS 4 IS
9
```

As you write more and longer programs you will probably make many errors. Everyone does. It does not hurt the computer and as long as it does not make you feel bad, no harm is done.

Radio Shack Users, READ THIS ! !

Before you correct any errors like this one, press the (**ENTER**) key. The reason is that any time you see the message

> **?SN ERROR IN LINE 10**

on the screen, your computer is expecting a special kind of command from you. (The manual that came with your computer will explain these special commands if you look for EDIT MODE information.) Pressing (**ENTER**) tells the computer that you will not be using these special commands.

E x e r c i s e s

In each Exercise the program is supposed to give the output to its left. It does not. Enter the program exactly as it appears. **RUN** it and see what output, if any, it gives. Finally, edit the program to give the output on the left.

EAT YOUR GREENS

1.
```
5  Clearscreen
10  PRINT "DO NOT "
20  PRINT "EAT YOUR GREENS"
```

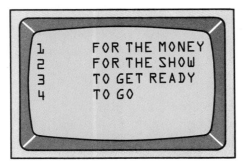

```
1    FOR THE MONEY
2    FOR THE SHOW
3    TO GET READY
4    TO GO
```

2.
```
5  Clearscreen
10  PRINT 1, "FOR THE MONEY"
20  PRINT 3, "TO GET READY"
30  PRINT 2, "FOR THE SHOW"
40  PRINT 4, "TO GO"
```

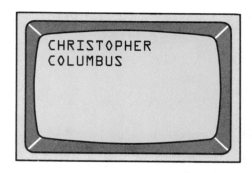

3. 5   Clearscreen
    10 PRINT "CHRISTOPHER"
    20 PRINT "HORATIO"
    30 PRINT "COLUMBUS"

4. 5   Clearscreen
    10 PRINT "BRUSH YOUR"
    20 PRINT "TEETH EVERY"
    30 PRINT "WEEK"

 **Chip's Challenges**

5. Enter the program exactly as it appears. **RUN** it and see what output, if any, it gives. Finally, edit the program to give the output on the left.

5   Clearscreen
10 PRINT MY NAME IS
20 PRINT PERCY P. PETTI

C H A P T E R   S U M M A R Y

1. A statement with a line number is stored but not executed by the computer.

2. A statement without a line number is executed but not stored by the computer.

3. A set of stored statements is called a program.

4. Entering the word **RUN** makes the computer execute a stored program.

5. Entering the word **LIST** makes the computer show a stored program.

6. Entering the word **NEW** makes the computer erase a stored program.

7. Editing a program means adding, erasing, or changing a line.

PROBLEM SET 4

Fill in the blanks.

1. You can store a statement in the computer by giving it a _____ number.
2. A _____ command tells the computer what to do with a stored program.
3. The system command _____ tells the computer to execute the program that is currently stored.
4. The system command _____ tells the computer to display the program that is currently stored.
5. The system command _____ tells the computer to erase the program that is currently stored.
6. Before you begin a new program, the system command _____ should be entered.
7. You do not use line numbers when entering a _____ command into the computer.
8. An instruction with a line number is stored but not _____ by the computer.
9. Adding, erasing, or changing a line of a stored program is called _____ the line.
10. Programmers do not count by ones when numbering program lines because they may wish to _____ a line into the program.

For Questions 11 to 14, use the program below.

```
NEW
5  Clearscreen
10  PRINT "THIS MESSAGE IS ON THE "
20  PRINT "NEXT "
30  PRINT "LINE"
```

11. What would happen if you entered RUN?
12. What would happen if you entered LIST?
13. What would happen if you typed the number 20 followed by (RETURN) or (ENTER) and then RUN?
14. What would happen if you entered NEW?

For Questions 15 to 18, use the program below.

```
NEW
5  Clearscreen
10  PRINT "6 + 10 = "
20  PRINT 2 * 8
```

15. What would happen if you entered RUN?
16. What would happen if you entered LIST?
17. What would happen if you typed 10 PRINT "2*8 = " followed by (RETURN) or (ENTER)?
18. What would happen if you entered NEW?

For Questions 19 and 20, use the program below.

```
NEW
5   Clearscreen
10  PRINT "GEORGE "
20  PRINT "WASHINGTON"
```

19. Describe what will happen if you type
15 PRINT "LIVES IN " followed by RETURN or
ENTER and RUN.

20. Describe what will happen if you type
15 PRINT "LIKES TO VISIT " followed by
RETURN or ENTER and RUN.

Try these on your computer. (Do not forget NEW and Clearscreen.)

21. Write a program that will produce the output below.

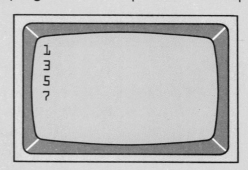

22. Write the program steps to produce the output below. Let the computer do the arithmetic.

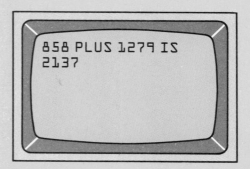

23. Write a program that will display the message

THE PRODUCT OF 915 AND 378 IS

on the top line and the answer on the next line. Let the computer do the arithmetic.

24. Write a program to display the message

3765 DIVIDED BY 145 IS

on the top line and the answer on the next. Let the computer do the arithmetic.

25. A Kubiks Rube costs $4.79. Bruce Engel sold 16 Kubiks Rubes for his school fundraiser. Write a program to compute and display the amount of money Bruce took in.

26. Betsy Dennis had these four examples to do for her math homework. Help Betsy do her homework by writing a program to perform the arithmetic and show the answers on the screen.

a. 1276
    1352
  + 1492

b. 32756
  − 14882

c. 348
  × 867

d. 176)442288

27. Write a program to print your name and the names of three of your friends.

28. The phrase, MY DEAR AUNT SALLY, brings much joy to people who love math. Write a program to print each word of the phrase on a separate line. (The phrase stands for **M**ultiplication, **D**ivision, **A**ddition, **S**ubtraction.)

 **Chip's Challenges**

29. Write a program which will give the output below.

```
TITLE:   LITTLE WOMEN
AUTHOR:  LOUISA MAE ALCOTT
```

30. Write a program which will display the message **THE AVERAGE OF 94, 72, 86 AND 88 IS** followed by the answer on the next line. Let the computer do the arithmetic.

Clockwise, from left: A computer with built-in disk drives; the correct way to hold a disk; a computer with a separate disk drive.

Disks and DOS

The part of the computer's memory where programs and variables are stored is temporary, or volatile, memory. When the computer is turned off—or when the command NEW is entered—the programs and variables are erased from the internal, built-in memory. If you wish to use a program more than one time, you have to re-enter it. Fortunately, there are devices, or extra pieces of equipment, that can be connected to a computer to save programs and other information for reuse. These devices give the computer additional external memory that is available when needed.

One of the most popular and efficient devices for saving programs is a **disk drive.** Most microcomputers use floppy disk drives. (The disks themselves are circular pieces of flexible plastic material. The disks are called floppy because they bend so easily. A magnetic floppy disk is like a small, very thin, phonograph record.) Disk drives may be built into the computer cabinet or may be separate pieces of equipment connected to the computer by a cable or wire. The cable carries information to the disk drive from the computer and back again.

A disk is used by a computer as you use a notebook to hold information you want to keep, may want to change, and will want to use lager.

When a disk is not being used, it should be stored in its special envelope, to keep it clean. Each disk is permanently enclosed in a heavy plastic jacket. The jacket is lined with a special material that protects the surface of the disk.

There is a small rectangular notch near the top right side of the disk jacket. This is called the **write-enable notch.** When it is not covered, the disk drive can write information on the disk. If you wish to prevent information from being written on the disk, the notch can be covered with a small tab, called a **write-protect tab,** that you will find in the package of disks.

A disk's surface is coated with magnetic material that allows the disk to pick up and hold many magnetic charges. The pattern of these charges forms a coded record of the statements of your program or of the information you want to keep. Part of the disk itself can be seen through the oblong windows in the front and the back of the jacket and through the circular hole in the center of the jacket.

It is important that you do <u>not</u> touch the exposed surface of the disk. Just a light touch on the surface can leave a fingerprint that can damage or destroy information stored on the disk. It is a good idea to handle disks very gently, placing your thumb on the label of the jacket and only your fingertips underneath.

Do <u>not</u> write on the label of the disk with anything but a soft felt-tip pen.

Do <u>not</u> expose disks to magnets. Because there is a magnetic field around wires that carry electricity, keep them away from electrical equipment. Magnets can remove rearrange the charges that represent information on the disks.

Do <u>not</u> store disks in places that are extremely hot or cold. Temperature can affect the way disks operate.

Do <u>not</u> bend or drop disks.

Do <u>not</u> leave disks where they can collect dust, smoke, or other foreign material.

A disk spins inside its jacket at a high rate of speed when it is in a disk drive and the drive is running. Even a tiny speck of dust can scratch the disk and make it useless. A part of the drive, called a **read/write head,** barely touches the exposed surface of the disk. The head can "read" the information from the disk. The computer copies, or LOADs, what is read into its internal, temporary memory. The head can also "write," or SAVE, information on a disk.

Important: Never insert a disk in a drive or remove a disk from a drive when the **read light,** a small red light on the front of the drive, is lit. You may damage or destroy the disk if you do.

When you are using a disk drive, you must use a special set of commands that are part of the computer's **disk operating system,** or **DOS.** Almost every microcomputer uses a different, unique DOS to direct the actions of its disk drives.

Before you can use a disk, it must be prepared using your computer's DOS command to initialize, or format, the disk. This command writes the information the drive needs to use on the disk, and gets the disk ready to accept your program. The special commands for preparing disks, using several popular microcomputers, follow.

Suppose you want to begin with your first disk. You might name it **DISK1**. First select a blank disk—or one you wish to erase. (The preparation process will remove any programs or information already stored on the disk.) Follow the directions for your system.

Apple: Type and enter this short program:

```
10  HOME
20  PRINT "THIS IS DISK1"
30  END
```

Then type **INIT HELLO** (RETURN)

DOS will write the short program with the name **HELLO** on the disk. It will run that program each time you use the disk. (Of course, you can make up your own greeting program.)

TRS-80: If you have a single disk drive, you will need to keep a copy of the DOS disk in the drive. To copy, or **backup,** that disk:

Type **BACKUP** (ENTER)
DOS will ask:
SOURCE DRIVE NUMBER?

Type **0** (ENTER)
DOS will ask:
DESTINATION DRIVE NUMBER?

Type **0** (ENTER)
DOS will ask:
SOURCE DISK MASTER PASSWORD?

Type **PASSWORD** (ENTER)
DOS will tell you when to change disks in the drive.

If you have two drives, put the blank disk in the top drive, drive 1.

Type **FORMAT** (ENTER)
DOS will ask:
FORMAT WHICH DRIVE?

Type **1** (ENTER)
DOS asks: **DISKETTE NAME?**

Type **DISK1** (ENTER)
DOS will ask: **MASTER PASSWORD?**

Press (ENTER)

Commodore 64:

Type **OPEN15,8,15** (RETURN)
Type **PRINT#15,"NEW0: DISK1,01"** (RETURN)

After you have written and tested a BASIC program, you can easily **SAVE** that program on your disk. First you must give the program a name. Program names must begin with a letter and may, after the first letter, contain either letters or digits. They should not (except as noted below) contain any blanks, punctuation, or special characters. If your program name contains no more than 8 characters, it can probably be used by any microcomputer's DOS. In these examples, your program will be named **PROGRAM1**.

Apple: Names may be up to 15 characters in length. They may contain periods, blanks (on Apple IIe), and several special characters. To save your program, type the command:

SAVE PROGRAM 1 (RETURN)

TRS-80 Model III/4: Names may be <u>no more than</u> 8 characters in length and may contain <u>no</u> special characters or blanks. Program names must be enclosed in quoation marks.

SAVE "PROGRAM1" (ENTER)

Commodore 64: Names should be <u>no more than</u> 8 characters in length and may contain <u>no</u> special characters or blanks. The program name must be enclosed in quotation marks. The device number, 8, must follow the program name.

`SAVE "PROGRAM1", 8` [RETURN]

It is suggested that you verify each **SAVE** on the Commodore by using the following command:

`VERIFY "PROGRAM1", 8` [RETURN]

When you **SAVE** a program on any computer, the DOS first instructs the read/write head to look at the **directory** or **catalog** of the disk. This is a record of the names of all the programs and collections of information stored and the place where they are written on the disk. If a program with the name you want to use is already stored on the disk, that program is <u>erased</u> and the new one is **SAVE**d in its place. If no program exists with the name you have chosen, the name is written in the record and the program **SAVE**d on the disk. Follow the instructions below to display the disk directory or catalog.

Apple: Type **CATALOG** [ENTER]

There may be more names in the catalog than can fit on the screen. The computer will stop listing them when the screen is full. Press any key to see the rest of the names.

TRS-80: Type `CMD"D:0"` [ENTER] (If you are not using BASIC, type DIR [ENTER])

(Zero is the number of the first, or bottom, drive built into the computer case.) If there are more program names than the screen can show, you can stop the listing by pressing the [BREAK] key.

Commodore 64:

Type **LOAD** `"$", 8` [RETURN]

(Commodore calls its first drive device 8.)

To load a program, follow these instructions.

Apple:
Type **LOAD PROGRAM1** [RETURN]

TRS-80:
Type **LOAD "PROGRAM1"** [ENTER]

Commodore 64:

Type **LOAD "PROGRAM1', 8** [RETURN]

SAVE, DIRECTORY or **CATALOG**, and **LOAD** are only three of the most frequently used disk operations available to your computer. There are many others. Look in your computer manual for more details and other disk operations.

What Do You Know?
1. What is a magnetic disk?
2. Why would the following not be permitted as program names?
   `$NAMES`
   `3BEARS`
   `DATA,DATA`
3. Name three ways in which the data on a disk may be damaged or destroyed.
4. What would happen if you gave two different programs the same name?

What Can You Find Out?
1. How is data stored on a disk?
2. What are tracks?
3. What are sectors?
4. What information, other than programs, might be stored on a disk?

What Do You Think?
1. What advantage does storing programs on disks have over storing them in the computer's memory or on magnetic tape?
2. When you erase a program from the computer's memory (by typing **NEW**), what effect does this have on programs saved on the disk?

CHAPTER 5

MEMORY AND MATHEMATICS

Values and Variables

Variables are used to label memory locations in the computer's Random Access Memory. Numeric variables store numbers to be used in arithmetic operations. String variables are used for all other values.

Storage Space for Numbers

DISCOVER FOR YOURSELF

Follow the steps below in order. For each **PRINT** statement, guess the computer's output. Write your guess on a sheet of paper. Check your answers by doing the exercise on your computer. Do not forget to press the (**RETURN**) or (**ENTER**) key after each line.

COMPUTER DISPLAYS

STEP

1. PRINT "A"
2. A = 8
3. PRINT A
4. A = 12
5. PRINT A
6. B = 6
7. PRINT "B"
8. PRINT B
9. PRINT A + B

WHAT DID YOU LEARN?

CHIP SAYS:
THE NUMBER 8 IS PLACED IN A MAILBOX THAT THE COMPUTER CALLS MAILBOX A.

Storage Area

Look at Steps 2, 4, and 6 in *Discover for Yourself*. The letters A and B in the statements are examples of variable names that store numbers. **Variable** names are used by the computer to store all kinds of information. How does the computer store information? It works something like this. Imagine the storage area of the computer to be many mailboxes, as in a large post office. When Step 2, A = 8, was entered, the computer placed the number 8 in one of the mailboxes and then labeled that mailbox A. Stored in the mailbox, A, at this time, is the number 8. When Step 3, **PRINT A**, was entered, the computer *went* to the mailbox called A, and printed, as it was instructed, the number 8. The **value** of A at this time is 8. Values of the variable stored in a mailbox can be changed. When Step 4, A = 12, was entered, the computer erased the number 8, from mailbox A and replaced it with the number 12. Note that Step 5 printed the value of A as 12 and <u>not</u> 8 because at this time the number 12 was stored in mailbox A and <u>not</u> 8.

CHIP SAYS: IN MAILBOX A, THE NUMBER 8 WAS REPLACED BY THE NUMBER 12.

Storage Area

There are other variable names that can be used to store numbers. Note that Steps 6 and 8 of the *Discover for Yourself* use the letter B as a name of a storage area (mailbox). Can you explain why the computer printed the number 6 in Step 8 and the number 18 in Step 9?

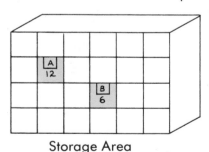

Storage Area

USE WHAT YOU HAVE LEARNED

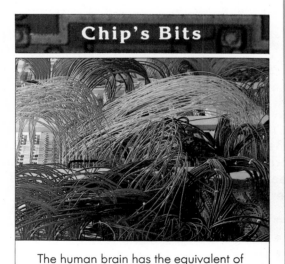

Chip's Bits

The human brain has the equivalent of one hundred thousand million computer connections. That equals enough storage for about one hundred trillion pieces of information. No computer can match that!

Memory Bank

Any <u>letter</u> of the alphabet can be used to store numbers in the computer. The names (letters) of the storage areas are called **variables**. *Since numbers are stored, the names (letters) of the storage areas are called* **numeric variables**.

1. Follow the steps below in order. For each **PRINT** statement, guess the output. Write your guess on a sheet of paper. Check your answers by doing the exercises on your computer. Do not forget to press the (**RETURN**) or (**ENTER**) key after each line.

COMPUTER DISPLAYS

STEP

 1. B = 5
 2. PRINT B
 3. G = 33
 4. PRINT G – B
 5. PRINT "G + B"
 6. I = 100
 7. PRINT B, I, G
 8. PRINT B + I + G
 9. PRINT B * G
10. PRINT 20 * B – I

2. Follow the steps in the stored program below. Guess what will be printed when the program is **RUN**. Write your guess on a sheet of paper.

```
10  E = 15
20  T = 20
30  C = 100
40  PRINT E * T / C        Output ___?___
```

Enter this program and **RUN** it. See if your guess was correct.

Chip's Challenges

3. Follow the steps in the stored program below. Guess what will be printed when the program is **RUN**. Write your guess on a sheet of paper. Enter the program and **RUN** it. See if your guess was correct.

```
10  A = 15
20  B = 30
30  A = A + B  ← Study this statement.
40  PRINT A * ( A + B )
```

5.2

Calculation by Computer

DISCOVER FOR YOURSELF

Follow the steps below in order. For each **PRINT** statement guess the computer's output. Write your guess on a sheet of paper. Check your answers by doing the exercises on your computer. Do not forget to press the **RETURN** or **ENTER** key after each line.

STEP

1. A = 6
2. PRINT A
3. B = 11
4. PRINT A, B
5. C = A + B
6. PRINT A, B, C
7. C = 2 * A + B
8. PRINT A, B, C

COMPUTER DISPLAYS

?
?
?
?

WHAT DID YOU LEARN?

CHIP SAYS: LOOK AT THE STATEMENTS AGAIN.

Look at the statements of Steps 1, 3, 5, and 7 again. How are these statements alike? Yes, each one contains the = symbol. These are called **Arithmetic** (pronounced a-rith-MET-ic) statements, even when no arithmetic is done.

Left side → What appears on the left side of the = symbol in each odd-numbered statement? A single variable name appears in each case. You can not place more than one variable name nor do any arithmetic on the left side of the = symbol.

Right side → Notice, however, that it is a different story on the right side of the = symbol. It is here that all of the arithmetic can be shown.

73

Now look back at the statements of Steps 6 and 8. What was printed as the value of C in Step 6? That is right, the number 17. In Step 8, what was printed as the value of C? The number 23 was printed. What do you suppose happened to the number 17? To understand what became of the number 17 it helps to know how a computer works on an <u>arithmetic</u> statement.

First, it looks at the right side of the = symbol and replaces every variable there with its current value.

Second, it does all of the arithmetic and comes up with a single number.

Third, it stores this number in the location labeled by the variable on the left. If the variable already has a value, the old value is erased and the new one is stored.

Look at the following four steps as an example. Even if you can guess the output in Step 4, read the information carefully. It is important for you to understand how the computer handles an arithmetic statement.

CHIP SAYS:
WHEN A COMPUTER MEETS AN ARITHMETIC STATEMENT, IT DOES THREE THINGS.

STEP

1. X = 5
2. Y = 9
3. Z = 3 * X – Y
4. PRINT X, Y, Z

COMPUTER DISPLAYS

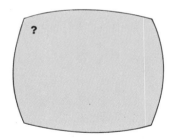

?

The statement of Step 1 says the current value of X is 5 and the statement of Step 2 says the current value of Y is 9. When the computer is given the statement of Step 3, it does the following:

First, on the right side of the = sign, the variables are replaced by their current values:

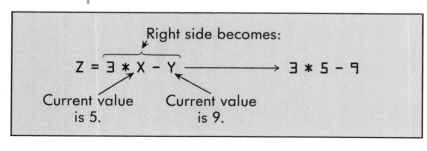

Right side becomes:

Z = 3 * X – Y ⟶ 3 * 5 – 9

Current value is 5.   Current value is 9.

Second, the arithmetic is done:

$$Z = 3 * 5 - 9 = \underbrace{15}_{becomes} - 9 = 6$$

Third, the number 6 is stored in Z, to become its current value:

$$Z = \longleftarrow \quad 6$$

Old value of Z is erased.

USE WHAT YOU HAVE LEARNED

The following exercises will help you to understand arithmetic statements. For each **PRINT** statement, guess the computer's output. Write your guess on a sheet of paper. Check your answers by doing the exercises on your computer.

STEP

1. X = 2 * 3 + 4
2. PRINT X
3. Y = 2 * X - 5
4. PRINT X, Y
5. Z = 2 * X + Y
6. PRINT Z, Y, X
7. Z = 6 + 4 * 2
8. PRINT Z

COMPUTER DISPLAYS

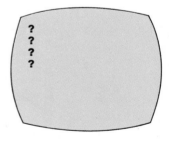

?
?
?
?

CHIP SAYS: STUDY CAREFULLY THE ARITHMETIC STATEMENT AT STEP 7.

You may be a little surprised at the last answer. Did you guess that 20 would be the output instead of 14? The computer always does its arithmetic in a special order. Of course, it works from left to right, but it does all multiplying or dividing <u>before</u> it does <u>any</u> adding or subtracting. If you did not get the computer's answer, try this one again, remembering to multiply 4 * 2 before you add.

E x e r c i s e s

1. Follow the steps below in order. For each **PRINT** statement, guess the output. Write your guess on a sheet of paper. Check your answers by doing the exercise on your computer. Do not forget to press `RETURN` or `ENTER` after each line.

STEP

COMPUTER DISPLAYS

1. L = 2 * 3
2. PRINT L
3. M = 1 + 4 * 2
4. PRINT L, M
5. N = M + L
6. PRINT L, M, N
7. PRINT 2 * L
8. M = 2 * L + 3 * M
9. PRINT L, M, N

2. Each of the following **PRINT** statements has more than one arithmetic operation. Guess what the computer will print. Be sure that you follow the computer's rules for arithmetic. Check your answers by doing the exercise on your computer.

a. PRINT 3 * 4/2 ___?___   b. PRINT 3 + 4/2 ___?___
c. PRINT 3 * 6 + 4/2 ___?___   d. PRINT 12/4 - 1 ___?___
e. PRINT 12/3 * 2 ___?___

3. Follow the steps in the stored program below. Guess what will be printed when the program is **RUN**.
   ```
   10   D = 3 + 3
   20   E = 15 - D
   30   F = 8 + D/2 + 3 * E
   40   PRINT D, E, F          Output ___?___
   ```
   Enter this program and **RUN** it. See if your guess was correct.

Chip's Challenges

Follow the steps in the stored programs below. Guess what will be printed when the program is **RUN**. Enter the programs and **RUN** them. See if your guess was correct.

4.
```
10   E = 48
20   T = 4
30   C = 6
40   E = E - T * C
50   T = E - T * C
60   C = (E - T * C)/C
70   PRINT E, T, C
```

5.
```
10   A = 12
20   B = 8
30   A = A + B
40   B = A + B
50   A = B - A
60   B = B - A
70   PRINT A, B
```

Memory Locations for Letters—and More

DISCOVER FOR YOURSELF

Follow the steps below in order. For each PRINT statement, guess the computer's output. Write your guess on paper. Check your answers by doing the exercise on your computer.

COMPUTER DISPLAYS

STEP

```
1.  A$ = "HI"
2.  PRINT A$
3.  B$ = "THERE"
4.  PRINT A$, B$
5.  PRINT B$, A$
6.  PRINT A$; B$
7.  A$ = "BYE"
8.  PRINT A$, B$
9.  A = 10
10. PRINT A, A$, B$
```

WHAT DID YOU LEARN?

Look at the statements of Steps 1, 3, and 7. In some ways they look like the arithmetic statements you saw in the last section. But do you notice any differences? Yes, two things are different. The variable on the left of the = symbol has a strange symbol, $, in it and the information on the right consists of letters, not numbers. These variables are called **string variables**. The $ sign is read "string."

String variables can even store the digits 0 through 9, but any numerals stored as strings of characters cannot be treated as numbers. You cannot do any arithmetic with them. Look at the statements of Steps 1 and 7. In the first statement,

```
A$ = "HI"
```

Memory Bank

*Variables that end with the $ symbol are called **string variables** and are used to store letters and other characters.*

the word **HI** was stored in **A$** and stayed there until the computer was given the statement of Step 7. For each of the **PRINT** statements of Steps 4, 5, and 6, the word **HI** was printed for **A$**. At Step 7, however, the word **HI** was erased and lost forever, replaced by the word **BYE**.

Look at the statement of Step 10 in *Discover for Yourself*. Does this tell you something about the wonderful **PRINT** statement? Notice that while you may not mix numeric and string variables in an arithmetic statement, you may certainly mix them in a **PRINT** statement. To store a word, name, message or any string of characters in a string variable, statements like those of Steps 1, 3, and 7 of *Discover for Yourself* are used. These statements are still called arithmetic statements.

USE WHAT YOU HAVE LEARNED

Follow the steps below in order. For each **PRINT** statement guess the computer's output. Write your guess on a sheet of paper. Follow up by doing the exercise on your computer. You may find it fun to make up your own examples, using string variables in **PRINT** statements and arithmetic statements to create interesting messages.

STEP

1. K$ = "KING"
2. L$ = "LOO"
3. PRINT L$; K$
4. D$ = "US"
5. T$ = "HER"
6. PRINT D$; T$
7. N$ = "GRIEF"
8. PRINT "GOOD" ; N$

COMPUTER DISPLAYS

CHIP SAYS:
EVERYTHING THAT YOU SHOULD KNOW ABOUT STRING VARIABLES IS SUMMARIZED HERE. READ CAREFULLY.

To make a string variable, simply place a $ symbol at the end of a variable name. Be sure that there are no blank spaces between the letter and the $ symbol. On the left side of the arithmetic statement, you may place only a single variable name. Nothing else is allowed! On the right side of the = symbol, you may have either of these conditions:

1. Another string variable, such as C$ = A$.

2. Any expression which has quotation marks ('') around it, such as

`M$ = "I LIVE AT 1313 MONSTER COURT"`

With a string variable on the left side of the statement, you may <u>not</u> have numeric variables (the kind used in the last section) or expressions without quotation marks on the right side of the = sign.

E x e r c i s e s

What, if anything, is wrong with each BASIC statement?

1. `K = "RIGHT"`   **2.** `B$ = "1777"`

3. `PRINT C, C$`   **4.** `T$ = GOODNIGHT`

5. `PRINT "GOOD MORNING"`   **6.** `A = A + D$`

7. Follow the steps below in order. For each `PRINT` statement, guess the computer's output. Write your guess on a sheet of paper. Check your answers by doing the exercise on your computer.

STEP

   1. `A$ = "CHIP"`
   2. `PRINT A$`
   3. `B$ = "SAYS"`
   4. `PRINT A$, B$`
   5. `PRINT B$, A$`
   6. `C$ = "HI"`
   7. `PRINT A$, B$, C$`
   8. `PRINT C$, B$, A$`
   9. `PRINT B$, A$, C$`
  10. `C$ = "BYE "`
  11. `PRINT A$, B$, C$, C$`
  12. `PRINT C$, A$`

COMPUTER DISPLAYS

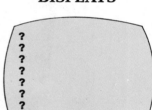

Chip's Challenges

8. Place the correct string variables and punctuation in each of the `PRINT` statements to the left so that the message displayed on the screen on the next page will be printed by the computer when the program is RUN. Try the program on your computer.

```
10  M$ = "TO "
20  A$ = "EASY "
30  R$ = "BASIC "
40  I$ = "LEARN "
50  E$ = "IS "
60  PRINT ___?___
70  PRINT ___?___
80  PRINT ___?___
90  PRINT ___?___
```

←   Place
←   string
←   variables
←   here

```
LEARN BASIC
BASIC IS EASY
TO LEARN BASIC IS EASY
EASY TO LEARN IS BASIC
```

Chip's Bits

The first microcomputer was sold as a kit for about $400. It was advertised in magazines in 1975. (It could also be bought completely assembled for about $600.) The Altair 8800, as it was called, had no ROM and only one-quarter K RAM. There was no keyboard and no monitor. But it was the very first personal computer.

MIXING NUMERIC AND STRING VARIABLES

Example 1: Gil Juarez was planting tomatoes in his garden. He knew that for every square foot of soil, he could produce three pounds of tomatoes.

The BASIC program below, when RUN, will determine the tomato harvest, or yield, for Gil's garden.

S = garden size, 12 sq. ft.	20 S = 12
Y = tomato yield or harvest.	30 Y = 3 * S
The value of Y is printed.	40 PRINT Y

When the program is RUN, the value 36 (representing 36 pounds of tomatoes) is printed.

Gil's neighbor Joe has a much larger garden. He has 31.5 sq. ft. in which to grow tomatoes. To find the number of pounds he could produce, just change line 20 from

20 S = 12   to   20 S = 31.5

On your computer, RUN the program to find Joe's yield of tomatoes.

Gil would also like to print the name of the owner of the garden as well as the yield on the computer. The program below will print Gil's name and the yield from his garden.

```
Gil's Program:   10   N$ = "GIL"
                 20   S = 12
                 30   Y = 3 * S
                 40   PRINT N$, Y
```

To do the same for Joe's garden, change lines 10 and 20 from

```
10 N$ = "GIL"   to   10 N$ = "JOE"
20 S = 12       to   20 S = 31.5
```

The new program will print, `JOE 94.5`, when it is RUN. Try it.

Example 2: Sal's class has a bowling team. He was elected secretary. Sal now has the job of finding the average score for his classmates every time they bowl three games. A BASIC program to find the average of three scores is shown below:

```
10 A = 110  ←──────────────── First score.
20 B = 130  ←──────────────── Second score.
30 C = 120  ←──────────────── Third score.
40 S = A + B + C  ←────────── Add up the scores.
50 T = S/3  ←──────────────── Calculate the average.
60 PRINT "THE AVERAGE IS "; T  ← Average printed.
```

Sal now must RUN the program. The computer will print, **THE AVERAGE IS 120.** Carla's scores were 125, 114, and 136. Sal will have to change only three lines to find Carla's average.

```
10  A = 110   will be   10  A = 125
20  B = 130   will be   20  B = 114
30  C = 120   will be   30  C = 136
```

To compute Bill's average, Sal retyped lines 10, 20, and 30 again. He used Bill's scores of 111, 90, and 90. When he entered RUN, the computer displayed the output on the left.

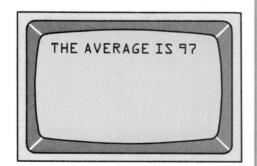

THE AVERAGE IS 97

Sal was not satisfied. He wanted the computer to print the names of his classmates above their average scores. To print Bill's name, he added the following two statements:

```
5 N$ = "BILL"    and    55 PRINT N$
```

Sal's new program:

```
5 N$ = "BILL"←─────── N$ keeps track of
10 A = 111            the name
20 B = 90
30 C = 90
40 S = A + B + C
50 T = S/3
55 PRINT N$
60 PRINT "THE AVERAGE IS "; T
```

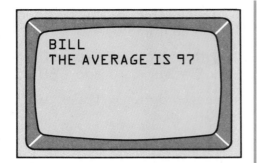

```
BILL
THE AVERAGE IS 97
```

Sal entered **RUN** and the computer displayed the output on the left.

Sal now has a program to compute the bowling averages for anyone in his class. For each person, he will retype lines 5, 10, 20, and 30.

Exercises

1. Change a line of Gil's program to store the name of Gil's other neighbor Johnny.
2. Change a line in Gil's program to store Johnny's garden size, 18.4 square feet.

What is the value of X in each of the program statements?

3. ```
   10  X = 5 * 3
   ```
4. ```
   10  X = 17 - 2
   ```
5. ```
   10  Y = 7
   20  X = 5 + Y
   ```
6. ```
   10  Y = 5
   20  X = 25/Y
   ```

What will the computer display (print) when each of the following programs is RUN?

7. ```
   10  N$ = "HELP"
   20  PRINT N$
   ```
8. ```
   10  N$ = "LIGHT"
   20  PRINT "MOON"; N$
   ```
9. Enter the following program and RUN.
   ```
   100  PRINT "BOWLING AVERAGES"
   110  N$ = "MARTY"
   120  A = 110
   130  B = 130
   140  C = 120
   150  S = A + B + C
   160  T = S/3
   170  PRINT N$
   180  PRINT "SCORES"
   190  PRINT A
   200  PRINT B
   210  PRINT C
   220  PRINT "AVERAGE IS "; T
   ```

Chip's Challenges

10. Using the string variable N$, change line 180 and delete lines 190, 200, and 210 in the program of Exercise 9 so that the computer prints on one line:
    ```
    MARTY SCORES ARE 110 130 120.
    ```

Name	At Bat	Hits
Soknic	122	34
Santine	133	42
Brown	99	20
Metlaw	140	45
Atkins	117	29
Yanokie	125	48
Quickman	135	51
Dobson	127	43
Hale	109	32

11. Write and **RUN** a computer program using numeric and string variables that will calculate the batting averages of the GLIBTON SEA HAWKS to the left.

CHAPTER SUMMARY

1. All information stored in a computer must be given a unique name, called a variable.
2. Letters of the alphabet, A, B, C, etc., are used to store numbers. These are called numeric variables.
3. An arithmetic statement is used to do arithmetic on the computer.
   It contains an = symbol that separates it into two parts:
   The left side, which can be only a single variable and nothing else.
   The right side, which may be numbers, variables, or both, with any amount of arithmetic indicated.
4. The computer works on the right side of an arithmetic statement by doing the following three things:
   First, each variable on the right side is replaced by its current value.
   Second, the arithmetic on the right side is done by the computer. The result is a single number.
   Third, this single number becomes the current value of the variable named on the left.
5. When the computer does a line of arithmetic, it works from left to right but does all multiplying and dividing before it does any adding or subtracting.
6. Variables which end with the $ symbol are called string variables. These are used to store letters and other characters.
7. There must not be any blank spaces between the letter and the $ symbol that names a string variable.

PROBLEM SET 5

Identify the error in each of the following BASIC PRINT statements.

1. PRINT $A   **2.** PRINT (HELLO)
3. PIRNT B   **4.** PRINT B + F$
5. PRINT 5B   **6.** PRINT R $

What would the computer display (print) for each of the following programs when RUN?

7. 10 K = 12   **8.** 10 X = 6
        20 PRINT K   20 Y = 8
9. 10 D = 13   30 Z = 10
        20 E = 14   40 Y = X * Y - Z
        30 PRINT "D + E"   50 PRINT X * Z - Y
10. 10 R = 42
        20 T = 7
        30 Q = R/T
        40 PRINT "THE QUOTIENT IS "; Q

Construct BASIC PRINT statements that will produce the following outputs on the video screen:

11. The statement, THIS IS A COMPUTER PROGRAM.
12. The value of F following the phrase, F IS EQUAL TO ___?___.
13. The values of A, B, and the sum, A + B, in the statement, THE SUM OF ___?___ PLUS ___?___ IS ___?___.
14. The value of 64 decreased by the product of 12 times 3 preceded by the phrase, THE ANSWER IS .

Each of the following PRINT statements has more than one arithmetic operation. What would the computer display (print) on the video screen?

15. PRINT 9 * 3 * 4   **16.** PRINT 14 * 2 + 8
17. PRINT 8 + 2/2   **18.** PRINT 112 - 36/3
19. PRINT 7 * 3 - 6/2   **20.** PRINT 9/3 + 6

Using the string variables below, what would the computer display for each of the following PRINT statements?

A$ = "ANDREA "
B$ = "BETH "
C$ = "HELLO "
D$ = "SAYS "
E$ = "CHIP "
F$ = "GOOD WORK "

21. PRINT A$; B$ **22.** PRINT C$; D$; E$
23. PRINT F$; A$; B$ **24.** PRINT A$; D$; C$

Using the string variables from Exercises 21-24, write **PRINT** statements for the following messages displayed on the video screen.

25.  CHIP SAYS HELLO ANDREA
26. ⟶ BETH SAYS GOOD WORK
27. ⟶ GOOD WORK BETH ANDREA
28. ⟶ HELLO CHIP ANDREA BETH
29. ⟶ CHIP SAYS GOOD WORK ANDREA BETH
30. ⟶ HELLO BETH HELLO ANDREA

Enter and **RUN** the programs. Guess the output of the computer before the program is **RUN**.

31.
```
10  B$ = "BASIC "
20  PRINT B$; "IS FUN"
```

32.
```
10  G = 14
20  R = 4
30  P = G * R - G
40  PRINT G, R, P
```

33.
```
10  F$ = "OF "
20  B = 120
30  E$ = "AVERAGE "
40  G$ = "IS "
50  C = 340
60  D = 86
70  S = B + C + D
80  A = S/3
90  PRINT E$; F$; B; C; D; G$; A
```

9 meters

21 meters

34. A farmer wishes to enclose a rectangular field with new fencing. Write, enter, and **RUN** a program that will calculate the amount of fencing (perimeter) the farmer will need. Use L and W for the measurements, length and width, of the rectangle. The formula for the perimeter of the rectangle is P = 2 * L + 2 * W.

35. The formula to change pounds to kilograms is K = P / 2.2. Write, enter, and **RUN** a program to change 44 pounds to kilograms. Print the output in the following form:

___?___ POUNDS = ___?___ KILOGRAMS

Use only numeric and string variables in the **PRINT** statement.

Chip's Challenges

36. Write, enter, and **RUN** the program of Ex. 34 above, using a different formula for the perimeter of the rectangle.

37. James Jacobs earns $3.40 per hour for the first 40 hours he works each week and $5.10 for each additional hour. Write, enter, and **RUN** a program to calculate James' earnings for a week he worked 56 hours. Include statements that will display (print) and label both the original information and the final answer.

38. Write, enter, and **RUN** a program that will display the triangular arrangement of stars shown to the left.

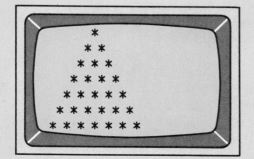

COMPUTER AWARENESS

What is a Computer?

A computer is a tool of the mind—it can help people think.

Why is a computer like a hammer or a toothbrush? If you said that each one is a tool designed to do its own special job, you have part of the answer. A hammer is designed to drive nails. If you've ever tried to do this with anything else—a rock, for example—you know why the hammer is made as it is. And if you've ever tried to clean your teeth without a toothbrush, you know how difficult and ineffective that can be.

A computer is also a tool. It doesn't drive nails or brush teeth, but it does something else: it helps people think.

Most tools help people work with their muscles. They extend or amplify what people can do with muscles. The hammer extends the pounding power of the carpenter, allowing him or her to make better, more effective use of the arm muscles. The toothbrush, with its hundreds of bristles, extends and makes more effective use of the up-and-down and back-and-forth motions of your hand as you clean your teeth.

In much the same way, the computer extends and makes more effective use of people's ability to think. It does many of the things that the human brain does, but it does them faster and it doesn't make mistakes.

It can store thousands of facts and recall any one of them almost instantaneously. It can carry out thousands of additions as fast as you can blink your eye. It can solve complicated problems in a tiny fraction of the time that it would take a human being.

A computer is like a hammer or toothbrush, then, because it is a tool designed to do its own special job—in this case, to solve problems. But that's only part of the answer.

The other part is that, like the hammer, the toothbrush, and all other tools, the computer can do nothing without people. A hammer is useless without someone to swing and direct it. A toothbrush cannot clean a single tooth without a person to give it its up-and-down and back-and-forth motion. (Or, in the case of an electric toothbrush, to turn it on and guide it.) So it is with the computer. Without someone to tell it what to do, the computer is as ineffective and unproductive as the hammer on the hardware store shelf or the toothbrush on the drugstore counter.

People must tell the computer exactly what to do and how to do it. They must tell it when to receive information and where and how to store that information. They must tell it when to add or compare two numbers and when and how to show an answer. They must even tell it when to stop.

The computer will do exactly what it is told to, nothing more and nothing less. Detailed instructions that tell it what to do must be written and given to the computer before it can perform even the simplest task. These directions are written in sets called programs. The people who write them are called programmers.

A program is a set, or series, of very simple but very detailed instructions. Think for a moment about some simple operation that you perform every day—putting a button through a buttonhole, for example. What do you actually do? What are the steps involved? You could write a program, giving each step in order. For example:

1. With the left hand, touch thumb and forefinger through buttonhole.
2. With right hand, grasp far edge of button (edge away from buttonhole) between thumb and forefinger with thumb nearest you.
3. As you push near edge of button into buttonhole, retract left forefinger from buttonhole.
4. As button edge goes through buttonhole, grasp it with thumb and forefinger of left hand.
5. While pushing far edge of button through hole with right thumb, pull fabric at outside edge of buttonhole to the right with right forefinger.
6. Grasp outside edge of fabric between thumb and forefinger of right hand and pull it down over button which is still held between thumb and forefinger of left hand.

That is a program for buttoning a man's shirt button. (For a garment with the button on the wearer's left and the buttonhole on the right—a woman's blouse, for example—left and right hands would be reversed.)

Now imagine if every movement of every muscle involved in this operation had also to be specified—including the arm muscles to position the hands in the proper place. You are beginning to get an idea of the amount of detail that has to go into the instructions for a computer.

This detail is necessary because there are relatively few things that a computer can actually do. All the many complex operations it performs are made up of combinations of these few simple things. A computer can:

1. Allow information to be entered.
2. Store information.
3. Move information from one place to another within the computer.
4. Display or print information.
5. Do arithmetic (on some computers only addition and subtraction can be done).
6. Compare two numbers.
7. Jump from one set of instructions to another.
8. Stop.

These simple steps are often called **primitive computer operations**. The programmer breaks down all the more complex things he or she wants the computer to do into such simple steps.

All of the computer's information, including its primitive operations, must be stored as numbers. Moreover, these numbers must be in a very simple system that uses nothing but ones and zeros, the **base two** or **binary** system. (The ordinary number system is the base ten or decimal system.) Programmers call the binary digits **bits**.

If everything is stored as numbers, how is it that you see letters and other characters on the computer keyboard and screen? The answer is simple: each key on the keyboard has its own coded binary number. When you touch a key, the computer converts your keystroke into the coded number for that key. For example, the letter A may have the coded number 65. When you touch the A key, the computer stores a string of ones and zeros that are the binary equivalent of 65. (The string of bits is called a **byte**. Most microcomputers use 8-bit bytes.)

When you ask the computer to display or print out information, the reverse happens: it converts the same string of ones and zeros back into A, and that is what you see on the screen or printout.

As you can see, the computer is not really very smart. It can only do simple operations with numbers. But because it can perform these operations very rapidly and very accurately and, more important, because many highly complex problems can be broken down and converted into these simple operations, it is an enormously valuable tool.

What Do You Know?
1. Why is a computer a tool?
2. What are the computer's primitive operations?
3. In what form is a computer's information stored?

What Can You Find Out?
1. What other kinds of number systems are there? Do people use any today beside the binary and decimal systems?
2. What is your computer's code for letters and characters?

What Do You Think?
1. Why was the base two or binary system chosen for computers?
2. Why do some people call computers *thinking* machines?

OUT OF ORDER

GOTO and FOR-NEXT Loops

The order in which instructions are completed can be changed by several BASIC statements. The GOTO statement directs the program to a specific line. A FOR-NEXT loop performs instructions repeatedly.

Program Jumps—From Line to Line

DISCOVER FOR YOURSELF | For each program below, trace the steps and guess the computer's output. Write your guess on a sheet of paper. Check your answers by doing the exercises on your computer. Do not forget to press the [RETURN] or [ENTER] key after typing each line.

PROGRAM

COMPUTER DISPLAYS

1.
```
 5  Clearscreen
10  A=5
20  B=9
30  PRINT A
40  PRINT B
```

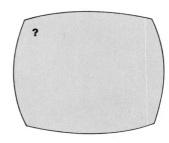

2. This program contains two new statements—GOTO and END. END may be used as the last step of a computer program. See what the GOTO statement does.

```
 5  Clearscreen
10  A=5
20  B=9
30  PRINT A
35  GOTO 50
40  PRINT B
50  END
```

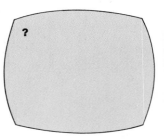

WHAT DID YOU LEARN?

In the first program, the computer follows the instructions in order, according to the line numbers. The output is:

> 5
> 9

Things are different in Program 2, however. There is a new statement in line 35, `GOTO 50`. This statement tells the computer to skip to line 50. The output for this program is:

> 5

The computer completely skips line 40. The value of B, 9, will never be printed.

Memory Bank

The `GOTO` *statement tells the computer to skip to the indicated line number.*

The computer can jump back as well as skip forward in a program, using the `GOTO` statement.

Consider the following program.

```
10  PRINT "HELLO"
20  PRINT "MY NAME IS"
30  GOTO 20
40  PRINT "BILL"
50  END
```

50 `END` ←——————— Used to mark the last step in this computer program.

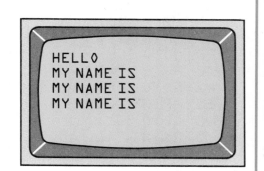

The computer would print the output on the screen to the left. Notice, `MY NAME IS` would be printed over and over again.

The computer runs the program in the following order, according to line number:

10, 20, 30, 20, 30, 20, 30, ...

The computer never prints `"BILL"` because it never gets to line 40.

The program is running in an **infinite** loop. Infinite is a mathematician's word for unending.

Some computers allow a space between `GO` and `TO`. Check this out on your system.

CHIP SAYS:
BE CAREFUL WHEN USING INFINITE LOOPS. YOU CAN ONLY STOP AN INFINITE LOOP BY USING A KEY SUCH AS BREAK. CHECK YOUR SYSTEM.

USE WHAT YOU HAVE LEARNED

CHIP SAYS:
TRACE THIS PROGRAM TO SEE IF YOU GET THE SAME OUTPUT.

```
5   Clearscreen
10   PRINT "YOU CAN"
20   GOTO 50
30   PRINT "AND JUMP"
40   GOTO 70
50   PRINT "HOP"
60   GOTO 90
70   PRINT "ALL AROUND"
80   GOTO 110
90   PRINT "SKIP"
100   GOTO 30
110   END
```

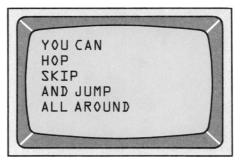

```
YOU CAN
HOP
SKIP
AND JUMP
ALL AROUND
```

As you can see, the GOTO statement can cause the computer to SKIP AHEAD or JUMP BACK.

CHIP SAYS:
IF YOU DID NOT GET THE SAME OUTPUT, TRY FOLLOWING THE TRACE SHOWN HERE.

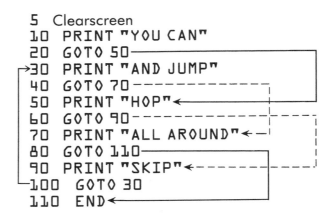

Order of line numbers	Computer action
5	Clears the screen.
10	Prints YOU CAN.
20	Skips ahead.
50	Prints HOP.
60	Skips ahead.
90	Prints SKIP.
100	Jumps back.
30	Prints AND JUMP.
40	Skips ahead.
70	Prints ALL AROUND.
80	Skips to 110.
110	Ends the program.

Caution:
Using the same line number twice in a GOTO statement, such as 20 GOTO 20, will result in an infinite loop. Use your system's (BREAK) key to stop an infinite loop.

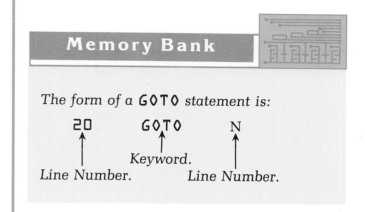

Memory Bank

The form of a GOTO *statement is:*

   20   GOTO   N

   ↑   ↑   ↑

 Line Number. Keyword. Line Number.

E x e r c i s e s

1. Each of the following contains exactly one error. Identify the error and write the statement correctly.
   a. 30 GOTO -25
   b. 50 TOGO 70
   c. 45 GONETO 30
   d. 50 GOTO .6

2. For each program, determine the output. After you trace the program, RUN it and check your answer.

   a.
   ```
   10   Clearscreen
   20   PRINT "HELLO"
   30   GOTO 50
   40   PRINT "GEORGIA"
   50   END
   ```

   b.
   ```
   10   Clearscreen
   20   PRINT "HELLO"
   30   GOTO 60
   40   PRINT "I AM HERE"
   50   GOTO 80
   60   PRINT "WHERE ARE YOU?"
   70   GOTO 40
   80   END
   ```

3. Supply the missing line numbers in the GOTO statements of this program to make it print:

   ROSES ARE RED, VIOLETS ARE BLUE,
   MATH IS FUN, COMPUTERS ARE, TOO!

   ```
   10   Clearscreen
   20   PRINT "ROSES ARE RED, ";
   30   GOTO
   40   PRINT "MATH IS FUN, ";
   50   GOTO
   60   PRINT "VIOLETS ARE BLUE,"
   70   GOTO
   80   PRINT "COMPUTERS ARE, TOO!"
   90   END
   ```

Chip's Challenges

4. Write a computer program that will make the computer print your name repeatedly.

6.2

Again . . . and Again . . . and Again

DISCOVER FOR YOURSELF

Trace the steps of the program below and guess the computer's output. Write your guess on a sheet of paper. Check your answers by running the program on your computer.

COMPUTER DISPLAYS

PROGRAM

```
5  Clearscreen
10  I=1
20  PRINT I
30  I=2
40  PRINT I
50  I=3
60  PRINT I
70  END
```

WHAT DID YOU LEARN?

The value of I changed from 1 to 2 to 3.

These values were printed on the screen.	Output
	1
	2
	3

Compare the program above to the one shown below.

Program	Output
5 Clearscreen	
10 FOR I = 1 TO 3	1
20 PRINT I	2
30 NEXT I	3
40 END	

The output is the same but the program is much shorter. This program contains two new statements.

```
10  FOR I = 1 TO 3
         ·
         ·
30  NEXT I
```
and

When used together, these statements and all lines in between them in a program form a new kind of loop, a **FOR—NEXT** Loop. Statement

```
10  FOR I = 1 TO 3
```

tells the computer to do two things:

1. Label the variable I and give it a beginning value, 1, and an ending value, 3.

2. Do all the program steps down to the **NEXT** statement three times, because the final value of I is 3.

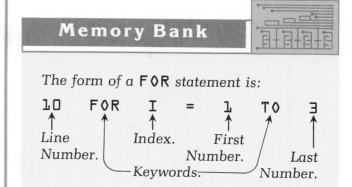

Memory Bank

The form of a **FOR** *statement is:*

```
10     FOR    I  =  1  TO  3
```

Line Number.

Index.

First Number.

Keywords.

Last Number.

When the computer sees a **FOR** statement, it repeats all the steps following, down to the **NEXT** statement, as many times as the **FOR** statement directs. This is called **looping**. During the loop, the value of the **index**—the variable in the **FOR** statement—changes from the beginning number, through the counting numbers, to the ending number.

Memory Bank

1. *The index can be any numeric variable.*
2. *The first value should be a whole number.*
3. *The last value should be a whole number.*
4. *There must be a* **NEXT** *statement for each* **FOR** *statement in a program.*

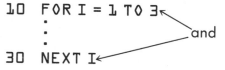

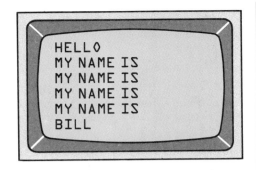

Trace each of the following programs. Compare your results with the output to the left after you run them.

Program 1 (Remember the infinite loop?)

```
5   Clearscreen
10   PRINT "HELLO"
20   FOR K = 1 TO 4
30   PRINT "MY NAME IS"        Loop
40   NEXT K
50   PRINT "BILL"
60   END
```

As you can see, only the steps between the FOR and NEXT statements are repeated.

Program 2

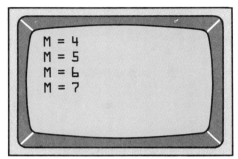

```
5   Clearscreen
10   FOR M = 4 TO 7
20   PRINT "M = ";M
30   NEXT M
```

Follow this trace of Program 2.

Program Statements	Explanation
5 Clearscreen	The screen is wiped clean.
10 FOR M = 4 TO 7	The loop begins with M = 4.
20 PRINT "M = ";M	The computer displays the value of M, 4. Note the spaces in the quotation marks and the semicolon.
30 NEXT M	This marks the end of the loop. The computer checks the value of the index, M. If M does not equal the final value, 7, the loop is run again.
20 PRINT "M = ";M	Since M does not equal 7, the computer increases M to the next number, 5. This is the value printed this time through the loop.
30 NEXT M	Again the value of M is checked. If M does not equal the final value, 7, the loop is run again.
.	
.	
.	

and so on.

The steps in the loop are repeated for M = 4, 5, 6, and 7, the last value. Once M = 7, the computer looks for the line number following the NEXT statement.

USE WHAT YOU HAVE LEARNED   Look at the partial program at the top of the next page. Supply the missing line so that the computer will count from 3 to 8, as shown.

```
Output        10
3             20  PRINT K
4             30  NEXT K
5
6
7             The FOR statement, 10  FOR K = 3 TO 8,
8             would cause the computer to count from 3 to 8.
```

E x e r c i s e s

1. Each of the programs below contains exactly one error. Identify the error, then rewrite the program correctly.

   a.
   ```
   10  FRO J = 1 TO 5
   20  PRINT J
   30  NEXT J
   ```
   b.
   ```
   10  FOR 5 TO 10
   20  PRINT L
   30  NEXT L
   ```

2. Determine the output of each of the following programs.

   a.
   ```
   5   Clearscreen
   10  FOR M = 1 TO 10
   20  PRINT "M = ";M
   30  NEXT M
   ```
   b.
   ```
   5   Clearscreen
   10  FOR X = 1 TO 5
   20  PRINT "LICKETY SPLIT"
   30  NEXT X
   ```

3. For each program below, supply the missing FOR statement which will make the computer print the output shown.

   a.
   ```
   5   Clearscreen       Output
   10
   20  PRINT N           5
   30  NEXT N            6
                         7
                         8
                         9
                         10
   ```
   b.
   ```
   5   Clearscreen       Output
   10
   20  PRINT "HELLO"     HELLO
   30  NEXT I            HELLO
                         HELLO
   ```

Chip's Challenges

4. Write a computer program that will make the computer display the output shown to the right. Use a FOR—NEXT loop.

   ```
   Output

   MY DOG
   HAS FLEAS
   MY DOG
   HAS FLEAS
   MY DOG
   HAS FLEAS
   ```

6.3

More About Loops

DISCOVER FOR YOURSELF Look at the programs below. Guess what the computer would display when each of the programs is RUN. Write your answers on a sheet of paper. Then enter the programs to see if you were correct.

PROGRAM

COMPUTER DISPLAYS

1.
```
5  Clearscreen
10  PRINT "MY ";
20  GOTO 50
30  PRINT "HAS ";
40  GOTO 70
50  PRINT "CAT ";
60  GOTO 30
70  PRINT "FUN ";
80  PRINT "AND FLEAS"
```

2. NEW
```
5  Clearscreen
10  FOR I = 1 TO 10
20  PRINT I
30  NEXT I
40  PRINT "READY OR NOT ";
50  PRINT "HERE I COME."
```

3. NEW
```
5  Clearscreen
10  PRINT "SEVENS TABLE"
20  FOR I = 1 TO 9
30  PRINT I; "*7 = "; I*7
40  NEXT I
```

4. NEW
```
5  Clearscreen
10  PRINT "SEVENS TABLE"
20  I=1
30  PRINT I; "*7 = ";I*7
40  I=I+1
50  GOTO 30
```

98

You have already seen the computer's remarkable ability to jump back or skip ahead in a program. It can also do many calculations over and over again.

In the first program, the GOTO statement was used to jump or skip around. Take a closer look.

Line 10 tells the computer to print MY.
Line 20 tells the computer to GOTO (go to) line 50.
Line 50 tells the computer to print CAT.
Line 60 tells the computer to go to line 30.
Line 30 tells the computer to print HAS.
Line 40 tells the computer to go to line 70.
Line 70 tells the computer to print FUN.
Line 80 tells the computer to print AND FLEAS.

The complete message is shown below:

MY CAT HAS FUN AND FLEAS

Program 4 prints the sevens table. This program never ends. You must (BREAK) the program. Program 3 prints the sevens table from 1 × 7 to 9 × 7.

Compare the output of these programs:

Program 3 Output	Program 4 Output
1*7 = 7	1*7 = 7
2*7 = 14	2*7 = 14
.	.
.	.
.	.
8*7 = 56	8*7 = 56
9*7 = 63	9*7 = 63
	10*7 = 70
	11*7 = 77
	.
	.
	.
	(Break)

In Program 3, the computer knew where to begin and end, as directed by the FOR statement:

FOR   I   =   1   TO   9

Begin at 1. ⟶   End at 9.

In Program 4, the computer is told where to begin in Line 20:

```
20  I = 1
         ↑
    Begin at 1.
```

However, the computer is not told where to end the sevens table. In Program 4, line 40 is the "count-by-ones" statement.

```
40  I = I + 1
             ↑
      Count by 1.
```

To understand the BASIC statement, $I = I + 1$, think of it this way:

    I is replaced by $I + 1$

Example: Suppose $I=3$ to begin. Then

    $I = I+1$ would be computed as
    $I = 3+1$
    $I = 4$←——The new value of I.

The FOR statement counts by one automatically. But suppose you want to count by 2, . . . or by 3, . . . or by 4? Try this program.

```
NEW
5  Clearscreen
10  FOR I = 1 TO 10 STEP 2
20  PRINT I
30  NEXT I
```

You should get the following output:

```
1
3
5
7
9
```

USE WHAT YOU HAVE LEARNED

Suppose you want to change Program 3 to print:

```
┌──→1 *7 = 7
├──→3 *7 = 21
├──→5 *7 = 35
├──→7 *7 = 49
├──→9 *7 = 63
└────These are all odd numbers.
```

To count by odd numbers, you start at one and count by 2. The FOR statement does this when you write it as:

Memory Bank

In the BASIC statement $I = I+1$, to get the new value of I, take the old value and add 1.

```
FOR  I  =  1  TO  9  STEP  2
```
Start at 1.   End at 9.   Count by 2.

Using this information, you can change Program 3 as follows:

```
NEW
5   Clearscreen
10   PRINT "SEVENS TABLE"
20   FOR I = 1 TO 9 STEP 2
30   PRINT I; "*7 = ";I*7
40   NEXT I
```

Add this to the FOR statement.

Try this on your computer. The output should look like this:

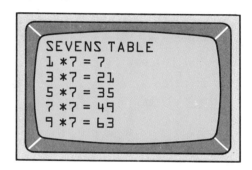

```
SEVENS TABLE
1 * 7 = 7
3 * 7 = 21
5 * 7 = 35
7 * 7 = 49
9 * 7 = 63
```

CHIP SAYS:
LOOK AGAIN AT THE FOR STATEMENT.

The FOR statement in Line 20 caused the odd numbers to be produced.

```
FOR  I  =  1  TO  9  STEP  2
```
Begin at 1. / End at 9. / Count by 2.
Keywords.

Can you change this FOR statement so that the products 14, 28, 42, 56, 70 are printed?

```
FOR  I  =  2  TO  10  STEP  2
```
Begin at 2. / End at 10. / Count by 2.
Keywords.

CHIP SAYS:
HERE IT IS, FOLKS!

How could you change the FOR statement to print the products 21, 42, 63, 84, and 105?

```
3 X 7 = 21
6 X 7 = 42
9 X 7 = 63
12 X 7 = 84
15 X 7 = 105
```

CHIP SAYS:
HERE IS THE
FOR STATEMENT!

The multipliers start at 3 and end at 15, counting by 3.

FOR I = 3 TO 15 STEP 3

Begin at 3.   End at 15.   Count by 3.

You can also count by 1/2s (use 1/2 = .5). Try the following program and compare your output to that shown.

Program	Output
NEW	
5 Clearscreen	1
10 FOR K = 1 TO 5 STEP .5	1.5
20 PRINT K	2
30 NEXT K	2.5
	3
	3.5
	4
	4.5
	5

This number makes the computer count by .5 (1/2).

You can count by any decimal number. Try some others.

Exercises

1. Write a **FOR** statement, using the variable K, to tell the computer to do the following:

	Begin at	End at	Count by
a.	1	50	1
b.	3	13	2
c.	11	121	11
d.	2	7	.1

2. What would the computer display if each of the following programs were **RUN**?

a. 10 FOR J = 1 TO 10
     20 PRINT J
     30 NEXT J

b. NEW
     10 FOR K = 3 TO 12 STEP 3
     20 PRINT K
     30 NEXT K

c. NEW
     10 FOR L = 1 TO 3 STEP .2
     20 PRINT L
     30 NEXT L

3. Copy and complete the following programs to have the computer begin at 2, end at 10, and count by .5.

a. NEW
```
10   PRINT "KG TO G"
20   PRINT "KG ", "G "
30   FOR
40   PRINT K, K*1000
50
```
b. NEW
```
10   PRINT "DOLLARS TO FRANCS"
20   PRINT "DOLLARS", "FRANCS"
30   FOR
40   PRINT D, 2.9*D
50
```
4. RUN the two programs in Problem 3.

Chip's Challenges

5. Write a program to display the 1089s table from 1×1089 to 9×1089. (What pattern do you find in the products?)

APPLICATIONS

COUNTING BACKWARD

The following program is dedicated to those brilliant scientists at NASA who launch the space shots. It counts backward from 10 to 1!

Program   Output

```
NEW
10   PRINT "SPACE SHOT"          SPACE SHOT
20   FOR N = 10 TO 1 STEP -1     10
30   PRINT N                     9
40   NEXT N                      8
50   PRINT "BLASTOFF"            7
                                 6
This number makes               5
the computer count              4
backward.                       3
                                 2
                                 1
                                 BLASTOFF
```

The FOR statement may be used to count backward as well as forward. The number following STEP makes the computer count backward. Look at the following examples.

Example 1:   FOR M = 10   to   1 STEP -1

Begin   End   Count back
at 10.   at 1.   by 1.

When used in a program, this FOR statement makes M count 10, 9, 8, . . . , 2, 1.

CHIP WONDERS: HAVE YOU NOTICED THAT WHEN NASA LAUNCHES A ROCKET THEY ALWAYS COUNT BACKWARD?

10,9,8,7,6,5,4,3,2,1...BLASTOFF!

Example 2: F0R K = 100 to 0 STEP -2

Begin   End   Count back
at 100.   at 0.   by 2.

Used in a program, this F0R statement would cause K to count 100, 98, 96, 94, 92, . . . , 4, 2, 0.

Add these steps to the rocket launch program and watch the rocket go "outta sight!":

```
60  PRINT "   *    "
65  PRINT "  * *   "
70  PRINT "  * *   "
75  PRINT "  * *   "
80  PRINT "  * *   "
85  PRINT "  * *   "
90  PRINT " ******* "
95  PRINT " ******* "
100  FOR L = 1 TO 20
110  PRINT
120  NEXT L
```

{ Be sure to count the spaces carefully.

Experiment 1: Find someone in your class who has a stopwatch or a watch displaying seconds. Then, enter this program:

```
NEW
5  Clearscreen
10  FOR L = 1 TO 1000
20  PRINT L
30  NEXT L
```

RUN . . . but wait! Do not press (ENTER) or (RETURN) yet! Start timing the moment you press (ENTER) or (RETURN). Stop the stopwatch the instant the program ends.

RUN the program two more times and compute the average time in seconds.

Experiment 2: Change line 20 of the program above to:

       20 PRINT L; "*9 = "; L*9

The program should print the first thousand values of the nines table. RUN the program three times and compute its average time.

Experiment 3: (The invisible counter.)
Take line 20 out of the program by entering:

       20

LIST the program.

CHIP WONDERS:
DID YOU EVER WONDER HOW LONG IT TAKES A COMPUTER TO COUNT TO 1000? TRY THESE EXPERIMENTS.

It should look like this:

```
 5   Clearscreen
10   FOR L = 1 TO 1000
30   NEXT L
```

The program tells the computer to count from 1 to 1000. Nothing is displayed. The program is finished when you see **READY** displayed. **RUN** it three times and find the average time.

CHAPTER SUMMARY

1. The **GOTO** statement tells the computer to take program statements out of their numbered order.

   It can skip ahead, bypassing several program statements.

   It can jump back to program statements already executed.

2. If a program repeats statements already executed it is said to enter a loop. Usually, the programmer must provide a method for the program to end a loop.

3. A **FOR-NEXT** loop allows the repeating of a sequence of program steps and keeps count of the times it is repeated. The loop must open with a **FOR** statement and close with a **NEXT** statement.

4. A **FOR** statement has this form:

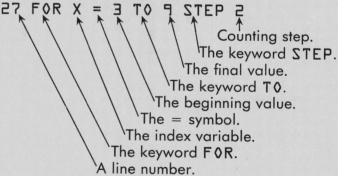

```
27 FOR X = 3 TO 9 STEP 2
```

Counting step.
The keyword **STEP**.
The final value.
The keyword **TO**.
The beginning value.
The = symbol.
The index variable.
The keyword **FOR**.
A line number.

5. The **NEXT** statement has this form:

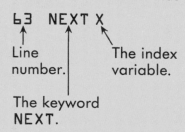

```
63  NEXT X
```

Line number.

The index variable.

The keyword **NEXT**.

PROBLEM SET 6

1. Each of the following contains exactly one error. Identify the error, then rewrite the line correctly.
   a. 20 GOETO 50   **b.** GOTWO 100
   c. GOTO END
   d. 10   FOUR I = 1 TO 900
   e. 20   FOR 5 TO 500
   f. 40   FOR 1 TO 10

2. **a.** If the old value of K is 2, what will the new value be if K = K + 5?   **b.** If the old value of X is 60, what will the new value be if X = X + 1?

3. Determine the output of each of the following programs:
   a. 5   Clearscreen
      10   FOR L = 1 TO 2
      20   PRINT L
      30   NEXT L
      40   PRINT "BUCKLE MY SHOE."
   b. 5   Clearscreen
      10   PRINT "I LIKE PEACHES ";
      20   GOTO 50
      30   PRINT "I AM THE NEATEST ";
      40   GOTO 70
      50   PRINT "I LIKE JAM"
      60   GOTO 30
      70   PRINT "KID THAT AM."

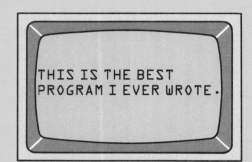

4. Complete the GOTO statement which would cause the computer to display the output on the left for each program.
   a. NEW
      5   Clearscreen
      10   PRINT "THIS IS THE BEST "
      20   GOTO
      30   PRINT "GOSH-DARN "
      40   PRINT "PROGRAM I EVER WROTE."
   b. NEW
      5   Clearscreen
      10   GOTO
      20   PRINT "MY NAME IS"
      30   GOTO
      40   PRINT "HI THERE!"
      50   GOTO
      60   PRINT "CHIP CIRCUITRY"

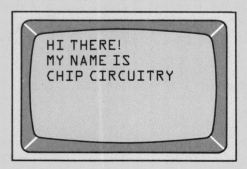

5. For each program below, determine the output.
   a. 5   Clearscreen
      10   FOR N = 2 TO 20 STEP 2
      20   PRINT N
      30   NEXT N

b. NEW
```
 5  Clearscreen
10  FOR J = 3 TO 12 STEP 3
20  PRINT J;" *5 = ";J*5
30  NEXT J
```
c.
```
 5  Clearscreen
10  FOR M = 2 TO 4 STEP .5
20  PRINT M
30  NEXT M
```
d.
```
 5  Clearscreen
10  FOR N = 8 TO 3 STEP -1
20  PRINT N
30  NEXT N
```

6. Complete the FOR statement in the program below to make the computer print the numbers 3, 6, 9, 12, and 15.
```
10  FOR
20  PRINT K
30  NEXT K
```

7. For each program below, write a FOR statement which will make the computer print the output shown.

a.
```
10
20  PRINT K;"*4 = ";K*4
30  NEXT K
```
Output
4
8
12
16
20

b.
```
10
20  PRINT M;"*3 = ";M*3
30  NEXT M
```
Output
12
21
30
39
48

For each of the following, write a program to solve the problem. Then RUN your program to test it.

8. Count backward from 20 to 10.
9. Count by 3 from 10 to 31.
10. Count by 5 from 100 to 120.
11. Count by .5 from 1 to 3.
12. Print an 8s table from 8 to 80.

Chip's Challenges

13. Write a program to print the squares of the numbers from 1 to 10.
14. Write a program to print the fractions 1/2, 1/3, 1/4, 1/5, . . . , 1/9.
Hint: notice that the denominators start at 2 and count by 1s to 9.

COMPUTER AWARENESS

From this computer control room, many operations can be controlled.

From Mainframes to Micros

In earlier sections you looked at the ancestors of computers. It is time now to bring the computer family tree up to date. Remember, like all family trees, it will continue to grow beyond the size it has reached today. One branch may die off, but others will continue. No one knows with certainty what the future generations will be like, but you can be quite sure that there will be future generations.

At present there are two branches in the family tree. Your computer, and most of those you are familiar with, belong to the **digital** branch. The second branch is called the **analog** branch. Consider first the digital branch of the computer family tree.

In the digital branch, computers come in all sizes. Many are very, very large. Many, like yours, are quite small. Some are even smaller— small enough to fit in a briefcase or a pocket.

Many large businesses and government agencies work with enormous, staggeringly large amounts of information. They use super-sized computers called **mainframes**. These giants of the computer family can do mammoth jobs, such as recording all of the long-distance calls made by a telephone company's customers. They can do as many as 100 million additions every second!

Very often, the people who use a mainframe never see the computer at all. Instead, they see the station or **terminal** at which they work. The word terminal means end. The computer terminal is at the end of wires connecting it to the mainframe. Terminals can be miles away from the computer, connected to it by telephone wires. Or they can be in the next room, or even in the same room as the mainframe. The distance makes no difference.

A terminal may look very much like your microcomputer. It may have a keyboard, screen, and printer similar to those you use. But the terminal's operations, or most of them, are performed by the mainframe. The mainframe receives input from the terminal and provides answers to it.

Many terminals can operate at the same time, sharing the same mainframe's storage space. They use its operations and sometimes perform operations of their own.

Smaller than the mainframe is the **minicomputer**. Despite its name, this is a sizeable piece of equipment, considerably bigger than your microcomputer. Like the mainframe, it may have terminals connected to it. In many ways, a minicomputer is just a smaller version of a mainframe. Because it is smaller, however, a minicomputer can usually handle less information than a mainframe. Generally, minicomputers cost less than mainframes but are more expensive than microcomputers.

Microcomputers are still smaller. They are given their name because of their small size and because they use microprocessors. Many microcomputers can do as much work as a minicomputer. Microcomputers can be connected to other micros in **computer networks**, usually using telephone wires. They can also communicate with minicomputers and with mainframes. Your computer is probably a microcomputer.

Mainframes, minicomputers, and microcomputers are all parts of the digital branch of the computer family tree. All do their work by **counting**.

Analog computers, those that belong to the second branch of the family tree, do not count. Instead, they **measure** their information.

Think of two watches. Both are equally accurate, governed by the vibrations in a quartz crystal. But one counts seconds and shows its results in numbers. There is no minute hand or hour hand, just a window that shows the hour and minute and second. The other watch is a measurer. Its hands move around a dial marked off to show twelve or twenty-four hours and, for the minute and second hands, sixty minutes and sixty seconds. The marks on the dial are measures of parts of the circle in which the hands move. They show, by an **analogy** or relationship, the passing of seconds, minutes, and hours. The first kind of watch is called a digital watch. The second kind is called an analog watch.

An analog computer, like the analog watch, does its work by measuring. Analog computers have a long history. Nearly one hundred years ago, a **bronze box** was found in the Mediterranean Sea. It was a machine, more than two thousand years old. The box simulated, or represented, something in nature. Moving gears simulated the movements of the sun and other stars and of the moon and planets. Because its gears could be moved faster than the heavenly bodies they represented, the box could be used to predict events. Sailors could find out where the sun would be at some future time. This information helped them travel where they wished. The bronze box was an analog computer.

A descendant of the bronze box was built at the beginning of this century. Designed by two Americans, Rollin A. Harris and E. G. Fisher, it was used to predict tides. The **Great Brass Brain**, as it was named, was in use at the United States Coast and Geodetic Survey until 1966. Like the bronze box, it imitated or simulated natural events.

During World War II, Dr. Vannevar Bush built an analog computer to simulate the actions of artillery shells. It was used to produce tables of numbers to direct the firing of weapons. It was a very slow computer, but it could do the work of one hundred people using mechanical calculators.

Today, digital computers are in the majority. But analog computers are still being built and used. Both sides of the family tree are alive and well and busy at work.

What Do You Know?
1. What are mainframes?
2. What are minicomputers?
3. Why are microcomputers given that name?
4. What are the two branches of the computer family tree?
5. What did Vannevar Bush use his computer for?

What Can You Learn?
1. Where are analog computers used today?
2. Can your computer communicate with other computers?
3. Does your school system use a mainframe or a minicomputer? How many terminals are connected to it?

What Do You Think?
1. Can any computer do both analog and digital tasks?
2. Will microcomputers ever be able to do the work of mainframes and minicomputers?

TIMERS AND COUNTERS

More about Loops

Sometimes, a computer's instructions are completed too quickly. FOR . . . NEXT loops can be used to slow the operation. In a program, loops may be enclosed in other loops.

Slower Computing

Whitney Lacsar likes to see his name printed on the computer screen. He wrote the program below and entered it. Study the program and answer the questions which follow:

```
10  Clearscreen
20  PRINT "WHITNEY LACSAR!!"
```

1. What would the screen display if Whitney typed LIST?

2. What would be displayed if Whitney typed RUN?
   Whitney was proud to see his name printed on the screen but decided that he would be much happier if his name would flash on and off.

3. Write the program step that would make the two steps above be repeated over and over.
   ```
   30  _____
   ```

4. Enter all of the steps above and RUN the program to see if it works. Use your own name instead of Whitney's.

5. Describe on a sheet of paper what happened when you entered RUN.

Did you enter this for Question 3 above?
```
30  GOTO 10
```
If you entered this, you saw that your name flashed on and off the screen very rapidly.

Whitney decided that the computer did its work much too quickly to please him. His friend, Alice, showed him how to use a **timing loop** to slow the computer down. Here is how.

1. Add these two steps between lines 10 and 20:

   ```
   15 FOR T = 1 TO 100
   16 NEXT T
   ```

2. Add these two steps between lines 20 and 30:

   ```
   25 FOR T = 1 TO 100
   26 NEXT T
   ```

Enter these statements and **LIST** the program. Notice that the computer has placed the added steps in the program at the proper places. Now enter **RUN** and see what is displayed. Your name now flashes on and off the screen at regular intervals. This program will not stop until you [**BREAK**] it.

Here is how the program works:

Line 10 clears the screen.

Lines 15 and 16 send the computer into a loop that simply keeps it busy looping 100 times. The actual time it takes depends upon the computer you are using. It should be about one-half of a second.

Line 20 prints your name.

Lines 25 and 26 are exactly like those in lines 15 and 16. They keep the computer busy and hold the name on the screen for a short time.

Line 30 sends the program back to line 10 which begins the process all over again.

Timing loops such as those above are used any time that the computer works too fast to suit your needs. Usually they are needed to keep output displayed on the screen long enough to be read. They have this form:

Memory Bank

Timing loops

A timing loop is a **FOR-NEXT** *loop which is used to slow down the computer's operation. It simply keeps the computer busy while you read what is displayed on the screen.*

```
35 FOR M = 1 TO 300←──────This number determines
36 NEXT M                 the length of the loop.
```

In line 35, the number **300** determines how long the timing loop takes. If you use a number less than **300**, the computer will complete the loop in a shorter time. If a number greater than **300** is used, the loop will take a longer time to be completed. Remember, if you wish to slow down your computer's display, use a greater number. If you wish to speed up your computer's display, use a lesser number.

USE WHAT YOU HAVE LEARNED

```
NEW
5  Clearscreen
10  PRINT "SPACE SHOT"
20  FOR N= 10 TO 1 STEP -1
30  PRINT N
40  NEXT N
50  PRINT "BLASTOFF"
```

CHIP WONDERS: HOW DID YOU ANSWER QUESTION 3 ?

The program on the left is the same countdown program that you saw in the last chapter. Study the program steps and see if you can answer the questions that follow:

1. Describe what the computer will do if you enter LIST.

2. Describe what the computer will do if you enter RUN.

3. How could you slow this program so that the countdown would take more time?

4. Enter the program and RUN it. You should be ready to type the steps which you will be adding below.

To slow this countdown, place a timing loop between lines 30 and 40. The number you place after the word TO in line 35 determines how much time it takes to count down from one number to the next. Enter the steps below. First LIST the new program to see that the added steps are correctly placed. Next RUN the program.

```
35  FOR T = 1 TO 400
36  NEXT T
```

Exercises

1. In Example 2 from the last chapter, (p. 104) you added statements that directed the computer to draw and launch a rocket ship. Add these steps to the countdown program above. Now place a timing loop in the program, between lines 110 and 120, to slow down the launch.

2. Have the computer print a message about one of your classmates. Use a timing loop to have the message flash on and off. It might be an amusing message such as:

BILLY SLATTERLY HAS THE CURLIEST TEETH IN TOWN!

3. Write a program to play this computer game with your friends. First give the computer a number (one with lots of digits). Have the computer print the number on the screen for a short time (use a timing loop). See if your friends can remember the number printed on the screen.

Chip's Challenges

4. The famous song "99 Bottles of Milk on the Wall" can be written on the computer in only a few program lines. Write the program to display this song. Add a timing loop so that the computer pauses briefly at the end of each verse.

7.2

Nested Loops,
a loop inside a loop inside . . .

```
NEW
10 Clearscreen
30 FOR K = 1 TO 4
40 PRINT K
50 NEXT K
```

Look at the program lines to the left. After you have studied them, see if you can answer the questions that follow:

1. Describe what the computer will do if you enter LIST.
2. Describe what the computer will do if you enter RUN.
3. Enter this program and RUN it. Write down the computer's output. Now add the following two lines to the program. LIST the new program to see that they have been correctly placed.
   ```
   20 FOR J = 1 TO 3
   60 NEXT J
   ```
4. Before you RUN this program, guess what the output will be. Write your guess on a sheet of paper.
5. Finally, RUN the program. Write down the computer's output.

Before you added lines 20 and 60 to the program, you probably guessed that this program would print the numbers 1, 2, 3, and 4, one number to a line. Were you a little surprised to see, after you entered the two new lines, that the computer printed the numbers 1 to 4 three times? To see why, first LIST the program.

```
10 Clearscreen
20 FOR J = 1 TO 3
30 FOR K = 1 TO 4
40 PRINT K
50 NEXT K
60 NEXT J
```

Notice that there are two **FOR − NEXT** loops in this program. The first one, which begins with line 20 and ends with line 60, lies entirely outside the other one. This is called an **outer loop**. The second loop, which begins with line 30 and ends with line 50, lies entirely inside the outer loop. This is called an **inner loop**. When two (or more) loops are placed like this in a program, they are said to be **nested**.

See how these nested loops work:

10 Clearscreen	Clears the screen.
20 FOR J = 1 TO 3	Begins the outer loop. The variable J is given the value 1. It will count to 3.
30 FOR K = 1 TO 4	Begins the inner loop. The variable K is given the value 1. It will count to 4.
40 PRINT K	Prints the value of K. This will happen 12 times.
50 NEXT K	Gives K its next value. This is the final step of the inner loop. It must be executed four times before the computer gets to line 60.
60 NEXT J	This is the final step of the outer loop. It gives J its next value. Each time J is given a new value, the entire inner loop, starting at line 30, will be executed again.

Memory Bank

Nested loops

When one loop lies entirely inside another loop, the loops are said to be **nested**. A loop that is completed within another loop is called an **inner loop**. A loop that encloses another loop is called an **outer loop**. Each time the **index** or variable of the outer loop is given a new value, the entire inner loop is executed.

USE WHAT YOU HAVE LEARNED

Look at the following program steps. Study the program and see if you can answer the questions that follow:

```
10  Clearscreen
20  FOR J= 1 TO 3
30  FOR K = 1 TO 4
40  PRINT J
50  NEXT K
60  NEXT J
```

1. Compare this program with that in the *Discover for Yourself* activity above. How are they different?

2. Guess what the computer's output would be if you entered **RUN**. Write your guess on a sheet of paper.

3. Enter this program and **RUN** it. Write the computer's output on a sheet of paper.

Line 40, **PRINT J**, is the only line which is changed from the *Discover for Yourself* program above. This program still prints 12 numbers, but it prints each of the numbers 1, 2, and 3, four times. Study this program carefully to be certain that you understand why this happens.

A word of caution!

When using nested loops you must be very careful to keep the inner loop entirely within the outer. The **NEXT** statement for the inner loop must come before the **NEXT** statement for the outer loop.

CHIP WONDERS: WHAT ABOUT THE 1ST QUESTION?

Correct

```
10  Clearscreen
20  FOR I = 1 TO 4 ←———————— OUTER LOOP ———┐
30  FOR J = 1 TO 3 ←———————— INNER LOOP ——┐ │
40  PRINT I,J                              │ │
50  NEXT J ←——————— This NEXT ends the inner loop. }┘ │
60  NEXT I ←——————— This NEXT ends the outer loop. }——┘
```

Incorrect

```
10  Clearscreen
20  FOR I = 1 TO 4
30  FOR J = 1 TO 3
40  PRINT I,J
50  NEXT I ←——————— These two NEXT statements are in
60  NEXT J ←——————— the wrong order.
```

Exercises

1. Study the program below and tell what will be displayed if the program is RUN.

```
10  Clearscreen
20  FOR K = 1 TO 3
30  FOR M = 2 TO 6 STEP 2
40  PRINT K, M
50  NEXT M
60  NEXT K
```

Enter this program and RUN it.

2. Study the program below and tell what will be displayed if the program is RUN.

```
10  Clearscreen
20  FOR N = 2 TO 6 STEP 2
30  FOR Z = 1 TO 3
40  PRINT Z
50  NEXT Z
60  NEXT N
```

Enter this program and RUN it.

3. Write the program steps needed to print the following set of numbers. Use a pair of nested loops to produce the numbers.

3, 5, 7, 3, 5, 7, 3, 5, 7

Chip's Challenges

4. Study the program below and determine what would be displayed if the program were RUN.

```
10  Clearscreen
20  FOR H = 1 TO 4
30  FOR D = 1 TO H
40  PRINT D
50  NEXT D
60  NEXT H
```

Enter the program and RUN it.

APPLICATIONS

Nested Loops

Tahia Plesch got a brand new digital watch for her birthday. It gave her a grand idea for a computer program. She would program her computer to be a digital clock. On top of the next page is how she started the program:

Chip's Bits

In the early 1960s, one company's mainframe computer could do 33,000 additions each second. It cost $280,000 and needed an air-conditioned room to work in. The Central Processing Unit was six feet wide and five feet high. The same company made a micro-computer twenty years later that was 200 times faster and cost less than $4,000.

CHIP WONDERS: DID YOU GET THIS FOR QUESTION 3?

```
NEW
10  Clearscreen
20  FOR S = 0 TO 59
50  Clearscreen
60  PRINT S
90  NEXT S
```

Enter Tahia's program and **RUN** it. See if you can help her, by answering the questions below.

1. Tahia wants **S** to stand for seconds. Why do you think she wanted **S** to count from **0** to **59**?

2. This program counts the seconds very carefully. Tahia noticed, however, that the seconds went by far too quickly. How could Tahia slow her clock?

3. Place a timing loop between lines 60 and 90. **RUN** the program and see how many seconds it takes to complete the entire program.

Your timing loop might have looked like this:

```
70  FOR T = 1 TO 300
80  NEXT T
```

Of course, you may have had a number other than **300** after the word **TO** in line 70. Chances are that your program did not take exactly 60 seconds. It will be necessary to try several different numbers in line 70 until you have it running correctly. Remember, if your clock runs too fast, place a greater number in line 70. If it runs too slowly, place a lesser number in line 70.

Tahia was delighted when she got her seconds working correctly. Before she continued with the clock, she **LIST**ed her program. It looked like this:

```
10  Clearscreen
40  FOR S = 0 TO 59
50  Clearscreen
60  PRINT S
70  FOR T = 1 TO 300   ←  You may have a
                          number other
                          than 300 here.
80  NEXT T
90  NEXT S
```

In order to have the clock count minutes, she had to add two lines and change another. Can you guess what these changes will be?

Chip's Bits

Time magazine's Person of the Year for 1983 was a Machine of the Year—the Computer. Like the men and women featured in earlier years, the machine had its picture on the cover and was the subject of stories about its achievements and its influence in the past year. All this was in the January 3, 1983, issue.

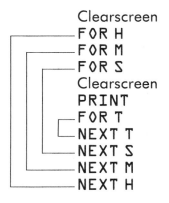

These are the lines she must add (M stands for minutes):

```
30 FOR M = 0 TO 59
100 NEXT M
```

Line 60 must be changed to read

```
60 PRINT M, S
```

Now when she LISTed her program it looked like this:

```
10 Clearscreen
30 FOR M = 0 TO 59
40 FOR S = 0 TO 59
50 Clearscreen
60 PRINT M, S
70 FOR T = 1 TO 300 ←    You may have a
80 NEXT T                number other
90 NEXT S                than 300 here.
100 NEXT M
```

Can you guess what is needed to place the hours in Tahia's clock? You were correct if you said that she needs to add two lines and change line 60 again. The changes are shown here:

```
20 FOR H = 0 TO 23
110 NEXT H
```

Line 60 will now read

```
60 PRINT H, M, S
```

Add these steps and **RUN** the program. You may not want the program to run until it is completed. If your timing loop is correct, it will take twenty-four hours to be finished!

The clock program has four nested loops in it. The outer loop counts the hours. Inside this loop is the one that counts minutes. The minute loop must complete sixty counts before the hour loop advances by one.

Within the minute loop is the loop that counts seconds. This also must count sixty times, before the minute loop advances once.

Finally, the timing loop in lines 70 and 80 controls the accuracy of the whole program. This loop lies completely within the loop that counts the seconds and must count about 300 (or so) times before the seconds can advance by one!

```
  Clearscreen
┌─FOR H
│┌─FOR M
││┌─FOR S
│││ Clearscreen
│││ PRINT
│││┌─FOR T
│││└─NEXT T
││└─NEXT S
│└─NEXT M
└─NEXT H
```

Tahia liked her program a lot, but she thought of a way to make the output look neater. Here is how she made the final change (on line 60, of course):

```
60  PRINT H; ":"; M; ":"; S
```

See if you can guess how her output will look when she **RUN**s this program now. Add this line to your program and **RUN** it.

USE WHAT YOU HAVE LEARNED

Kim had a brown paper bag full of green, red, and yellow gum drops. Three times he reached into the bag for gum drops and ended up with two greens and a yellow. He was delighted with his catch but wondered about the many different ways there are to mix the three colors, green, red, and yellow. He decided to write a computer program to help him. In his program, the number 1 stands for green, 2 stands for red, and 3 stands for yellow. Three nested loops are used to do all of the mixing or combining.

The Program

```
10  Clearscreen
20  FOR A = 1 TO 3
30  FOR B = 1 TO 3
40  FOR C = 1 TO 3        ⎰Quite a mixture of
50  PRINT A; B; C,← ⎱commas and semi-
60  NEXT C⎱              colons.
70  NEXT B ⎱← These variables come in the
80  NEXT A⎰    reverse order of those in the
              FOR statements.
```

When Kim ran his program, he was shocked to see that there were 27 different ways to combine the colors. The output is to the left.

Here is how Kim interpreted these numbers:

G G G	G G R	G G Y
G R G	G R R	G R Y
G Y G	G Y R	G Y Y
R G G	R G R	R G Y
R R G	R R R	R R Y
R Y G	R Y R	R Y Y
Y G G	Y G R	Y G Y
Y R G	Y R R	Y R Y
Y Y G	Y Y R	Y Y Y

Key:
G green   R red   Y yellow

```
RUN

111    112    113
121    122    123
131    132    133
211    212    213
221    222    223
231    232    233
311    312    313
321    322    323
331    332    333
```

E x e r c i s e s

1. In the clock program, the computer goes through the timing loop 300 times each second. That means that it goes through the timing loop 60 * 300 = 18 000 times in a minute. Use your computer to determine how many times it would go through the timing loop in twenty-four hours!

2. A shoebox contained blue and yellow pencils. Lois reached in for two pencils. Write a program to give all possible combinations of the two colors, blue and yellow.

3. Dennis has a plastic coin bank that contains pennies, nickels, dimes, and quarters. He picks four coins out of his bank. Write a program to give all possible combinations of the four types of coins.

Chip's Challenges

4. Laverne Schuster asked Kim if she could have four of his gumdrops. Kim, always good-natured, invited her to pick them from his bag. Write a program to give all possible mixes for four gumdrops, from the bag of green, red, and yellow gumdrops.

CHAPTER SUMMARY

1. When a FOR-NEXT loop is contained entirely within another, the loops are called nested loops.

2. A loop which is contained within another is called an inner loop. The other loop is called an outer loop.

3. The index, or variable, of an inner loop must count through its entire range before the variable of the outer loop advances once.

4. When loops are nested, each loop must begin with a FOR statement and end with a NEXT statement. The FOR statement of an inner loop must follow the FOR statement of an outer loop. The NEXT statement of an inner loop must come before that of an outer loop.

5. Any number of FOR-NEXT loops may be nested, depending only on the amount of memory available.

PROBLEM SET 7

Copy and complete the following programs and fill in the missing variable names.

1.
```
10  FOR I = 1 TO 3
20  FOR J = 1 TO 4
30  PRINT J
40  NEXT_____
50  NEXT_____
```

2.
```
10  FOR M = 1 TO 10
20  FOR N = 1 TO 20
30  FOR P = 1 TO 5
40  PRINT P
50  NEXT_____
60  NEXT_____
70  NEXT_____
```

Find the error or errors in the programs below. Tell how you would correct each error.

3.
```
10  FOUR K = 1 TO 3
20  FOR L = 1 TO 3
30  PRINT L
40  NEXT L
50  NEXT K
```

4.
```
10  FOR S = 1 TO 4
20  FOR T = 2 TO 10 STEP 2
30  PRINT T
40  NEXT S
50  NEXT T
```

5.
```
10  FOR A = 5 TO 7
20  FOR B = ONE TWO THREE
30  PRINT A, B
40  NEXT B
50  NEXT A
```

Study the lines of the programs below. What would be the output of each if RUN were entered?

6.
```
10  FOR X = 1 TO 3
20  FOR Y = 1 TO 2
30  PRINT Y
40  NEXT Y
50  NEXT X
```

7.
```
10  FOR M = 2 TO 4
20  FOR N = 1 TO 3
30  PRINT N
40  NEXT N
50  NEXT M
```

8.
```
10  FOR K = 1 TO 5 STEP 2
20  FOR Y = 1 TO 3
30  PRINT K
40  NEXT Y
50  NEXT K
```

9.
```
10  FOR Z = 1 TO 5 STEP 2
20  FOR W = 1 TO 2
30  PRINT W
40  NEXT W
50  NEXT Z
```

10.
```
10  FOR X = 4 TO 1 STEP -1
20  FOR Y = 1 TO X
30  PRINT Y
40  NEXT Y
50  NEXT X
```

11.
```
10  FOR A = 1 TO 3
20  FOR B = 1 TO 2
30  FOR C = 1 TO 3
40  PRINT C
50  NEXT C
60  NEXT B
70  NEXT A
```

12. Write the program steps to have the message below printed on the screen over and over (and over). Include a timing loop so that there is about a half-second pause between the lines of the message.

THIS MESSAGE SEEMS TO GO ON AND ON

13. Write the program steps to print the same message as in Problem 12 above. Have only the part of the message which appears below repeated.

AND ON

14. Write the program steps to have the computer print a secret message (such as the one below) on the screen. Keep the message on the screen for a short time with a timing loop. See how many of your classmates can tell you the message.

MEET ME FOR A SECRET
CAPTAIN OREGANO FAN CLUB MEETING
AFTER SCHOOL UNDER THE BANYAN TREE

15. Study the program steps below. What would be the output if RUN were entered?
```
10  Clearscreen
20  PRINT "THIS MESSAGE GETS FASTER";
30  FOR I = 100 TO 1 STEP -1
40  PRINT " AND FASTER ";
50  FOR K = 1 TO I
60  NEXT K
70  NEXT I
```

16. Write the program steps to have the numbers from 99 to 1 printed, with a timing delay after each number.

17. Write the program steps to have the following set of numbers printed four times. Use nested loops to produce them.

3,5,7,9

18. Write a program to have the following set of numbers printed, using nested loops to produce the numbers.
1,1,1,1,3,3,3,3,5,5,5,5

19. Write a program to have your name and address flash on the screen about two times a second.

20. Write a program to have the computer print the following set of numbers. Use nested loops to give the numbers.
6,6,6,5,5,5,4,4,4,3,3,3,2,2,2,1,1,1

21. A wooden box contains apples, oranges, and bananas. Lester reaches in three times for fruit. Write a program to show every possible combination of the three fruits.

22. Regina has green, blue, black, and red socks in her bureau drawer. Each morning she reaches into her drawer for two socks. Write a program to display all possible pairs of the socks.

 **Chip's Challenges**

23. The song "1 little, 2 little, 3 little Indians" has long been a favorite. Write a program with FOR-NEXT loops to print the words to the song. Use a timing loop to delay the output between verses.

24. Using nested loops, write a program to have the following printed on the screen:
1
1 2
1 2 3
1 2 3 4
1 2 3 4 5

25. Write a program to draw the figure below on the screen. Make it rise slowly to the top of the screen. See the Rocket Launch program for a guide.

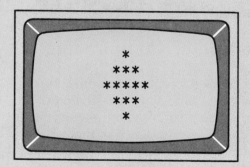

Hint: Have a FOR-NEXT loop do PRINT ten times before drawing the figure. This will place the figure near the bottom of the screen.

26. Jenny keeps nickels, dimes, and quarters in a jar. Each day she reaches into the jar and takes out five coins. Write a program to give all possible combinations of these kinds of coins.

Computer Components

The interior of a mainframe shows both its size and the complex wiring it uses.

Take a look at your computer. Neat, is it not? Tidy. Its keyboard, with which you are getting very familiar, is very much like that of an electric typewriter. Its screen is like that of your television set at home.

You know something about what is inside it, too. You know that it contains a microprocessor. You know that this microprocessor is the heart of your computer.

What else does your computer contain? There are many wires.

There are a few switches. And there are thousands and thousands of electrical gadgets, many of them with strange sounding names.

All the electrical devices are connected by wires to form electric **circuits**. (A circuit is an unbroken path that electricity takes from its source, through the devices it runs, and back to the place where it started.) All of the computer's operations are carried out by special circuits. Circuits send information to various

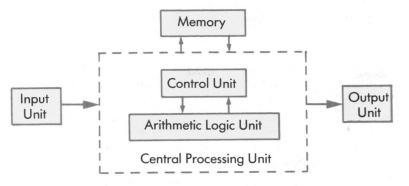

Memory

Control Unit

Input Unit → Arithmetic Logic Unit → Output Unit

Central Processing Unit

parts of the computer. Circuits compare two items of data to see if they are the same. Circuits display information on the screen. There are thousands and thousands of different circuits, waiting to be turned on or off, in even the smallest computer.

These circuits have been sorted or classified into five major groups. Each of these groups is a **component** of the computer. These components are:

1. **Input**
2. **Output**
3. **Memory**
4. **Arithmetic Logic Unit**
5. **Control Unit**

The diagram above shows how these components are related.

Let's look at each of these components.

1. The **Input Unit** is usually a keyboard. Many other input devices, however, such as **magnetic tape**, **magnetic disks**, or **punched cards**, can be used. But most information begins at a keyboard.

All information entered through the Input Unit is translated into electrical impulses. Remember that each key has a code of ones and zeros. In electric circuit terms, a one means the circuit is turned on, and a zero means it is turned off. Therefore each character on the keyboard, is converted into a string of ons and offs. The entered information, in the form of such strings of ons and offs, is sent into the computer's Central Processing Unit. It is then stored in the Memory until needed.

2. The **Output Unit** is often a video display screen, similar to a TV screen. Some computers have a **printer** as an additional output device. Information can also be output to magnetic tape or disk, but it cannot be seen in that form.

3. The **Memory Unit** is where all the information is stored. You can think of the Memory Unit as consisting of thousands of **locations**, like mailboxes. Each location has a number, which is called its **address**. Addresses always begin at zero and continue in sequence 0,1,2,3, etc. Every location can hold a number, which is called the **contents** of the address. The contents of a particular location can change many times during a program, but the address of the location never changes. A location is always identified by its address, and the address is an important part of the computer's instructions.

Information can be sent from the Memory Unit to one of three other units:

a. To the Arithmetic Logic Unit, where it is called **data** and arithmetic operations are performed on it.

b. To the Control Unit, where it is called an **instruction** and is used to direct the computer's actions.

c. To the Output Unit, where it is displayed (or printed, etc.)

4. The **Arithmetic Logic Unit** is where all the arithmetic is performed. A very important part of this unit is the **arithmetic register**. The register can hold only one number at a time. The other number used in the operation must be brought from the Memory Unit. The number from the Memory Unit can be added to, subtracted from, multiplied by, or divided into the number in the register. The answer is then put into the register, replacing the number that was there originally.

5. The **Control Unit** directs all the computer's actions. Two important parts of this unit are the **instruction pointer** and the **instruction register**.

The pointer tells the computer where its next instruction is located. When the computer is first turned on, an address is loaded into the pointer. The instruction at the location identified by this address is brought to the Control Unit, and the address in the pointer is increased by one, for example, from 2 to 3 or from 6 to 7. (The pointer can only count by one. However, instructions can be given that permit a new number to be sent to the pointer. These are called **branching** or **jumping** instructions.)

The instruction register receives the instruction pointed to by the pointer. Most instructions consist of two parts, an instruction code, which tells the computer what to do, and an address, which tells it what to do it to, that is, where to find the information on which the operation is to be performed. The Control Unit interprets the instruction and carries it out.

As you saw on the diagram, the Control Unit and the Arithmetic Logic Unit together are called the **Central Processing Unit (CPU)**. (Sometimes this is known simply as the Processor.)

The microprocessor, which is at the heart of your computer, is its Central Processing Unit. The thousands of circuits that make it up fit on a tiny chip of silicon, like a piece of glass, smaller than your smallest fingernail. This chip is sealed in a plastic box about the size of a corn chip. Metal prongs come out of this box, to which wires can be attached to make the necessary electrical connections. It is this little plastic box and the tiny chip inside it that enable the computer to do all the many truly amazing things it can do.

What Do You Know?
1. What are the five components of a computer?
2. What are three kinds of input devices? Which is most commonly used?
3. In addition to the video display screen, what other output devices can be used?
4. Where is information stored in a computer?
5. Where do computers compute?

What Can You Learn?
1. How does a computer compare information?
2. How does a computer multiply and divide?

What Do You Think?
1. Are there any other input devices, besides those mentioned, being used in your community?
2. Does computer information stored on tape or disks make sounds?

COMING INPUT—GOING OUTPUT

Numeric and Alphabetic Values

Information, or data, may be entered from the keyboard, while a program is RUNning. The INPUT statement instructs the computer to accept the data entered and to store it in a variable location.

Data from the Keyboard

DISCOVER FOR YOURSELF

For each of the following programs, guess the computer's output. Then RUN the program to check your answers. Remember to enter NEW before each program.

COMPUTER DISPLAYS

PROGRAM

```
1.  10   A = 10
    20   B = 20
    30   PRINT "A = ";A,
    40   PRINT "B = ";B
    50   PRINT "A+B = ";A+B
```

```
2.  10   A$ = "COMPUTERS "
    20   B$ = "ARE "
    30   C$ = "FUN"
    40   PRINT A$;B$;C$
```

```
3.  10   PRINT "WHAT'S YOUR NAME?"
    20   X$ = "SHIRLEY"
    30   PRINT X$
```

```
4.  10   A$ = "COMPUTERS "
    20   B$ = "ARE "
    30   C$ = "FUN"
    40   PRINT A$+B$+C$
```

WHAT DID YOU LEARN?

You should have the output shown below for Program 1.

```
A = 10          B = 20
A+B = 30
```

The comma at the end of line 30 caused the computer to continue printing on the same line.

For Program 2, you should have the output shown on the next page.

COMPUTERS ARE FUN

String variables were used and all the strings were printed on the same line because of the semicolons.

The output for Program 3 appears below.

WHAT'S YOUR NAME?
SHIRLEY

Program 4 may have been a bit of a surprise to you. The output appears below.

COMPUTERS ARE FUN

Now you are going to see how to improve each of these programs by using the **INPUT** instruction.

This is what an **INPUT** statement looks like.

10 INPUT N

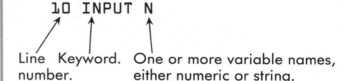

Line   Keyword.   One or more variable names,
number.   either numeric or string.

Here are rewrites of the four programs from *Discover for Yourself*, using the **INPUT** statement.

Examples:

1. The screen at the left shows Program 1, page 130, with lines 10 and 20 altered. After entering **RUN**, a *?* is displayed. The computer does not doubt your **RUN** command. It is waiting for data, a value for the variable named in the **INPUT** statement. In this case, enter 10, the value you want for A, then press **RETURN** or **ENTER**.

Your screen would   RUN
now show this. Note   ?10
that another ques-   ?
tion mark has ap-
peared.

Of course, the program listing would also appear.

The computer is waiting for a second piece of data. Enter 20, the value of B.

Memory Bank

Strings

You can join strings together by placing a + between the variable names.

Memory Bank

INPUT statement

The **INPUT** instruction causes the computer to do the following:

1.   *Stop* **RUN**ning *the program.*
2.   *Display a* ?.
3.   *Wait for data (information) to be entered.*

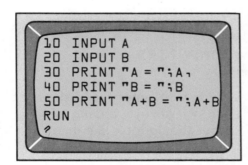

```
10  INPUT A
20  INPUT B
30  PRINT "A = ";A,
40  PRINT "B = ";B
50  PRINT "A+B = ";A+B
RUN
?
```

CHIP SAYS:
NOTE THE ? —
YOUR COMPUTER
MAY ALSO SHOW
A CURSOR.

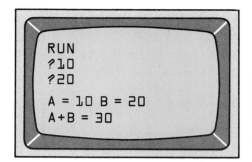

```
RUN
?10
?20

A = 10 B = 20
A+B = 30
```

Your screen should now look like the one on the left. As soon as you entered the second value, 20, the computer completed the program.

The advantage of using the **INPUT** statement in this program is that you can **RUN** the program again and enter new numbers. But you do not have to re-type lines 10 and 20. Try it. Just enter **RUN** again. When the question marks appear, enter 15, then 30.

2. The **INPUT** statement can also be used with string variables. Change Program 2, page 102, to that shown below.

```
10   INPUT A$
20   INPUT B$
30   INPUT C$
40   PRINT A$;B$;C$
RUN
```

Lines 10, 20, and 30 have been changed, using **INPUT**. When the **?** appears this time, type the word **COMPUTERS**, press the space bar, then press ⬚**RETURN**⬚ or ⬚**ENTER**⬚. The space will prevent run-on words in your output.

You should get another **?** following **COMPUTERS**.

```
RUN
?COMPUTERS
?
```

Continue to enter the rest of the words after each **?**, always ending with a space. Your output should look like this:

```
RUN
?COMPUTERS
?ARE
?FUN
COMPUTERS ARE FUN
```

3. Program 3 can be used to personalize your output. Simply change line 20 to
```
20   INPUT X$
```
and **RUN** the program. Your output should be similar to the output shown below.

```
10   PRINT "WHAT IS YOUR NAME?"
20   INPUT X$
30   PRINT X$
RUN
WHAT IS YOUR NAME?
?
```

Chip's Bits

The magnetic telegraph, invented by the American painter Samuel F.B. Morse, used a pattern of electric signals similar to a computer's. The signals stood for letters and numbers. Combinations of long and short signals are used in the Morse Code, which is now used mainly in radio telegraphy, where the short signals are known as "dits" and the long ones as "dahs."

When the **?** appears, type your name and enter it. You should get a display similar to this.

```
10  PRINT "WHAT IS YOUR NAME?"
20  INPUT X$
30  PRINT X$
RUN
WHAT IS YOUR NAME?
?ALLEE OOP ◄───────── Your name typed in
ALLEE OOP ◄            here and printed out
                       └here.
```

Now, dress up your program. Change line 30, as shown. Then **LIST** and **RUN** the program. Your output should be similar to that shown below.

```
10  PRINT "WHAT IS YOUR NAME?"
20  INPUT X$
30  PRINT "MY NAME IS ";X$ ◄── Here is a new line 30.
RUN                        ╲── Did you put a space here?
WHAT IS YOUR NAME?
?ALLEE OOP ◄─────────── Type your name here, where
MY NAME IS ALLEE OOP              you see ALLEE OOP
```

It is also possible to combine lines 10 and 20 into a single line. First, eliminate lines 10 and 20 as written. To do this, simply enter the lines shown below.

```
10  Clearscreen
20  INPUT "WHAT IS YOUR NAME";X$
```

LIST the program to be sure the changes have been made. **RUN** the program. This time you should get the following line displayed on your screen.

```
WHAT IS YOUR NAME? ◄──  Your computer may dis-
                        play a flashing cursor at the
                        end of this line.
```

This **?** was not in the **INPUT** statement, line 20. It was displayed by the computer, which prints the string and adds the **?**. Now type and enter your name. Your display should look like this.

```
WHAT IS YOUR NAME? ALLEE OOP
MY NAME IS ALLEE OOP
```

Your name displayed   Your name typed in
here by computer.   here by you.

A word about string variables. Recall from Chapter 5 the form of a statement using a string variable:

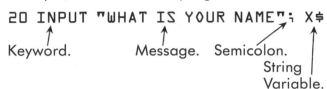

```
10  X$ = "SHIRLEY"
```
String   Quotation
Variable.   Marks.

You were told to use quotation marks when using string variables. However, it is not necessary to include quotation marks when you enter the data while the program is running. For example, look at the last program's line 20.

```
20 INPUT "WHAT IS YOUR NAME"; X$
```

Keyword.   Message.   Semicolon.
                                      String
                                      Variable.

This statement directs the computer to print the message WHAT IS YOUR NAME, display a ?, then pause to wait for data. You need only enter your name, without quotation marks.

> Note: Your system may or may not display a ? after a message in an INPUT statement. Check this out.

4. For further illustration of the use of the INPUT statement, look at Program 4, page 102. Replace lines 10, 20, and 30 with these lines.

```
10  INPUT "ENTER A NOUN ";A$
20  INPUT "ENTER A VERB ";B$
30  INPUT "ENTER A NOUN ";C$
40  PRINT A$+B$+C$
```

Now RUN the program, typing in the words COMPUTERS, ARE, and FUN. Your display will look like this. Caution! Remember to type a blank space after each word of data, before entering it.

Memory Bank

INPUTting strings

In an INPUT statement:

1. *A message must be in quotation marks.*
2. *There must be a semicolon between the message and the variable.*
3. *Enter data for a string variable without quotation marks.*

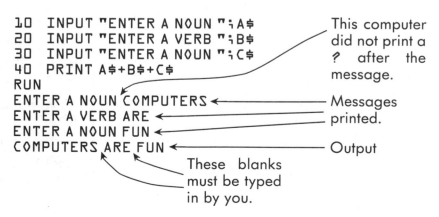

```
10  INPUT "ENTER A NOUN ";A$
20  INPUT "ENTER A VERB ";B$
30  INPUT "ENTER A NOUN ";C$
40  PRINT A$+B$+C$
RUN
ENTER A NOUN COMPUTERS
ENTER A VERB ARE
ENTER A NOUN FUN
COMPUTERS ARE FUN
```

This computer did not print a ? after the message.

Messages printed.

Output

These blanks must be typed in by you.

USE WHAT YOU HAVE LEARNED

```
ENTER YOUR NAME JOLLY CHOLLY
ENTER YOUR AGE 13
ENTER BEST FRIEND'S NAME ALICE
MY NAME IS JOLLY CHOLLY
MY AGE IS 13
BEST FRIEND'S NAME IS ALICE
```

Complete the **INPUT** statements in the program shown below to direct the computer to display the output to the left.

Program

```
10  INPUT_____
20  INPUT_____      Copy and complete lines
30  INPUT_____      10, 20, and 30.
40  PRINT "MY NAME IS ";A$
50  PRINT "MY AGE IS ";B$
60  PRINT "BEST FRIEND'S NAME IS ";C$
```

Do not forget the semicolons and quotation marks. The string variables you should use can be found in the **PRINT** statements.

Exercises

1. Each line below contains exactly one error. Identify the error, then write the line correctly.
   a. `10  PUTIN A$`   **b.** `INPUT A`
   c. `10  "ENTER A NUMBER";X`
   d. `10  INPUT "ENTER A NUMBER",Y`
   e. `10  "WHAT IS YOUR NAME?";N$`
   f. `INPUT "ENTER YOUR HEIGHT";H`

2. Rewrite each program below using **INPUT** statements without messages.
   a. `10  A=55` ⎱ ←——— Replace these two lines.
       `20  X=100` ⎰
       `30  PRINT "A*X = ";A*X`
   b. `10  PRINT "ENTER A NUMBER"`
       `20  N = 3.1415` ←——————┐
       `30  PRINT "ENTER ANOTHER NUMBER "` ⎞
       `40  R = 100` ←——————— Replace these
       `50  P = R*N`   two lines.
       `60  PRINT "THE PRODUCT IS ";P`

3. Rewrite the program in 2b above, using **INPUT** statements which include the messages in lines 10 and 30.

4. Determine the output of each of the following programs.
   a. `10  INPUT "ENTER A NUMBER ";C`
       `20  INPUT "ENTER ANOTHER NUMBER ";D`
       `30  PRINT "THEIR SUM IS ";C+D`
       `40  PRINT "THEIR PRODUCT IS ";C+D`
       Data: C=15, D=25
   b. `10  INPUT "WHAT IS YOUR NAME?";N$`
       `20  INPUT "HOW OLD ARE YOU?";O$`
       `30  PRINT "HELLO ";N$`
       `40  PRINT "YOUR AGE IS ";O$`
   Assume the name entered is Svengali and the age is 150 years. Your answer should include everything displayed after **RUN** is typed and entered.

5. Determine the output for each program below. Assume the given data would be entered correctly.

a.
```
10   INPUT "ENTER A NOUN ";A$
20   INPUT "ENTER A VERB ";B$
30   INPUT "ENTER A NOUN ";C$
40   PRINT B$ + A$ + C$
```
Data: COMPUTERS
          ARE
          FUN

b.
```
10   PRINT "AREA OF A RECTANGLE "
20   INPUT "ENTER THE LENGTH IN CM ";L
30   INPUT "ENTER THE WIDTH IN CM ";W
40   A = L * W
50   PRINT "AREA IS ";A;" SQUARE CM"
```

Data: 20
             10

c.
```
10   INPUT "ENTER A FRIEND'S NAME ";A$
20   INPUT "FRIEND'S FAVORITE COLOR ";B$
30   INPUT "YOUR ZIP CODE ";C$
40   PRINT A$;" WEIGHS ";C$;" POUNDS "
50   PRINT "BECAUSE ";A$;" EATS ";B$;" ICE CREAM"
```
Data: TOM, GREEN, 21218

d.
```
10   INPUT "ENTER A PET ";P$
20   INPUT "ENTER A TEACHER'S NAME ";T$
30   INPUT "ENTER YOUR FAVORITE COLOR ";C$
40   INPUT "ENTER YOUR FAVORITE SNACK ";S$
50   INPUT "ENTER YOUR NAME ";N$
60   PRINT "DEAR DR. ";T$
70   PRINT "MY ";P$;" HAS A ";C$;" TAIL."
80   PRINT "HE ATE ";C$;" ";S$;" ."
90   PRINT "CAN YOU HELP MY ";P$;"?"
100   PRINT "THANK YOU,"
110   PRINT N$
```
Data: DOG, PIERCE, PINK, POPCORN, DOT

Chip's Challenges

6. Write a computer program that will display the message

JOHN LOVES MATH

or any other message. Each message should contain three words, a noun, a verb, and another noun. The output should look like this:

ENTER A NOUN (You enter a noun.)
ENTER A VERB (You enter a verb.)
ENTER ANOTHER NOUN (You enter a noun.)

Then print the message in the same order.

8.2

More Input about INPUT

Look at the program at the right. Guess the output you would get using the numbers:

```
10  INPUT A
20  A = A + 1
30  PRINT A
```

a. 1   **b.** 10   **c.** 100

Did you get the following results?

a. ?1   **b.** ?10   **c.** ?100
　　2　　　　　　11　　　　　　101
　　　　　　　　　Output

Use this idea in this program below. Note the blank space at the end of the quoted message in line 30 and at the beginning of the message in line 40. Try the program. Your output should look like this, assuming your age is 13.

```
10  INPUT "YOUR AGE ";A
20  A=A+1
30  PRINT "NEXT YEAR YOU WILL BE "
40  PRINT A;" YEARS OLD"
RUN
YOUR AGE 13
NEXT YEAR YOU WILL BE
14 YEARS OLD
```

Now suppose a friend uses this program and enters 12 YEARS after the ?, (or blank, depending on your system.) The output might look like that shown at the left.

An error message is sent by the computer when someone tries to enter letters for a numeric variable.

Your system might show ?REDO, or give some other error message. Simply re-type the age without the word YEARS. The program should run correctly.

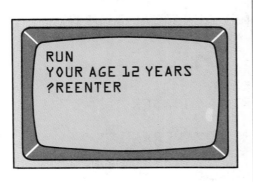

```
RUN
YOUR AGE 12 YEARS
?REENTER
```

Memory Bank

INPUT errors

Never·try to **INPUT** *non-numeric data for numeric variables.*

To avoid this kind of error, you, the programmer, can use a message in the **INPUT** statement to help the user. Simply change line 10 to:

```
10  INPUT "ENTER YOUR AGE IN YEARS ";A
```

This message tells the user to enter only a numeric value. Such a message, or any similar message, appearing in an **INPUT** statement is called a **prompt**. Such messages are helpful to the user of a program.

WHAT DID YOU LEARN?

Points to remember:
1. A statement such as **10 PRINT** can be used to skip lines in output.
2. Messages, called prompts, can help the user of a program understand the program.

USE WHAT YOU HAVE LEARNED

Study the program below.

These lines prompt the user to enter name.

These lines prompt user to enter grades.

What do you think these lines do?

```
10   Clearscreen
20   PRINT "AVERAGE PROGRAM"
30   PRINT
40   INPUT "ENTER YOUR FIRST NAME ";F$
50   INPUT "ENTER YOUR LAST NAME ";L$
60   PRINT "ENTER YOUR GRADES "
70   INPUT "MATH ";M
80   INPUT "LANGUAGE ";L
90   INPUT "SCIENCE ";S
100   INPUT "SOCIAL STUDIES ";H
110   A = (M + L + S + H)/4
120   PRINT
130   PRINT "NAME ";L$;",";F$
140   PRINT
150   PRINT "GRADES ";M;" ";L;" ";S;" ";H
160   PRINT
170   PRINT "AVERAGE IS ";A
```

This program instructs the computer to accept a student's name and grades. The student's average is computed. The name, grades, and average are displayed. The output is shown at the top of the next page.

```
RUN
AVERAGE PROGRAM

ENTER YOUR FIRST NAME? ALLEE
ENTER YOUR LAST NAME? OOP
ENTER YOUR GRADES
MATH?80
LANGUAGE?90
SCIENCE?80
SOCIAL STUDIES?90

NAME      OOP,ALLEE

GRADES 80 90 80 90

AVERAGE IS 85
```

Trace the steps of the program.

Line(s)	Explanation
10	Clears the screen.
20	Prints a title for the program.
30	Skips a line.
40 and 50	Prompts the user and allows entry of the user's first and last names.
60	Prompts the user for the next few lines.
70, 80, 90, 100	Halts the program for **INPUT** of the user's grades, one at a time.
110	Computes the average.
120	Prints a blank line—that is, skips a line.
130	Prints the title, **NAME**, followed by the user's name, last name first. Note how the comma in line 130 made the computer skip spaces before printing the user's name—**OOP,ALLEE**. Remember, in a **PRINT** statement, the comma causes the computer to skip to the next print zone, or field.
140	Skips a line.
150	Prints the title, **GRADES**, followed by the user's grades. The blanks in quotation marks, (**" "**), put spaces between numbers.
160	Skips a line.
170	Prints the user's average.

E x e r c i s e s

1. Rewrite lines 70, 80, 90, and 100 of the **INPUT** Application program, p. 110, to enter grades for Art, Music, Shop, and Reading.

2. Rewrite each **INPUT** statement below to include an appropriate prompt.
   a. 10 INPUT X
   To enter the user's weight in pounds.
   b. 10 INPUT Y$
   To enter the user's favorite car.
   c. 10 INPUT N
   To enter the user's height in inches.

3. Change the **AVERAGE PROGRAM**, p. 138, to compute the average of five grades, with Reading as the fifth grade to be entered.

Chip's Challenges

4. Write a computer program to compute the unit price of an item purchased at the supermarket. Use the formula

   P = C/N   where   P = unit price
                           C = cost of item
                           N = number of units of item

   For example, if a 10 oz jar of roasted nuts costs $1.80, the unit price would be computed as follows:

   C = 1.80   P = 1.80/10
   N = 10   P = .18

   The unit price is 18 cents per ounce. Your output should look like this:

   ENTER THE COST? (User enters cost)
   NUMBER OF UNITS IS? (User enters number of units of item)
   UNIT PRICE IS (Computer prints value of P)
   Run the program using the following items:
   64 ounce bottle of Kong Kola for $1.20
   2 liter bottle of floor wax for $2.85

CHAPTER SUMMARY

1. In a **PRINT** statement, string variables can be joined by using + signs.
2. The **INPUT** statement causes the computer to:
   a. Stop running the program.
   b. Display a **?**.
   c. Wait for data to be entered.
3. The form of the **INPUT** statement is:

   10   INPUT   N

   Line   Keyword.   Variable which may
   Number.   be numeric or string.

4. Messages called prompts may be displayed by **INPUT** statements.
5. When using a prompt in an **INPUT** statement, the form is: A semicolon.

   10 INPUT "MESSAGE" ; X

   The prompt in   The variable.
   quotation marks.

6. As a rule, always enter data for a string variable in an **INPUT** statement without quotation marks.
7. Never try to **INPUT** non-numeric data for numeric variables.

PROBLEM SET   8

1. Determine whether each of the following statements is valid or invalid. If invalid, rewrite the statement correctly.
   a. INPUT X
   b. 35 INPUT X$
   c. 20 PUTIN A$
   d. 40 INPUT 1X
   e. 30 INPUT X,INPUT Y
   f. 70 INPUT "ENTER YOUR NAME";N$
   g. 80 INPUT "ENTER AGE",A
   h. 60 INPUT ENTER MATH GRADE;G
   i. 50 INPUT X; "ENTER WEIGHT"
   j. 55 INPUT "YOUR NAME IS?";N$

2. Rewrite each program, using INPUT statements.

   a. 10 A = 50
       20 B = 80
       30 C = A+B
       40 PRINT C

   b. 10 PRINT "TEN PRODUCTS"
       20 X = 15
       30 FOR I = 1 TO 10
       40 P=X*I
       50 PRINT P
       60 NEXT I

3. What is the output for Program 2b above?

4. Write INPUT statements to enter the given data and assign it to the given variable in a program. Use line number 40 and do not use prompts.
   a. Enter 98.6, assign to T.
   b. Enter SUZIE WOOZIE, assign to N$.
   c. Enter 32, assign to F.

5. Rewrite the Average Program p. 138, to compute the average of grades in Physical Education, Shop, Home Economics, and Band.

6. Write a computer program which will accept input of your age in years, then calculate the number of days, the number of hours, and the number of minutes you have lived. (Use 1 year = 365 days.)

7. Write a computer program to accept input of your weight in pounds, then compute the number of ounces you weigh.

8. What would be displayed or printed by the computer as a result of running the following programs?
   a. 10 INPUT "LENGTH IN INCHES ";L
       20 INPUT "WIDTH IN INCHES ";W
       30 A = L * W
       40 PRINT "AREA IS ";A;" SQ. IN."
   b. 10 INPUT "ENTER RADIUS IN INCHES ";R
       20 A = 3.14 * R * R
       30 PRINT "AREA IS ";A;" SQ. IN."

9. Change one line in each of the programs of Problem 8 to compute the areas in feet. Then, change the PRINT statement to properly label the answer.

10. Run the following program, using your own personal

data. First guess the output, then compare your guess to the computer's output.

```
10   INPUT "WHAT IS YOUR NAME? ";N$
20   INPUT "WHAT IS YOUR FAVORITE SNACK? ";S$
30   INPUT "WHAT IS YOUR FAVORITE ROCK GROUP? "; R$
40   PRINT
50   PRINT "HELLO, ";N$
60   PRINT "I ALSO LIKE TO LISTEN TO ";R$
70   PRINT "AND EAT ";S$
```

11. Write a computer program, using prompts, which will accept a person's name and the number of miles from home to school, then compute the distance in feet. (1 mile = 5280 feet.)

12. The area of a right triangle with base b and height h is found using the formula A = .5 × b × h. Write a program which will let the user enter the base and the height of any right triangle, and then compute its area. Use **INPUT** statements with prompts.

13. Make the necessary changes to direct the program in 8a to compute the perimeter of a rectangle in inches.

14. Make the necessary changes to instruct the program in 8b to compute the circumference of a circle.

15. Write a program to make the computer print or display the message below.

> Dear   (friend)
> I have a pretty   (color)
> pet   (pet)   .
> My pet eats   (cereal)   .

Use **INPUT** statements to enter the data indicated in parentheses. Use prompts to help another user.

Chip's Challenges

16. Juanita just bought her first new car and wants to check the fuel economy. Write a computer program to help her do this. To compute the number of miles per gallon, use the formula: N = D/G

where   N = number of miles per gallon

D = distance driven

G = number of gallons of gasoline consumed

Your output should look like this:

ENTER DISTANCE IN MILES (You enter value of D)
ENTER GALLONS OF GAS USED (You enter value of G)
ECONOMY RATING IS (Computer prints value of N)
MILES PER GALLON

Use the figures below to run the program.
Juanita drove 345 miles and purchased 12.7 gallons of gas when she filled the tank.

COMPUTER AWARENESS

Getting Data In and Out

By using a modem, this computer can receive and transmit data over telephone wires.

The most common input device for computers is the keyboard. The most common output device is the video screen. The letters on the keyboard are arranged like those on the typewriter, because that arrangement is familiar to most people. The back of the video screen is coated with phosphorus, a chemical element. When the video receives a coded signal, an electron gun behind the screen is fired. Electrons hit the phosphorus and energize tiny particles of the phosphorus, causing it to light up. The pattern of the particles lit forms the character images you see.

The keys you press on the keyboard are switches. Each sends a particular message to the computer. A special part of the computer, called the **character generator,** contains patterns of dots to match each message or code. These patterns are translated into signals that the video tube can interpret by a device called a **modulator.**

Keyboard entries and video images are extremely useful, but they are not permanent. Other devices, called **peripherals,** have to be used for permanent data storage and for records.

Many computers use cassettes for storage of input and output. Ordinary cassette recorders can be used for software (programs) and for data. They are economical, but they are not really fast enough for most computer use.

Most computers in schools and offices use disks for storage. The ones most commonly used for microcomputers are called floppy disks, and are 5¼ inches across. Other floppy disks are 8 inches across. Disks are read by a special peripheral called a disk drive. A floppy disk can store as many as 500,000 bytes of information.

There are also hard disks. A hard disk can store up to 50 **megabytes** of data. (A megabyte is one million bytes.)

There are other kinds of input devices besides the keyboard. When a program is running, a **light pen** can be used to send data to the computer. When the pen is pointed at a character on the screen, it sends an electronic signal to the computer.

Some computers have **joysticks.** Their movement sends coded electronic signals to the computer.

When a computer user wants to see a program's output on paper, he or she uses a **printer.** The least expensive kind of printer uses heat-sensitive paper. This **thermal printer** can produce about fifty characters a second.

Dot matrix printers are usually faster. Some of them can produce as many as two hundred characters a second. Some even contain microprocessors of their own.

The star of the printer family is the **daisy wheel printer.** Its output looks exactly as if it had come from a typewriter. It gets its name from the print head, a hub with 96 or more arms arranged around it like the petals of a daisy. Different print heads are available for most daisy wheel printers, so the user has a choice of type styles and sizes.

A very important peripheral device is the **modem.** A modem changes the computer's pattern of electric pulses into signals that can be sent over telephone wires. This is called **modulation.** The modem can also change the signals that come over the telephone lines back into computer pulses. This is **demodulation.** The two processes, modulation and demodulation, give the modem its name.

A variety of other input and output devices are used for special purposes. These include **optical mark readers** (which can read certain kinds of type), bar code readers (which read the marks on supermarket packages), **graphics pads, digitizers, plotters,** and **reel-to-reel tapes.**

What Do You Know?
1. Why are the letters on a computer keyboard arranged the same way as the letters on a typewriter?
2. What is a disadvantage of keyboard entries and video images?
3. What is the main advantage of the cassette for storing data? What is its main disadvantage?
4. What does a modem do?

What Can You Find Out?
1. What is another name for the video screen tube?
2. What does *thermal* mean?
3. What is a matrix?
4. Do disks come in other sizes?

What Do You Think?
1. Can a computer be made to accept input from a human voice?
2. What is the best way to store computer input and output?

CHAPTER 9

WHERE THE INFORMATION GOES

READ-DATA Statements

When many values are to be used in a program, they may be assigned to variables using a READ statement. This statement requires a DATA statement to supply the values it will use.

9.1

Values into Variables

DISCOVER FOR YOURSELF

Look at the programs below. Trace the steps and guess the computer's output. Write your guess on a sheet of paper. Check your answers by entering the programs and RUNning them.

PROGRAM

COMPUTER DISPLAYS

1.
```
NEW
10  A = 1
15  A$ = "MONEY"
30  PRINT A; " FOR THE "; A$
50  END
```

2.
```
NEW
20  READ A, A$
30  PRINT A; " FOR THE "; A$
40  DATA 1, MONEY
50  END
```

3.
```
NEW
10  FOR I = 1 TO 2
20  READ A, A$
30  PRINT A; " FOR THE "; A$
40  DATA 1, MONEY, 2, SHOW
45  NEXT I
50  END
```

WHAT DID YOU LEARN?

Programs 1 and 2 printed the same message,

    1 FOR THE MONEY

Program 1 used variables in the statements,

    10 A = 1
    15 A$ = "MONEY"

to input information. Program 2 used **READ** and **DATA** statements,

```
20   READ A, A$
40   DATA 1, MONEY
```

to input the <u>same</u> information. When the computer reaches a **READ** statement in a program, it searches for a **DATA** statement and assigns the information listed in the **DATA** statement to the variables in the **READ** statement. In Program 2, the statement,

```
20   READ A, A$
```

directed the computer to search for the **DATA** statement,

```
40   DATA 1, MONEY
```

The computer assigned

1 to **A**   and   **MONEY** to **A$**

```
20   READ A, A$
40   DATA 1, MONEY

10   A = 1
15   A$ = "MONEY"
```
THESE ARE EQUIVALENT.

Did you notice a difference? That is right! The strings in the **DATA** statement are not enclosed in quotation marks. However, quotation marks must be used if the string has a comma in it. For example, if **BALTIMORE, MD** is a string in a **DATA** statement, then **BALTIMORE, MD** must be enclosed in quotation marks. Can you think of the reason why this is so? That is correct! Without quotation marks the computer would consider **BALTIMORE, MD** as two strings rather than one string.

In Program 3, the computer executed the statement,

```
20   READ A, A$
```

twice. The <u>first time</u> the computer came to the **READ** statement,

```
20   READ A, A$
```

it searched for the **DATA** statement,

```
40   DATA 1, MONEY, 2, SHOW
```

It assigned

1 to **A**   and   **MONEY** to **A$**

and then the computer printed

1 FOR THE MONEY

CHIP SAYS:
NOTICE THAT THE READ AND DATA STATEMENTS ARE EQUIVALENT TO THE VARIABLE STATEMENTS.

Note: The computer reads (uses) information in **DATA** statements in the <u>order list-ed</u>.

Memory Bank

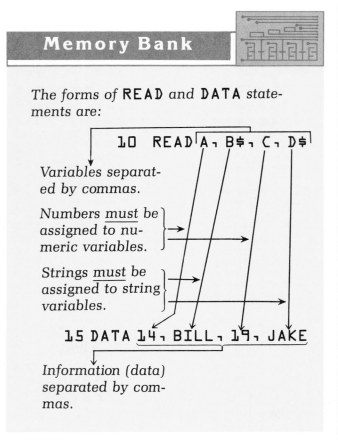

The forms of **READ** and **DATA** statements are:

10   READ A, B$, C, D$

Variables separated by commas.

Numbers *must* be assigned to numeric variables.

Strings *must* be assigned to string variables.

15 DATA 14, BILL, 19, JAKE

Information (data) separated by commas.

USE WHAT YOU HAVE LEARNED

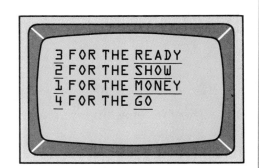

```
3 FOR THE READY
2 FOR THE SHOW
1 FOR THE MONEY
4 FOR THE GO
```

The <u>second</u> <u>time</u> the computer came to the **READ** statement,

20   READ A, A$

it again searched for the **DATA** statement,

40   DATA 1, MONEY, 2, SHOW

Because it had already **READ**

1 and **MONEY**

the computer assigned

2 to A and **SHOW to A$**

and printed

2 FOR THE SHOW

> <u>Note</u>: Without special instructions, the computer reads (uses) information in **DATA** statements <u>only</u> <u>once</u>.

---

*CAUTION: Never end a **DATA** statement with a comma!*

Look at the screen to the left. Complete the **DATA** statement of the program so that the computer will print the rhyme shown on the screen. Enter and **RUN** the program to check your answer.

```
NEW
10   FOR I = 1 TO 4
20   READ A$, A
30   PRINT A; " FOR THE "; A$
40   DATA _____  ←——— List information here
45   NEXT I
50   END
```

Do not forget! You must separate numbers and strings in **DATA** statements with commas. You must assign strings to string variables and numbers to numeric variables.

What do you think would happen if there were not enough information listed in **DATA** statements? Try it in the program above, using

40   DATA FISH, 5, DATE, 8, DISH, 6

Exercises

The **READ** or **DATA** statement in the following exercises may or may not be correct. If the statement is incorrect, give the reason.

1. `10  READ, A, B, C`
2. `10  DATA 14;17;25`
3. `10  DETA 42, 55, 3`
4. `10  READ F G J L`
5. `10  REED E, E$, F$, G`
6. `10  DATA X, Y, Z, A, B, K`
7. `15  DATA 982, 143, MAINE`
8. `10  READ W`

9. Consider each of the following pairs of **READ** and **DATA** input statements. Determine the value assigned to each variable.

   a. `20  READ A, B`
       `25  DATA 456, 654`

   b. `20  READ X, Y$, G$, Z`
       `25  DATA 245, MONEY, BANK, 999`

   c. `20  READ G, E, T`
       `25  DATA 98, 56, 77`

   d. `20  READ R$, T$, D, J`
       `25  DATA RING, BELL, 55, 43`

10. Rewrite this computer program using a **READ** statement to enter data.

    ```
    NEW
    10  A = 45
    20  K = 38
    30  P = 56
    40  X = (A + K + P)/3
    50  PRINT X
    60  END
    ```

11. Enter the programs—the one shown and your version—of Problem 10 and **RUN** them. Check the outputs of each program.

12. For each program below, trace the steps and guess the computer's output. Write your guess on a sheet of paper. Check your answers by entering and **RUN**ning them.

    a.
    ```
    NEW
    20  READ R, Q
    25  DATA 16, 18
    30  READ T$, P
    35  DATA JOSH, 2
    40  S = R + Q * P
    45  PRINT T$, S, R, P, Q
    50  END
    ```

    b.
    ```
    NEW
    20  READ B$, K, T$
    25  DATA BIKES, 10, SPEED
    30  PRINT K, T$, B$
    35  READ J$, Y$, D
    40  DATA RIDE, EASY, 2
    45  PRINT Y$, D, J$
    50  END
    ```

 Chip's Challenges

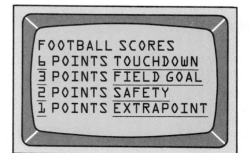

FOOTBALL SCORES
6 POINTS TOUCHDOWN
3 POINTS FIELD GOAL
2 POINTS SAFETY
1 POINTS EXTRAPOINT

13. Write a program whose output will be the same as that shown on the screen to the left. Use **READ** and **DATA** statements to input the information underlined. Enter the program and **RUN** it.

9.2

More Information about Data

Look at the program below. Trace the steps and guess the computer's output. Write your guess on a sheet of paper. Check your answer by entering the program and RUNning it.

CHIP SAYS:
MANY READ AND DATA STATEMENTS MAY BE IN A PROGRAM.

PROGRAM

```
NEW
5  DATA 1, 2, 3
10  READ A, B, C, D, E
15  DATA 4, 5, 6
20  DATA 7, 8
25  READ F, G, H, I, J
30  DATA 9
35  READ K, L
40  PRINT " A = "; A; " B = "; B; " C = "; C
45  PRINT " D = "; D; " E = "; E; " F = "; F
50  PRINT " G = "; G; " H = "; H; " I = "; I
55  PRINT "J = "; J; " K = "; K; " L = "; L
60  DATA 10, 11, 12
65  END
```

COMPUTER DISPLAYS

?

WHAT DID YOU LEARN?

The computer assigns information in DATA statements to variables in READ statements in a specific order. When the computer reaches the statement,

    10 READ A, B, C, D, E

it searches for the DATA statement in the program with the lowest line number, no matter where that DATA statement is in the program.

    5 DATA 1, 2, 3

Then it assigns the information listed in the DATA statement to the variables in the READ statement.

150

```
5  DATA 1, 2, 3
10 READ A, B, C, D, E
```

The computer assigns

1 to A, 2 to B, and 3 to C

There are not enough numbers listed in the **DATA** statement to assign to all of the variables in the **READ** statement. The computer then searches for the **DATA** statement with the <u>next lowest</u> line number in the program

```
15 DATA 4, 5, 6
```

The computer then assigns the information listed in this **DATA** statement to the variables, D and E, of the **READ** statement.

```
10  READ A, B, C, D, E
15  DATA        4, 5, 6
```

The computer assigns

4 to D and 5 to E

When the computer comes to the next **READ** statement,

```
25 READ F, G, H, I, J
```

it again searches for the **DATA** statement with the lowest line which contains the first piece of information not yet assigned to a variable.

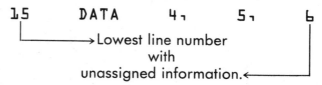

```
15      DATA     4,    5,    6
```
→Lowest line number
            with
unassigned information.←

> The computer normally uses information in **DATA** statements <u>only once</u>. It passes over information in **DATA** statements which has been assigned previously.

The computer then assigns the unused information of the **DATA** statement to the variables of the **READ** statement.

```
15 DATA 4, 5, 6
25 READ    F, G, H, I, J
```

There are not enough numbers listed in this **DATA** statement to assign to the variables of the

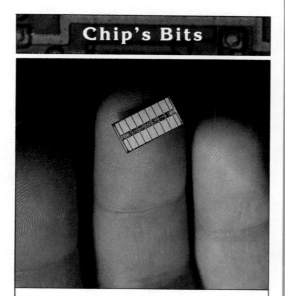

Chip's Bits

Every new computer has more memory than the ones that preceded it. Scientists are working to make small memories hold even more information than they can now. In the next few years they think they will be able to store a million bits on one memory chip!

CHIP WONDERS: DO YOU REMEMBER THIS?

The Cyber 205 is one of the world's most powerful computers. Built by Control Data Corporation, it can do 400 million calculations every second. Two American universities, Colorado State and Purdue, are among the users of Cyber 205.

READ statement. The computer then searches for the **DATA** statement with the next lowest line number in the program.

    20 DATA 7, 8

The computer then assigns the information listed in this **DATA** statement to the variables of the **READ** statement.

    20 DATA   7, 8
               ↓   ↓
    25 READ F, G, H, I, J

This process continues until all the variables of the **READ** statements have been assigned values listed in **DATA** statements as shown in the table below.

READ statements		Assignments		DATA statements
		A ← 1		
		B ← 2		5 DATA
10 READ	{	C ← 3	}	
		D ← 4		
		E ← 5	}	15 DATA
		F ← 6		
		G ← 7	}	20 DATA
25 READ	{	H ← 8		
		I ← 9	}	30 DATA
		J ← 10		
35 READ	{	K ← 11	}	60 DATA
		L ← 12		

Programmers usually group all **DATA** statements together. This simplifies the work of the computer when it is told to **READ** a value for a variable. It also makes it possible to change the **DATA** statements easily, if necessary.

USE WHAT YOU HAVE LEARNED

Terry Fermal wrote the program on the top of the next page, which describes the way information in **DATA** statements is assigned to variables in **READ** statements. Trace Terry's program to determine what information is assigned to which variables and the message which Terry prepared. Enter and **RUN** her program on your computer to check your answer.

PROGRAM

```
NEW
5   DATA LINE
10   READ J$, K
15   READ A, M$, D$
20   DATA 5, 35, FIRST
30   READ R, B$, E
35   DATA NUMBER, 20
40   DATA SMALLEST, 40, THEN
50   READ G$
55   PRINT B$, J$, D$
60   PRINT K, M$, G$
65   PRINT R, G$, A, G$, E
70   END
```

CHIP WONDERS: WHAT INFORMATION IS ASSIGNED TO THE VARIABLES OF TERRY'S PROGRAM?

J$ = ___?___
K = ___?___
A = ___?___
M$ = ___?___
D$ = ___?___
R = ___?___
B$ = ___?___
E = ___?___
G$ = ___?___

COMPUTER DISPLAYS

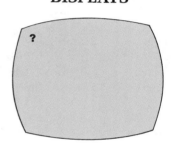

?

Memory Bank

DATA Statements

DATA statements may be placed <u>anywhere</u> in a program, at the beginning, in the middle, or at the end of the program. Wherever the **DATA** statement is, the computer will find it.

What do you think would happen if you placed a **DATA** statement after the **END** statement in a program? Try this with Terry's program by changing line number 40 to line number 75 and deleting line 40. Then enter her program and **RUN** it. Did you think that the **END** statement had to be the last statement in a program?

E x e r c i s e s

1. Consider each of the following sets of READ and DATA statements. Determine the information assigned to each variable.

a.
```
20   READ A, B, C, D$, E$
30   DATA 1782, 1942
35   DATA 2603, DAY
40   DATA NIGHT
```

b.
```
100  DATA 17, 14, JOHN, MARY
110  READ R, M
120  READ B$, D$, A, F$
130  DATA 15, LOVES
```

2. Determine the output for each of the following programs.

a.
```
NEW
10   READ A$, B$, C
15   DATA HAS, DOG
20   READ D$, E$
25   DATA 110, MY, FLEAS
30   PRINT D$; B$; A$; C; E$
35   END
```

b.
```
NEW
15   DATA 4
20   DATA SCORE, 7
5    DATA AGO, AND, YEARS
25   READ A$, B$
30   READ C$, D, E$
35   READ F
40   PRINT D; E$; B$; F; C$; A$
45   END
```

3. Check your answers to Exercise 2 above by entering the programs and RUNning them.

4. Write the PRINT statement for the program of Exercise 2a above that will make the computer display the message,
   HAS MY DOG 110 FLEAS
   Check your answer by entering the program on your computer and RUNning it.

Chip's Challenges

5. Determine the output of the following program. Check your answer by entering the program and RUNning it.
```
NEW
5    T = 0
10   PRINT "EMPLOYEE", "TOTAL HOURS"
15   FOR I = 1 TO 5
20   READ A$, B, C, D
25   E = B + C + D
30   PRINT A$, E
35   T = T + E
40   NEXT I
45   PRINT
50   PRINT "TOTAL HOURS WORKED = "; T
55   DATA RODRIGUIZ, 6, 5, 7
60   DATA FITZGERALD, 3, 2, 5
65   DATA MCHENNY, 6, 4, 3
70   DATA JACKSON, 5, 2, 4
75   DATA ROSEBERGER, 4, 7, 2
80   END
```

6. Melodie Coznofsky purchased the sporting equipment listed in the table on the next page for the prices shown.

Item	Price
Tennis racquet	$17.46
Golf balls	$28.50
Fielder's glove	$16.95
Football helmet	$19.99
Soccer ball	$10.88

Write a computer program that will use **READ** and **DATA** statements to input the information given and print a table such as the one above. Enter the program and **RUN** it.

CHAPTER SUMMARY

1. **READ** and **DATA** statements are used to input information (data) in a computer program.
2. **READ** and **DATA** statements must go together in a program.
3. A string in a **DATA** statement is not enclosed in quotation marks unless it has a comma in it.
4. The computer uses information in **DATA** statements in the order it is listed. Usually, the information is used only one time.
5. Information in **DATA** statements must be assigned to appropriate variables. Numbers must be assigned to numeric variables and strings must be assigned to string variables.
6. Several **READ** and **DATA** statements may be used in one program.
7. The form of the **READ** statement is

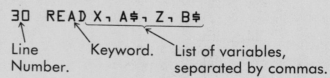

Line Number.   Keyword.   List of variables, separated by commas.

8. The form of the **DATA** statement is

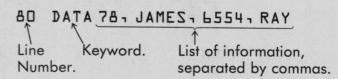

Line Number.   Keyword.   List of information, separated by commas.

9. **DATA** statements may be placed anywhere in the program.
10. The computer assigns information (data) in **DATA** statements to variables in **READ** statements using the **DATA** statement with the lowest line number first. Then the next lowest line number is used, and so on, until all variables of the **READ** statements have been assigned information (data) from the **DATA** statements.

The **READ** or **DATA** statements in the following problems may or may not be correct. If the statement is incorrect, give the reason.

1. 10   REID A, X, R   **2.** DATA 14, 19, MARIE
3. 95   READ P, Q, 15   **4.** 17   DATUM JOE, ALEX
5. 64   READ, A, B$, X, Z$ **6.** 17   DATA A, B, C

Consider each of the following sets of **READ** and **DATA** input statements. Determine the value assigned to each variable.

7.   10   READ A, C, B$
         15   DATA 18, 19, JOSHUA
8.   20   READ X$, Y$, B
         25   DATA ZERO, "BALTIMORE, 21209", 1407
9.   10   DATA FOX, RABBIT, RUN
         15   READ R$, T$, B$
10. 30   READ D, E$, C, B, A$
         35   DATA 101, NINETY, 90, 83, FIRST

Rewrite the following computer programs using **READ** and **DATA** statements to input the information. Enter and **RUN** both programs, the program shown and the program you wrote, and compare the outputs.

11. NEW
         10   X = 44
         20   Y = 82
         30   Z = 123
         40   A = X + Y - Z
         50   PRINT A
         60   END

12. NEW
         10   L = 8
         15   W = 2
         20   A$ = "AREA "
         25   S$ = " SQUARE "
         30   C$ = " CM"
         40   PRINT A$; L * W; S$; C$
         45   END

13. NEW
         10   INPUT C
         15   INPUT D
         20   INPUT E
         25   S = (C + D)/E
         30   PRINT S
         35   END
         RUN
         ?17
         ?19
         ?4

14. NEW
         5   D$ = "WILDCATS"
         10   E = 14
         15   F = 13
         20   A$ = "ROYALS"
         25   B = 20
         30   C = 7
         35   G$ = "MINNOWS"
         40   H = 18
         45   I = 9
         50   PRINT "TEAM", "WON", "LOST"
         55   PRINT
         60   PRINT D$, E, F
         65   PRINT A$, B, C
         70   PRINT G$, H, I
         75   END

Consider each of the following sets of **READ** and **DATA** input statements on the next page. Determine the value assigned to each variable.

15.
```
50   READ R, S, T
60   READ X, Y, Z
70   DATA 15, 20
80   DATA 19, 18
90   DATA 20, 15
```

16.
```
20   DATA BLANKS, VARIABLES
25   DATA 101, 103, 105
5    DATA CHIP, KNOWS
10   READ A$, B$
15   DATA 14, BASIC
30   READ A, C$, D$
35   READ E$, F
40   READ G, H
```

17.
```
5    DATA 45, SNOW
10   READ A
15   DATA INCHES, BLIZZARD
20   READ B$, C$, D$
```

18.
```
5    DATA 1
10   READ A, B$
15   DATA SETS, 47, 32
20   READ C, D, E$, F$
25   DATA SCREEN, VIDEO, 18, TYPE
30   READ E, G$, F, H
35   DATA 1001, 1002, PAPER
40   READ P$, R$
45   DATA FINIS
```

Trace the steps of the following programs to determine the computer's output. Write your answers on a sheet of paper. Check your answers by entering and running the programs.

19.
```
NEW
5    DATA MORTALS, ARE
10   DATA ALL, HUMANS
15   READ A$, B$, C$, D$
20   PRINT D$; B$; C$; A$
25   PRINT C$; D$; B$; A$
30   PRINT C$; A$; B$; D$
35   END
```

20.
```
NEW
5    DATA 3, 5, 9, 10
10   FOR I = 1 TO 10 STEP 3
15   READ A, B
20   A = (A + B) * I
25   PRINT I, A
30   NEXT I
35   DATA 7, 6, 4, 2
40   END
```

21. Write a program, using **READ** and **DATA** statements, which will output the information shown on the screen below and print the average of the test scores for each student.

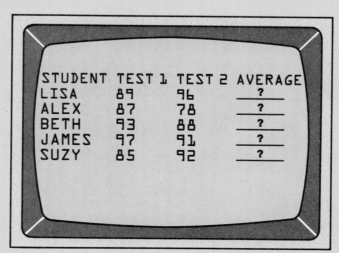

STUDENT	TEST 1	TEST 2	AVERAGE
LISA	89	96	?
ALEX	87	78	?
BETH	93	88	?
JAMES	97	91	?
SUZY	85	92	?

Chip's Challenges

22. Determine the value assigned to each variable of the following set of READ and DATA statements.

```
20   DATA 1
10   DATA 2, 3
45   DATA 4, 5, 6
5  DATA 7, 8, 9, 10
40   DATA 11, 12, 13, 14, 15
30   DATA 16, 17, 18, 19, 20, 21
106  READ A, B, C, D, E, F
107  READ G, H, I, J, K
108  READ L, M, N, O
109  READ P, Q, R
110  READ S, T
112  READ U
```

23. What (if anything) will be the output of the following program? Check your answer by entering and RUNning it.

```
NEW
5  FOR J = 1 TO 2
10   DATA 3, BETH, 9
15   FOR I = 1 TO 3
20   READ A, B$
30   DATA MARIE, 13, BILL
25   PRINT B$; A
35   NEXT I
40   NEXT J
45   END
```

Did you get an error message which indicated not enough data listed? Do you know why?

24. Wendel Sampson, President of Jackson's Student Savings and Loan Company, computes the interest owed each depositor at the end of the year using the formula,

Interest = Principal × Rate × Time

where 5% is the rate and time is expressed in years. Write a program, using READ and DATA statements, that will produce the following output.

DEPOSITOR	PRINCIPAL	TIME	INTEREST
DUGGAN	$ 37.00	2	?
ESCALOT	$115.50	1	?
SMITH	$ 95.25	3	?
LAURETTE	$103.50	2	?
WESSDALE	$ 56.50	4	?
ARUNELL	$ 78.50	3	?
TOTAL INTEREST = ?			

COMPUTER AWARENESS

Of these hundreds of silicon chips, only about half will eventually be used in computers.

A Closer Look at the Inside

The heart of your computer, its microprocessor, began as part of a crystal of silicon grown in a special vacuum oven. On a slice of the crystal, about as thick as your fingernail and about four inches in diameter, were printed hundreds of copies, side by side, of a complicated pattern of circuits and electronic parts. The slice was heated in a furnace where chemicals entered the silicon wherever there were circuit lines, changing it so that electricity could flow through the circuits. (Electricity cannot flow through untreated silicon. It can only follow the paths where the chemicals have been absorbed.)

The patterns were tested to see if they worked. (Only about half usually pass the test.) Then they were cut apart into chips smaller in area than your smallest fingernail. The successful chips were sealed in their wired packages. One of them is now in your computer.

As you have seen, the microprocessor is the Central Processing Unit or CPU of your computer. It is the computer's boss. Like an orchestra conductor, it directs everything the computer does, from the instant

159

you turn the computer on until you turn it off.

The CPU turns the instructions the computer receives into electrical on and off signals. It controls their operation. With its arithmetic logic unit, it combines and compares data. It keeps track of the location of instructions and data with its **address buffers**, or storage spaces. It regulates input and output with **input/output buffers**. It holds information it needs to use often in its **registers**, or special memory locations, and it stores results of the work of the arithmetic logic unit in a special register called an **accumulator**.

The microprocessor is timed by a tiny quartz clock that "ticks" millions of times each second. Each tick marks the entry of one **bit**, either a pulse of electricity (a one,) or no pulse (a zero).

Transistors in the circuits act as switches. These switches are combined to form **gates**. The condition of a gate, the combination of open and closed switches, determines the way electricity flows through the circuit.

The CPU's circuits are connected to the rest of the computer by **busses** or tracks. The three most important kinds of busses are:

1. The **Address bus**, which carries information about the location of data.
2. The **Control bus**, which carries directions for the entry of data.
3. The **Data bus**, which carries information to be written to memory.

Busses connect the CPU to the **Read Only Memory (ROM)**. ROM is a permanent storehouse of instructions. It holds special programs that direct the operations of the computer. It contains the **interpreter**, which translates BASIC statements to the computer's language. ROM puts the greeting on the screen when the computer is turned on. ROM makes the **prompt** and cursor appear. As computers develop further, more and more ROM is being included in them.

Busses also connect the CPU to the **Random Access Memory (RAM)**. (In fact, both kinds of memory are random-access, available when needed. A better name for RAM would have been Read/Write Memory.) RAM is like a chalkboard which can be erased after work has been done on it. RAM is erased by turning the computer off, by pressing the reset button, or by entering NEW.

What Do You Know?
1. Why are the silicon slices baked with chemicals in a furnace?
2. What part of the CPU locates instructions and data?
3. What part of the CPU holds frequently used information?
4. What are the tracks that connect the CPU to the rest of the computer called?
5. What is ROM? RAM?

What Can You Find Out?
1. What are some of the computer's gates called?
2. How much ROM does your computer have?
3. What does *bootstrap* mean in connection with computers?
4. What is PROM?

What Do You Think?
1. Why do so many chips fail the test in the manufacturing process?
2. How do gates in a computer work?

CHAPTER 18

QUESTIONS AND ANSWERS

IF-THEN Statement

Computers make decisions, based on the answers *computer* questions. The IF-THEN statement asks a que tion and uses information in memory to answer it. Th answer determines the computer's next action.

10.1

What Comes Next?

DISCOVER FOR YOURSELF For each program, guess the computer's output. Write your guess on a sheet of paper. Check your answers by entering and running the programs. Do not forget to press the [RETURN] or [ENTER] key after typing each line.

COMPUTER DISPLAYS

PROGRAM

1.
```
10  FOR I=1 TO 5
20  READ X
30  PRINT X
40  NEXT I
50  DATA 3,12,35
```

2.
```
10  J=1
20  PRINT J
30  J=J+1
40  GOTO 20
```

3.
```
10  N$="MARY"
20  PRINT "HI, ";N$
30  PRINT "HOW ARE YOU?";
40  INPUT R$
50  PRINT "GOOD"
60  PRINT "THAT IS TOO BAD"
```

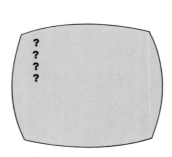

WHAT DID YOU LEARN?

Was there anything wrong with Program 1? No. The computer, however, told you that it was OUT OF DATA IN LINE 20. The computer expected to READ five numbers but line 50 gave it only three. In this chapter, you will learn how the computer can decide if it has read the last number in a list.

Was there anything wrong with Program 2? No. The program just never ended after you entered RUN. You will learn how the computer can *decide* when you want it to stop printing. (Do you think it is the computer deciding or it is you telling the computer how to decide?) Program 3 was an attempt to begin a conversation with the computer. Not much of a conversation, was it? While the computer will never become a psychiatrist, you can certainly try to make it look more professional.

To understand how the computer can make a decision, you must understand how to ask computer questions. Below are three *computer* questions and three *people* questions. Do you see the difference?

<u>People Question</u>

How is the weather?
What is for dinner?
Where were you yesterday?

<u>Computer Question</u>

Is A = 5?
Is N$ = "NO"?
Is X larger than 2
and B$ = "OK"?

<u>Differences</u>

1. People questions may have many possible answers. Question: How is the weather? Possible answers: Hot, cold, cloudy, sunny, hazy, rainy

   Computer questions must have exactly two answers. Question: Is A = 5? Possible answers: YES or NO (or TRUE or FALSE)

Chip's Bits

On/Off is all it knows

A switch can be on or off to represent a number, answer a question, or provide some other kind of information. A computer is able to store information or perform calculations because it is a system of switches connected together in a precise and logical way.

YES

STOP

NO

GO

Computers are often compared to the human brain, but the brain is far more powerful. Computers work with electronic gates. Usually, two signals enter a gate and only one comes out. The human brain works with neurons. A neuron can accept as many as 10,000 signals and send one out. And there are no computer gates that can make "maybe" decisions as a neuron can.

2. People can ask about what is in the memory of others. Question: Where were you yesterday?

Computers can *ask* only about what is in their own memories. Question: Is N$ = "NO"? (N$ is a value stored in the computer's memory.)

Memory Bank

Questions

A computer can:

1. Ask only questions that will have yes or no answers.

2. Ask only questions about what is in its own memory.

USE WHAT YOU HAVE LEARNED

Can you think of computer questions to prevent the difficulties of the programs in the *Discover for Yourself* activity? For Program 1, you might have the computer <u>ask</u>: Is X = 35? If the answer is YES, the computer might be directed to END the program and avoid the error message.

In Program 2, the computer could <u>ask</u>: Is J = 20? You could direct the computer to stop counting if the answer to the question is YES. For the last program, the question might be: Is R$ = "GOOD"? Then the program could display a comment that suited the reply.

How do people respond after they have their questions answered? Of course, it depends on the question and its answer. In general, people can respond in many ways.

Example 1:

Question: What is the weather like outside?
Answer: Raining.

People responses:
>No baseball game today.
>I had better wear my raincoat.
>I should stay home so I will not catch a cold.
>Great weather for ducks.

Example 2:

Question: Where are you going, Red Riding Hood?

Answer: To my grandma's.

Wolf responses:
>I had better get there first.
>Where does your grandma live?
>Does your grandma have wolf insurance?

What can a computer do after it answers a question YES or NO? You will find that out as you learn how to ask a question in BASIC.

E x e r c i s e s

For Exercises 1 to 9, determine whether the questions are *people* questions or *computer* questions. What are some possible answers for each of the questions?

1. Is 2 + 2 = 5?
2. What are your favorite colors?
3. During what months is major league baseball played?
4. Is A = 12?
5. Is algebra a difficult subject?
6. How long is your program?
7. Is ft. the abbreviation for feet?
8. What is your address?
9. Is 7 greater than 12?

Chip's Challenges

10. Determine whether this question is a *people* or a *computer* question. What are some possible answers?
Is 8 = 4*2 and is 8 greater than 10?

11. Suppose you were searching for a matching pair of socks in a drawer. What questions, having YES or NO answers, would you ask yourself?

And Then He Said . . .

DISCOVER FOR YOURSELF

For each of the programs below, decide on two different answers to the questions asked. Guess the computer's output if each program were RUN twice, using the answers you chose. Write your guesses on a sheet of paper. Then enter each program and RUN it two times, using your answers.

COMPUTER DISPLAYS

PROGRAM

```
1.  10   PRINT "WHAT IS YOUR FAVORITE COLOR";
    20   INPUT Y$
    30   IF Y$ = "BLUE" THEN PRINT "VERY GOOD"
    40   PRINT "THANK YOU FOR THE INFORMATION"
```

```
2.  10   PRINT "I WILL PRINT A MESSAGE IF YOU GUESS"
    20   PRINT "THE NUMBER I AM THINKING OF"
    30   PRINT "WHAT IS YOUR GUESS";
    40   INPUT G
    50   IF G=25 THEN GOTO 80
    60   PRINT "SORRY, ";G;" IS THE WRONG NUMBER"
    70   END
    80   PRINT "PROGRAMMING IS FUN"
```

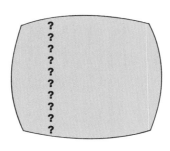

WHAT DID YOU LEARN?

Here is what might have happened when the first program was RUN, if you first answered BLUE and then YELLOW:

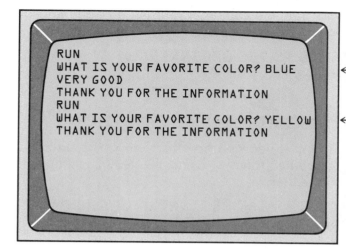

```
RUN
WHAT IS YOUR FAVORITE COLOR? BLUE
VERY GOOD
THANK YOU FOR THE INFORMATION
RUN
WHAT IS YOUR FAVORITE COLOR? YELLOW
THANK YOU FOR THE INFORMATION
```

← This is what you entered.
Is Y$ = "BLUE"? YES

← Is Y$ = "BLUE"? NO

Line 30 asked the *computer* question. The value you supplied decided the computer's output.

If you had guessed the computer's number was 25 the first time and 51 the next time, the second program's output would be:

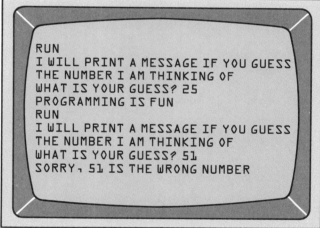

```
RUN
I WILL PRINT A MESSAGE IF YOU GUESS
THE NUMBER I AM THINKING OF
WHAT IS YOUR GUESS? 25
PROGRAMMING IS FUN
RUN
I WILL PRINT A MESSAGE IF YOU GUESS
THE NUMBER I AM THINKING OF
WHAT IS YOUR GUESS? 51
SORRY, 51 IS THE WRONG NUMBER
```

Line 50 asked the *computer* question: Is G = 25? The value you gave G decided the computer's output. If your guess was 25, line 50 sent the computer to line 80 and you saw the message. If your guess was not 25, the answer to the *computer* question was NO and the computer displayed line 60.

You learned earlier in this text why every program line is given a number. The computer carries out the instructions in the program one line at a time, beginning with the first line number. Then it does the line with the next greatest number and so on. Line numbers are

Chip's Bits

Computers of the future may use a different kind of crystal for their integrated chips. Gallium arsenide is made of two elements, gallium and arsenic. It lets electrons travel five times faster than silicon does. It also produces only one one-hundredth of the heat that silicon produces.

the path the computer follows through the program. For example,

```
10   PRINT "THIS IS THE BEGINNING OF THE PATH"
20   X = 7
30   Y = 4
40   PRINT X + Y
50   PRINT "THIS IS THE END OF THE PATH"
```

You also learned how to change the path the computer follows, using the GOTO statement. For example,

```
10   PRINT "THIS IS THE BEGINNING OF THE PATH"
20   PRINT "WHAT IS YOUR NAME";
30   INPUT N$
40   PRINT "HAVE A GOOD DAY, ";N$
50   GOTO 20
```

The GOTO statement tells the computer to go to another line in the program and to follow the instructions there. That other line may be backward or forward, within the program. The GOTO statement changes the path the computer follows.

There is another statement that changes the computer's path through a program: the IF-THEN statement. This time, however, the computer asks a *computer* question first. The path changes only if the answer is YES. If the answer is NO, the computer goes on doing its job as though nothing had happened, and follows the normal path.

Here is what the IF-THEN statement looks like:

IF   *computer* question   THEN   do this if the answer is YES
↑   ↑
Keyword.   Keyword.

(People say "IS"—computers *say* "IF".)

Look at these examples.

```
20   IF Y$ = "BLUE" THEN PRINT "VERY GOOD"
```
↑   ↑   ↑   ↑
Keyword.   Keyword.
     Computer question: Do this if the answer is YES.
     Is Y$ = "BLUE"?

This is what line 20 tells the computer:

Print "VERY GOOD" only if the value of Y$ is

BLUE and go on to the next line.
Otherwise, (when the answer to the question, Is Y$ = "BLUE"?, is NO) just go on to the next line.

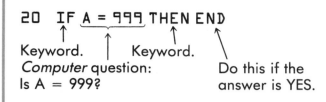

```
20  IF A = 999 THEN END
```

Keyword.   Keyword.
Computer question: Do this if the
Is A = 999?   answer is YES.

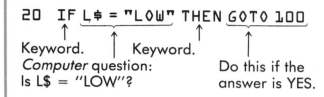

```
20  IF L$ = "LOW" THEN GOTO 100
```

Keyword.   Keyword.
Computer question: Do this if the
Is L$ = "LOW"?   answer is YES.

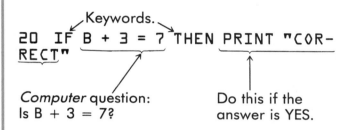

Keywords.

```
20  IF B + 3 = 7 THEN PRINT "COR-
RECT"
```

Computer question: Do this if the
Is B + 3 = 7?   answer is YES.

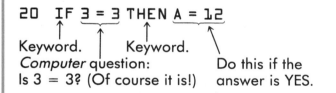

```
20  IF 3 = 3 THEN A = 12
```

Keyword.   Keyword.
Computer question: Do this if the
Is 3 = 3? (Of course it is!)   answer is YES.

Chip's Bits

ELIZA, a program written by MIT professor Joseph Weizenbaum, can carry on a conversation with a computer user. It cannot make up new ideas to talk about, however. It uses what it is told in order to continue the conversation.

Memory Bank

Keyword.   A computer question.   Any BASIC statement to be done when the answer is YES.

```
IF I = 20 THEN PRINT "I HAVE
IT"
```

Keyword.

USE WHAT YOU HAVE LEARNED

Josey Williams enjoyed keeping her classmates informed about different things. She was often asked, for example, to name the birthstones of various months. Josey decided to make the computer look smart by writing a program to print the birthstone when a month was entered.

Here is Josey's program:

```
10 PRINT "JOSEY'S BIRTHSTONE PROGRAM"
20 PRINT "MONTH, PLEASE";
30 INPUT M$
40 IF M$ = "JANUARY" THEN S$ = "GARNET"
50 IF M$ = "FEBRUARY" THEN S$ = "AMETHYST"
60 IF M$ = "MARCH" THEN S$ = "BLOODSTONE"
70 IF M$ = "APRIL" THEN S$ = "DIAMOND"
80 IF M$ = "MAY" THEN S$ = "EMERALD"
90 IF M$ = "JUNE" THEN S$ = "AGATE"
100 IF M$ = "JULY" THEN S$ = "RUBY"
110 IF M$ = "AUGUST" THEN S$ = "SARDONYX"
120 IF M$ = "SEPTEMBER" THEN S$ = "SAPPHIRE"
130 IF M$ = "OCTOBER" THEN S$ = "OPAL"
140 IF M$ = "NOVEMBER" THEN S$ = "TOPAZ"
150 IF M$ = "DECEMBER" THEN S$ = "TURQUOISE"
160 PRINT "THE BIRTHSTONE FOR ";M$;"IS";S$
```

RUN the program, entering several different months.

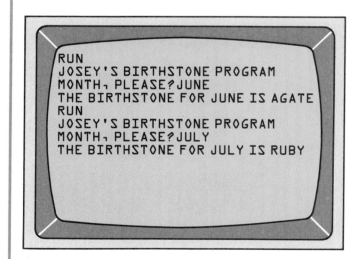

```
RUN
JOSEY'S BIRTHSTONE PROGRAM
MONTH, PLEASE?JUNE
THE BIRTHSTONE FOR JUNE IS AGATE
RUN
JOSEY'S BIRTHSTONE PROGRAM
MONTH, PLEASE?JULY
THE BIRTHSTONE FOR JULY IS RUBY
```

Josey used the **IF-THEN** statement to decide which month a classmate had entered. **S$** was then given a string value, depending on the value of **M$**. Josey did not have to worry about memorizing the birthstones anymore.

E x e r c i s e s

For Exercises 1 to 5, determine whether the IF–THEN statements are correct or incorrect.

```
1.  30  IF A IS EQUAL TO 2 THEN GOTO 50
2.  30  IF A + B = 3 THEN C = 5
3.  30  IF A$ = "BILL" THEN WRITE "GOOD LUCK"
4.  30  IS X=5 THEN Y=3
5.  30  IF L$ = "FEET" THAN Y$ = "YARDS"
```

In Exercises 6 to 9, what would the computer print if the programs were RUN?

```
6.  10  A = 3
    20  B = 4
    30  C = 5
    40  IF B = 3 THEN GOTO 80
    50  PRINT "GOOD BYE"
    60  END
    80  PRINT "HELLO"
7.  10  A = 3
    20  B = 4
    30  C = 5
    40  IF A = B – 1 THEN GOTO 80
    50  PRINT "GOOD BYE"
    60  END
    80  PRINT "HELLO"
8.  10  A = 3
    20  B = 4
    30  C = 5
    40  IF 2*A – B = 5 THEN GOTO 80
    50  PRINT "GOOD BYE"
    60  END
    80  PRINT "HELLO"
9.  10  A = 3
    20  B = 4
    30  C = 5
    40  IF A + B = C + 2 THEN GOTO 80
    50  PRINT "GOOD BYE"
    60  END
    80  PRINT "HELLO"
```

Chip's Challenges

10. Change Josey's program to print each month's flower after the month is entered.

10.3

More Decisions

DISCOVER FOR YOURSELF

For each of the following programs, guess what the computer will display. Write your guesses on a sheet of paper. Check your answers by entering and running the programs.

COMPUTER DISPLAYS

PROGRAM

1.
```
10   J = 1
20   PRINT J
25   IF J = 20 THEN END
30   J = J + 1
40   GOTO 20
```

2.
```
10   J = 1
20   PRINT J
25   IF J = 20 THEN END
30   J = J + 2        Changed from J = J + 1
40   GOTO 20
```

WHAT DID YOU LEARN?

In the first program of the *Discover for Yourself* activity, the computer stopped counting at 20. Line 25 *asked* the *computer* question: Is J = 20? A NO answer let the computer go on counting. A YES answer made the program END.

The second program was very different! You had to use the (BREAK) key to stop the counting. The value of J was never 20. The computer printed 1, then 3, 5, 7, 9, 11, 13, 15, 17, 19, 21, and so on. Fortunately, there is a way to make the computer stop when J becomes greater than 20. BASIC has a set of Decision Symbols, of which = is only one.

Memory Bank

BASIC Decision Symbols

=   Is equal to.

>   Is greater than.

<   Is less than.

<> Is not equal to.

>= Is greater than or equal to.

<= Is less than or equal to.

To have the computer stop when J is greater than 20, the computer must *ask* the question: Is J greater than 20? If the answer is YES, the program ends. Do you remember the symbol for greater than?

```
10  J = 1
20  PRINT J
25  IF J > 20 THEN END←Is J greater than 20?
30  J = J + 2
40  GOTO 20
```

If this program were RUN, the computer would print 1, 3, 5, 7, 9, 11, 13, 15, 17, 19, and 21, then END.

What do you think would happen if you made the following changes?

```
10  J = 1
20  PRINT J
25  IF J < 20 THEN END←Is J less than 20?
30  J = J + 2
40  GOTO 20
```

Only the number 1 would be printed. Why?

```
10  J = 1
20  PRINT J
25  IF J = 20 THEN END←
30  J = J + 2         Is J equal to 20?
40  GOTO 20
```

Chip's Bits

The science of electronics changes so rapidly that it is difficult to keep informed about all the new inventions and discoveries. It's estimated that more than half of everything electrical engineers learn in college is out of date three years after they graduate!

The preceding program would never end. Why?

Here are some examples of correct IF-THEN statements using BASIC Decision Symbols:

```
20   IF A > B THEN GOTO 50
20   IF X > Y + 3 THEN A$ = "GREAT"
20   IF A <> 5 THEN PRINT "A IS NOT EQUAL TO 5"
20   IF R >= 7 THEN PRINT "R COULD BE 7 OR 8 OR . . ."
```

USE WHAT YOU HAVE LEARNED

Everyone in Lillian Johnson's class was required to sell fifteen candy bars to help finance the class play. For every candy bar sold, after the first fifteen, Lillian's classmates received two bonus points, to be used when buying tickets. Lillian decided to have the computer find the bonus points. Here is her program:

```
10   Clearscreen
20   PRINT "STUDENT NAME ";
30   INPUT N$
40   PRINT "CANDY BARS SOLD ";
50   INPUT C
60   IF C <= 15 THEN GOTO 120
70   B = C - 15
80   P = 2 * B
90   PRINT N$;" BONUS POINTS ";P
100   GOTO 20
120   PRINT N$;" NOT ELIGIBLE FOR A BONUS"
130   GOTO 20
```

The program allows you to enter a name, N$, and the number of candy bars sold, C. Line 60 checks to see if the number of bars sold was 15 or less. If it is less than or equal to 15, then line 120 is executed next. The student is not eligible for a bonus. If the answer to the question, Is C <= 15?, is NO (C must be greater than 15), then line 70 is executed. B is the number of candy bars beyond the required 15 that were sold. P is the number of bonus points. Line 90 prints the student's name and the number of bonus points earned. This program, by the way, does not end. It always goes back to line 20. By changing line 130 and adding the following lines to the end of the program, Lillian can decide when to stop.

```
130   PRINT "ANY MORE NAMES (YES OR NO)";
140   INPUT A$
150   IF A$ = "YES" THEN GOTO 20
160   END
```

In addition, line 100 should be changed to:

```
100  GOTO 130
```

Lillian's program now looks like this:

```
10   Clearscreen
20   PRINT "STUDENT NAME ";
30   INPUT N$
40   PRINT "CANDY BARS SOLD ";
50   INPUT C
60   IF C <= 15 THEN GOTO 120
70   B = C - 15
80   P = 2 * B
90   PRINT N$;" BONUS POINTS ";P
100  GOTO 130
120  PRINT N$;" NOT ELIGIBLE FOR A BONUS"
130  PRINT "ANY MORE NAMES (YES OR NO)";
140  INPUT A$
150  IF A$ = "YES" THEN GOTO 20
160  END
```

This is what Lillian saw when she ran the program:

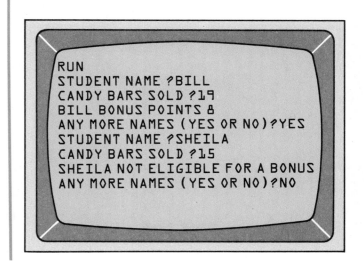

```
RUN
STUDENT NAME ?BILL
CANDY BARS SOLD ?19
BILL BONUS POINTS 8
ANY MORE NAMES (YES OR NO)?YES
STUDENT NAME ?SHEILA
CANDY BARS SOLD ?15
SHEILA NOT ELIGIBLE FOR A BONUS
ANY MORE NAMES (YES OR NO)?NO
```

E x e r c i s e s

For Exercises 1 to 4, write the IF-THEN instruction for the given situations. Use 70 for the line number.

1. Print "NO SERVICE CHARGE" when A is greater than 10.
2. Add X to Y when Z is not equal to 500.
3. Go to line 85 when A$ is not "TRUE".
4. Print 1776 when the sum of X and Y is greater than the sum of A and B.

What will be printed when the following programs are RUN?

5.  ```
    10   A = 1
    20   B = 5
    30   IF A < 3 THEN PRINT A
    40   IF A = 5 THEN PRINT "HARRY"
    50   PRINT B
    ```

6.  ```
    10   A$ = "TOM"
    20   B$ = "GEORGE"
    30   IF A$ <> B$ THEN GOTO 80
    40   END
    80   PRINT A$;" AND ";B$
    ```

7.  ```
    10   FOR I = 1 TO 5
    20   READ X$
    30   PRINT X$
    40   IF X$ = "END" THEN END
    50   NEXT I
    60   DATA JACK, SPRAT, COULD, END
    ```

Chip's Challenges

8. Change Lillian's program to give two bonus points for each candy bar sold, after the first 15, as long as the total is less than 25. Have it give three bonus points for each additonal candy bar of the 25 or more sold.

APPLICATIONS

PROBLEM SOLVING

The Flag

Did you notice, in Exercise 7 above, that the FOR-NEXT loop should have gone through five cycles and it actually went through only four? The IF-THEN statement looked for the value, END, for X$ and ended the program. Since there was not enough data to go through five cycles, the IF-THEN statement was used to tell the computer when to stop reading data. Data processing people call this "using a **flag**." Look at some flag examples.

Example 1: No More Milk

```
10   READ J
20   DATA 99,98,97,96,95
30   PRINT J;" BOTTLES OF MILK ON THE WALL"
40   PRINT J;" BOTTLES OF MILK"
50   PRINT "IF ONE BOTTLE HAPPENS TO FALL"
60   GOTO 10
```

This is a variation of the famous school bus song. Here it is RUN.
```

```
99 BOTTLES OF MILK ON THE WALL
99 BOTTLES OF MILK
IF ONE BOTTLE HAPPENS TO FALL
98 BOTTLES OF MILK ON THE WALL
98 BOTTLES OF MILK
IF ONE BOTTLE HAPPENS TO FALL
97 BOTTLES OF MILK ON THE WALL
97 BOTTLES OF MILK
IF ONE BOTTLE HAPPENS TO FALL
96 BOTTLES OF MILK ON THE WALL
96 BOTTLES OF MILK
IF ONE BOTTLE HAPPENS TO FALL
95 BOTTLES OF MILK ON THE WALL
95 BOTTLES OF MILK
IF ONE BOTTLE HAPPENS TO FALL
OUT OF DATA LINE 10
```

How can you prevent the error message from appearing? You can do it by placing an **IF-THEN** statement in the program and using the last number in the **DATA** statement to stop the program. Here is a solution.

```
10   READ J
20   DATA 99,98,97,96,95 ←——Flag.
30   PRINT J;" BOTTLES OF MILK ON THE WALL"
40   PRINT J;" BOTTLES OF MILK"
50   PRINT "IF ONE BOTTLE HAPPENS TO FALL"
55   IF J = 95 THEN END
60   GOTO 10
```

Using a flag to tell when to stop doing a task is a very common technique in business programs.

In Program 1 of the first *Discover for Yourself* activity, a flag could have been used to stop the program before that nasty error message was printed. The flag may be any number that will never be data in a program. For example, if you know that the number 999 will never be used, you could use it as a flag. Shown below are the old and the new programs for that activity:

Old

```
10   FOR I = 1 TO 5
20   READ X


30   PRINT X
40   NEXT I
50   DATA 3,12,15
```

New

```
10   FOR I = 1 TO 5
20   READ X
25   IF X = 999 THEN END  ←——Flag.
30   PRINT X
40   NEXT I
50   DATA 3,12,15,999
```

Example 2: The Sales Report

This program will list the names of classmates and the total number of candy bars each sold. Every day, new names can be added as sales increase.

```
5   PRINT "NAME","SALES"
10    READ N$
20    IF N$ = "END" THEN END
30    READ S
40    PRINT N$, S                    Flag.
50    GOTO 10
60    DATA SMITH,25
70    DATA JONES,21
80    DATA JACKSON,8
100    DATA END
```

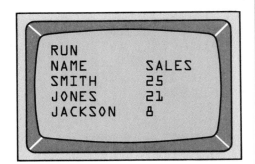

```
RUN
NAME        SALES
SMITH       25
JONES       21
JACKSON     8
```

Line 20 checks to see if the value **END** was read. If it was, then the program ends. The value **END** is the flag.

Error Trapping

Did you ever play a Guess-the-Number game, in which you had to guess a number between 1 and 10? There was always someone who chose 12 or 0 as the guess. The following is a Guess-the-Number program in which you enter the number and someone else tries to guess it. Beware if the number guessed is not between 1 and 10!

```
10    PRINT "WHAT IS THE NUMBER TO GUESS "
20    INPUT A
30    Clearscreen
40    PRINT "WHAT IS YOUR GUESS (BETWEEN 1 AND 10)";
50    INPUT G
60    IF G > 10 THEN GOTO 40
70    IF G < 1 THEN GOTO 40          Error traps.
80    IF A = G THEN GOTO 110
90    PRINT G;" IS NOT THE NUMBER - TRY AGAIN"
100    GOTO 40
110    PRINT "CONGRATULATIONS, THAT IS MY NUMBER"
120    PRINT "DO YOU WANT TO PLAY AGAIN (YES OR NO)";
130    INPUT A$
140    IF A$ = "YES" THEN GOTO 10
150    END
```

A is the number you put in for your friend to guess. G is your friend's guess. Lines 60 and 70 will not accept values greater than 10 or less than 1, respectively. Line 80 checks to see if your friend has made the correct guess. If it is correct, then line 110 sends congratulations. Otherwise, your friend is asked to try again. **Error trapping** is a term used by data processing people. It includes making sure that there are IF—THEN statements in programs to prevent people from entering numbers that are obviously wrong.

The Psychologist

In the first *Discover for Yourself* activity, you tried to have a conversation with the computer. Without IF—THEN statements, the conversation was not very good. Below is a program that makes your computer seem a little human when it is RUN.

```
5   Clearscreen
10   PRINT "WHAT IS YOUR NAME";
20   INPUT N$
30   PRINT "HOW ARE YOU TODAY?"
40   PRINT " (OK OR AWFUL)";
50   INPUT S$
60   IF S$="OK" THEN PRINT "GOOD, ";N$;" I FEEL OK TOO"
70   IF S$="AWFUL" THEN PRINT "THAT IS TOO BAD"
80   PRINT "WHAT IS YOUR FAVORITE SUBJECT ";N$;
90   INPUT L$
100   PRINT L$;" IS MY FAVORITE SUBJECT"
110   PRINT "I AM CERTAINLY HAPPY TO HAVE A CHANCE TO"
120   PRINT "SPEAK TO YOU ";N$
130   PRINT "DO YOU WANT TO DO IT AGAIN (YES OR NO)";
140   INPUT A$
150   IF A$ = "YES" THEN GOTO 30
160   END
```

Here is a sample session.

```
WHAT IS YOUR NAME?JODY
HOW ARE YOU TODAY?
(OK OR AWFUL)?OK
GOOD, JODY I FEEL OK TOO
WHAT IS YOUR FAVORITE SUBJECT JODY?AARDVARK ANATOMY
AARDVARK ANATOMY IS MY FAVORITE SUBJECT
I AM CERTAINLY HAPPY TO HAVE A CHANCE TO
SPEAK TO YOU JODY
DO YOU WANT TO DO IT AGAIN (YES OR NO)?NO
```

Fortunately, you do not have to pay your computer $50 an hour for a talk session.

CHAPTER SUMMARY

1. A computer can make decisions based on questions that have a YES or NO response. It can *ask* only about what is in its memory.
2. The computer statement that makes a decision is the IF-THEN statement.
3. The IF-THEN statement consists of:

Keyword.   Keyword.

20 IF A = 5 THEN PRINT "MY LUCKY NUMBER"

Computer question: Do this if the answer is YES.
Is A = 5?

4. The computer question may include any of the BASIC Decision Symbols. They are:
   =   Equal to.
   <   Less than.
   >   Greater than.
   <= Less than or equal to.
   >= Greater than or equal to.
   <> Not equal to.

PROBLEM SET 10

1. Determine whether the following IF-THEN statements are correct or not correct.
   a. 20   IF A+B = 3 THEN GOTO 40
   b. 20   IF X > 3 THEN PRINT "THREE"
   c. 20   IS A$ = "NO" THEN PRINT "PUNT"
   d. 20   WHATIF S = 3 THEN INPUT A
   e. 20   IF X IS LESS THAN 3 THEN READ A
2. For each set of instructions below, what will be the computer's output?

a.
```
10   READ A,B
20   IF A=B THEN GOTO 50
30   PRINT A; "NOT =";B
40   GOTO 10
50   PRINT A;"=";B
60   GOTO 10
70   DATA 20,30
```

b.
```
10   READ A,B
20   IF A=B THEN GOTO 50
30   PRINT A;"NOT =";B
40   GOTO 10
50   PRINT A;"=";B
60   GOTO 10
70   DATA 40,40
```

c.
```
10   READ N$
20   IF N$="END" THEN END
30   READ A
40   IF N$="CHOCOLATE" THEN C=2 * A
50   IF N$="BOOKS" THEN C=5 * A
```

```
60   IF N$="TOYS" THEN C=10 * A
70   PRINT A;N$;" RECEIPTS = ";C
80   GOTO 10
90   DATA CHOCOLATE,12,TOYS,5
95   DATA BOOKS,14,END
```

3. Write an **IF—THEN** statement to:
   a. Print "OK" if X is greater than 5.
   b. Go to line 70 when A$ is "BILL".
   c. Input a value for Z if the sum of X and Y is 7.
   d. Print "OVERTIME DUE" when H is greater than 40.

4. What would be the output if the following program were RUN?
```
10   READ A,B
20   IF A < 5 THEN PRINT A + B
30   IF A >= 5 THEN PRINT A * B
40   GOTO 10
50   DATA 3,4,4,7,5,6,6,2
```

5. The following program will print baseball batting averages, using **READ** and **DATA** statements. B is the number of times at bat, H is the number of hits, and A is the batting average.
```
5   FOR K = 1 TO 3
10   READ B
20   READ H
30   A = H/B
40   PRINT " AT BAT ";B
50   PRINT " HITS ";H
60   PRINT "AVERAGE ";A
70   NEXT K
80   DATA 100,30,63,14,55,9
```
   a. Add an **IF—THEN** statement so that the program will end when 999 is **READ** for the value of B.
   b. Alter the program so that you can also print the names of the batters. (Use the names of your classmates.)
   c. Change the program so that a message will be printed if a batting average is greater than .300.

6. What would be printed if the following program were RUN?
```
10   READ X,Y
20   IF Y = 0 THEN GOTO 50
30   A = X / Y
40   GOTO 60
50   A = Y / X
60   PRINT A
70   GOTO 10
80   DATA 10,5,3,0,4,2,25,5
```

7. Alter the program of Problem 6 to print the values of Y and X. Add a flag so that the **OUT OF DATA IN LINE 10** message will not be printed.

8. Change the Guess-the-Number program on page 178 to guess a number between 10 and 20.

9. Larry was having trouble with his nines table. He wrote the following program to help him drill:

```
10   FOR I = 1 TO 9
20   PRINT I;" * ";9;" = ";
30   INPUT A
40   IF A = I * 9 THEN PRINT "CORRECT"
50   IF I * 9 <> A THEN PRINT "WRONG"
60   NEXT I
```

   a. RUN this program to see that it actually is a nines table drill.

   b. Change the program to make it an eights table drill.

   c. Change the program so that it prints the correct answer when Larry makes a mistake.

   d. Change the program to do addition tables instead of multiplication tables.

10. Write a program to count from 1 to 99 by twos, without using FOR-NEXT statements.

11. Packages shipped from New York to Pittsburgh are charged at the following rates:

   $43 per ton for the first fifteen tons.

   $25 per ton for each ton after the first fifteen.

The program below will compute the shipping cost, after the number of tons is input.

```
10   PRINT "NUMBER OF TONS ";
20   INPUT T
30   IF T > 15 THEN GOTO 60
40   C = T * 43 ←──────────── Cost is 43 * number of tons.
50   GOTO 80
60   N = T - 15 ←──────────── N is the number of tons greater than fifteen.
70   C = 15 * 43 + N * 25 ←── Cost is $43 for the first fifteen tons and $25 for each extra ton.
80   PRINT "SHIPPING CHARGE IS $";C
90   GOTO 10
```

   a. RUN the program to see that it computes the correct shipping charge.

   b. Change the program to compute the shipping charges from Pittsburgh to Dayton: $88 per ton for the first twenty-two tons and $63 per ton for each ton after that amount.

   c. Change line 90 to ask if you want to compute more charges.

12. Using Problem 11 as a guide, write a program to solve this problem:

The Hothouse Fuel Company charges two rates for heating oil, depending on the amount delivered. If the customer takes delivery of less than 100 gallons of heating oil, the rate charged is $1.27 per gallon. The rate becomes $1.21 for each gallon of heating oil after the first 100 gallons. Compute the charges for the customers shown below with the number of gallons each purchased.

Customer	Purchases
A. J. Sweeney	96 gallons
U. X. McFarland	106 gallons
F. E. Oliver	83 gallons
R. M. Lyter	125 gallons

13. Ms. O'Casey is the timekeeper for the Tarwell Paving Company. She would like to have a program that computes the salary for each employee in the following manner:

If the employee works 40 or fewer hours, he or she is paid the regular hourly rate. The employee receives an amount equal to the number of hours multiplied by the regular hourly rate.

If the employee works more than 40 hours, he or she is paid one and one-half times the regular hourly rate for each hour after the 40 hours. This amount is added to his or her 40-hour salary.

Write a program for Ms. O'Casey to calculate the pay for the employees listed below.

Employee	Regular Rate	Hours Worked
A. Albrecht	$4.50	40 hours
J. Bergman	$7.85	45 hours
H. Wilson	$5.33	38 hours

14. The cost of a taxi ride from the airport is $1.10 per mile for the first five miles and $.95 for each additional mile. Write a program to find the cost of the taxi ride for any distance, from one mile to twenty-five miles.

15. Write a program to accept two numbers and print the lesser number.

16. Write a program to accept two numbers and print the greater number.

Chip's Challenges

17. Veeza Charge-It has the following yearly finance charges:
23% for the first $500.
19% for each dollar after the first $500.
Write a program to find the yearly finance charges for purchases of $250, $1800, $525, and $2122. Remember: To find the finance charge, multiply the purchase by the rate.

Planning Programs

Good programmers often use diagrams to help them plan programs.

Anyone who knows the vocabulary and syntax of a computer language can write a program. *Good* programmers often think of programming as a kind of problem-solving activity.

Programmers who write useful and/or entertaining programs usually spend much time planning. They begin by deciding exactly what kind of problem they are trying to solve. Then they describe the steps they

need to take to solve the problem, in ordinary English sentences.

Remember the Number Guess program on page 166? Before deciding how to make the *computer* play the game, the programmer might have thought of the way that *human* players do it:

1. Human 1 thinks of a number but does not tell Human 2 what it is.

2. Human 1 says "What is your guess (between 1 and 10)?"
3. Human 2 makes a guess.
4. If the guess is less than 1, Human 1 repeats the question.
5. If the guess is greater than 10, Human 1 repeats the question.
6. If the guess is right, Human 1 congratulates Human 2 and asks "Do you want to play again?"
7. If the guess is wrong, Human 1 repeats the first question.

In this game, the problem to be solved is: Are two numbers the same?

After they list the problem-solving steps and before they write any of the program's statements, good programmers think and plan every detail of the program.

They think about the data the computer will need to use. They think of how the bits and pieces of data are related to each other and to the results they want from the program.

They think about the way the computer will get the data that it needs. (This program has data—secret numbers and guesses—entered from the keyboard.)

They decide what information to include in the program. (The computer has to be told what the least and greatest numbers can be.)

They decide what the person using the program will have to enter from the keyboard. (They decide what prompts to use and what error traps are needed.)

They think about variable names. (Good programmers often try to make the variable names show the kind of values they hold. For example, they may decide G would be a good variable to hold the Guess the program's user enters.)

Good programmers also think about the actions the computer will have to perform. They decide which operations will be used. They decide what will be compared to make the decisions. (The guess has to be compared to three numbers—the least possible, the greatest possible, and the secret number.)

They decide what monitor displays will look like.

Finally, good programmers design the **structure** or organization of the program's parts.

They may begin the design stage by thinking of program **modules** or pieces of the program. Each module is a group, or **block,** of program statements.

Some programmers might use a **block diagram** such as this to design a number guessing game:

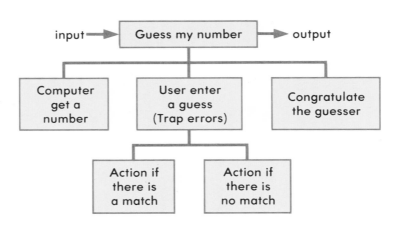

Other programmers might think of a program's structure in levels.

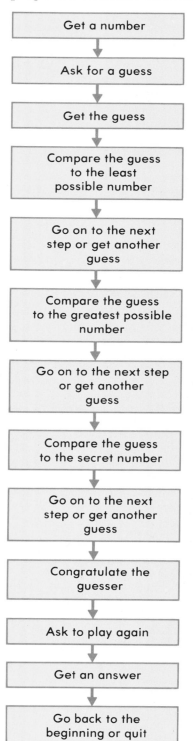

Get a number

↓

Ask for a guess

↓

Get the guess

↓

Compare the guess to the least possible number

↓

Go on to the next step or get another guess

↓

Compare the guess to the greatest possible number

↓

Go on to the next step or get another guess

↓

Compare the guess to the secret number

↓

Go on to the next step or get another guess

↓

Congratulate the guesser

↓

Ask to play again

↓

Get an answer

↓

Go back to the beginning or quit

The top or first level is the general purpose of the program. The second level is the set of major blocks of program statements. Other, lower levels are smaller blocks of statements that will be used by the major blocks.

For the number guessing game, a **top-down** block diagram like the one at the left could be used to plan the program's structure.

Good programmers then make detailed plans for each module, using the block diagram as a program skeleton.

Finally, they are ready to begin coding, translating the plans into BASIC program statements.

Are you a good programmer?

What Do You Know?
1. What is a module?
2. What is a block diagram?
3. What is the structure of a program?
4. How is a block diagram used?

What Can You Find Out?
1. Look at a listing of a program you like.
    a. Can you identify the major blocks of the program?
    b. Did the programmer help you? How?

What Do You Think?
1. Which stage of the programming process is the most important: problem-solving, thinking and decision-making, designing, or coding?
2. Which stage is the most difficult?
3. Which stage is the most fun?
4. Which stage would take YOU the most time?

CHARTING THE COURSE

Flowcharts and Branching

Diagrams to plan or to explain programs are called flow charts. They trace a path through the program, from beginning to end, sometimes branching to different parts of the program.

11.1

Pathways through Programs

1. The following steps describe the process you might follow in placing a phone call to a friend, if, on your first try, the line was busy. Rearrange the steps in logical order.

   a. Dial a friend's number.
   b. Hold conversation.
   c. End call. Conversation completed.
   d. Tell friend goodbye.
   e. Identify yourself.
   f. Dial friend's number again.
   g. Friend answers telephone.
   h. End call. The line is busy.

2. The steps listed below describe what you might do to prepare a peanut butter sandwich. Rearrange the steps in a logical sequence.

   a. Place two pieces of bread together to make a sandwich, peanut buttered sides touching.
   b. Remove two slices of bread.
   c. Pick up knife.
   d. Use knife to get some peanut butter from jar.
   e. Spread peanut butter on bread using knife.
   f. Continue spreading peanut butter until both slices of bread are covered.
   g. Open jar.
   h. Open bread package.
   i. Get peanut butter, knife, and loaf of bread.
   j. Eat and enjoy.

COMPARE YOUR RESULTS WITH THESE

1. Here is a logical sequence for problem one.

   a. Dial friend's number
   h. End call. The line is busy.
   f. Dial friend's number again.
   g. Friend answers telephone.
   e. Identify yourself.
   b. Hold conversation.
   d. Tell friend goodbye.
   c. End call. Conversation completed.

2. Here is one of several possible correct answers for Problem 2. If yours differs, you can determine whether or not you are correct by following your directions to make a sandwich at home.

   i. Get peanut butter, knife, and loaf of bread.
   g. Open jar.
   h. Open bread package.
   b. Remove two slices of bread.
   c. Pick up knife.
   d. Use knife to get some peanut butter from jar.
   e. Spread peanut butter on bread using knife.
   f. Continue spreading peanut butter until both slices of bread are covered.
   a. Place two pieces of bread together to make a sandwich, peanut buttered sides touching.
   j. Eat and enjoy.

Chip's Bits

The use of transphasors, which react to light the way transistors react to electricity, could make computers one thousand times faster. Transistors can switch in one billionth of a second, but transphasors can switch in one thousandth of that time—in one trillionth of a second! Research on transphasors is going on as this book is being written.

WHAT DID YOU LEARN?

The answers to the two exercises above represent logical, step-by-step procedures for solving problems. They are similar to the easy-to-follow instructions you may have used to assemble a toy or a model. Such instructions are often accompanied by illustrations or pictures to help you follow the procedure. A computer program is a logical sequence of steps. It, too, can be accompanied by an illustration which helps you follow the program steps in order. Such an illustration is called a **flow chart**. Look at the flow chart shown on the next page.

Flow Chart

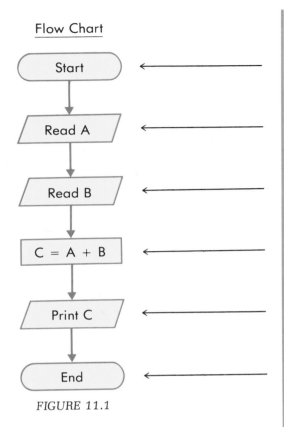

FIGURE 11.1

Explanation

Start — Marks beginning of program.

Read A — Enter a value and assign to variable A.

Read B — Enter a value and assign to variable B.

C = A + B — Compute the sum and assign to C.

Print C — Output the value of C.

End — Marks end of program.

A flow chart can be a useful tool in helping to understand or to plan computer programs. Many different symbols may be used in flowcharts. Only five of these are used in this book. Four of the symbols are used in the flow chart above and are described below.

Symbol

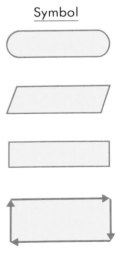

Meaning

Terminal—marks the beginning and end of a program.

Input/output—used to indicate `READ`, `INPUT`, and `PRINT` instructions.

Process—used to indicate addition, subtraction, multiplication, division, and exponentiation. Also used to assign values, such as A = 6.

Arrow—indicates direction or flow of the process.

Look at the program and flowchart on the next page. Each may be used to find the area of a circle after the radius is entered.

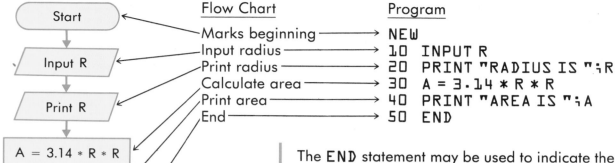

Flow Chart | Program
Marks beginning → NEW
Input radius → 10 INPUT R
Print radius → 20 PRINT "RADIUS IS ";R
Calculate area → 30 A = 3.14 * R * R
Print area → 40 PRINT "AREA IS ";A
End → 50 END

FIGURE 11.2

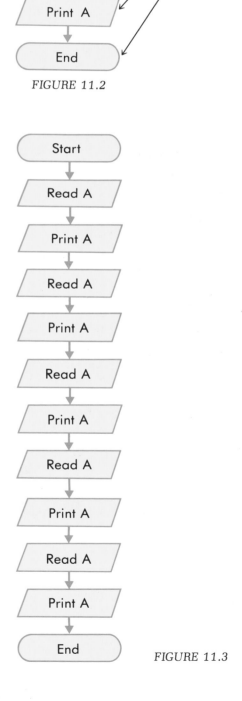

FIGURE 11.3

The **END** statement may be used to indicate the end of a BASIC computer program. However, it is not necessary. In this text, it is frequently omitted. Although the **NEW** statement may not be needed at the beginning of a program, it is good practice to use it. By following the arrows of the flow chart, each step is reached in its proper order.

Memory Bank

Flow charts

A computer program is a logical sequence of steps used to solve a problem. A flow chart may be used to help understand a program.

Study the flow chart at the left.

If you wished to write a computer program for the problem solution illustrated by the flow chart in figure 11.3, it would be necessary only to write each step in the BASIC language. **NEW** would be used to correspond to the flow chart step, Start. The BASIC statement **END** may be used to replace the flow chart step, End. In fact, the completed program would look so much like the flow chart that one might ask if it is really necessary to construct the flow chart at all. Certainly, if all flow charts were as simple as this one, it would not be necessary.

Notice that the same two steps are repeated.

A simpler way to show this would be to write the first **READ** and **PRINT** instructions and then direct the computer to go back and do these

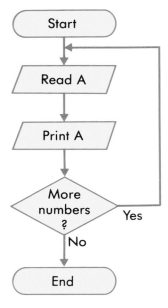

FIGURE 11.4

over and over again. However, there is no way to tell when the last number has been reached. Some way to make a decision which indicates whether the problem is finished or not is needed. Such a decision may be based on a question such as, "Is this the last number?" A No response would send the program back to the beginning. A Yes response would let it continue, to reach the final statement. Placing a question such as this in a flow chart involves the use of another flow chart symbol, the diamond.

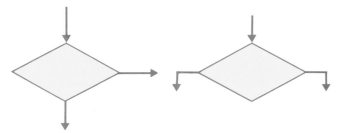

The **diamond** is for decisions. It has only one arrow pointing into it and two arrows pointing out of it.

The computer has the ability to make decisions. This ability eliminates the need of tedious repetition of steps in a program. The computer does this by branching to an indicated part of the program. The flow chart of Figure 11.4 illustrates this.

In the flow chart in Figure 11.4, the decision statement, in the form of a question, is placed in the diamond. The decision to be made is whether to end the program or to repeat the READ and PRINT instructions. An answer of Yes to the question directs the flow of the problem back to the READ instruction. A No answer directs the flow forward to the End instruction.

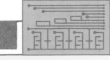

Memory Bank

Decision Diamond

The decision diamond of a flow chart must contain a question whose answer is Yes or No as shown to the left. Program flow follows the branch of the arrow with the answer to the question.

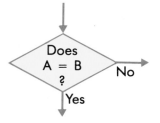

USE WHAT YOU HAVE LEARNED

The flow chart shown on the left illustrates how to input a list of names and print them. A portion of the program is shown beside the flow chart. Copy and fill in the missing instructions to complete the program.

Flow Chart

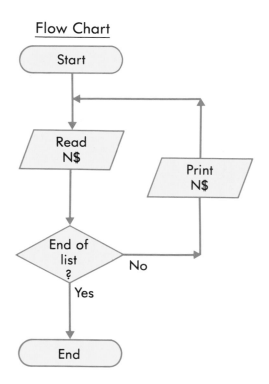

Program

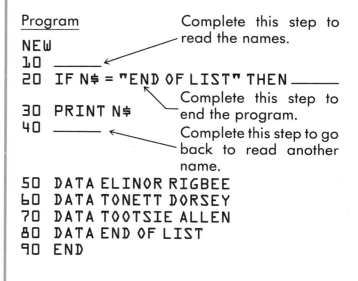

```
NEW
10  _____          Complete this step to
                     read the names.
20  IF N$ = "END OF LIST" THEN _____
30  PRINT N$         Complete this step to
                     end the program.
40  _____          Complete this step to go
                     back to read another
                     name.
50  DATA ELINOR RIGBEE
60  DATA TONETT DORSEY
70  DATA TOOTSIE ALLEN
80  DATA END OF LIST
90  END
```

Notice the last data statement, line 80. The string, **END OF LIST**, is the test value of **N$** in line 20. It is also the question asked in the decision diamond of the flow chart.

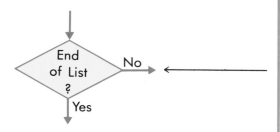

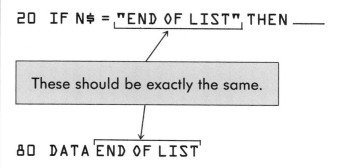

```
20  IF N$ = "END OF LIST" THEN ____
```

These should be exactly the same.

```
80  DATA END OF LIST
```

Compare your answers to the lines below.

10 READ N$ corresponds to

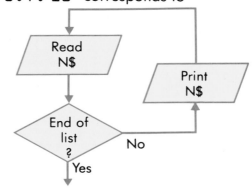

```
20  IF N$ = "END OF LIST" THEN 90
```
corresponds to

```
40  GOTO 10  corresponds to
```

E x e r c i s e s

1. Sketch the flow chart symbol which is used to:
   a. Make a decision.
   b. Read in a value.
   c. Calculate the value of A+B and assign it to S.
   d. Mark the end of a flow chart.

2. Use the flow chart on page 162 to determine the value of C for:
   a. A = 15, B = 40
   b. A = 56, B = 34

3. Use the flow chart in Figure 11.2 to determine the value of A for:
   a. R = 10
   b. R = 5

4. Refer to the program on page 191. What would be printed if:
   a. R = 10
   b. R = 5

5. Refer to the program on page 193. What would be printed as a result of RUNning the program?

Flow Chart

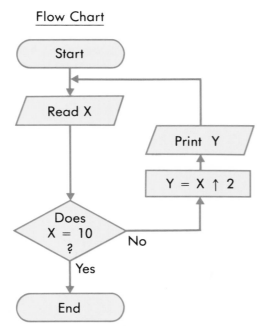

6. Copy and complete lines 10, 20, 30, and 50 of the program corresponding to the flow chart on the left.

Program

```
NEW
10  _____
20  IF X=10 THEN _____
30  _____
40  PRINT Y
50  _____
60  DATA 2
70  DATA 4
80  DATA 6
90  DATA 8
100  DATA 10
110  END
```

Chip's Challenges

7. The flow chart shown at the left can be used to find the volume of a rectangular container and the number of gallons of fluid it can hold. Write the program steps to solve the problem. Begin with line number 10.

Flow Chart

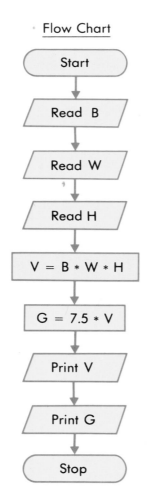

Go with the Flow

Flow Chart

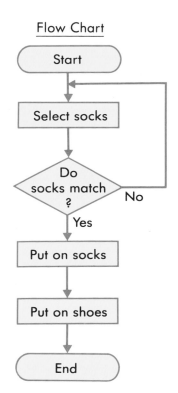

FIGURE 11.5

Branching to Repeat

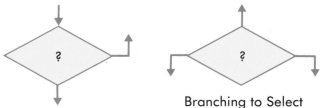

Branching to Select

Frank Merriwell opened his sock drawer and discovered that his socks were not properly paired. The flow chart in Figure 11.5 illustrates how Frank paired his socks. Trace through the flow chart to see the process.

Process

Frank picked a pair of socks from the drawer.

He compared the two socks to determine if they match.

Once Frank found a matched pair, he put them on.

He then put on his shoes.

This flow chart is an example of **branching to repeat**.

Memory Bank

There are two kinds of branching.
1. *Branching to repeat.*
2. *Branching to select.*

Look at the flow chart at the top of the next page. This flow chart illustrates **branching to select**. Here is how it works.

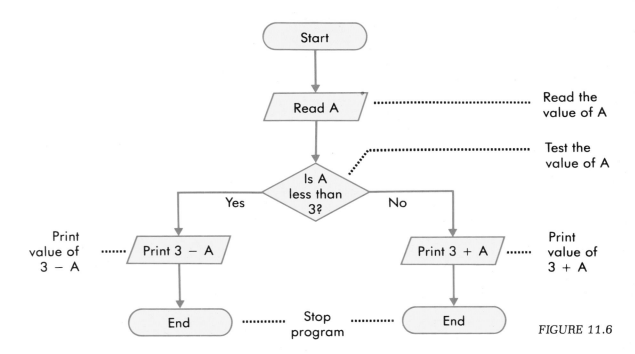

Read the value of A

Test the value of A

Print value of 3 − A

Print value of 3 + A

Stop program

FIGURE 11.6

USE WHAT YOU HAVE LEARNED

Study the examples below.

Example 1: Kent Clark has been assigned the task of printing a list of the names and telephone numbers of subscribers to his paper, the Daily Star. First, Kent developed the flow chart to the left. He then wanted to write the computer program. Help Kent by copying and supplying the missing computer steps.

Program

```
NEW
10  READ _____
20  IF N$=_____ THEN_____
                Complete these lines.
30  PRINT N$, P$
40  GOTO_____

50  PRINT                      This line skips
                               a line.
60  PRINT "END OF LIST"
70  DATA ELINOR RIGBEE, 529 6725
80  DATA TONETT DORSEY, 302 1111
90  DATA TOOTSIE ALLEN, 999 0001
100  DATA END OF LIST, 99999
110  END
```

This flow chart is an example of **branching to repeat**. Look at the last data entry, line 100, and at the **IF** statement in line 20.

Flow Chart

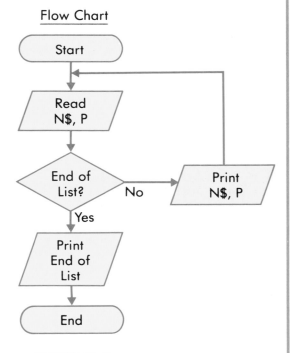

FIGURE 11.7

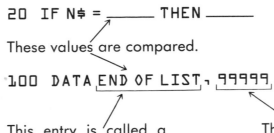

20 IF N$ = _____ THEN _____

These values are compared.

100 DATA END OF LIST, 99999

This entry is called a "trailer record".

This entry is needed because line 10 causes the computer to look for two pieces of data.

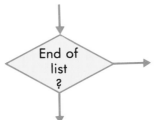

End of list ?

Line 20 is the "test" line. To see how to complete line 20, simply look at the contents of the decision diamond in the flow chart to the left and the PRINT line in the program.

Line 20 is completed as follows:

20 IF N$ = "END OF LIST" THEN 50

Line number of PRINT.

The last data entry, called the **trailer record**, is determined from the test line. In this case, the test value of N$ is the string, END OF LIST. Therefore, the trailer record is also the string, END OF LIST. Almost anything may be used as the trailer record. The only restriction is that the trailer record must agree with the test value. For example, the following would also work.

20 IF N$ = "LINUS" THEN 50
       .
       .
       .
100 DATA LINUS, 99999
110 END

In this program, the computer will read a name and phone number, then test to see if it is the last name (trailer record). If it is not the last name, the information is printed. If the last name has been read, the message "END OF LIST" is printed. Did you complete lines 10 and 40? If so, you should agree with these lines.

10 READ N$, P$
40 GOTO 10

Another way to end the program would be:

20 IF N$ = "END OF LIST" THEN END

Then you could eliminate line 50, 60, and 110.

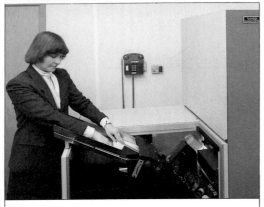

Chip's Bits

Paper files may be eliminated by an IBM document analysis system. The computer "reads" information on papers, using a laser, and stores it at the rate of one page every fifteen seconds. The system even provides for the storage of graphics. It can recognize 256 different shades of gray!

Flow Chart

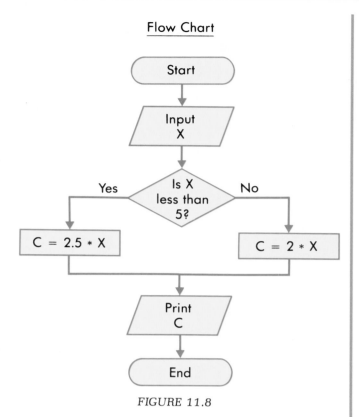

FIGURE 11.8

Diamond

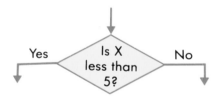

Example 2: The Giant Gizmo Company sells Green Gizmos according to the following:

Five or more cost $2.00 each.

Fewer than 5 cost $2.50 each.

Dottie Parlon works in the billing department. She used the flow chart in Figure 11.8 to write the program. Pretend you work with Dottie. Copy and complete the program.

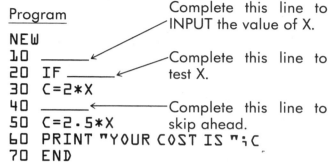

Program

```
NEW
10 _____        Complete this line to
                  INPUT the value of X.
20 IF _____     Complete this line to
                  test X.
30 C=2*X
40 _____        Complete this line to
50 C=2.5*X        skip ahead.
60 PRINT "YOUR COST IS ";C
70 END
```

This program and flow chart illustrate **branching to select**. In this case, only one value is entered. Therefore, no trailer record is needed. Instead of repeating a process, the computer decides which one of two processes to choose. The choice depends on the answer to the test question in the diamond. Compare the diamond to the partially completed line 20 below.

These must agree.

```
20 IF X < 5 THEN _____
```

This program will:

Input the number of Gizmos ordered, X.

Test to decide how to compute the cost.

Compute the correct cost.

Print the cost in a message to the customer.

The completed lines should be:

```
10 INPUT X
20 IF X < 5 THEN 50
     .
     .
     .
40 GOTO 60
```

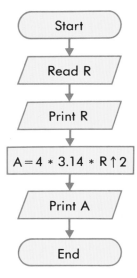

FIGURE 11.10

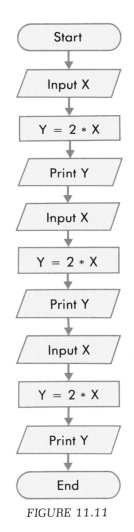

FIGURE 11.11

1. Refer to the flow chart in Figure 11.8. Determine the value of C for:
   a. X = 3
   b. X = 5
   c. X = 25

2. Refer to the flow chart in Figure 11.9. What would be printed if the value read in for N is 7 and the following numbers are input?
   a. 5
   b. 9
   c. 7

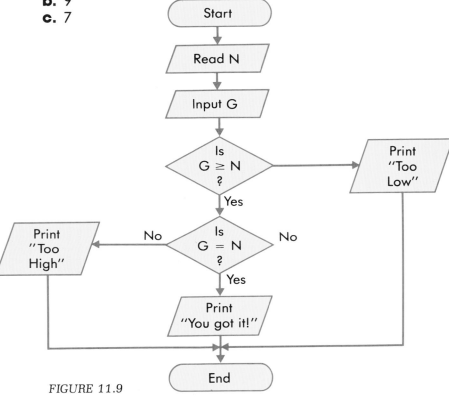

FIGURE 11.9

3. Refer to the flow chart in Figure 11.10. What would be the value of A for:
   a. R = 10
   b. R = 5

Chip's Challenges

4. Draw a flow chart using a decision diamond which would do the same thing as the flow chart in Figure 11.11.

5. Draw a flow chart which would illustrate how to read a number, M, and compare it to 21. If M is less than 21, print M. If M is greater than or equal to 21, print 21.

CHAPTER SUMMARY

1. A flow chart is a diagram showing the order of steps to be followed in solving a problem.
2. The flow chart symbols are:

   a. To indicate Start or End.

   b. To indicate operation or assignment.

   c. To indicate READ, INPUT, or PRINT.

   d. To indicate a decision.

   e. To indicate the flow.

3. The decision diamond has only one arrow going in and two arrows going out.
4. In a program or flow chart you may:
   a. Branch to repeat.   b. Branch to select.
5. A trailer record is used to end a loop.
6. A flow chart solution for a particular problem is not the only solution possible.

PROBLEM SET   11

1. The steps followed by Audrey Luiz in doing her homework are shown below. Make a flow chart using these steps.
   a. Audrey collects her materials and opens her book.
   b. Audrey sharpens her pencil.
   c. Audrey gets a drink of water.
   d. Audrey turns on the T.V.
   e. If there is a good program playing, she watches it and then goes back to the first step. If there is not a good show on T.V., she does her homework.
   f. Stop.

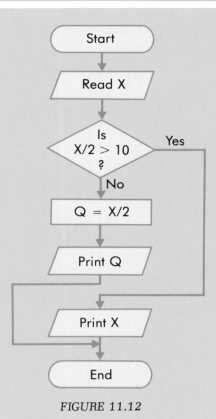

FIGURE 11.12

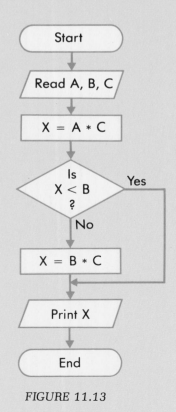

FIGURE 11.13

2. Follow the instructions given in the flow chart in Figure 11.12 and determine what will be printed when the following data is entered.
   a. X = 12   **b.** X = 23
3. Study the program below. Draw a flow chart to illustrate the program.
```
NEW
10  READ A
20  READ B
30  IF A>10 THEN 60
40  PRINT B
50  GOTO 80
60  PRINT A
70  DATA 34,16
80  END
```
4. What would be printed if the program above were RUN?
5. What would be printed if the program above were changed to 70 DATA 10,0?
6. Write the program corresponding to the flow chart in Figure 11.12.
7. For the flow chart in Figure 11.13, determine the value of X if:
   a. A = 4, B = 9, C = 2   **b.** A = 10, B = 4, C = 3
8. The formula for calculating distance is d = rt where d stands for distance, r stands for rate, and t stands for time. Distance equals rate multiplied by time. Construct a flow chart to read values for rate R, time T, and compute and print the distance D.
9. Write the program corresponding to the flow chart you prepared in Problem 8.
10. Determine the value of D in Problem 9 if:
    a. R = 60, T = 3
    b. R = 45, T = 4.5
11. Write an **IF** statement to test the value of A, as shown in the decision diamond. If the answer to the test value is Yes, the program should go to line 80.

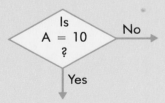

12. What trailer record would be needed to end a program with the decision diamond in Problem 11?
13. Given a program with this test statement:
    IF X = 98.6 THEN 110
    which of the following is a correct trailer record?
    a. 110   **b.** 98.6
    c. 96.8 + 110   **d.** 99999

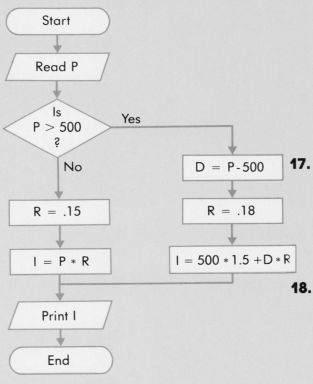

FIGURE 11.14

14. Copy and complete line 80 in the program shown. This line should contain the trailer record which would end the program.

```
NEW
10  READ A
20  PRINT A
30  IF A = 100 THEN 90
40  PRINT A * A
50  GOTO 10
60  DATA 5
70  DATA 20
80  DATA_____
90  END
```

15. In a flow chart, what figure represents each of the following?
   a. The flow of the problem.
   b. The start of the chart.
   c. A decision.
   d. An operation.

16. The flow chart in Figure 11.14 will convert feet (F) and yards (Y) to meters (M). The program steps, without their line numbers, are shown in scrambled order. Match each program step with its appropriate line number in the flow chart. Note that **DATA** statements have been omitted.
   a. $M1 = .91*Y$
   b. END
   c. $M = M1 + M2$
   d. PRINT "METERS =",M
   e. $M2 = .30 * F$
   f. READ Y, F

17. The EWELL PAYOFF Loan Company charges 15 percent interest for the first 500 dollars borrowed, and 18 percent interest for any amount greater than 500 dollars. Using the flow chart on the left, trace the steps to determine the interest (I) charged to each of the following people:
   a. Sydney Oswinkle, who borrowed 435 dollars.
   b. Roxanne Scott, who borrowed 640 dollars.

18. Write the **IF** statement illustrated by each of the following flow chart segments.

a.

b.

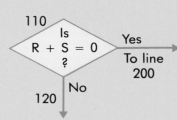

FIGURE 11.15

Chip's Challenges

19. Sandy is a sales representative for a crankshaft manufacturing company. She receives a commission of 8 percent for the first $10 000 sales and 12 percent for any sales beyond that amount. Prepare a flow chart which determines Sandy's commission (C) for any sales amount (S).

20. The following flow chart illustrates a computer guessing game. Pretend you are the programmer. Copy and complete the program steps which contain a blank.

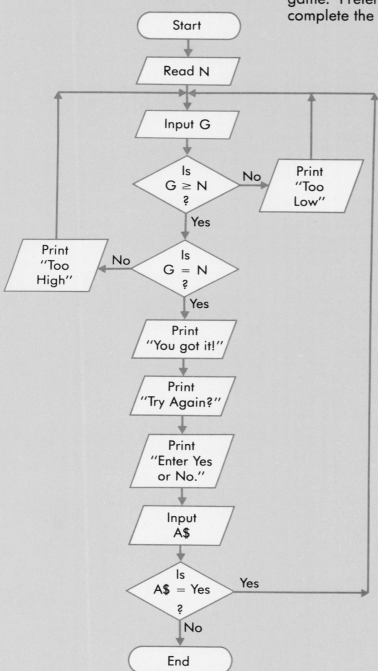

Program
NEW
10 _____
20 _____
30 IF _____
40 PRINT _____
50 GOTO _____
60 IF _____
70 PRINT _____
80 GOTO _____
90 PRINT "YOU GOT IT"
100 PRINT "TRY AGAIN?"
110 PRINT "ENTER YES OR NO"
120 _____
130 IF _____
140 END

COMPUTER AWARENESS

Electronic Files

Sophisticated computer systems can handle vast quantities of data.

Besides being a fast and accurate "number cruncher" or calculating machine, a computer is a record keeper. It can accept all kinds of information. It can do things with that information, such as arrange and combine it. It can store or file information. And it can show the results of its work.

This work is called data processing. Facts—data—are put into a form that can be entered into the computer. Data entry can be from a keyboard, from punched cards, from computer tapes, from disk storage, or from other special input devices. Two of these special devices are the bar code readers found in supermarkets and the special marked card readers that some schools use to score tests.

Each unit of data forms a **field**. A set of related fields is called a **record**. A collection of records is a **data file**. In a class data file in a school, the collection of records would be the names and grades of all the students in the class. A record would be one student's name and grade. The student's last name, first name, and separate grades would be the fields for that student's record.

The computer can sort and arrange data, using its Arithmetic

Logic Unit. (Remember, letters are stored by a **numeric** or number code.)

Imagine three boxes or memory locations. Suppose the computer has been instructed to put the information in the first two boxes in alphabetical order. It finds a B (code 66) in the first box and an A (code 65) in the second. The sorting program instructs it to copy B into a third memory location, for temporary storage. Then it can copy A into the first box, erasing B. A is still in the second box, however, so the program instructs the computer to copy B into the second box, where it belongs, erasing A.

Special software—programs—can direct the **hardware**, the computer and its peripherals, to search for specific data, arrange this data in special categories, total the values of the data, and use the data in other programs, to write letters, or to send bills.

Some data files, such as those of banks and retail stores, have to be changed frequently. Keyboards and cash registers in the bank or store can be connected directly to the organization's computer. A bank computer, for example, records each deposit and withdrawal as it is made, keeping the customer's account record up to date. A store computer can record the kind of merchandise sold and subtract the item from its inventory, the record of all the things it has in stock. When the computer finds that the store is running out of something, it can inform the manager.

Some files are **data bases**, sets of records that are more or less permanent. Lawyers may use data bases that record past legal decisions, saving hours of research in a law library. Schools keep records of all students and their achievements. Town, city, and county governments keep lists of registered voters and taxpayers.

People often complain that computerized record keeping results in many mistakes. Mistakes do occur, but they are almost always human errors, not computer errors. They are usually the result of either careless preparation of data to be entered into the computer or human error in entering correct data. The computer can only do what it is instructed to do, and it can do it only with the data that it is given.

Some so-called computer errors come from another cause, error in programming. These, too, are human errors. Programmers, after all, are human beings, too.

What Do You Know?
1. What is data processing?
2. In data processing, what is a field?
3. What is a record?
4. What is a data file?
5. What part of the computer sorts data?

What Can You Find Out?
1. Does your school use computerized records to schedule classes?
2. How does the bar code reader help the manager of a supermarket?
3. What is a network?

What Do You Think?
1. How might "computer errors" be reduced or eliminated?
2. Is it safe to keep important records in computer data banks?
3. Should duplicates of important records be kept somewhere else?

PROGRAMMING TOP TO BOTTOM

Good Programming Practices

Good programs require good planning. Planning to INITIALIZE, PROCESS, and OUTPUT information can help the programmer to write subprograms, which combine to make good programs.

12.1

Before BASIC

DISCOVER FOR YOURSELF

Lee and Anton were going to make lemonade for their class to sell in the annual Elmer A. Fernsdorff Founders' Day celebration. They found this recipe, which serves twelve.

8 lemons
6 cups of water
1 cup of sugar

Squeeze lemons into water, add sugar and stir with ice, the recipe adds.

1. If they wanted to serve only six people, how many lemons and how much water and sugar would they need?

2. Suppose that they wanted to serve 24 people. How would they adjust the recipe?

3. Their class has 32 students. How many lemons would they need to make lemonade for their class?

4. They would expect to serve about 300 at the Founders' Day celebration. How would they change the recipe for this many people?

WHAT DID YOU LEARN?

Lee wondered how many lemons would be needed for the big day. He suggested that they write a computer program to convert the recipe for large numbers of people. After he and Anton did some thinking, they came up with these ideas:

1. Whoever was using the program should enter the number of people who would be served.

2. The computer should print out how many lemons, and how many cups of water and sugar would be needed to make that much lemonade.

That was the easy part! Now, they discovered, it would be necessary to put their ideas into the computer. They asked Mr. Pierce, their teacher, for help. Mr. Pierce grinned and wrote these three words on the board:

INITIALIZE   PROCESS   OUTPUT

He explained that computer programs can usually be divided into three main parts. Whenever you have trouble beginning, you can start by thinking about each of these three parts.

INITIALIZE (pronounced i-NISH-uh-lize) means getting data ready. In this part, variables are named and their beginning values given. Data may also be entered with `READ` or `INPUT` statements. In the lemonade program, you would do these four things:

1. Set the number of lemons, L, to 8.
2. Set the amount of water, W, to 6.
3. Set the amount of sugar, S, to 1.
4. `INPUT` the number, N, to be served.

PROCESS means making the computer do the computing or other processing needed for the program. In the lemonade program, this means changing the amounts of lemons, sugar, and water needed to serve the number of people entered in the initialization part of the program.

OUTPUT means displaying the answers or the information calculated in the processing part. In the lemonade program, the number of lemons and the amount of sugar and water needed must be displayed.

Chip's Bits

The United States government is the world's largest user of computer hardware and software. It spends $15 billion every year on computers! In 1982, the federal government owned more than 18,000 computers of all sizes. Some were small microcomputers. Others were huge CRAYIS computers, among the most powerful ever built.

Memory Bank

Program Planning

When you plan a program, think first of these three major parts:

INITIALIZE   PROCESS   OUTPUT

Do not worry (yet) about writing the BASIC statements of the program.

Now that Lee and Anton had their program well planned and organized, they felt much better about writing the actual BASIC statements. They could now consider each of these parts as a small, separate program (which Mr. Pierce called a **subprogram**). That, they agreed, made the job of programming much easier.

They both agreed that the first subprogram, the initializing, would be pretty easy. Here is what they wrote:

INITIALIZE

```
10  Clearscreen
20  L = 8
30  W = 6
40  S = 1
50  INPUT N
```

The next subprogram, the processing, made them do some heavy thinking. Anton reasoned that since the recipe served 12, they could divide each ingredient by 12 to serve one. Then they could simply multiply this number by N. That would make it serve N people. Here is this part of the program:

PROCESS

```
60  A = N*L/12
70  B = N*W/12
80  C = N*S/12
```

The final subprogram turned out to be the easiest part of all. This is what they wrote.

OUTPUT

```
90   PRINT A
100  PRINT B
110  PRINT C
```

Memory Bank

Subprograms

After you have planned your program and organized it into major parts, think of each of the parts as a separate subprogram. Write the BASIC statements for each subprogram.

USE WHAT YOU HAVE LEARNED

Toni played on the class softball team and wanted to find her batting average. She had 36 times at bat and 13 hits. She also knew that she had to divide Times at Bat by Number of Hits to calculate the average.

1. Help Toni plan a computer program by organizing the problem into three major parts:

   Initialize, Process, and Output.

CHIP WONDERS:
DID YOUR PROGRAM LOOK LIKE THIS?

2. Write the program statements for each of the three parts above.

```
10   Clearscreen      INITIALIZE
20   T = 36
30   H = 13
40   A = H/T          PROCESS
50   PRINT A          OUTPUT
```

E x e r c i s e s

1. Angelos wanted to find the average for the three math tests he had taken. He received scores of 68, 72, and 81. Describe each of the three major parts of a BASIC program to compute his test average. Use the variable names X, Y, and Z for the test scores and A for the average.
2. Toni wished to change her batting average program so that she could enter Times at Bat and Number of Hits (T and H) using **INPUT** statements. Describe each of the three major parts of this new program.
3. Write the programs for each of the two exercises above.

Chip's Challenges

4. Sometimes one of the three program parts is missing from a problem. For example Gil Juarez wanted to store the words HOW, NOW, BROWN, COW (using the string variables H$, N$, B$, C$) and have them printed out in every different order possible.
   a. Determine which of the three major parts is missing from this problem.
   b. Describe each of the other two parts.
   c. Write the program steps for this program.

12.2

Keep the User Informed

```
10    Clearscreen
20    L = 8
30    W = 6
40    S = 1
50    INPUT N
60    A = N*L/12
70    B = N*W/12
80    C = N*S/12
90    PRINT A
100   PRINT B
110   PRINT C
```

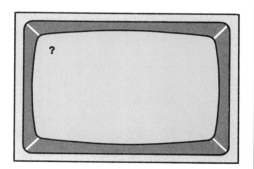

Lee and Anton were very proud of their lemonade program and wanted to try it out. To the left is the program as they entered it:

Study the Lemonade Program and answer the questions below.

1. If you enter **RUN**, what will you be asked to enter?
2. If you enter **RUN** and then enter the number 36, what will be the computer's response?

Enter the program. Follow the directions below and answer the questions.

3. Enter **RUN** and describe the appearance of the computer screen.
4. If you had not seen the program, would you know what the computer was requesting? What could you do to the program to make sure the user knows what is needed?

Lee and Anton asked Penny to **RUN** their Lemonade Program. When Penny entered **RUN**, on the left is what she saw on the screen.

Is this what you saw on your screen? She did not know what the computer was asking for. Did it want a number? Two numbers? A name? Lee and Anton both agreed that someone using the program needed to know the kind and amount of information requested by the computer. Mr. Pierce, with his friendly grin, suggested that they use a prompt. (The prompt was explained in Chapter 8.)

He pointed out that prompting the user makes the program and the computer seem much friendlier. He mentioned that only one item should be entered for each **INPUT** statement and that every **INPUT** statement needed a prompt.

Memory Bank

INPUT Prompts

An **INPUT** statement should not ask for more than one piece of data.

Every **INPUT** statement should prompt the user, telling what kind of data is needed and for what the data will be used.

Now Lee and Anton wrote the following new statements:

```
45  PRINT "THIS IS A RECIPE FOR LEMONADE."
46  PRINT "HOW MANY PEOPLE TO BE SERVED?"
```

They LISTed their program and saw this:

```
10   Clearscreen
20   L = 8
30   W = 6
40   S = 1
45   PRINT "THIS IS A RECIPE FOR LEMONADE."
46   PRINT "HOW MANY PEOPLE TO BE SERVED?"
50   INPUT N
60   A = N*L/12
70   B = N*W/12
80   C = N*S/12
90   PRINT A
100   PRINT B
110   PRINT C
```

Enter this program so that you can **RUN** it with Penny. See what output you get when you answer the computer that you want to serve 36 people. Do you see the same problem with the output that Penny saw?

After Penny ran the program the screen looked like that to the left.

Penny was a bit impatient when she saw the final output. She had no idea what was meant by the three numbers 24, 18, and 3. Of course, Lee and Anton knew what the numbers represented. They also knew that their program needed a little more work. Mr. Pierce said that their output needed **labels**.

Memory Bank

Labels

All output from a program must be labeled so that the user knows what the output means. The programmer should make the labels a part of every PRINT statement.

Lee changed the end of the program by rewriting the last three PRINT statements. He also added another at line 85. This is how they looked:

```
85  PRINT "FOR "; N;" PEOPLE YOU NEED"
90  PRINT A; " LEMONS"
100  PRINT B; " CUPS OF WATER"
110  PRINT C; " CUPS OF SUGAR"
```

Can you guess the output from these four PRINT statements? Enter the program and RUN it. See if your guess was correct.

Exercises

1. Look at Angelos' problem in the first set of exercises for this chapter (p. 211). Change this program so that the three test scores are entered through **INPUT** statements. Be sure to prompt all input and label all output.

2. Look at Toni's batting average program (Exercise 2, p. 211). Write the BASIC statements for this program. Be sure to include prompts for input and labels for output.

3. The program below prints the larger of two numbers. Rewrite the program so that it prompts the input of the two numbers by printing:
PLEASE ENTER THE 1ST NUMBER
PLEASE ENTER THE 2ND NUMBER
Finally, it should label the output by printing:
THE LARGER NUMBER IS _____
The program is below:
```
10  Clearscreen
20  INPUT A
30  INPUT B
40  IF A >= B THEN PRINT A
50  IF B > A THEN PRINT B
```

Chip's Challenges

4. Write a program to pick out and print the largest of three numbers. The input of the three numbers should be prompted and the output of the largest should be labeled.

12.3

Make Friends with a Computer

Sometimes it is necessary to go back to a program and make some changes. If the program is very short, this is not difficult. For a long program, however, this can be a hard thing to do. It would be very helpful if you could place statements in the program itself that would help you to identify the important parts of the program.

Study the program below. After you have studied it, try to answer the questions which follow.

```
10   Clearscreen
20   FOR I = 1 TO 16
30   PRINT "*"
40   NEXT I
50   FOR I = 1 TO 6
60   PRINT "**************"
70   NEXT I
80   FOR I = 1 TO 10
90   PRINT "*"
100  NEXT I
```

1. What is the output for the FOR−NEXT loop in lines 20 through 40?

2. What is the output for the FOR−NEXT loop in lines 50 through 70?

3. What is the output for the FOR−NEXT loop in lines 80 through 100?

4. If the program were RUN, how would you describe the output?

5. Enter this program and RUN it. Did you guess the correct output?

Alice, who wrote this program, called it "Raise the Flag." RUN the program again and see if it looks like a flag and a flagpole to you. (For your computer, it may need a few changes before it looks very much like a flag and pole.)

Before making any of these changes, you should identify what the different parts of the program do. You can then place BASIC statements in the program, which will describe each part of the program. The keyword, REM, permits you to do this. Here is how it works:

16   REM ANYTHING YOU WISH TO PLACE HERE

Line   Keyword.   Any Combination of Characters
Number.   You Wish.

The keyword REM stands for REMark. It lets you put any kind of messages or remarks in your program. When the program is RUN, the computer simply ignores REM statements. It passes right by them to the next statement. When a program is LISTed, however, the REM statements appear. They make a program much easier to read and understand. See how much easier Alice's program is to understand when several REM statements are added.

```
10   Clearscreen
15   REM THIS LOOP DRAWS THE FLAGPOLE
20   FOR I = 1 TO 16
30   PRINT "*"
40   NEXT I
45   REM THIS LOOP DRAWS THE FLAG
50   FOR I = 1 TO 6
60   PRINT "**************"
70   NEXT I
75   REM THIS LOOP RUNS THE FLAG UP THE POLE
80   FOR I = 1 TO 10
90   PRINT "*"
100   NEXT I
```

Now it is a simple matter to locate any part of the program that you wish to change. It may be, for example, that on your computer the flag is run too far up the pole. Perhaps it is not run far enough up the pole. You can easily find the loop which controls this (lines 80 to 100). If you wish to adjust the raising of the flag, you can change the last number in line 80. You may need to experiment to find the value that looks best on your screen. You could also use a timing loop to slow down the part that runs the flag up the pole.

Memory Bank

Documentation

(Doc-you-men-TAY-shun) *This means any directions, instructions, remarks, or comments which help a person reading or running your program. They can be* REM *statements,* PRINT *statements,* INPUT *statements, or even notes and comments that you write about your program.*

Programs, especially long programs, should have much documentation. Each part of the program should be described or identified in a REM statement. The variables in the program should be identified in a REM statement. At the very beginning of the program a REM statement should be used to identify the program and the programmer. Of course, any of these REM statements can be replaced by PRINT statements that do similar things.

USE WHAT YOU HAVE LEARNED

The program below prints a well-known song. It contains several REM statements. The REM statements have no remarks or comments. Study the program and see if you can write the remarks on a sheet of paper for each part of the program.

```
10    Clearscreen
20    REM _____
30    FOR I = 1 TO 4
40    REM _____
50    READ A$
60    REM _____
70    PRINT A$
80    PRINT A$
90    PRINT
100   NEXT I
110   DATA ARE YOU SLEEPING?, BROTHER JOHN
120   DATA MORNING BELLS ARE RINGING, DING DONG DING
```

CHIP WONDERS: WHAT DID YOU WRITE FOR LINE 20 ?

The REM statement in line 20 should tell about the loop which follows it. It should mention that each time through the loop, a line of the song is read and printed twice.

Exercises

1. The program below is Angelos' average program. Provide the documentation for this program by copying and completing the REM statements.

```
10   Clearscreen
15   REM _____
20   A = 68
30   B = 72
40   C = 81
50   REM _____
60   S = A + B + C
70   REM _____
80   A = S/3
90   PRINT "THE SUM IS "; S
100  PRINT "THE AVERAGE IS "; A
```

2. The program below is the one that flashes Whitney's name on and off the screen. Provide the documentation by copying and completing the REM statements.

```
10   Clearscreen
20   REM _____
30   PRINT "WHITNEY LACSAR ! !"
40   REM _____
50   FOR I = 1 TO 100
60   NEXT I
70   REM _____
80   Clearscreen
90   REM _____
100  FOR I = 1 TO 100
110  NEXT I
120  GOTO 20
```

Chip's Challenges

3. Study the program below and determine what it does. Provide the documentation by copying and completing the REM statements.

```
10   Clearscreen
20   REM _____
30   PRINT "FRACTION","DECIMAL"
40   REM _____
50   FOR I = 1 TO 10
60   REM _____
70   FOR J = 1 TO I
80   REM _____
90   PRINT J; "/";I, J/I
100  NEXT J
110  NEXT I
```

12.4

Best Face Forward

It is a good feeling to write a computer program that really works. You should feel very proud to see the results of your program. If you can make your output interesting and easy to understand, you can feel even better. One way to improve output is by having it appear in a chart or graph. See how this can be done.

DISCOVER FOR YOURSELF

Look at the **DATA** statement below. It lists the months from September to June. Following each month is a number. The number represents the number of school days in that month.

```
210  DATA SEP,18,OCT,22,NOV,21,
DEC,15,JAN,18,FEB,20,MAR,17,
APR,22,MAY,19,JUN,16
```

1. Write a **READ** statement that will accept a single month and its corresponding number of school days.

2. Write the program statements that will make the **READ** statement repeat until all of the data is entered.

3. Write the program steps to have the data printed as it is read. The names of the months should be in one column and the numbers of days should be in another column.

4. Write the program statement that will place the following heading at the top of each column:

CHIP WONDERS: DID YOUR PROGRAM LOOK LIKE THIS?

MONTHS   NO. OF SCHOOL DAYS

(Helpful hint - In a **PRINT** statement, separate the variable names with commas. Your computer will print them in columns for you.)

```
10   Clearscreen
20   PRINT "MONTHS","NO. OF SCHOOL DAYS"
30   FOR I = 1 TO 10
40   READ A$,N
50   PRINT A$, N
60   NEXT I
210  DATA—see the data on previous page.
```

WHAT DID YOU LEARN?

In this activity, you discovered that output can be neatly printed in columns. By placing commas between variable names, you made the computer keep the month names and the number of days in line. Even your column headings were lined up correctly because you separated them by commas.

Chip's Bits

So many different moves are possible in a chess game that no computer can yet defeat a human chess master all the time. If the computer tried to check every possible move at the rate of one billion moves each second, it would take billions of years to make each decision! Possibly the best chess-playing program for microcomputers is SARGON, originally written in 1978 by Don and Kathe Spracklen. In its current version, SARGON can check about 250 positions each second.

Memory Bank

Columns of Output

You can print up to three columns of output (four on some computers) on each line by using a **PRINT** *statement such as:*

50 PRINT A, B, C

Use commas to separate the variables. The headings can appear in a statement such as:

20 PRINT "1ST HEADING", "2ND HEADING"

To be safe, do not use more than twelve characters inside each pair of quotation marks.

Now, take another look at the **DATA** statement in line 210. This data can be shown in the form of a bar graph. The following screen display shows this.

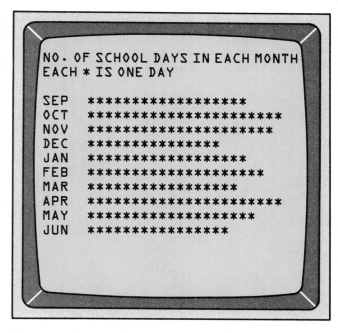

```
NO. OF SCHOOL DAYS IN EACH MONTH
EACH * IS ONE DAY

SEP   *******************
OCT   ************************
NOV   **********************
DEC   ****************
JAN   ********************
FEB   **********************
MAR   ******************
APR   *************************
MAY   ********************
JUN   ****************
```

You can have the computer display the bar graph by changing the program. First, see how the use of the semicolon affects a **PRINT** statement.

You would expect every **PRINT** statement to make the computer begin a new line of output. Indeed, this does happen, unless the last thing to be printed was followed by a comma or semicolon.

If a **PRINT** statement ends with a comma, the next thing printed will be on the same line, unless the computer is already at the end of that line. Blank spaces are added by the computer so that everything printed will fall into columns. There will be three such columns (four on some computers) in any line.

If a **PRINT** statement ends with a semicolon, the next thing printed will begin right where the last thing left off. Usually, no blanks will be added by the computer. If blanks are needed, the programmer must supply them.

To see how this works, try the statements below:

Try This First	Try This Next	Finally, Try This
1 PRINT 5	1 PRINT 5,	1 PRINT 5;
2 PRINT 6	2 PRINT 6,	2 PRINT 6;
3 PRINT 7	3 PRINT 7	3 PRINT 7
RUN	RUN	RUN

In the bar graph program, you will use some PRINT statements that end with semicolons. These will allow the printing to continue on the same line. Other PRINT statements will contain neither commas nor semicolons. These will be used to give you a new line.

Here is how the bar graph program will work:
1. Headings will be printed.
2. The following steps will be done 10 times, once for each month:
   The month name and number of days are read;
   The month name is printed, followed by blanks;
   In a FOR-NEXT loop one * is printed for each day. The program for the bar graph is below.

Program   Comments

```
5  Clearscreen
10  PRINT "NO. OF SCHOOL DAYS IN EACH MONTH"
20  PRINT "EACH * IS ONE DAY"
30  FOR I = 1 TO 10  ←——————— Loop to read months.
40  PRINT             ←——————— This gives a new line.
50  READ A$, N        ←——————— Month and days read.
60  PRINT A$;"   ";←——————— The semicolon keeps
                               the printing on the same
                               line.

70  FOR K = 1 TO N    ←——————— This loop prints the bar,
80  PRINT "*";        ←——————— one * for each day. The
90  NEXT K                     semicolon keeps the
100  NEXT I                    printing on the same
210  DATA (same as above)      line.
```

Enter this program and RUN it. Do you agree that it makes your output look more interesting? You will see that the name of every month in the DATA statement contains only 3 letters. The bar graph would not look as good if some names contained more letters than others. You can experiment with the DATA statement and see for yourself. (You can make a bar graph if the names do not all have the same number of letters. You will learn how in Chapter 14.)

The bar graph program can be used for many kinds of data. What do you think would happen, however, if the data for one line contained more *s than fit on a line? The bar would span more than one line and not look at all like a bar. In this case, it is necessary to use a scale. This means that you let each * stand for more than one item. You can add two lines to the program and change a few others to take care of this.

The number entered in line 4 is called a **scaling factor** and will tell how many items each * stands for. You may have to run the program many times, trying different numbers each time, before you find the correct scaling factor. Notice that we STEP by the scaling factor in the FOR-NEXT loop that begins in line 70.

```
3    PRINT"EACH * STANDS FOR HOW MANY ITEMS";
4    INPUT S ←                              → These steps are added
5    Clearscreen
10   PRINT "THE HEADING FOR YOUR GRAPH"
20   PRINT "EACH * STANDS FOR ";S;" ITEMS"
30   FOR I = 1 TO 10
40   PRINT
50   READ A$, N                            → These steps are changed
60   PRINT A$; "   ";
70   FOR K = 1 TO N STEP S
80   PRINT "*";
90   NEXT K
100  NEXT I
210  DATA (The data for your bar graph goes here.)
```

USE WHAT YOU HAVE LEARNED

Name	Number of Points
Janis	102
Marty	98
Peggy	121
Molly	83
Betty	84

CHIP WONDERS: WHAT WAS THE SCALING FACTOR YOU USED?

The Fernsdorff Quasars won the basketball championship. They gave their five leading scorers prizes. The table to the left shows the winners and the number of points scored by each during the season.

Use the program above to make a bar graph for the players and their scores. RUN the program several times using a larger value for the scaling factor S each time. Find the smallest value of S that allows each bar to fit on one line.

The value of S depends on your computer. If your computer allows 40 characters on a line, you may have used a value of 4 for S. If your computer has 64 characters on a line, you may have used a value of 3. Line 30 should look like this:

```
30 FOR I = 1 TO 5
```

since only 5 names will appear in the DATA statement.

E x e r c i s e s

The table below gives the average daily temperatures for one week. Use the information in this table for Exercises 1-3 below.

Day of Week	Average Temperature
Mon	32
Tue	27
Wed	20
Thr	18
Fri	25

AVERAGE DAILY TEMPERATURES FOR DEC 14 – DEC 18

1. Use the information in the table to make a **DATA** statement. Give the **DATA** statement the line number 210.

2. Use a program such as the one you wrote in *Discover for Yourself* to **READ** the data in your **DATA** statement from Exercise 1 above. **PRINT** the days and average temperatures in a table similar to the one shown. The information should be printed in columns. The columns should have these headings:

   DAY   AVERAGE TEMPERATURE

3. Use the information in the **DATA** statement from Exercise 1 to make a bar graph. The bar graph should have this heading and description:

   AVERAGE DAILY TEMPERATURES FOR ONE WEEK EACH * STANDS FOR 1 DEGREE

Chip's Challenges

4. The table below gives bowling scores for Jane, Nick, Andy, Bill, and Mary. Each one bowled three games. Write a program which reads in the information, calculates the average for each of the bowlers, and displays each bowler's name and average in a bar graph.

Name	1st Game	2nd Game	3rd Game
Jane	68	54	58
Nick	72	64	68
Andy	50	48	52
Bill	60	62	64
Mary	78	80	84

12.5

Read it Again

Mitzi wrote the program below to **READ** and **PRINT** a list of her favorite words. The words are in the **DATA** statement in line 210.

```
5   Clearscreen
10  FOR I = 1 TO 5
20  READ A$
30  PRINT A$
40  NEXT I
50  FOR I = 1 TO 5
60  READ A$
70  PRINT A$
80  NEXT I
210  DATA EARTHWORMS,
CLOTHESPINS, ONIONS,
BILLBOARDS, BOTTLECAPS
```

Note: this is not the last item in the **DATA** statement.

If Mitzi's program is **RUN**, it may cause the computer to print an error message. If you cannot determine what could go wrong, look at the questions below. They may help.

1. How many times must the **READ** statement in line 20 be carried out to complete the **FOR-NEXT** loop?

2. How much data is needed to complete the **FOR-NEXT** loop?

3. How many items are there in the **DATA** statement?

4. How many times must the **READ** statement in line 60 be carried out in completing the **FOR-NEXT** loop?

5. Will the computer be able to complete the program?

225

WHAT DID YOU LEARN?

The **READ** statement in line 20 is expected to accept five items of data. The **READ** statement in line 60 is also expected to accept five items of data. This totals ten items. Since the **DATA** statement has only five items, the computer will run out of data and print an error message.

Mitzi realized that if she added five more words to the **DATA** statement there would be enough data. She decided, however, to place a **RESTORE** statement between lines 40 and 50. She entered this:

    45 RESTORE

and then entered **RUN**. She was filled with joy to see her favorite words printed on the screen not once but twice!

Here is how the **RESTORE** statement works:

1. The first **READ** statement in a program causes the computer to select the first item in the first **DATA** statement in the program. Think of this as placing a **pointer** at that item.

    When **I = 1**, the statement

    20 READ A$

    makes the computer search for the first **DATA** statement and place a pointer on **EARTHWORMS**, the first item in the statement. At this time,

    A$ = "EARTHWORMS"

    and **EARTHWORMS** is printed.

        ← Pointer

    210 DATA EARTHWORMS,CLOTHESPINS,ONIONS,
    BILLBOARDS,BOTTLECAPS

2. Each time an item is read, the pointer is moved to the next item.
    When **I = 2**, the statement

    20 READ A$

moves the pointer to `CLOTHESPINS`, the second item in the `DATA` statement. At this time,

`A$ = "CLOTHESPINS"` (`EARTHWORMS`

has been erased.)

and `CLOTHESPINS` is printed.

← Pointer

`210  DATA EARTHWORMS,CLOTHESPINS,ONIONS,`
`BILLBOARDS,BOTTLECAPS`

The first five items are read in this way.

3. If a `DATA` statement has no more items, the pointer is moved to the next `DATA` statement in the program. In Mitzi's program this does not happen. There is only one `DATA` statement.

4. The `RESTORE` statement moves the pointer back to the very first item in the very first `DATA` statement. This permits all of the data to be read again.

← Pointer

`210  DATA EARTHWORMS,CLOTHESPINS,ONIONS,`
`BILLBOARDS,BOTTLECAPS`

The five items can now be read again.

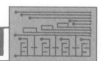

Memory Bank

The RESTORE Statement

When the `RESTORE` statement is encountered, the data pointer is moved back to the first item in the first `DATA` statement in a program. This permits all of the data to be `READ` again. This can happen as many times in a program as you want.

USE WHAT YOU HAVE LEARNED

Use the same **DATA** statement that Mitzi used in her program:

```
210  DATA EARTHWORMS,CLOTHESPINS,ONIONS,
BILLBOARDS,BOTTLECAPS
```

Write a program that will **READ** only the first four items and **PRINT** them two times. Use Mitzi's program as your guide.

CHIP WONDERS:
DID YOU CHANGE
LINES 10 AND 50?

You only had to change two statements in the entire program. Line 10 becomes:

```
10 FOR I = 1 TO 4
```

and line 50 becomes:

```
50 FOR I = 1 TO 4
```

All other lines stay the same!

E x e r c i s e s

1. Write a program such as the one Mitzi wrote to have each item in this **DATA** statement **READ** and **PRINT**ed twice.
```
170  DATA RICH MAN,POOR MAN,BEGGAR MAN,
THIEF
```

2. Write a program such as the one Mitzi wrote to have each item in the **DATA** statement used three times.
```
180  DATA DOCTOR,LAWYER,INDIAN CHIEF
```

3. Write a program such as the one Mitzi wrote to have each number in this **DATA** statement used four times.
```
300  DATA 5280, 98.6, 3.14, 1776, 1620,
54.40
```

Chip's Challenges

4. Enter the following **DATA** statement carefully.

```
200  DATA ALL,ALL,DOGS,CATS,LOVE,LOVE,
CATS,MICE
```

Write a program similar to Mitzi's, to read the list twice. Have it read the items two at a time. The first time the list is read, have only the first word of each pair printed. The second time have the second word printed. This should give you two separate messages.

12.6

Data on Demand

The **DATA** statement below is Mitzi's list of favorite words. They should be used to answer the questions that follow.

```
210  DATA EARTHWORMS, CLOTHESPINS, ONIONS,
BILLBOARDS, BOTTLECAPS
```

DISCOVER FOR YOURSELF

1. If Mitzi entered and ran the following program lines, what would be the computer's output?

```
10  READ A$
20  PRINT A$
```

2. If Mitzi entered and ran the following program lines what would be the computer's output?

```
10  READ A$
20  READ A$
30  PRINT A$
```

3. If Mitzi entered and ran the following program lines, what would be the computer's output?

```
10  FOR I = 1 TO 4
20  READ A$
30  NEXT I
40  PRINT A$
```

4. Enter each set of program lines from Questions 1, 2, and 3. RUN each program and see if you were correct in guessing the output.

WHAT DID YOU LEARN?

For Question 2, did you say that the word **CLOTHESPINS** would be displayed by the computer? The first **READ** statement read the first **DATA** item. At that time **A$**, had the value **EARTHWORMS**.

229

The second **READ** statement read the second **DATA** item. Then A$ had the value **CLOTHES-PINS**. The value **EARTHWORMS** was erased. The **PRINT** statement made the computer display the current value of A$, **CLOTHESPINS**.

In Question 3, the first four **DATA** items were read in the **FOR-NEXT** loop. Each of the first three of these was erased as the next was read. Only the fourth one, **BILLBOARDS**, was printed.

Clever Mitzi wrote a program using her list of favorite words and another list of five words. The program has the computer make up slogans using these two lists. It can make up twenty-five different slogans!

Before looking at her program, look at the two lists of words:

First List	Second List
SAVE	EARTHWORMS
STAMP OUT	CLOTHESPINS
CONSERVE	BOTTLECAPS
BEAUTIFY	ONIONS
CONTROL	BILLBOARDS

Mitzi's program asks the user for two numbers, each no greater than 5. The first number selects a word from the first list. The second number chooses a word from the second list. The two words are combined to make a slogan. Enter Mitzi's program and see what slogans you can make.

```
5   Clearscreen
10    REM SLOGAN GENERATOR
20    PRINT "ENTER 2 NUMBERS BETWEEN 1 & 5"
30    PRINT "WHAT IS THE FIRST NUMBER";
40    INPUT F
50    PRINT "WHAT IS THE SECOND NUMBER";
60    INPUT S
65    REM THIS LOOP READS THE LIST UP TO
66    REM THE FIRST SELECTION
70    FOR I = 1 TO F
80    READ A$
90    NEXT I
95    REM PRINTS THE FIRST PART OF SLOGAN
96    PRINT "HELP "; A$;
100   REM ALLOWS THE DATA TO BE READ AGAIN
110   RESTORE
115   REM LOOP READS PAST FIRST LIST
```

```
116   REM READS TO SECOND SELECTION
120   FOR I = 1 TO 5+S
130   READ A$
140   NEXT I
145   REM PRINTS LAST HALF OF SLOGAN
150   PRINT " OUR NATION'S "; A$
200   DATA SAVE,CONSERVE,STAMP OUT,
BEAUTIFY,CONTROL
210   DATA EARTHWORMS,CLOTHESPINS,
BOTTLECAPS,ONIONS,BILLBOARDS
```

After Mitzi ran her program the output looked like this:

```
ENTER 2 NUMBERS BETWEEN 1 & 5
WHAT IS THE FIRST NUMBER? 3
WHAT IS THE SECOND NUMBER? 2
HELP STAMP OUT OUR NATION'S CLOTHESPINS
```

After Mitzi had entered the two numbers, F had the value 3 and S had the value 2. Lines 70, 80, and 90 make the computer READ the first three DATA items. The first two were erased and only the third item was printed. Where was the data pointer at that time? That is right, it was pointing to the item STAMP OUT.

The RESTORE in line 110 places the pointer back at the first DATA item. Lines 120 through 140 will make the computer read 7 (5 + S) items of DATA. The first six of these will be erased and the last item will be printed. In this RUN, the third item from the first list and the second item from the second list will be placed in the slogan.

In Chapter 14 of this book, you will see how to make the computer pick the numbers F and S for you and surprise you with its own slogan.

Did you notice that when the computer printed the question:

WHAT IS THE FIRST NUMBER?

it placed a question mark after it? There was no question mark indicated in the PRINT statement in line 30 and yet one appeared on the screen! On Mitzi's computer (and many others), the INPUT statement causes a question mark to appear on the screen. Mitzi knew this. She placed a semicolon at the end of line 30. She knew then that the next thing printed would be placed immediately after the letter R in the word NUMBER. The next thing, of course, was the computer's own question mark.

Memory Bank

The pair of statements,

```
20  PRINT "WHAT NUMBER";
30  INPUT X
```

will print the message

WHAT NUMBER?

on the screen and allow a number to be entered immediately after the question. Notice the semicolon in line 20.

USE WHAT YOU HAVE LEARNED

CHIP SAYS:
TRY THE QUESTIONS ON YOUR COMPUTER.

Use Mitzi's slogan program above to answer the following questions:

1. If the numbers 2 and 5 were entered, what would the output be?

2. If the numbers 4 and 1 were entered, what would the output be?

3. What numbers would have to be entered for the program to make up this slogan?

HELP CONTROL OUR NATION'S ONIONS

4. What numbers would have to be entered for the program to display this slogan?

HELP SAVE OUR NATION'S BILLBOARDS

Exercises

1. Write **PRINT** and **INPUT** statements that will make the computer display the following question and accept a response:
HOW MANY NUMBERS WILL YOU ENTER?

2. Write **PRINT** and **INPUT** statements that will make the computer display the following and accept a response:
DO YOU WANT TO RUN THIS PROGRAM AGAIN?

3. Mitzi wished to add the word SUPPORT to her first list and the word CATFISH to her second list. Of course she would have to change the **DATA** statements, lines 200 and 210, to do this. She would also have to change the number 5 in line 20 to the number 6.
a. Name one other line that must be changed.
b. Write this new line.

Chip's Challenges

4. Look at the two lists of words below. Write a program to read any word from the first list and combine it with any word from the second list. Use Mitzi's slogan program as a guide. The two words selected should have the word OF printed between them.

First List	Second List
HERD	CATTLE
PACK	DOGS
SCHOOL	FISH
COVEY	PIGEONS
CLOWDER	CATS
PRIDE	LIONS
RAG	COLTS

CHAPTER SUMMARY

1. Many computer programs can be organized into three parts:
   Initialize, Process, and Output.

2. Each of the three parts can be thought of as a smaller program, called a subprogram.

3. Only one value should be entered in each **INPUT** statement.

4. All data entered through an **INPUT** statement should be prompted by **PRINT** statements that tell what kind of data is needed and what the data is for.

5. All data displayed by the computer should be labeled.

6. The appearance of much output can be improved by having it appear in tables and bar graphs.

7. A **REM** statement allows you to place any message, comment, or instruction in a program. The computer, when it executes a program, ignores all **REM** statements.

8. Programs, especially long programs, should be well documented. This means that variables should be described, parts of the program labeled, and instructions for the use of the program given.

9. If a PRINT statement ends with a comma or semicolon, the computer continues the next output on the same line. A comma allows three (four on some computers) columns, with enough blanks between to have the output appear in columns. A semicolon allows many items to appear on a line without blanks between them.

10. The RESTORE statement moves the data pointer back to the first item in the first DATA statement.

PROBLEM SET   12

1. Many computer programs can be organized into three parts called _____, _____, and _____.

2. Each of the three parts can be thought of as a small program called a _____.

3. Initialization means entering data through a _____ statement or through an _____ statement.

4. All arithmetic is performed in the _____ part of a program.

5. If a program needs data from the keyboard, it should _____ the user by telling what kind of data is needed, how much is needed, and for what it will be used.

6. A program should label all _____ that it produces.

7. Comments can be placed within a program by using _____ statements.

8. Each PRINT statement begins a new line of output unless the PRINT statement ends with either a _____ or a _____.

9. If _____ are used to separate variables in a PRINT statement, the output will be lined up in columns.

10. The _____ statement moves the data pointer to the first item in the first DATA statement.

11. Two numbers labeled X and Y are entered into the computer. The first is subtracted from the second and the result, called Z, is printed. Identify each of the three major parts of this program.
   Initialize _____
   Process _____
   Output _____

12. Write the program for Problem 11 above.

13. Three numbers called A, B, and C are entered, added together and the result, S is printed. Identify each of the three major parts of this program.
   Initialize _____
   Process _____
   Output _____

14. Write the program for Problem 13 above.

15. An object falls towards the earth at a rate given by this formula: F = 16*T*T

(T stands for the number of seconds the object has fallen and F stands for the number of feet it has fallen.) The value of T is entered and the number of feet fallen is displayed. Identify the three major parts of this program.

Initialize _____

Process _____

Output _____

16. Write the program for Problem 15. Prompt the input with the statement:

HOW MANY SECONDS

Label the output with the statement:

THE OBJECT HAS FALLEN _____ FEET.

17. Jackercrack Popcorn costs 38 cents an ounce. Write a program which will allow someone to enter a number, N, to stand for the number of ounces. Have the computer find and display the cost of the popcorn. Be sure to prompt the input and label the output.

18. Write a program which will accept, through INPUT statements, a person's name, address, city, state, ZIP code, and phone number. Each of the entries should be prompted. Have the information printed out in the following form. (If you are quite clever, have the comma placed between the city and state.)

LEVERING P. HAMMOND

5280 ONE MILE LANE

PATRIOT HEIGHTS, NJ 01776

314-1592

19. The program below will accept three numbers and print the largest number. Provide documentation for the program by completing the REM statements.

```
5   Clearscreen
10  REM THIS PROGRAM WILL _____ (complete
    this)
20  PRINT "PLEASE ENTER 3 NUMBERS"
30  PRINT "1ST NO. ";
40  INPUT A
50  PRINT "2ND NO. ";
60  INPUT B
70  PRINT "3RD NO. ";
80  INPUT C
90  REM _____
100  L = A
110  REM _____
120  IF B > L THEN L = B
130  IF C > L THEN L = C
140  REM _____
150  PRINT "THE LARGEST NUMBER IS"; L
```

20. The program below will accept two numbers and will add the numbers, subtract the numbers, multiply the numbers, and divide the numbers. Provide documentation, input prompts, and labels for the output.

```
5   Clearscreen
10   PRINT "PLEASE ENTER TWO NUMBERS."
20   PRINT "_____"; (Place input prompt here)
30   INPUT A
40   PRINT "_____"; (Place input prompt here)
45   INPUT B
50   REM _____
60   S = A + B
70   REM _____
80   D = A - B
90   REM _____
100  P = A * B
110  REM _____
120  Q = A/B
130  REM _____
140  PRINT "_____"; S (Place output label here)
150  PRINT "_____"; D (Place output label here)
160  PRINT "_____"; P (Place output label here)
170  PRINT "_____"; Q (Place output label here)
```

21. Lee and Leslie opened six bags of cashew nuts and counted the nuts in each bag. The results are shown in the **DATA** statement below. Use the **DATA** statement in a program to print out the results in a table. Be sure to have headings for each column.

```
280  DATA 1ST BAG,22,2ND BAG,19,3RD
BAG,24,4TH BAG,18,5TH BAG,26,
6TH BAG,21
```

22. Use the **DATA** statement in Problem 21 and have the results printed in the form of a bar graph.

23. The students in Mr. Pierce's class could tell when it was a sunny or gloomy day by whether Mr. Pierce told many jokes or not. He tells many jokes on a bright sunny day. One week they counted his jokes. The results are in the **DATA** statement below. Write a program to have the results printed in a bar graph. Can you tell anything about the weather for that week?

```
300  DATA MON,16,TUE,5,WED,18,THU,19,
FRI,3
```

24. The members of the Fernsdorff Achievers Club are selling pattimint peppers to raise money. The **DATA** statement below lists the club members and the number of pattimint peppers sold by each. Write a program to have the data printed in a bar graph.

```
310  DATA MARY,38,JOAN,45,ANDY,39,
BILL,54,DALE,18,LISA,41,SLIM,14,
IGGY,22
```

You will probably need a scaling factor to have this bar graph properly printed.

Chip's Challenges

25. The DATA statement below contains the first and last names of some famous characters:
250 DATA DONALD, DUCK, CHARLIE, BROWN, ROAD, RUNNER
Write a program to enter each of the six names and print each first name with the incorrect last names. For example, some of the mismatched names would be:
DONALD BROWN
DONALD RUNNER
   etc. . .
Be sure to provide documentation by using REM statements.

26. Write a program that will accept any number (less than 100) and then print out every pair of whole numbers whose sum is the number entered. Be sure to prompt all input, label all output, and document the program with REM statements. The output should appear like this:
1 AND 49 = 50
2 AND 48 = 50
3 AND 47 = 50
   and so on . . .

Towns	Rivers
FIDDLIN	ROOF
PLAYIN	ROCKS
TUBUCKS	NOZE
STEPPIN	TABLE
KETTLE	STOVE

27. Some towns and rivers seem to go together, like Straford-on-the-Avon. In the first list on the left are five imaginary towns. There are five imaginary rivers in the second list. Use Mitzi's slogan program as a guide to write a program that will put these towns and rivers together, with the expression -ON-THE- between each pair.

28. An aphorism (AF-ur-iz'm) is a saying, such as:
MONEY IS THE ROOT OF EVIL.
You can replace the word MONEY with any word from the first list below. The word ROOT can be replaced by any word from the second list and the word EVIL by words from the third list. Use Mitzi's slogan program as a guide and the lists of words as DATA to write an aphorism program. The phrase IS THE should come between the first two words of each saying and the word OF should come between the last two words of each saying.

MONEY words	ROOT words	EVIL words
JOY	SOURCE	LIFE
SLEEP	PIGPEN	SONG
NOISE	CAUSE	THOUGHT
REMORSE	SNAKEPIT	FEELING
FEAR	SEASONING	KNOWLEDGE

Sights and Sounds

The Experimental Music Center at the Massachusetts Institute of Technology.

Computers are calculating machines, capable of almost incredible speed and accuracy. They are record keepers, able to hold and locate, at a moment's notice, vast quantities of data.

But computers are more than this. Partly because they can calculate and store data, they are important aids in making decisions. In some cases, they make decisions themselves, determining, for example, the right mixture of gasoline and air for an automobile engine at a specific moment. (Of course, such decisions are directed by programs.)

More often, however, computers provide data on which decisions can be based, and combine and present these data in different ways.

The data may be presented in the form of words and numbers. Often, however, it is easier to understand and work with a **graphic display** of the data than with words and numbers.

Computers make it possible to prepare accurate graphic displays of information quickly. Special software can prepare the graphics from user data. It can send the graphic display to a printer or plotter, or put it on the video screen.

One kind of special graphics printer is a **jet ink printer.** This device shoots tiny dots of colored ink at the paper. Jet ink printers can make the dots overlap to create different shades of colors.

A **digital plotter** is also used for graphics. (Digital means that the plotter is directed by number codes.) Some digital plotters have a robot arm that can select pens of different colors to draw graphs and charts. Plotters can also produce transparencies of graphics.

A computer's video graphics depend on the kind of **display chip** in the computer. Display chips determine the size of the smallest amount of screen area that the user can control A graphic display is made of tiny pieces, each of which fills one of these small screen areas. These tiny pieces of graphics are called **pixels.** If the screen is divided into many pixels (and the pixels are, therefore, very small), the result is **high resolution graphics.** There is great detail, and curved lines appear very smooth. (High resolution graphics can have more than 50 000 pixels to use!) Computers with **low resolution graphics,** using only two or three thousand pixels, show curves as sets of straight lines.

Some computers go even further with video graphics. They can provide animated graphics, which are moving pictures on the video screen.

Graphics instructions are input to the computer by special software and by data supplied by the user. Instructions can also be input by special hardware. For example, a joystick, similar to a computer game control, can be used to move the cursor and create graphics.

A **digitizing tablet** is another graphics input device. A stylus can be moved over the shape to be drawn. When the stylus is stopped, a button is used to send the computer the **coordinates** of the point the stylus is touching. (Coordinates tell how far over and how far down the point is on the drawing or diagram.)

Video digitizers can also be used to input information. These devices translate pictures into data that record shades and tones of colors in the form of numbers that the computer can understand.

Some graphics software can produce diagrams that look three-dimensional. The program can compute the angles to show an object in perspective and make it look more realistic. Still other software can produce stereo graphics. Like 3-D movies, these require special glasses for viewing them. The computer displays two views, one for each eye, alternately, creating a very real-looking object.

A special application of computer graphics is called CAD/CAM, for Computer-Aided Design/Computer-Aided Manufacture. Engineers give the computer information about their needs and the formulas for computing measurements. The computer produces the design. The engineer can change some data in order to see a different design. When the design meets all of the engineering requirements, the computer can produce the charts and diagrams needed to build the real thing. It can also direct the operations of the machinery that produces the product.

Computer graphics make it possible for you to see things that you have only been able to imagine. An old proverb says that one picture is worth a thousand words. Computer graphics has given people, as never before, the ability to create, and make use of, that one picture.

Some computers contain special chips called **synthesizers** that permit them to be programmed to make sounds or to produce music.

All sounds are simply vibrations of air. If the vibrations repeat regularly, the sound is said to be *pitched.*(If the vibrations are irregular, the sound is just noise.) Sound travels through air in waves, similar to waves in water. The height of a wave determines its loudness or *volume.* The distance between the peaks of two waves, the wavelength, determines the *pitch* of the sound, how high or how low it is.

Wave motion can be graphed and points on the graph digitized, or represented as numbers. Using special commands or special software, a computer can send binary codes to its synthesizer. The synthesizer then sends signals to an **amplifier** that magnifies, or strengthens, the signals. The strengthened signals travel to a loudspeaker that vibrates at different rates to make different sounds. The delays between the bits of the codes determine the pitch of the sound.

Symthesizers may be all digital, all analog, or combinations of both. When they are used in electronic instruments, analog circuits produce very smooth waveforms. The Commodore 64, which uses an analog filter in its synthesizer, can produce very musical sounds.

Computers are helping to record music, too. Digital disks are prepared by directing a computer to convert music to binary codes, or bits. (There can be as many as 15 billion bits of information in one hour of music!)

The codes are used to make **compact disks** that are played by lasers.

Computers can be musical instruments. In 1968, Walter Carlos produced a very popular recording called "Switched-On Bach." Carlos' instrument was a Moog Synthesizer.

Computers can even be programmed to compose music. The first such music, "Illiac Suite for String Quartet," is more than 25 years old.

Many computer scientists are working to produce realistic speech synthesis, so that computers can recognize and reproduce human speech. Speech is much more difficult to "teach" a computer than music. Think how many more human sounds there are than musical tones. Think of the many combinations of sounds a computer would have to "know" to recognize the vocabulary humans use. Now think of all the accents you can find in a single language. Limited computer speech reproduction and recognition is already possible. Scientists will need to use huge quantities of memory to make computers communicate as people do.

What Do You Know?
1. How does a jet ink printer create graphics?
2. What controls a digital plotter?
3. What is a pixel?
4. What is a coordinate?
5. What is a synthesizer?

What Can You Find Out?
1. How many pixels does your computer allow you to control?
2. Can your computer produce sounds?

What Do You Think?
1. Why are graphics important to businesses?
2. Are graphics programs difficult to write?

FOR USE AND REUSE

Subroutines

Subroutines are used to organize a program's sub-programs. They also provide for repeated use of sets of program statements.

13.1

Reusable Routines

DISCOVER FOR YOURSELF

Perry, who wrote the program below, called it "Perry's Billboard". Study the program steps below.

```
10   Clearscreen   17 blank spaces
20   A$ = "              ↓              "
30   B$ = "*******************"
40   C$ = "        P E R R Y        "
50   D$ = "        E W I N G        "
```

Enter the statements above. As you add each of the statements below, guess what output it would produce. Write your guess on a sheet of paper. Enter RUN after Statement 5 and check your answers.

STATEMENT	COMPUTER DISPLAYS

1. 60 PRINT "*"; A$; "*"   ?
2. 70 PRINT "*"; B$; "*"   ?
3. 80 PRINT "*"; C$; "*"   ?
4. 90 PRINT "*"; D$; "*"   ?
5. 100 PRINT "*"; B$; "*"   ?
RUN

WHAT DID YOU LEARN?

Do you think Perry's output looks very much like a billboard? He added the following lines to his program. Enter them and RUN the program.

```
110  FOR K = 1 TO 6
120  PRINT "*"; A$; "*"
130  NEXT K
```

Perry noticed that six of the lines in his program looked very much alike. Lines 60, 70, 80, 90, 100, and 120 were very similar, except for the string variable in each. He thought it would be very pleasant if he had to type only one **PRINT** statement that could be used six times in the program. He learned that by using a **subroutine** (pronounced SUB-roo-teen) he would realize his fondest dreams.

Memory Bank

Subroutine

A subroutine is a set of program steps that can be executed from any place in a program. After execution of the subroutine, program flow continues from the point at which the subroutine was called.

Mr. Pierce explained subroutines this way. Sometimes, when you are reading a book, you meet a word you do not know. How do you get help? You leave the book and turn to a dictionary. After using the dictionary, you return to your place in the book. (Of course, the wise reader will place a bookmark in the book to make the return easier.)

A subroutine is like the dictionary. The **main program**, or **drive program**, is like the book. The drive program *calls* on the subroutine for help. The computer *marks* the place in the program where the call was made. Then it returns to this place when it leaves the subroutine.

You may use a dictionary many times in reading a book. Similarly, a subroutine can be called many times during a program. In fact, a subroutine can even be called from another subroutine.

Chip's Bits

Many of the records you buy or listen to on the radio are digital recordings. Some live broadcasts are also digitized. Digitizing turns sound waves into sets of numbers that stand for the things that make the sound special such as pitch, loudness, and tone quality or timbre. The computer usually has to work with 40,000 numbers each second to make the music sound "live."

Usually, all subroutines are placed at the end of a program. The first statement in a subroutine should be a REM statement stating the purpose of the subroutine.

The statement that calls a subroutine from a drive program is the GOSUB statement. It has this form:

```
95  GOSUB 1000
```

Line ↑ Keyword.   Line number of the first
Number.   statement
                  in the subroutine.

When the computer encounters this statement, it does the following things:

1. It remembers the location of this statement in the program.

2. It jumps to the first statement of the subroutine.

3. It executes the statements of the subroutine until it encounters a RETURN statement.

4. When it meets a RETURN statement, it returns to the drive program statement which immediately follows the GOSUB statement.

The RETURN statement occurs in the subroutine and causes the computer to leave the subroutine and return to the drive program. It has this form:

```
1020  RETURN
```

Line ↑   Keyword.
Number.

Perry wrote this subroutine for his billboard program:

```
NEW
1000  REM SUBROUTINE TO PRINT A LINE
1010  PRINT "*"; Z$; "*"
1020  RETURN
```

He placed this statement just before the subroutine: 999 END

This was to keep the computer from entering the subroutine by mistake. He tested his subroutine by writing this drive program:

```
10  Clearscreen    17 blank spaces
20  A$ = "          ↓          "
30  B$ = "*******************"
40  C$ = "      P E R R Y      "
50  D$ = "      E W I N G      "
60  Z$ = A$
65  GOSUB 1000
```

Do you know what statement follows line 65? If you have been entering Perry's lines with him, type LIST. Your screen will display this:

```
10  Clearscreen    17 blank spaces
20  A$ = "          ↓          "
30  B$ = "*******************"
40  C$ = "      P E R R Y      "
50  D$ = "      E W I N G      "
60  Z$ = A$
65  GOSUB 1000 ←————————— Jump to line 1000.
999 END ←————————— Return here.
1000  REM SUBROUTINE TO PRINT A LINE
1010  PRINT "*"; Z$; "*"
1020  RETURN
```

Were you surprised to see line 999 following 65? Now enter RUN. Here is what you should see printed:

```
*            *      17 blank spaces
```

When the computer executed line 60, it placed the value of A$, (17 blank spaces), in Z$. Line 65 caused a jump to the subroutine beginning at line 1000. Line 1000, a REM statement, is ignored but line 1010 is executed and the output above is displayed. The RETURN statement in line 1020 causes a jump back to statement 999, which immediately follows line 65.

Chip's Bits

Doctors are experimenting with computer-based devices to help paralyzed people use their hands—and even walk. The computer sends signals to muscles to make them move. The doctors are hoping to build very tiny computers that can be implanted in paralyzed arms, hands, and legs.

USE WHAT YOU HAVE LEARNED

Add each set of statements below to Perry's new program. As you add the statements, guess what output they will produce. Write your guess on a sheet of paper. Enter RUN after Set 5 and check your answers.

STATEMENT

COMPUTER DISPLAYS

1. 70   Z$ = B$
75   GOSUB 1000
2. 80   Z$ = C$
85   GOSUB 1000
3. 90   Z$ = D$
95   GOSUB 1000
4. 100   Z$ = B$
105   GOSUB 1000
5. 110   Z$ = A$
115   FOR K = 1 TO 6
120   GOSUB 1000
130   NEXT K
RUN

E x e r c i s e s

1. Write the program statements that would *call* Perry's subroutine to have the following output displayed:

    * H E L P ! *

2. Write the program statements that would *call* Perry's subroutine several times and have the following lines of output displayed:

    * H E L P   S T A M P *
    *   O U T   *
    * B I L L B O A R D S *

3. Write a subroutine beginning at line 2000 that will **PRINT** two blank spaces followed by a string variable. Do not forget the **REM** statement or the **RETURN** statement.

4. Use your subroutine from Exercise 3 to draw a long arrow pointing down the screen. First, in a **FOR-NEXT** loop, use it to draw the symbol **!** (exclamation point) five times. Next use it to draw the letter **V**.

Chip's Challenges

5. Using a subroutine similar to Perry's Billboard subroutine, write a program to place your name in a box in the center of the screen.

APPLICATIONS

PLANNING AROUND SUBROUTINES

The use of subroutines makes the job of planning a program much easier. It lets you break a program into its parts and treat each part separately.

The steps below are recommended in planning any program that is more than a few lines long.

1. Outline the major parts of the program. Do not actually write the BASIC statements. Describe the subroutines, what they will do, and their beginning line numbers. This outline, with a few modifications, will become the drive program.

2. Write each subroutine separately. Each subroutine should complete just one task.
3. Subroutines should be placed after the drive program, in the order they are to be used.
4. All data should be placed in **DATA** statements after the last subroutine.
5. Place a **REM** statement at the beginning of each subroutine. Also, place a **REM** statement before each subroutine call in the drive program.

These steps will be illustrated by using Mitzi's Slogan program from the last chapter (p. 230).

I. Outline of Mitzi's Slogan Generator
    A. Get two numbers, F and S, to select words from the lists. This will be done in a subroutine beginning at line 1000.
    B. Pick the first word from the first list. This will be done in a subroutine which begins at line 2000. Store the first word as the variable F$.
    C. Pick the second word from the list. This can use the same subroutine as above. Store the second word as S$.
    D. Print the two words in the message. This can be done in a subroutine which begins at line 3000.
    E. Place the **DATA** statements in lines 4000 and up.

II. The writing of the subroutines
    A. This subroutine will be like the input routine in Mitzi's program. It will begin at line 1000 with a **REM** statement.

Chip's Bits

In 1934, the German government began to use a code machine called Enigma. This machine was invented by Hugo Koch, a Dutchman. In England, Alan M. Turing built a machine that could simulate Enigma. This machine, called The Bomb, was used to decode German messages in World War II.

```
1000    REM ENTER TWO NUMBERS
1010    PRINT "ENTER TWO NUMBERS BETWEEN 1 AND 5"
1020    PRINT "WHAT IS THE FIRST NUMBER";
1030    INPUT F
1040    PRINT "WHAT IS THE SECOND NUMBER";
1050    INPUT S
1060    RETURN
```

This subroutine can be tested by entering GOSUB 1000. The computer will wait for the entry of two numbers. After the numbers have been entered, type PRINT F, S. Enter to see the numbers.

B. The second subroutine will begin at line 2000 with the REM statement:

```
2000    REM PICK A WORD FROM THE LIST
2010    RESTORE
2020    FOR I = 1 TO N
2030    READ A$
2040    NEXT I
2050    RETURN
```

This cannot be tested until the DATA statements are written. Write these statements next.

```
4000    DATA SAVE, etc. . . .
4010    DATA EARTHWORMS, etc. . . .
```

Now the subroutine can be tested by entering:

```
N = 2  ◄————————— Use any number
GOSUB 2000        from 1 to 10.
PRINT A$
```

C. This subroutine will begin at line 3000 with the REM statement:

```
3000    REM PRINT A SLOGAN
3010    PRINT "HELP "; F$; " OUR NATION'S "; S$
3020    RETURN
```

III. The drive program. This consists mostly of subroutine calls and follows the outline from **I.A.** above.

```
10    REM SLOGAN GENERATOR
20    Clearscreen
30    REM GET TWO NUMBERS
40    GOSUB 1000
50    REM GET FIRST WORD
60    N = F
70    GOSUB 2000
80    F$ = A$
90    REM GET SECOND WORD
100   N = 5 + S
```

```
110   GOSUB 2000
120   S$ = A$
130   REM PRINT SLOGAN
140   GOSUB 3000        This keeps you from entering
999   END               the subroutines by mistake.
```

> The final program is certainly longer than the original program. You do not always make your programs shorter by using subroutines. You do, however, make them easier to plan, read, and understand. This becomes <u>very important</u> when you have to look for errors and make corrections.

E x e r c i s e s

1. Suppose that Mitzi wished to have ten words in each list. The **DATA** statements, of course, would have to be changed to contain the extra words. Only two other lines in the entire program would need changing, lines 100 and 1010. Make the necessary changes.

2. The subroutine below is a timing loop, in which the variable N determines the time interval. A large value of N causes a long interval and a small value causes a shorter interval. Write program statements to set the value of N to 500 and call the subroutine. Be sure to place an **END** statement after the **GOSUB** statement.

```
5000   REM TIMING LOOP SUBROUTINE
5010   FOR T = 1 TO N
5020   NEXT T
5030   RETURN
```

3. Write a drive program to have your name flash on and off the screen. Use the timing loop subroutine from Exercise 2 twice; once to hold your name on the screen and again to keep the screen cleared. Use the steps below to plan the program:
   1. Clear the screen.
   2. Set the value of N and call the Timing Subroutine.
   3. Print your name.
   4. Set the value of N and call the Timing Subroutine.
   5. Repeat each of the steps above.

Chip's Challenges

4. Rewrite the program in Exercise 4 (p. 233), using subroutines to plan and organize it. Use Mitzi's program to develop an outline, write the subroutines, and write the drive program.

13.2

Errors to Avoid

Using subroutines gives you new chances to make errors. In this section you will see some of the common errors and ways to avoid them.

Some of the exercises below may cause an error message to appear on your screen. (All the errors will be explained later.)

DISCOVER FOR YOURSELF

Enter the following program statements exactly as they appear. After each set of statements has been entered, guess what output will be produced. Write your answers on a sheet of paper. Enter RUN and check your answers.

COMPUTER DISPLAYS

STATEMENT

1.
```
100   REM PRINT LINE 1
110   PRINT "THIS IS LINE 1"
150   RETURN
RUN
```

2.
```
10   Clearscreen
20   GOSUB 100
RUN
```

3.
```
NEW
10   GOSUB 60
20   GOSUB 80
30   END
60   REM SUBROUTINE #1
70   PRINT "THIS IS LINE 1"
80   REM SUBROUTINE #2
90   PRINT "THIS IS LINE 2"
100   RETURN
RUN
```

```
4. NEW
   10  GOSUB 100
   20  END
   100  REM A POOR SUBROUTINE
   110  GOSUB 100
   120  RETURN
   RUN
```

WHAT DID YOU LEARN?

Ada Lovelace is called the first programmer because she thought of many of the ideas used in programs today. She wrote about reusable instructions such as subroutines, loops, and branches based on decisions.

Memory Bank

Blocking Subroutine Entry

*Always block the entry to a subroutine by placing an **END** statement just before the first line of the subroutine. This will prevent entering the subroutine by mistake.*

In Set 1, did you get an error message like this?

RETURN WITHOUT GOSUB ERROR IN 150

Here is what happened. When the computer executes a **GOSUB** statement, it *marks* its place by storing the line number of the **GOSUB** statement in a list. On meeting a **RETURN** statement, it takes this number off the list and returns to the line indicated. If there is no number on the list, as happened in this set, it cannot **RETURN** and an error message is displayed.

Memory Bank

Entering subroutines

*You must enter a subroutine by using a **GOSUB** statement. Otherwise, the subroutine's **RETURN** statement will give you an error message.*

The same error occurred in Set 2. In this program the computer entered the subroutine twice; once by executing the **GOSUB 100** statement in line 20 and again, after the **RETURN**, by executing the statements following line 20. The second time it reached line 150, there was no line number in the **RETURN** list. This error can be avoided by writing this statement:

99 END

In Set 3, you probably did not get an error message. If you look at the output, you see that it is probably not what the programmer intended. The following line is printed twice:

THIS IS LINE #2

It appears that the programmer forgot to place a **RETURN** statement at the end of the first subroutine. This kind of error is especially annoying because the computer does not recognize it as an error. This can be corrected by writing the following statement:

75 RETURN

Were you surprised by the outcome of Set 4? It appeared that your computer was doing nothing at all. If you were patient and permitted the computer to run for a while perhaps you got this strange message:

OUT OF MEMORY

Line 110 is a line of the subroutine that calls itself! While this is permitted, it produces an unexpected result. Each time the subroutine is called, the computer stores the return line number in its **RETURN** list. After very, very many of these subroutine calls, the list takes up the entire memory of the computer! In general, it is poor programming to have a subroutine call itself. It should be avoided.

USE WHAT YOU HAVE LEARNED

Each of the following programs has an error in a subroutine or a subroutine call. Find and correct the errors. If you enter these programs, type them exactly as they appear, even if they seem incorrect.

1.
```
10   FOR I = 1 TO 5
20   GOSUB 125
30   NEXT I
125  PRINT "THIS IS LINE #"; I
130  RETURN
```
(Hint: see Set 2 in *Discover for Yourself.*)

2.
```
10   GOSUB 200
20   GOSUB 100
30   END
100  PRINT "ENTER THE SECOND NUMBER";
110  INPUT X
200  PRINT "ENTER THE FIRST NUMBER";
210  INPUT X
220  RETURN
```
(Hint: see Set 3 in *Discover for Yourself.*)

E x e r c i s e s

Find and correct the error in each program.

1.
```
10   PRINT "NOW YOU SEE IT – "
20   GOSUB 100
30   Clearscreen
40   PRINT "NOW YOU DON'T!"
50   GOSUB 100
```

```
100  FOR K = 1 TO 200
110  NEXT K
120  RETURN
```
2.
```
10   PRINT "ENTER A NUMBER FROM 1 TO 10";
20   INPUT X
30   GOTO 100
40   END
100  FOR K = 1 TO X
120  PRINT K
130  NEXT K
140  END
```

Chip's Challenges

3. Find and correct the error in the following program.
```
10   B$=" FIRST "
20   FOR J = 1 TO 10
30   GOSUB 200
40   NEXT J
50   END
100  PRINT B$
110  B$ = " NEXT "
200  PRINT "NUMBER "; J; "IS";
220  GOSUB 100
230  RETURN
```

CHAPTER SUMMARY

1. A subroutine is a set of program statements that performs a special task. It can be used many times in a program.

2. Subroutines can be used to help organize and plan a program. A program's processing can be completely done in subroutines. The part of the program which calls on these subroutines is the drive program or main program.

3. The statement which calls a subroutine is GOSUB and it has this form:

   45   GOSUB 2000

   Line number.   Keyword.   Number of the first line in the subroutine.

4. The computer stores the line number of the GOSUB statement that calls a subroutine and returns to this statement. On RETURN, it executes the statement immediately following the GOSUB statement.

5. The computer executes the statements of a sub-routine until it meets a **RETURN** statement. It takes from the **RETURN** list the last number it placed there and returns to that line of the program.

6. The **RETURN** statement has this form:

2050 RETURN

Line number.   Keyword.

7. The first statement of a subroutine should be a **REM** statement which describes the subroutine.

8. All subroutines should be placed at the end of the drive program.

9. An **END** statement must come between the end of the drive program and the first subroutine. This blocks the computer from entering the sub-routine by mistake.

PROBLEM SET 13

In Problems 1 to 5, find and correct the errors in the statements:

1. 35 GOSUD 2100

2. 40 RETURN 50

3. RETURN

4. 200 GOSUB 200

5. 60 RETRUN

In Problems 6 to 10, use the program statements below:

```
499  END
500  REM READ SUBROUTINE
510  RESTORE
520  FOR L = 1 TO N
530  READ D$
540  NEXT L
550  RETURN
560  DATA CAT,DOG,BEAR,SHEEP,APE,MONKEY
```

6. What would be printed as a result of the following?
```
10  N = 3
20  GOSUB 500
30  PRINT D$
```

7. What would be printed as a result of RUNning the following?
```
10  N = 6
20  GOSUB 500
30  PRINT D$
```

8. Write the program steps which call the **READ SUBROU-TINE** above and cause the word **APE** to be printed.

9. Write the program steps which call the **READ SUBROU-TINE** above to print the word **SHEEP**.

10. What would be printed as a result of RUNning the following program?

```
10   N = 1
20   GOSUB 500
30   C$ = D$
40   N = 6
50   GOSUB 500
60   PRINT "MY "; C$; " IS A "; D$
```

Use the following program steps in completing Problems 11 to 15.

```
499   END
500   REM NUMBER READER
510   RESTORE
520   FOR K = 1 TO X
530   READ W
540   NEXT K
550   RETURN
560   DATA 5,7,9,2,3,6,1
```

11. What would be printed as a result of RUNning the following program?
```
10   X = 2
20   GOSUB 500
30   PRINT W
```

12. Write the program steps which call the **NUMBER READ-ER** subroutine above and cause the number 6 to be printed.

13. Write the program steps which call the **NUMBER READ-ER** subroutine and print the number 9.

What would be printed as a result of RUNning the following programs?

14.
```
10   X = 1
20   GOSUB 500
30   Y = W
50   X = 5
60   PRINT X+Y
```

15.
```
10   S = 0
20   FOR X = 1 TO 6
30   GOSUB 500
40   S = S + W
50   NEXT X
60   PRINT S
```

16. Write a subroutine that will print the following statement. Write the program steps to call the subroutine.
    HELP ! I AM TRAPPED INSIDE THIS COMPUTER !

17. Write a subroutine that will find the sum of three numbers, A, B, and C. Write a program to call this subroutine and print the sum.

18. Write a subroutine that will accept a number, N, from the drive program and cause N blank lines to be printed on the screen. Write a program calling the subroutine. Have 4 blank lines separate these two lines of text:

Important: TRS-80 users;
Begin your program with this
statement;

`1  CLEAR 500`

```
THIS IS LINE 1
THIS IS LINE 2
```

19. Use the subroutine in Problem 18 in a program that prints your name, address, and phone number on three separate lines. Your name should be on the top line, your phone number on the bottom line, and your address in the middle of the screen.

20. Write a program that will read three numbers, find their sum, and print the result. Have the reading, processing, and printing done in separate subroutines. Write a drive program that calls the subroutines. Use the following statement for `DATA`.

`4000  DATA 1620, 1492, 1776`

21. Write a program that will `INPUT` four numbers and find their average. Have the input, processing, and output done in separate subroutines. Write a drive program to call the subroutines.

22. Write a program that reads the four words below and prints them in reverse order. Have the reading and printing done in subroutines.

`COW, BROWN, NOW, HOW`

23. Write a program for Problem 15 in Problem Set 11 (p. 235), using subroutines to do the initialization, processing, and output.

24. Write a program for Problem 17 in Problem Set 11 (p. 235), using subroutines to do the input and output.

25. Write a program for Problem 18 in Problem Set 11 (p. 235), using subroutines for the input and output.

Chip's Challenges

26. Rewrite Alice's RAISE THE FLAG program (p. 215) so that each of the three parts is done in a subroutine.

27. Rewrite the BAR GRAPH program (p. 222) so that each of these parts is done in a subroutine.
a. The printing of the headings.
b. The reading of the data.
c. The printing of each bar.
Write a drive program which calls each of these subroutines.

28. Rewrite the program for Problem 27 in Problem Set 11 (p. 237) using subroutines for these parts:
a. The `INPUT` of the two numbers.
b. The selection of the words from the lists.
c. The printing of the final phrase.

29. Rewrite the program for Problem 28 in Problem Set 11 (p. 237) using subroutines for these parts.
a. The `INPUT` of the two numbers.
b. The selection of the words from the lists.
c. The printing of the final phrase.

Astronauts Anna and William Fisher experiencing zero gravity as part of their NASA training.

Role Playing and Reality

As you have seen, computers can be very helpful in the process of making decisions. One of the ways in which they can do this is through simulation.

A simulation is an imitation or model of a real situation. By studying what happens in the simulation, you can learn what is likely to happen in the real situation.

A computer simulation is a model of a system of some kind, either a real system or one that exists only in someone's imagination. It is built from facts that are known—or are created—about that system. Sometimes ideas and theories that underly or that grow from the system are also included. Usually the computer model includes only a part of the system, the part that the programmer wants to study.

Computer simulations were first used by government agencies. Now their use is much more widespread, and they are used in business, industry, education, and other settings.

For a computer simulation, a data base, the set of facts and ideas that describe an environment, for example, is stored in the computer. Then, information changing some of the conditions of the environment can be input. The effects of the changes or **interventions** can be studied without disturbing the real system or environment.

Suppose you are considering building a dam in a particular place. A computer simulation can help you understand what the effects of the dam will be on the surrounding countryside. It can also show what will happen in times of excessive rainfall, in periods of drought, and under other conditions. You can change the design of your simulated dam by what you input to the computer and then immediately see how the changes affect the whole system.

Many decisions to build dams, to provide irrigation, to change waterways, or to locate roads are based on simulations of this kind.

Computer simulations can teach, also. Some of these simulate historical events. You can "make history" by your inputs to the program! Scientific experiments can also be simulated. Students can see the results of chemical reactions that would be too dangerous or too difficult to perform in the classroom—and the results of experimenter errors! Other programs simulate business decisions, to show how an economy operates, or allow a student to "rule" an imaginary land and thus learn about leadership and decision making.

Businesses use simulations in product testing. Computers can simulate the stresses and weight loads on bridges, for example, so engineers can design safe and lasting structures. Architects use computer simulations both to design buildings that will stand up to earthquakes and winds and to make sure the buildings will fit the owners' purposes.

NASA uses simulations to test space vehicles and condition their crews. Aeronautical engineers use them to test wing and body designs before a plane is built. Their uses are almost endless!

The success of a computer simulation depends on the amount and the kind of information selected for the data base by the programmer. The computer can only provide instant access to that data base. It can use these data only in the equations developed by the programmer. All of its work could be done by a human being, but not so fast or so accurately. In this instance, as in so many others involving complex decisions, the computer is not a decision maker. With its vast memory and its electronic speed, however, it is an important, and increasingly indispensable, aid in making informed, timely decisions.

What Do You Know?
1. What is a simulation?
2. What is a data base?
3. Who were the first users of computer simulations?
4. What can you learn from a simulation?

What Can You Find Out?
1. Does your school have any computer simulations you can use?
2. How does NASA simulate conditions in space?
3. Do any companies in your community use computer simulations?

What Do You Think?
1. Would computer simulations be a good way to learn math?
2. Is it easy to create a good data base?

COMPUTER DELIGHTS

BASIC Functions

Built-in computer functions help programmers do difficult jobs easily. TAB, RND, and INT help work with numbers. LEFT$, RIGHT$, and MID$ are used with strings.

Move it Over

Look at the programs below. Trace the steps and guess the computer's output. Write your result on a sheet of paper. Think of **TAB** as meaning "move in from the left side of the screen." It will help you to determine the output of Program 2. Check your answers by entering the programs and RUNning them.

<table>
<tr><td align="center">PROGRAM</td><td align="center">COMPUTER
DISPLAYS</td></tr>
</table>

1. ```
   NEW
   10  A$ = "JACK"
   20  FOR I = 1 TO 5
   30  PRINT A$
   40  NEXT I
   50  END
   ```

2. ```
   NEW
   10  A$ = "JACK"
   20  FOR I = 1 TO 5
   30  PRINT TAB(I); A$
   40  NEXT I
   50  END
   ```

The programs are almost identical. A simple inspection reveals that **TAB(I)** in line 30 of Program 2,

```
30  PRINT TAB(I); A$
```

must be responsible for the difference in the outputs.

Program 1

```
RUN
 JACK ⎫
 JACK ⎪
 JACK ⎬  output
 JACK ⎪
 JACK ⎭
```

Program 2

```
RUN
  JACK
   JACK
    JACK ⎫ output
     JACK
      JACK
```

The **TAB** function is an instruction to the computer that produces an effect similar to that of the tab key on a typewriter. It instructs the computer to <u>indent</u>, counting from the first print position on the left. When the computer encounters a **TAB** function, for example, **TAB(5)**, in a **PRINT** statement, it begins printing in the 6th (5 + 1) print position, counting from the first print position on that line.

> The number of spaces indented varies from system to system, so check your computer system to determine the number of spaces indented.

For example, in Program 2, the first time through the loop,

with I = 1, **TAB(1)** in line 30 directed the computer to print **JACK**, starting in the 1 + 1 = 2 print position.

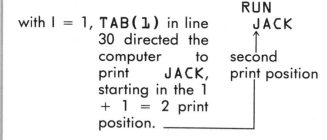

```
          RUN
           JACK
            ↑
         second
         print position
```

The second time through the loop,

I = 2. **TAB(2)** in line 30 caused the computer to print **JACK** starting in the 2 + 1 = 3 print position.

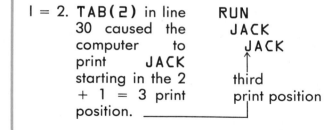

```
          RUN
           JACK
            JACK
             ↑
          third
          print position
```

CHIP SAYS:
CHECK THIS OUT.

This process continued until all values of I were assigned and JACK was printed as shown below.

Loop Sequence	Print Statement	Print Position
		RUN
I = 1	30 PRINT TAB(1); A$	2 ——→JACK
I = 2	30 PRINT TAB(2); A$	3 ——→JACK
I = 3	30 PRINT TAB(3); A$	4 ——→JACK
I = 4	30 PRINT TAB(4); A$	5 ——→JACK
I = 5	30 PRINT TAB(5); A$	6 ——→JACK

output

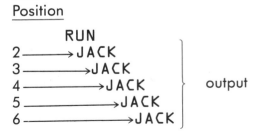

Memory Bank

TAB function

The **TAB** function is written:

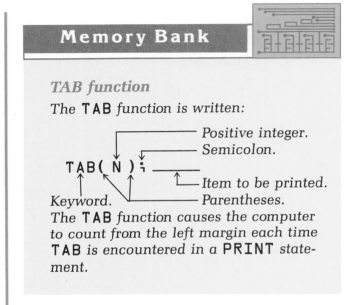

TAB(N); — Positive integer. — Semicolon. — Item to be printed.
Keyword. — Parentheses.

The **TAB** function causes the computer to count from the left margin each time **TAB** is encountered in a **PRINT** statement.

USE WHAT YOU HAVE LEARNED

Ms. Lisa Compton, Vice-President in charge of motor sales at the Monfaber Motor Company, needed to develop a graph that would show the number of cars sold each month, as listed.

Monfaber Motor Sales	
Month	*Number*
January	8
February	10
March	22
April	23
May	21
June	22
July	20
August	15
September	18
October	11
November	8
December	7

Because she knew that a bar graph is an excellent way to display information, Ms. Compton decided to prepare one. Her company's sales can be read clearly from a bar graph. Using an asterisk, * , to represent a car sale, she identified a month with 20 or more car sales as GOOD and one with less than 20 as FAIR. Ms. Compton wanted to display the monthly sales in the form,

JANUARY ******** FAIR

By first thinking of the three major parts of a computer program,

INITIALIZE   PROCESS   OUTPUT

Ms. Compton wrote the program listed below.

Lisa Compton's Program

```
10  Clearscreen
11  REM MONFABER MONTHLY CAR SALES
12  REM OUTER LOOP READS MONTH AND SALES
13  FOR I = 1 TO 12
15  READ A$, N
16  PRINT
20  PRINT A$; " ";                                        ──two blank spaces
23  REM INNER LOOP PRINTS ASTERISK FOR EACH CAR SOLD
25  FOR J = 1 TO N
30  PRINT "*";
35  NEXT J
40  IF N> = 20 THEN PRINT " GOOD";
45  IF N < 20 THEN PRINT " FAIR";                         two blank spaces
50  NEXT I
55  DATA JANUARY,8,FEBRUARY,10,MARCH,22,APRIL,23,MAY,21
56  DATA JUNE,22,JULY,20,AUGUST,15,SEPTEMBER,18
57  DATA OCTOBER,11,NOVEMBER,8,DECEMBER,7
60  END
```

Study Ms. Compton's program. Can you identify the steps in her program which are INITIALIZE, PROCESS, and OUTPUT? Enter the program and RUN it. What did you observe? It does not quite look as it should, does it? Except for the months, the information is not properly indented. Sales trends are not easily recognized from this display. What do you think can be done in order to improve Ms. Compton's bar graph? That is correct! Use TAB functions to print the asterisks and the words starting at the same print position in each line. The month with the most letters in its name is SEPTEMBER with 9. If two print positions are left blank after SEPTEMBER, all asterisks can be printed starting at the 12th print position using TAB(11); in line 30. The greatest number of cars, 23, was sold in APRIL. If two print positions are left blank after printing the 23 asterisks, the words, GOOD or FAIR, can be printed starting at the 37th print position using TAB(36); in lines 40 and 45.

12th print position   37th print position

```
APRIL        ***********************  GOOD
          .                 .
          .:                .
          .                 .
SEPTEMBER    ******************        FAIR
```

12th print position   37th print position

```
30  PRINT TAB(11); "*";
40  IF N > = 20 THEN PRINT TAB(36); "GOOD";
45  IF N < 20 THEN PRINT TAB(36); "FAIR";
```

CHIP SAYS:
IN MS. COMPTON'S PROGRAM, RETYPE THESE LINES AND RUN IT.

The outputs of Ms. Compton's program are shown below.

```
JANUARY   ********  FAIR
FEBRUARY  **********  FAIR
MARCH     ***********************  GOOD
APRIL     ************************  GOOD
MAY       *********************  GOOD
JUNE      **********************  GOOD
JULY      ********************  GOOD
AUGUST    ****************  FAIR
SEPTEMBER ******************  FAIR
OCTOBER   ***********  FAIR
NOVEMBER  ********  FAIR
DECEMBER  *******  FAIR
```

Without the use of the **TAB** function

```
JANUARY   ********                      FAIR
FEBRUARY  **********                    FAIR
MARCH     ***********************       GOOD
APRIL     ************************      GOOD
MAY       *********************         GOOD
JUNE      **********************        GOOD
JULY      ********************          GOOD
AUGUST    ****************              FAIR
SEPTEMBER ******************            FAIR
OCTOBER   ***********                   FAIR
NOVEMBER  ********                      FAIR
DECEMBER  *******                       FAIR
```

With the use of the **TAB** function

As you can see, the second one displays the output in a more effective manner. What time of the year does the Monfaber Motor Company sell the most cars?

Exercises

1. Determine if the following **TAB** functions are correct. If the function is not correct, write it correctly.

   a. `10   PRINT TB(11); A`
   b. `10   PRINT TAB(16.5); "BUBBLES"`
   c. `10   PRINT TAB(20); "X = "; TAB(25); "ANDROIDS"`
   d. `10   PRINT TAB 19 ; "MONTHLY PAYMENTS"`

2. Use a **TAB** function with a **PRINT** statement to label Ms. Compton's second output displayed on page 264, using the column headings:

   MONTH   CAR SALES   RATING

3. Insert the **PRINT** statement of Problem 2 in Ms. Lisa Compton's program. Enter the program and **RUN** it.

Chip's Challenges

Game	Team	Opponent
1	43	37
2	39	22
3	54	41
4	35	38
5	47	45
6	41	28
7	36	40
8	41	39
9	56	48

4. Maria Feriolla is the manager of the basketball team. Maria wants to write a computer program that will display the team scores in an easily read form.

Write a program for Maria that will display all the information shown at the left in table form. Enter the program and **RUN** it.

5. Write a program with **TAB** functions to produce the output as shown on the screen below. Enter your program and **RUN** it.

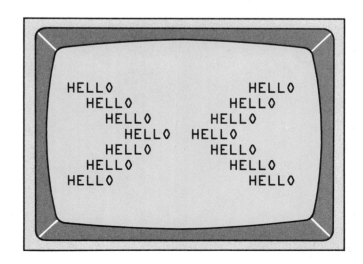

14.2

Chop and Round

DISCOVER FOR YOURSELF

Look at the programs below. Trace the steps and guess the computer's output. Write your result on a sheet of paper. Check your answers by entering the programs on your computer and RUNning them.

PROGRAM

COMPUTER DISPLAYS

1. NEW
```
10   FOR J = 1 TO 5
20   READ X
30   PRINT "X = "; X
35   NEXT J
40   DATA 1.7, 2.36, 3.51, 4 , 5.9
50   END
```

2. NEW
```
10   FOR J = 1 TO 5
20   READ X
30   PRINT "X = "; INT(X)
35   NEXT J
40   DATA 1.7, 2.36, 3.51, 4 , 5.9
50   END
```

WHAT DID YOU LEARN?

In Program 1, the computer read each number listed in the **DATA** statement and then printed the number read.

```
X = 1.7
X = 2.36
X = 3.51
X = 4
X = 5.9
```

In Program 2, the computer read each number listed in the **DATA** statement and then printed only an **integer**, a number with no decimal point or numbers following the point.

```
X = 1
X = 2
X = 3
X = 4
X = 5
```

What do you think was the reason for the computer printing only an integer in Program 2? That is correct, `INT(X)` in line 30.

The `INT` function performs a very special and simple operation. It converts the number called the **argument** into the largest integer that is less than or equal to the number. The output for Program 2 is shown in the table below. The computer read the numbers listed in the `DATA` statement, the `INT` function converted each number into an integer, and that integer was printed.

Data	Conversion	Output
1.7	INT(1.7) = 1	X = 1
2.36	INT(2.36) = 2	X = 2
3.51	INT(3.51) = 3	X = 3
4	INT(4) = 4	X = 4
5.9	INT(5.9) = 5	X = 5

Memory Bank

INT function

The `INT` *function is written:*

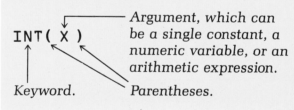

`INT( X )`

Argument, which can be a single constant, a numeric variable, or an arithmetic expression.

Keyword.   Parentheses.

The `INT` function can be used either by itself or as a part of any BASIC arithmetic expression. Shown below are some examples of BASIC statements containing `INT` functions.

Example 1 The statement

```
20  PRINT INT(X + Y)
```

will cause the quantity X + Y to be calculated and converted to an integer. This integer is then printed.

Example 2 The statement

```
30  A = B * INT(C/D)
```

will cause the quotient C/D to be converted to an integer which will be multiplied by B, and the result assigned to A.

Example 3 The statement

`30  IF INT(X/Y) * Y = X THEN PRINT X`

will cause the quotient X/Y to be converted to an integer that will be multiplied by Y and if the product equals X, then X will be printed.

USE WHAT YOU HAVE LEARNED

Recall the lemonade program prepared by Lee and Anton in Chapter 12.

```
20   L = 8
30   W = 6
40   S = 1
45   PRINT "THIS IS A RECIPE FOR LEMONADE"
50   PRINT "HOW MANY PEOPLE TO BE SERVED?"
55   INPUT N
60   A = N * L/12
70   B = N * W/12
80   C = N * S/12
85   PRINT "FOR "; N; " PEOPLE YOU NEED"
90   PRINT A; " LEMONS"
100   PRINT B; " CUPS OF WATER"
110   PRINT C; " CUPS OF SUGAR"
120   END
```

Enter this program and **RUN** it to determine the recipes for lemonade that will serve 61 and 71 people. As you observe from your screen, the recipes are not expressed as whole numbers. It is difficult to measure such quantities accurately. A more practical lemonade program would guarantee that recipe quantities would be expressed as whole numbers. Can you think of a way to do this? That is correct! Use the **INT** function to change the numbers A, B, and C in the lemonade program to integers. But wait! Is this what you really want to do?

Look at the screen to the left. Shown are the recipes for lemonade that will serve 61 and 71 people. The **INT** function used in the lines of the program

```
90   PRINT INT(A); " LEMONS"
100   PRINT INT(B); " CUPS OF WATER"
110   PRINT INT(C); " CUPS OF SUGAR"
```

would cause the computer to print the recipes as integers. Try this on your computer and compare the outputs as shown on next page.

```
THIS IS A RECIPE FOR LEMONADE
HOW MANY PEOPLE TO BE SERVED?
?61
FOR 61 PEOPLE YOU NEED
40.6667 LEMONS
30.5 CUPS OF WATER
5.08333 CUPS OF SUGAR
READY
RUN
THIS IS A RECIPE FOR LEMONADE
HOW MANY PEOPLE TO BE SERVED?
?71
FOR 71 PEOPLE YOU NEED
47.333 LEMONS
35.5 CUPS OF WATER
5.91667 CUPS OF SUGAR
```

Output without INT

FOR 61 PEOPLE YOU NEED
40.6667 LEMONS ─────────→
30.5 CUPS OF WATER
5.08333 CUPS OF SUGAR

FOR 71 PEOPLE YOU NEED
47.333 LEMONS
35.5 CUPS OF WATER
5.91667 CUPS OF SUGAR ──→

Output with INT

FOR 61 PEOPLE YOU NEED
40 LEMONS
30 CUPS OF WATER
5 CUPS OF SUGAR

FOR 71 PEOPLE YOU NEED
47 LEMONS
35 CUPS OF WATER
5 CUPS OF SUGAR

In the recipe for 61 people, should 40.6667 LEMONS be converted to 40 LEMONS? In the recipe for 71 people, should 5.91667 CUPS OF SUGAR be converted to 5 CUPS OF SUGAR? Certainly not! The quantities need to be rounded to the nearest whole number. Can you think of a way to do this?

The following examples demonstrate how the INT function can be used to round to the nearest whole number.

Examples

		Observation
1.	INT(4.1 + .5) = INT(4.6) = 4	4.1 is rounded to 4
2.	INT(7.3 + .5) = INT(7.8) = 7	7.3 is rounded to 7
3.	INT(8.5 + .5) = INT(9.0) = 9	8.5 is rounded to 9
4.	INT(3.7 + .5) = INT(4.2) = 4	3.7 is rounded to 4
5.	INT(5.9 + .5) = INT(6.4) = 6	5.9 is rounded to 6

The INT function can be used to round a number, X, to the nearest whole number using the form,
    INT(X + .5)

Use the INT(X + .5) function to round the quantities of the lemonade recipe. Enter the program and RUN it. Compare your output to that shown on the screen to the left. It was produced using the INT(X + .5) function in the lines,

```
90  PRINT INT(A + .5); " LEMONS"
100  PRINT INT(B + .5);
" CUPS OF WATER"
110  PRINT INT(C + .5);
" CUPS OF SUGAR"
```

Check your output to verify that the numbers in the recipe have been rounded to the nearest whole number.

```
THIS IS A RECIPE FOR LEMONADE
HOW MANY PEOPLE TO BE SERVED?
?61
FOR 61 PEOPLE YOU NEED
41 LEMONS
31 CUPS OF WATER
5 CUPS OF SUGAR
READY
RUN
THIS IS A RECIPE FOR LEMONADE
HOW MANY PEOPLE TO BE SERVED?
?71
FOR 71 PEOPLE YOU NEED
47 LEMONS
36 CUPS OF WATER
6 CUPS OF SUGAR
```

1. Determine if the following **INT** functions are correct. If not, write them correctly.
   a. `20  PRINT NIT(7.93)`
   b. `20  PRINT INT 17.2`
   c. `20  A = INT(19.3 * 14.1)`
   d. `20  INT(25.4) = C`

2. Determine the value of X in each of the following statements.
   a. `20  X = INT(9.9)`
   b. `20  X = C * INT(A)` where A = 4.9 and C = 11.3
   c. `20  X = INT(F/D) + INT(F * D)` where D = 8 and F = 52.
   d. `20  X = INT((A + B)/(A − B))` for A = 17.3 and B = 14.2

3. Trace the steps of this program to determine the computer's output. Write your answer on a sheet of paper. Check your answer by entering the program and **RUN**ning it.

```
NEW
10  FOR K = 1 TO 4
20  READ A, B
30  IF INT(A/B) = A/B THEN GOTO 50
40  PRINT B; " IS NOT A FACTOR OF "; A
45  GOTO 60
50  PRINT B; " IS A FACTOR OF "; A
60  NEXT K
65  DATA 8, 4, 16, 10, 19, 6, 85, 5
70  END
```

Length		Width	
7.3	in.	5.2	in.
14.52	cm	8	cm
25.7	ft	13.1	ft
3.9	m	2.1	m

4. The area of a rectangle is given by the formula, A = L * W, where L is the length and W is the width of the rectangle. Write a computer program that computes the area of the rectangles listed in the chart to the left.

Output your answers and data under the column headings,   **LENGTH   WIDTH   AREA**   and round the area of the rectangle to the nearest square unit.

Chip's Challenges

5. What is the value of X in each of the following statements?
   a. `20  X = INT(INT(9.1)/INT(6.5))`
   b. `20  X = INT(-8.3) + INT(-3.8)`

6. Write a computer program that inputs two numbers, X and Y, and determines whether or not Y is an exact divisor of X. (Hint: See Exercise 3 above.) Use labels and prompts to assist the user. Enter your program and **RUN** it, using X = 2288 and Y = 16.

14.3

Pick a Number

DISCOVER FOR YOURSELF

Enter the following program and RUN it. Do not try to guess the computer's output at this time.

PROGRAM

COMPUTER DISPLAYS

```
NEW
10 PRINT RND( 1 )
15 END
```

TRS - 80 users put a zero here.

?

Record the computer's output on a sheet of paper. RUN the program three more times, each time guessing the computer's output.

RUN

COMPUTER DISPLAYS

FIRST

?

SECOND

?

THIRD

?

271

WHAT DID YOU LEARN?

No, there is nothing wrong with your computer. The expression,

RND(1)   TRS - 80 users put a zero
      ↑ ─────────here.

in the program is an instruction to the computer to produce a random number with a value between 0 and 1. A random number is one that is produced according to no rule or procedure. That is why the computer printed a different number each time the program was executed. Shown below is a computer program and its output when the program was executed. Type and **RUN** the program on your computer. Compare your output with the output shown.

Random Numbers Program	Output Random Numbers
NEW	.734801
	.208048
10 FOR K = 1 TO 10	.627633
	.358479
20 PRINT RND(1)	.137551
30 NEXT K	.127641
	.175054
40 END	.809923
	.888876
	.787622

Memory Bank

RND function

The **RND** function may be written:

                                    ┌─ TRS - 80 users
                                    │ use zero for the
                          ↓   argument.
              RND (1)
              ↗   ↖   ↖
        Keyword.   Parentheses.

It generates a random number between 0 and 1. The **RND** function can be used in any valid BASIC expression.

USE WHAT YOU HAVE LEARNED

Sometimes it is necessary to pick a number between 1 and 10, or 0 and 100, or between some other specified pair of numbers. This can be done using the **RND** and **INT** functions as shown in the following examples.

Example 1

Since	`RND(1)`	is a number between 0 and 1,
then	`10 * RND(1)`	is a number between 0 and 10.
Therefore,	`INT(10 * RND(1))`	is an integer between 0 and 10, including 0.

Example 2

Since	`RND(1)`	is a number between 0 and 1,
then	`20 * RND(1)`	is a number between 0 and 20.
Therefore,	`INT(20 * RND(1))`	is an integer between 0 and 20, including 0.

Example 3

Since	`RND(1)`	is a number between 0 and 1,
then	`15 * RND(1)`	is a number between 0 and 15
and	`15 * RND(1) + 5`	is a number between 5 and 20.
Therefore,	`INT(15 * RND(1) + 5)`	is an integer between 5 and 20, including 5.

Test the conclusions in the examples above.

TRS-80 users may substitute:

1) `RND (10) - 1`
2) `RND (20) - 1`
3) `RND (15) + 4`

Enter and RUN the Random Numbers Program each time replacing `RND(1)` or `RND(0)` in line 20 with the expressions in the examples.

Random numbers are useful in simulating events that do not have totally predictable outcomes, such as flipping a coin. If you tossed a coin 100 times, how many heads and tails would you expect? That is correct. You would expect 50 heads and 50 tails. Try it! This event can be simulated by the computer using the RND and INT functions. Tossing a coin 100, 1000, or more times can be a tedious job. The computer can be programmed to "toss" the coin for you.

Lee and Anton had difficulty with this problem until Mr. Pierce, their teacher, reminded them of the three main parts of any computer program:

INITIALIZE   PROCESS   OUTPUT

Lee and Anton agreed that they would instruct the computer to generate at random, a 0 or 1, where 0 would represent a tail and 1 would represent a head. Lee suggested that they use the expression,

$$INT(2 * RND(1))$$

to do this. Anton agreed. He suggested that they instruct the computer to print a T for each 0 and an H for each 1. Lee thought that this was a great idea. They agreed that the computer should count and print the total number of heads and the total number of tails. Lee and Anton then wrote the program shown below. Study their program and identify the steps which are INITIALIZE, PROCESS, and OUTPUT.

TRS-80:

1 = TAILS
2 = HEADS
Then RND(2) produces what you want.

Flipping a Coin

```
10   REM FLIPPING A COIN
20   REM THE RND FUNCTION
30   H = 0
40   T = 0
50   FOR J = 1 TO 100
60   X = INT(2 * RND(1))
70   IF X = 1 THEN GOTO 110
80   PRINT "T";
90   T = T + 1
100   GOTO 130
110   PRINT "H";
120   H = H + 1
130   NEXT J
140   PRINT
150   PRINT "NUMBER OF HEADS", H
160   PRINT "NUMBER OF TAILS", T
170   END
```

Lee and Anton ran their program ten times to see how close the head and tail counts came to each other. The results of their runs are given in the table below.

Run Number	Heads Number	Tails Number
1	41	59
2	53	47
3	52	48
4	42	58
5	39	61
6	47	53
7	57	43
8	45	55
9	49	51
10	43	57
Total	468	532

Lee and Anton expected that the number of heads and the number of tails would be about the same. In their experiment, there were 468 heads and 532 tails. Enter their program and RUN it ten times. Compare your results with theirs.

Exercises

1. Correct the error in each of the following **RND** functions.
   a. `10  PRINT RDN(1)`
   b. `10  PRINT RND 1`
2. What is the range of numbers generated by the following expressions?
   a. `14 * RND(1)`
   b. `25 * RND(1) + 10`
   c. `INT(30 * RND(1))`
   d. `INT(40 * RND(1) + 15)`
3. Write a BASIC expression that would randomly select a number from each of the following range of numbers:
   a. Any number between 0 and 8.
   b. Any number between 10 and 20.
   c. Any integer between 1 and 50, including 1.
   d. Any integer between 7 and 40, including 7.
4. Write a computer program to simulate flipping a coin 25 times. Use BASIC functions to select the integers 1 or 2. Print **TAILS** if 1 is selected and **HEADS** if 2 is selected. Enter and **RUN** your program.
5. A standard **die** is a cube with a different number of spots (one to six) on each face or side of the cube. Write a computer program to simulate tossing a die 20 times and print, with appropriate labels, the number of times each face appeared on top when the die was tossed 20 times.

Chip's Challenges

6. Write a computer program to simulate tossing two dice (dice is plural for die) ten times. Have the computer display, with appropriate labels, the number represented by the face of each die and the sums of the numbers.
7. **a.** Write a computer program to print the message,
      SAVE THE WHALES
      randomly selecting the print position on the line.
   b. Using a timing loop, alter the program in Exercise 7a to flash the message,
      SAVE THE WHALES
      ten times on the screen, randomly selecting the print position on the line.
   c. Using a timing loop, alter the program in Exercise 7b to flash the message,
      SAVE THE WHALES
      ten times on the screen, randomly selecting the line on which the message is to be printed and randomly selecting the print position on that line.

14.4

Bits of Strings

DISCOVER FOR YOURSELF

Enter the following experiments and RUN them. Do not try to guess the program outputs until you have RUN the computer experiments.

1. EXPERIMENT

```
NEW
10   FOR J = 1 TO 4
20   A$ = "GOOD"
30   PRINT LEFT$(A$,J)
40   NEXT J
50   END
```

PROGRAM   **COMPUTER DISPLAYS**

```
NEW
10   FOR J = 1 TO 4
20   B$ = "NEWS"
30   PRINT LEFT$(B$,J)
40   NEXT J
50   END
```

2. EXPERIMENT

```
NEW
10   FOR K = 1 TO 4
20   C$ = "EXIT"
30   PRINT RIGHT$(C$,K)
40   NEXT K
50   END
```

PROGRAM   **COMPUTER DISPLAYS**

```
NEW
10   FOR K = 1 TO 4
20   D$ = "FAST"
30   PRINT RIGHT$(D$,K)
40   NEXT K
50   END
```

3. EXPERIMENT

```
NEW
10  FOR L = 1 TO 4
20  E$ = "SECONDHAND"
30  PRINT MID$(E$,L,L)
40  NEXT L
50  END
```

PROGRAM

```
NEW
10  FOR L = 1 TO 4
20  F$ = "PERFORMANCE"
30  PRINT MID$(F$,L,L)
40  NEXT L
50  END
```

COMPUTER DISPLAYS

WHAT DID YOU LEARN?

The functions, LEFT$, RIGHT$, and MID$, selected certain characters of a string. With LEFT$, the selection began at the left of the string. With RIGHT$, it began at the right of the string. With MID$, the characters were selected by counting from a particular character of the string.

In Program 1, the expression
LEFT$(B$,J)

selected left characters of the string variable, B$.

When J = 1, {selected 1 character}

LEFT$(B$,1) = N   NEWS

When J = 2, {selected 2 characters}

LEFT$(B$,2) = NE   NEWS

When J = 3, {selected 3 characters}

LEFT$(B$,3) = NEW   NEWS

When J = 4, {selected 4 characters}

LEFT$(B$,4) = NEW   NEWS

In Program 2, the expression
RIGHT$(D$,K)

selected right characters of the string variable, D$.

When K = 1, {selected 1 character}

RIGHT$(D$,1) = T   FAST

When K = 2, {selected 2 characters}

RIGHT$(D$,2) = ST   FAST

When K = 3, {selected 3 characters}

RIGHT$(D$,3) = AST   FAST

When K = 4, {selected 4 characters}

RIGHT$(D$,4) = FAST   FAST

Memory Bank

LEFT$ function

The LEFT$ *function is written:*

A string.
An integer.

LEFT$(M$, K)

Keyword. Parentheses.

Memory Bank

RIGHT$ function

The RIGHT$ *function is written:*

A string.
An integer.

RIGHT$(M$, K)

Keyword. Parentheses.

The LEFT$ function selects a specific number of characters counting from the <u>left</u> of the string. The RIGHT$ function selects a specific number of characters counting from the <u>right</u> of the string.

Look at Program 3 and its output. The MID$ function in Program 3 selected a specific number of characters counting from a <u>particular</u> character of the string.

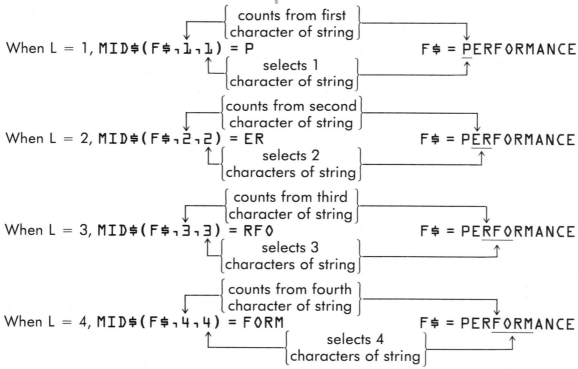

When L = 1, MID$(F$,1,1) = P — counts from first character of string — selects 1 character of string — F$ = PERFORMANCE

When L = 2, MID$(F$,2,2) = ER — counts from second character of string — selects 2 characters of string — F$ = PERFORMANCE

When L = 3, MID$(F$,3,3) = RFO — counts from third character of string — selects 3 characters of string — F$ = PERFORMANCE

When L = 4, MID$(F$,4,4) = FORM — counts from fourth character of string — selects 4 characters of string — F$ = PERFORMANCE

In the expression, MID$(F$,M,J) the integers M and J do not have to be equal as in Program 3. What would be printed by the computer if line 30 in Program 3 were

30 PRINT MID$(F$,7,3) ?

The computer would search for the 7th character of the string, PERFORMANCE. The 7th character is M. The computer would then select three characters of the string, beginning with the 7th character. The computer would print MAN.

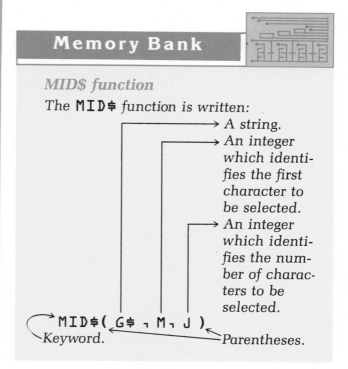

Memory Bank

MID$ function

The MID$ function is written:

→ A string.

→ An integer which identifies the first character to be selected.

→ An integer which identifies the number of characters to be selected.

→ MID$(G$, M, J)
Keyword.   Parentheses.

USE WHAT YOU HAVE LEARNED

Miles Remeris, Program Manager of the Winside Corporation, instructed Mrs. Sally White, Programmer Trainee, to write a program. This program would read an employee's name such as,   MAX BAUER
with only one blank space separating the first and last names and print the employee's name in the form,   BAUER, MAX
Sally knew that the expressions LEFT$(A$, 3) and RIGHT$(A$, 5) could be used to identify the first name, LEFT$(A$, 3) = MAX, and the last name, RIGHT$(A$, 5) = BAUER, if A$ = "MAX BAUER". Because not all first names are three characters long and not all last names are only five characters in length, Sally had to find a way to use these functions to identify the first and last names of any employee.

Sally consulted with her Supervisor, Ms. Erasette, who introduced her to the LEN function. The **LEN** function calculates the length of a string. With this information, Sally was able to complete the assignment given to her by Mr. Remeris. Study Sally's program carefully.

Chip's Bits

The blind may be able to see some day through tiny video cameras that send pictures to a computer which changes them to electrical pulses. These go to electrodes attached to the part of the brain that is used for seeing. With progress in miniaturization, the entire device could be concealed in a glass eye and a pair of eyeglass frames.

Sally's Program

```
5   REM REVERSING FIRST AND LAST NAMES
10  READ A$
12  REM ONE BLANK BETWEEN NAMES
15  DATA MAX BAUER
17  REM LENGTH OF STRING IS L
20  L = LEN(A$)
23  REM THIS LOOP FINDS THE BLANK
25  FOR K = 1 TO L
30  IF MID$(A$,K,1) = " " THEN GOTO 40
35  NEXT K
40  F$ = LEFT$(A$,K)
45  L$ = RIGHT$(A$,L - K)
50  PRINT L$; ","; F$
55  END
```

CHIP SAYS:
REMEMBER THE
BLANK BETWEEN
NAMES.

An important idea which enabled Sally to write the program is contained in line 30. Do you know what it is? That is correct! This **IF** statement, with the **MID$** function, tests for and identifies the position number of the blank which separates the first name from the last name in the string variable, **A$**.

Enter and **RUN** Sally's program to verify that the first and last names are reversed. Use your first and last name in the **DATA** statement.

Exercises

1. Determine the error in each of the following expressions:
  a. LEF$(B$,6)
  b. MID(A$,J,3)
  c. RIGHT$(D$,A$)
  d. MID$(A,4,1)
  e. LEFT$(8,B$)
  f. RIGHT$(J$ J)

2. Determine the characters of the strings selected by each of the following expressions:
  a. LEFT$(F$,5) where F$ = "Reversing"
  b. LEFT$("BASIC",2)
  c. MID$(C$,5,3) where C$ = "Challenge"
  d. RIGHT$(S$,4) where S$ = "String"
  e. RIGHT$("SOLID",3)
  f. MID$(M$,7,4) where M$ = "Expression"

3. What is the value of L in each of the following statements?
  a. 10 L = LEN(A$) where A$ = "Statements"
  b. 10 L = LEN("VALUABLE")
  c. 10 L = LEN(C$) where C$ = "Good Luck"
  d. 10 L = LEN("SEE YOU SOON")

4. Write a computer program that inputs (Use **INPUT** statement) an individual's name, such as
MARY GOLINSKY
and prints the name in the form, GOLINSKY, MARY
Use **INPUT** statements with appropriate prompt(s).

5. Change Sally's program to read the names of the employees in the Widget Department of the Winside Corporation and print each name, last name, followed by a comma, first.

Winside Corporation Widget Department

Employees

1. Maria Perez
2. Humphrey Tootsberry
3. Melanie Johnson
4. Iona Washington
5. Michael Duggin
6. Sam Bassnelle

Chip's Challenges

6. Determine the value of L in each of the following statements.
   a. `10  L = LEN(T$ + T$)` where T$ = "Tom"
   b. `10  L = LEN(A$ + B$)` where A$ = "Good Night"
   and B$ = "Pleasant Dreams"
7. Change Sally's program to read in any number of employee names and print their names, last name first, followed by a comma.
8. Write a program to read in an individual's full name, first name, middle name, and last name, such as
   `JOHN ANTHONY MAGINTI`
   and then print the name in the form,
   `MAGINTI, JOHN ANTHONY`

Enter and `RUN` your program, using the list of employees from the OREC Section of the Winside Corporation.

Winside Corporation OREC Section

Employees

1. Mary Sue Jones
2. John Anthony Maginti
3. Corlesse Jo Manner
4. Bob Orlando Moton

CHAPTER SUMMARY

1. The `TAB` function, following `PRINT`, instructs the computer to indent a specified number of spaces from the left margin.
2. The `TAB` function can be used to output information in columns.
3. The `INT(N)` function instructs the computer to select the greatest integer which is less than or equal to N.
4. The `INT` function can be used to "round off" any number.

5. The RND function produces a random number.

6. The RND function is useful in simulating events which do not have totally predictable outcomes.

7. The LEFT$ function selects a specific number of characters, counting from the left of the string.

8. The RIGHT$ function selects a specific number of characters, counting from the right of the string.

9. The MID$ function selects a specific number of characters, counting from a particular character of the string.

10. The LEN function calculates the length of the string.

PROBLEM SET 14

1. Each of the following TAB functions is incorrect. Write each TAB function correctly.
   a. 20   PRINT TAB 13; K
   b. 20   PRINT TAB(258); "SALES"
   c. 20   PRINT TAP(5); "GREAT"
   d. 20   PRINT TB(15); A + B

2. Illustrate the computer output of each of the following statements, showing the print positions of the output.
   a. 10   PRINT "Y ="; TAB(10); "NANCY"
   b. 10   PRINT TAB(6); "Y ="; TAB(15); "MARIJO"
   c. 10   PRINT TAB(7); "A + B ="; TAB (15); 5
   d. 10   PRINT "ITEM NO.";
      20   PRINT TAB(16); "NO. SOLD"

3. Each of the following INT functions is incorrect. Write each INT function correctly.
   a. 30   PRINT INT 14.2   b. 30   PRINT NIT(8.4)
   c. 30   PRINT INT(*)   d. 30   PRINT INT 5

4. Determine the value of N in each statement.
   a. 10   N = INT(32.8)
   b. 10   N = INT(19.3 + 21.8)
   c. 10   N = INT(D/N) where D = 32 and N = 5
   d. 10   N = INT(-6.2)
   e. 10   N = K + INT(G)
      where K = 35.5 and G = 5.6
   f. 10   N = INT(B + C)/INT(B - C)
      where B = 4.5 and C = 2.3

5.
   a. Write a BASIC statement using the INT function to round a number A to the nearest whole number.
   b. Write a BASIC statement using the INT function to round the product of two numbers, X and Y, to the nearest whole number.

6. Each of the following RND functions is incorrect. Write each RND function correctly.

a. `10 PRINT RND 1` **b.** `10 PRINT RDN(1)`

7. What is the range of numbers produced by the following expressions?

a. `12 * RND(1)` **b.** `INT(12 * RND(1))`
c. `25 * RND(1) + 8` **d.** `RND(1) + 10`
e. `INT(30 * RND(1) + 25)`
f. `INT(100 * RND(1) + 1)`

8. Write a BASIC expression which would randomly select a number from each of the following ranges of numbers:

a. Any number between 0 and 10.
b. Any number between 10 and 30.
c. Any integer between 1 and 60.
d. Any integer between 3 and 53.
e. Any integer between 1 and 32, including 1 and 32.

9. Determine the error in each of the following expressions.

a. `LEFT(A$, 5)` **b.** `RIGHT$ "MONEY",5`
c. `MIDDLE("CASE",3, 2)` **d.** `MIDS(M$, 6, 3)`
e. `LEF$("TIME", 7)` **f.** `RIGTH$(C$,8)`

10. Determine the characters of the strings selected by each of the following expressions.

a. `LEFT$(A$,4)` where A$ = "happiness"
b. `MID$("FOLLOW", 2, 4)`
c. `RIGHT$(J$,5)` where J$ = "joyfully"
d. `MID$(K$,2, 2)` where K$ = "kite"
e. `LEFT$(B$, 9)` where B$ = "select integer"
f. `RIGHT$("RIGHT", 3)`

11. Write BASIC expressions using a LEFT$, MID$, or RIGHT$ function to select the specified characters of the strings.

a. ADS of A$ = "HEADS"
b. BAT of B$ = "BATTLE"
c. TT of C$ = "CATTLE"
d. EFFECT of E$ = "EFFECTIVE"
e. JECTIV of F$ = "OBJECTIVE"
f. BY of G$ = "GOOD BYE"

12. What would be printed as a result of executing each of the following sets of statements? Assume X = 25, Y = 50, and Z = 75.

a.
```
10  PRINT "SUM OF";
20  PRINT X; "PLUS"; Y;
30  PRINT "IS"
40  PRINT TAB(9); Z
```

b.
```
10  PRINT "X =",
20  PRINT TAB(16); "Y =",
30  PRINT TAB(31); "Z ="
40  PRINT X, Y, Z
```

13. Determine the output of the program on the next page. Write your answer on a sheet of paper. Enter and RUN the program to verify your answer.

```
5   Clearscreen
10  PRINT TAB(7); "STUDENT NO.", TAB(20); "AVERAGE"
20  FOR I = 1 TO 3
30  READ N, A, B, C
40  PRINT TAB(11); N, TAB(20); (A + B + C)/3
50  NEXT I
60  DATA 45, 65, 75, 80
70  DATA 62, 75, 85, 95
80  DATA 39, 90, 90, 84
90  END
RUN
```

14. Mr. Thomas rented a building for his factory. The building contained five rooms with the following floor dimensions:

    Room 1 — 10 meters by 12 meters
    Room 2 — 13 meters by 25 meters
    Room 3 — 35 meters by 70 meters
    Room 4 — 12 meters by 18 meters
    Room 5 — 16 meters by 28 meters

    Write, enter, and RUN a program that would calculate the area of floor space in each room and the total area of floor space in the factory. Print output data using TAB functions, with appropriate column headings. Print the total floor space in sentence form.

15. Follow the steps of the program below and answer the following questions. Repeat the program using all the data listed.

```
10  READ X
20  DATA 1, 2, 37, 55, 24, 88, 13, 64
30  IF INT(X/2) * 2 = X THEN GOTO 60
40  PRINT X, "NO"
50  GOTO 70
60  PRINT X, "YES"
70  END
```

    a. Determine the output for each data value.
    b. What is printed when the input is an even number?
    c. What is printed when the input is an odd number?

16. Using a FOR - NEXT loop, enter and RUN the program of Problem 15 above, outputting the answers in appropriate sentence form.

17. Write a program step using an IF-THEN statement and an INT function to determine if a number Y is divisible by 29. Use line numbers 30 and 90, in that order, for the IF-THEN statement.

18. Construct a BASIC statement using the RND function to pick a number from 0 to 12, inclusive.

19. Write a computer program to simulate flipping a coin 50 times. Use BASIC functions to select randomly the integers 1 or 2. Print HEADS if 1 is selected and TAILS if 2 is selected. Enter and RUN your program.

20. Write a computer program to simulate tossing a die 30 times and print, with appropriate labels, the number of times each face appeared on top of the die.

21. Determine the output of this program. Write your answer on a sheet of paper. Enter and RUN the program to verify your answer.

```
5   Clearscreen
10   READ A$
15   DATA ANDREA MARIE DUGGAN
20   L = LEN(A$)
25   FOR K = 1 TO L
30   IF MID$(A$,K,1) = " " THEN GOTO 40
35   NEXT K
40   F$ = LEFT$(A$,K)
45   N$ = RIGHT$(A$, L - K)
50   G = LEN(N$)
55   FOR J = 1 TO G
60   IF MID$(N$,J,1) = " " THEN GOTO 70
65   NEXT J
70   M$ = LEFT$(N$, J)
75   L$ = RIGHT$(N$, G - J)
80   PRINT L$; ","; M$; F$
85   END
```

22. Change the program of Problem 21 to read the names of the employees in the Driblet Department. Print each name, last name first, followed by a comma, then the first and middle names.

**Winside Corporation
Driblet Department**

Employees

1. Liza Mary Anders
2. Robert Joe Martinez
3. Sam Lorenz Bolt
4. Nancy Ann Alesczyk
5. Margaret Sally Jones

23. Determine the output of the program to the right. Write your answer on a sheet of paper. Enter and RUN the program to verify your answer.

```
NEW
10   FOR J = 1 TO 4
20   A$ = "GOOD"
25   B$ = "LUCK"
30   PRINT   TAB(15);
LEFT$(A$,J),
35   PRINT   TAB(20);
RIGHT$(B$,J)
40   NEXT J
45   END
```

 Chip's Challenges

24. A business firm decides to give each employee a bonus of one-twelfth of his or her annual salary. Write, enter, and RUN a computer program to determine the amount of bonus paid by the firm to each employee and the

total value of the bonuses. The annual salaries are $10 500, $9850, $11 500, $8840, $9000, $7700, $15 000, $14 560, $25 000, and $19 000. Display your output in a table form using the headings:

EMPLOYEE NUMBER   SALARY   BONUS

Be sure to label the total bonus paid.

25. Write a computer program with **TAB** function to produce the output shown on the screen below. Enter your program and **RUN** it.

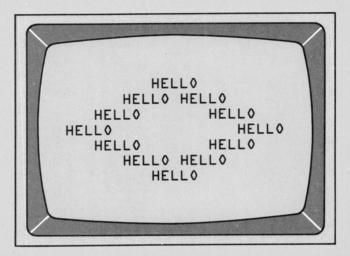

26. What is the value of X in each statement?
a. `30  X = INT(INT(65.4)/INT(-14.6))`
b. `30  X = INT(INT(-9.80) + INT(10.7)) * INT(45.8)`

27. Write a computer program that determines if a number X is exactly divisible by 5. Print the output, using appropriate sentence form.

28. Write, enter, and **RUN** a computer program which will randomly select one word from each of the columns to the left. Then print a message in the form,
    Name **HAD A** Size Item
Use a **FOR-NEXT** loop and a timing loop to flash ten messages on the screen. See Mitzi's Slogan Generator on page 230.

Name	Size	Item
MARY	LITTLE	LAMB
JOHN	BIG	FOOT
MERLE	TINY	CAR
HARRY	GREAT	NOSE

29. Determine the value of L in each of the following statements:
a. `10  L = LEN(B$ + B$)` where B$ = "BOOM"
b. `10  L = LEN(A$ + G$)` where A$ = "ADIOS"
        and G$ = "AMIGO"

30. Write a computer program to read the full names of individuals and then print only those names with less than sixteen letters in their full name. Print names selected with last name first, followed by comma, then first and middle names. Enter and **RUN** your program using the employees listed in the OREC Section of the Winside Corporation in Exercise 8 on page 281.

COMPUTER AWARENESS

These scientists are using computers to find oil reserves.

Society's Servant

Solving a problem is something like writing a computer program. The problem solver needs to gather data (initialize); arrange or combine the information, discarding extra data (process); and reach a solution (output).

Today, people are solving problems that use information that may be constantly changing, impossible to see, or dangerous to collect. The data processing involves long and complicated formulas and equations. Reaching a solution could be so slow that its results would be useless.

Because computers can store vast amounts of information and process it quickly and accurately, so-ciety uses them to solve many varied problems. Researchers are developing problem-solving **algorithms**, sets of steps used to relate data collected for a particular problem. Engineers and scientists are designing special input devices called sensors to collect the information to make the algorithm work. The sensors are analog devices that measure changing conditions. Their output is translated into digital signals for computers to use.

The United States Geological Survey uses a computer system at Mount Saint Helens. Tilt meters, installed inside the volcano, measure changes in the crater floor. These sensors send readings to the computer every ten minutes. The computer, using special software, analyzes the data to show trends in the tilt or inflation of the crater floor. As a result, scientists can now predict eruptions thirty minutes before they actually occur. This allows them to explore the crater safely, since they have adequate warning of an eruption.

Other sensors gather information for computers about conditions below the earth's surface. Some of these sensor-computer systems are used by archaeologists to locate sites of vanished cities. Others are used in mining and petroleum drilling operations. One system is being used in Venice, Italy. Engineers using it hope it will help keep the city from sinking below the sea.

Computers are also used to control hazardous manufacturing processes. Sensors monitor extreme heats, deadly gases, and dangerous chemicals. Data from the sensors are translated to digital information for the computer. The computer can display or otherwise indicate that information for its operators. It can also send data to devices that operate valves, regulators, or other control machinery.

Some cities are solving traffic problems with computerized traffic control systems. Sensors measure traffic patterns at intersections. They record the numbers of cars travelling in each direction. This information is sent to the computer in the control center. The computer analyzes the data and compares it to data that describe the best possible movement of the traffic. If the real and ideal conditions do not match, the computer calculates changes for the timing of traffic lights. The changes are trans-

lated into commands the signal lights' control boxes can use. The timing of the light's red and green periods is changed, to keep traffic moving.

On the space shuttles *Columbia* and *Challenger*, computers serve as flight engineers. Sensors monitor conditions inside and outside the ships. The computers constantly compare data received with data stored in their memories. They calculate required changes and translate the changes into commands the shuttles can understand. The computers also translate the pilots' actions into appropriate directions for the ship. The computers ''know'' where the ship is, and direct the firing of jets (in space), and the movement of airfoils (in the atmosphere) to control its movements. The pilots have to learn only one set of responses. The computers translate these responses into appropriate action of jets or airfoils depending on whether the ship is in space or in the atmosphere.

What Do You Know?
1. Why are computers useful in solving society's problems?
2. What is an algorithm?
3. For what are sensors used?
4. How do computers help keep traffic moving?

What Can You Find Out?
1. Does your community have a computerized traffic control system?
2. Do any manufacturers in your area use computer controlled processing?

What Do You Think?
1. Does society have some problems that computers cannot help solve?

SUMMING IT UP

Accumulating Values

The task of averaging a set of numbers requires the operations of addition and division. Accumulating and counting, in a loop, can computerize the job.

Totals to Average

DISCOVER FOR YOURSELF

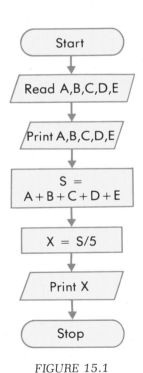

FIGURE 15.1

Cara Carr, a payroll supervisor at Glacial Products, used the flow chart in Figure 15.1 to write a computer program. The program was used to find the average weekly salary of the five employees in the Cog Department. The computer output of Cara's program is shown below. Study the flow chart and the program to answer the questions.

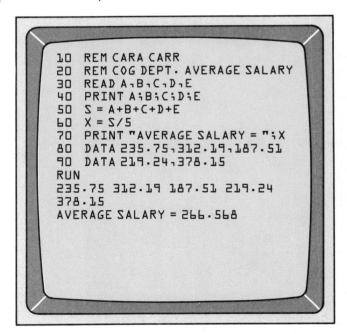

```
10   REM CARA CARR
20   REM COG DEPT. AVERAGE SALARY
30   READ A,B,C,D,E
40   PRINT A;B;C;D;E
50   S = A+B+C+D+E
60   X = S/5
70   PRINT "AVERAGE SALARY = ";X
80   DATA 235.75,312.19,187.51
90   DATA 219.24,378.15
RUN
235.75 312.19 187.51 219.24
378.15
AVERAGE SALARY = 266.568
```

1. What were the salaries of each of the five employees?

2. What was the average of the salaries of the employees in the Cog Department?

3. How many numbers are averaged in Cara's program?

4. What changes in Cara's program are necessary so that it will calculate the average of the weekly salaries: $233.50, $195.45, $311.87, $212.39?

WHAT DID YOU LEARN?

As you can see, many changes are required to calculate the average of four values. The original program is limited to calculating the average of five and only five values. Listing variables in the **READ** statement is not, in this case, the best way to input the data. Finding the average of ten salaries would require naming ten variables in the **READ** statement: **30 READ A, B, C, D, E, F, G, H, P, Q.** This is an awkward way to input data. Since each number read does not need its own variable name, a For-Next loop can be used to input data in the program.

The list of variables in the **READ** statement can be thought of as one **READ** instruction, repeated several times. For example, **30 READ A, B, C, D** corresponds to the **READ** instruction repeated four times. Consider the instructions illustrated in the partial flow chart in Figure 15.2. The program reads and prints four numbers by repeating the instructions four times.

The program, however, does not perform the addition of the numbers—a necessary step for calculating an average. The addition must be performed by **accumulating** a sum each time a number is read. This is similar to the task performed by a cash register or adding machine. A variable, called the accumulator, is selected to store the accumulated sum. The variable in this example is S. Consider the statement, $S = S + A$, which has been included in the partial flow chart in Figure 15.3. This BASIC statement accumulates a sum. Each time a number A is read by the computer, that number is added to the previous value of S and automatically stored in the accumulator, replacing the previous sum. This process is repeated four times. Each time a number is read, a new sum results. After the fourth time through the loop, the value of S is the sum of the four numbers read by the computer.

When the first number A is read by the computer, it must be added to the previous value of S. However, there is no previous value of S at this point.

An initial value must be assigned to the variable S that will clear the accumulator. This is similar to clearing an adding machine or calculator to start with zero.

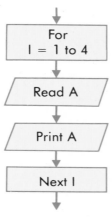

FIGURE 15.2

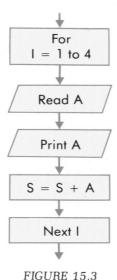

FIGURE 15.3

Memory Bank

Accumulating a Sum

1. The sum of several numbers may be accumulated by a BASIC statement such as `30  S=S+A`.
2. First set the value of the accumulator variable to zero, for example, `10  S=0`.

The step, S = 0, in the flow chart in Figure 15.4 clears the accumulator. Use the data entries 233.50, 195.45, 311.87, 212.39 and follow the instructions to see how accumulating works.

USE WHAT YOU HAVE LEARNED

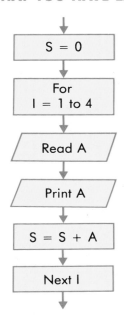

FIGURE 15.4

Step	Instruction	Explanation
1	S = 0	The value of 0 is assigned to S.
2	For I = 1 TO 4	The For-Next loop is started.
3	Read A	The value 233.50 is assigned to A.
4	Print A	The number 233.50 is printed.
5	S = S + A	The value 0 + 233.50 is assigned to S.
6	Next I	End of the loop. I is incremented by 1.
7	Read A	The value 195.45 is assigned to A.
8	Print A	The number 195.45 is printed.
9	S = S + A	The value 233.5 + 195.45 is assigned to S. S = 428.95 at this point.
10	Next I	End of the loop. I is incremented by 1.

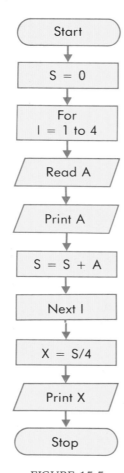

FIGURE 15.5

11 The loop is executed two more times until the sum, S = 953.21, is accumulated. Each time the **READ** statement is executed by the computer, a number listed in a **DATA** statement is read.

Cara Carr rewrote her average salary program, using a For-Next loop to input data. This is shown in the flow chart in Figure 15.5. As you can see, Cara chose S as the variable to use as the accumulator. The statement, S = S + A, accumulates the total.

The output of the program, using the data entries 233.50, 195.45, 311.87, 212.39, is shown below.

```
10   REM CARA CARR'S
20   REM COG DEPT. AVERAGE SALARY
30   S = 0
40   FOR I = 1 TO 4
50   READ A
60   PRINT A
70   S = S + A
80   NEXT I
90   X = S/4
100  PRINT "AVERAGE SALARY = ";X
110  DATA 233.50,195.45,311.87,
212.39
RUN
233.5
195.45
311.87
212.39
AVERAGE SALARY = 238.3025
```

Note that Cara has eliminated the long list of variables in the **READ** statement. The program, however, only calculates the average of four numbers. The **FOR** statement 40 FOR I = 1 TO 4, and the division statement, 90 X = S/4, must be changed to calculate an average of numbers other than four. For example, if eight numbers are to be averaged, then these statements must become 40 FOR I = 1 TO 8 and 90 X = S/8. Later you will discover how to adjust a program to calculate the average of different quantities of numbers without changing program steps.

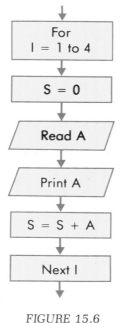

FIGURE 15.6

The statement S = 0, which clears the accumulator, has a specific place within a program. It must be placed before the loop that controls the reading of the numbers. In Cara's program the placement is before the FOR statement.

Study the flow chart in Figure 15.6. What step immediately follows the FOR step? As you can see, the statement S = 0 follows the FOR step. Thus, S = 0 is within the FOR-NEXT loop. Each time the loop is executed, the value of S will be set to 0. For example, assume the number 233.50 has been read in and the loop executed one time. At the end of the first cycle, the value of S is 233.50. Execution of the program continues, re-entering the loop. The very next step sets the accumulator S equal to 0, erasing the previous total, 233.50. Suppose the value 195.45 is read in during the next cycle. Do you see that the value of S at the completion of that cycle will be 195.45? Remember, the step S = 0 must only be executed one time for a set of numbers to be summed. Therefore, avoid placing this step within the loop.

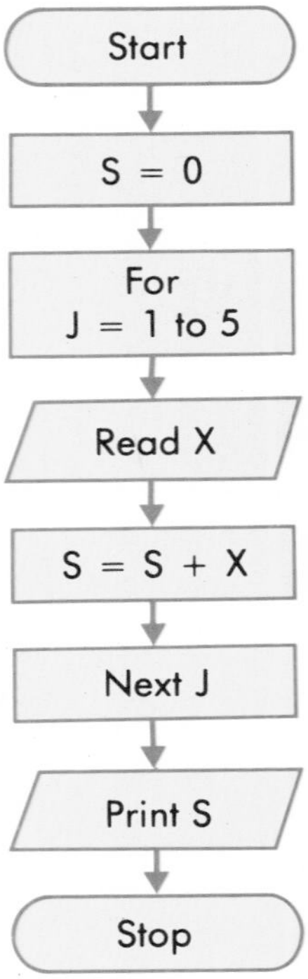

Memory Bank

Accumulating and FOR-NEXT loops

1. When accumulating a sum, the first value of the accumulator must be zero.
2. Use a statement such as S = 0.
3. Always place this statement before the FOR-NEXT loop.

Exercises

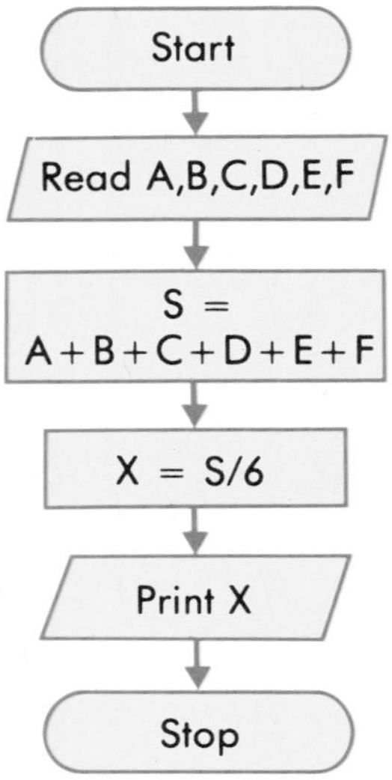

1. Refer to Figure 15.7 to complete the following:
   a. Change one flow chart symbol to accumulate the sum of ten numbers.
   b. Add one flow chart step to find the average of the five numbers and one to print the average.
2. Rewrite the flow chart in Figure 15.8 to enter six numbers and find their average. Use accumulating techniques.
3. Change two lines in Cara's Average Salary program, p. 293, so that the output will include $ signs. In other words, instead of 195.45, print $195.45.

Chip's Challenges

4. Write a program to print the sum of fifty numbers, using a FOR-NEXT loop and accumulating techniques. Refer to Exercise 1 above.
5. How would you alter the program in Exercise 4 above to find the sum of any number of data entries?

FIGURE 15.7

FIGURE 15.8

Count on Your Computer

DISCOVER FOR YOURSELF

```
10   REM ACCUMULATING
20   S = 0
30   FOR J = 1 TO 4
40   READ X
50   S = S + X
60   NEXT J
70   A = S/4
80   PRINT A
90   DATA 70
100  DATA 80
110  DATA 80
120  DATA 70
```

WHAT DID YOU LEARN?

Look at the program at the left. Answer the following questions.

1. How many numbers are **READ** in?

2. What is the initial value of the accumulator, S?

3. What arithmetic operation is indicated in line 70?

4. What would be the output of the program if it were **RUN?**

This program may be used to find the average of four numbers. In order to find the average, you must:

1. Find the sum of the four numbers.

2. Divide the sum by 4.

Lines 20 through 60 accumulate the sum of the four numbers. The average is computed by the instruction A = S/4 in line 70.

By applying what you have learned, you can write a program to find the average of any number of numbers. Look at the program on the next page.

Line 20 enters the number of values to be averaged. Lines 30 through 70 enter the values and accumulate their sum. Line 80 computes the average of "N" values. Line 90 outputs the average. Line 100 indicates the number of values whose average will be computed.

```
10   REM THE AVERAGE OF N NUMBERS
20   READ N
30   S=0
40   FOR J= 1 TO N
50   READ X
60   S=S+X
70   NEXT J
80   A=S/N
90   PRINT "THE AVERAGE IS ";A
100   DATA 6,57.3,16.9,31.5,48.2,61.3,58.7
RUN
THE AVERAGE IS 45.65
```

In this case, the average of 50 numbers could be computed. The lines following line 100 would contain the numbers to be averaged.

More about Accumulating—Generating Data Internally

The average program is an example of accumulating the sum of addends (numbers to be added) which are entered through a READ statement. As it is entered, each number is added to the partially accumulated sum. There are occasions when you may want to accumulate the sum of certain values which result from statements other than READ or INPUT statements.

Example: Find the sum of the integers from 1 to 19, inclusive.

A possible solution is to read in the value of each integer to be added, as is shown in the program below.

```
10   REM ACCUMULATING 19 NUMBERS
20   S=0
30   FOR I = 1 TO 19
40   READ N
50   S=S+N
60   NEXT I
70   PRINT S
```

This solution would require 19 data entries, one for each of the integers. Refer to the program as you go through the following table. Note the value of the index I, and compare it to the value of N, the number entered by the READ statement.

Chip's Bits

One of the early investigators of Boolean Logic is better known as the author of *Alice in Wonderland* and *Through the Looking Glass*. Lewis Carroll's real name was Charles Lutwidge Dodgson, an English mathematician who lived from 1832 to 1898. He invented and marketed a game of logic that used Boolean Algebra.

Time through the loop	Value of I	Value of N	Value of S
1st	1	1	1
2nd	2	2	3
3rd	3	3	6
4th	4	4	10
.	.	.	.
.	.	.	.
.	.	.	.
19th	19	19	190

You probably noticed that the value of I and the value of N were the same at each step of the program. In other words, the values of N could easily have been generated within the loop. The step S = S + N may be changed to the statement S = S + I to obtain the same result. This change would eliminate the need for the READ and DATA statements in the program. This more efficient solution and its output are shown below.

```
10  REM ACCUMULATING 19 NUMBERS
20  S=0
30  FOR I = 1 TO 19
40  S=S+I
50  NEXT I
60  PRINT "THE SUM IS ";S
RUN
THE SUM IS    190
```

USE WHAT YOU HAVE LEARNED

The Board of Directors of the Glacial Products Company requires that each department of the company submit, at its annual meeting, the average of the employees' wages for that department.

Maria Gonzales, of the Glacial Products Computer Center, found that the number of employees is not the same for each department. Each time a department's average wage was calculated, she had to determine the number of employees in the department. To do this, she had to count the employees listed on the department's Payroll Data Sheet. She remembered that a counting loop can be used to count the number of times a statement or a sequence of statements is executed. The count, when data entry is terminated, can be used as the divisor to calculate the average. In her program solution, Maria used a trailer record to terminate the entry of data and the accumulation of the sum. She knew that the trailer number, 99999, would be read, but not included, in the accumulation of the sum. As each data number other than the trailer record is read:

1. The number is added to S.

2. The counter I is increased by 1.

When the trailer number, 99999, is read:

1. The average is computed.

2. The average is printed.

3. Execution of the program is terminated.

The TEMP Department of the Glacial Products Company sent the Computer Center the Payroll Data Sheet shown below.

Glacial Products Company	
Payroll Data Sheet	TEMP Dept.
Employee	Salary
1. Fitzgerald, Michael	12,400
2. Motill, Janice	10,824
3. Johnson, George	11,780
4. Spinoza, Carlita	14,355

Maria's program and its output are shown below.

```
10   REM MARIA GONZALES
20   REM AVERAGE PROGRAM
30   REM TEMP DEPT.
40   S=0
50   I=0
60   READ X
70   IF X=99999 THEN 110
80   S=S+X
90   I=I+1
100  GOTO 60
110  A=S/I
120  PRINT "THE AVERAGE IS ";A
130  DATA 12400,10824,11780,14355,99999
RUN
THE AVERAGE IS 12339.75
```

E x e r c i s e s

1. Change two lines of the program in *Discover for Yourself* to find the average of six numbers.

2. What would the computer print as a result of running the following program?

```
10   REM PROBLEM 2
20   S=0
30   FOR I = 1 TO 4
40   S=S+I
50   NEXT I
60   PRINT S
```

3. What would the computer print as a result of running the program below, using the following data?
   Data: 10, 20, 30, 40, 50

```
10   REM PROBLEM 3
20   S=0
30   FOR I = 1 TO 5
40   READ X
50   S=S+X
60   NEXT I
70   PRINT S
```

4. Add one line to the program above to find the average of the five numbers. Change one line to print the average instead of the sum.

5. What would the computer print as a result of running the following program, with the data given?

```
10   REM PROBLEM 5
20   S=0
30   READ X
40   IF X=99999 THEN 70
50   S=S+X
60   GOTO 30
70   PRINT "THE SUM IS ";S
80   DATA 100,125,150,175,99999
```

6. Change two lines in the program of Exercise 5 to use 32767 as the trailer record.

Chip's Challenges

7. Rewrite the program of Exercise 5 to find the average of the numbers 85, 90, 75, 88, 93, and 94. Use 32767 as a trailer record.

C H A P T E R   S U M M A R Y

1. The sum of several terms may be accumulated by a BASIC statement such as
   30 S = S + A

2. Before accumulating a sum, the value of the accumulator must be set to zero. This can be done by using a statement such as
   10 S = 0
   where S is the accumulator.

3. Always place the statement S=0 in the program before the FOR-NEXT loop.

4. When finding the average of accumulated numbers, place a statement such as
   A = S/N
   after the FOR-NEXT loop.

PROBLEM SET 15

1. In the statement S = S + X, the variable S is called the ___?___.

2. In finding the sum of several numbers by accumulating, always set the value of the accumulator to ___?___ before finding the sum.

3. Each program that follows is incorrect. Identify the error, then write the program correctly.

   a.
   ```
   10  FOR I = 1 TO 5
   20  S=0
   30  S=S+I
   40  NEXT I
   50  PRINT S
   ```
   This program should find the sum of the numbers from 1 to 5.

   b.
   ```
   10  S = 0
   20  FOR K = 10 TO 15
   30  NEXT K
   40  PRINT S
   ```
   This program should find the sum of the numbers from 10 to 15.

c.
```
10  S = 1
20  FOR K = 1 TO 4
30  S = S+K
40  NEXT K
50  PRINT S
```
This program should find the sum of the numbers from 1 to 4.

d.
```
10  S = 0
20  READ X
30  FOR M = 1 TO 4
40  S = S + X
50  NEXT M
60  PRINT S
70  DATA 34,45,67,56
```
This program should find the sum of the numbers given in the **DATA** statement.

e.
```
10  S=0
20  FOR L= 1 TO 5
30  READ X
40  S = S + X
50  NEXT L
60  A = S/X
70  PRINT "AVERAGE = ";A
80  DATA 90,70,80,90,80
```
This program should find the average of five numbers.

4. What would be printed as a result of **RUN**ning the following programs?

a.
```
10  S = 0
20  FOR M = 1 TO 3
30  S = S + M
40  NEXT M
50  PRINT S
```

b.
```
10  S = 0
20  FOR I = 1 TO 5
30  READ X
40  S = S+X
50  NEXT I
60  PRINT S
70  DATA 10,20,30,40,50
```

c.
```
10  S = 0
20  FOR J = 1 TO 5
30  READ X
40  S = S + X
50  NEXT J
60  A = S/5
70  PRINT A
80  DATA 10,12,14,16,18
```

5. What would be printed as a result of RUNning the following programs?

   a. 10 S = 0
   20 FOR K = 2 TO 8 STEP 2
   30 S = S + K
   40 NEXT K
   50 PRINT S

   b. 10 S = 0
   20 FOR M = 3 TO 11 STEP 2
   30 S = S + M
   40 NEXT M
   50 PRINT S

6. What would be printed as a result of RUNning the following program, using the sets of DATA statements given in each part?

   Program   10 S = 0
   20 READ N
   30 FOR J = 1 TO N
   40 READ A
   50 S = S+A
   60 NEXT J
   70 PRINT "SUM = ";S

   DATA statements
   a. 80 DATA 5,86,82,78,66,92
   b. 80 DATA 4,70,80,90,80

7. What would be printed as a result of RUNning the following program, using the sets of DATA statements given in each part?

   Program   10 S = 0
   20 READ X
   30 IF X = 99999 THEN 60
   40 S = S + X
   50 GOTO 20
   60 PRINT S

   DATA statements
   a. 70 DATA 35,55,75,45,99999
   b. 70 DATA 20,30,40,50,60,70,99999

8. Using the partial program below, complete the FOR statement so that the program will compute the sum for each of the sets of numbers that follow.

   10 S = 0   Copy this program and
   20 FOR I = _____   complete line 20.
   30 S = S + I
   40 NEXT I
   50 PRINT S

   a. 1, 5, 9, 13, 17
   b. 28, 38, 48, 58, 68, 78

c. 6, 12, 18, 24, 30, 36, 42
d. 11, 22, 33, 44, 55, 66, 77, 88, 99
e. 5, 10, 15, 20, 25, 30, 35, 40, 45, 50

9. Write a computer program to find the sum of:
   a. The consecutive integers from 25 to 50.
   b. The consecutive odd integers from 19 to 73.

10. Write a computer program to find the average of the following numbers:
    102.5, 98.6, 32, 3.14, 66.6

11. Write a computer program to find the average of "n" numbers read in. RUN the program to find the average of the numbers given in Problem 10 above.

Chip's Challenges

Write and RUN a computer program using the accumulating techniques of this chapter for each of the following problems. Results should be printed in sentence form, whenever possible.

12. Tyrone Wilson consulted on five jobs and each job paid a different hourly wage. Find the amount of money Tyrone earned in the week he worked the following hours, at the indicated wages:

    10 hours at $9.50 per hour
     8 hours at $8.75 per hour
     7 hours at $9.25 per hour
     6 hours at $7.95 per hour
     4 hours at $9.75 per hour

13. Louise Lane is the team statistician for Hitech High School's basketball team. She wants to find the total number of points scored during the week. The table shows the scoring record of each player. Field goals (FG) count 2 points each and free throws, (FT) count 1 point each. Write a computer program to help Louise find:
    a. The total points scored by the entire team during the week.
    b. The average number of points scored by each player (there were four games played).

Player Name	Number of FG	FT
Akeem	11	6
Bodell	9	7
Jones	7	10
Morgen	12	7
Smith	10	9
Sturtz	9	9
Wilson	4	4
Zink	3	1

COMPUTER AWARENESS

Rights and Responsibilities

Computers have been used for many different purposes. Unfortunately, they have also been abused and misused.

Computers have been used to help commit crimes, and crimes have been committed to obtain computer data belonging to others. Computers have been used to violate people's privacy and to raise questions about their reputations.

Right now, no matter who you are or where you are, there is almost certainly somewhere a computer that contains data about you.

Hospitals, schools, and busi-

Keeping records is an important computer job. Keeping records safe is a human task.

nesses all maintain **data banks**. The United States government, with all its agencies, has the largest set of computer data banks in the world.

All of these files are confidential. None of the record keepers is allowed by law to share the information collected without your permission. In most cases you are permitted to look at the files that are kept about you. Any corrections that you wish to make must be included in your file.

Most businesses use special collections of data called credit ratings. When customers want to buy something on credit (using payments spread over several months or years), the business asks their permission to get a credit rating. They get this from a credit bureau.

Credit bureaus maintain data banks with personal information about people who use credit to make purchases. By law, only data that affect the credit rating can be included. The credit bureau is allowed to supply its reports only to companies that have a right to know.

Sometimes, however, mistakes find their way into the data bank, mistakes that make a customer seem to be unreliable. Such mistakes can mean that a customer whose bills have always been paid on time is nonetheless denied the right to buy something on credit.

Such customers can demand additional information from the business. They can demand to know why credit has been refused. And they can ask that their version of the "error" be included in the file. The original denial of credit remains as a fact, however, even though the correction will be included in future reports.

Credit information more than seven years old must be removed from the data bank. This helps to correct old errors. It also, however, removes evidence of long-term reliability.

Other information about people, their money, and what they do with it is kept by banks, social agencies, and tax-collecting departments. Most people want this information to be kept confidential. They know records are needed, but they are concerned about the availability of so much personal information. They are afraid it might be used, without their permission, by people who have no right to see the data.

These people have a right to be concerned. Data security is impor-

tant. Unauthorized use of information can hurt you and other people. It can hurt businesses. It can hurt governments.

Because of the dangers of unauthorized use, companies and agencies that have data banks use many kinds of security measures. Employees are often required to wear special identification badges with their pictures on them. Software often includes codes or passwords that only authorized persons know. Until these codes are input, the software will not run. Hardware can often be locked. Other hardware will not operate until the user is identified by stored information. Still other hardware is programmed to notify security guards if it is used improperly. There are even special systems to make data appear unreadable to those who are not supposed to see it.

Unfortunately, none of these security systems—or any others yet developed—are foolproof. Data security still depends on the people who use data, whether legally or illegally.

Many people have discovered ways to gain access to data banks illegally. Criminals have transferred money from the bank accounts of others to their own. They have stolen business secrets and plans from computer memories. They have altered vital business information for their own purposes. They have even stolen millions of dollars from large banks.

Not all these people succeed, of course. Many times, their activities, and their identities, are detected by other computers! Local governments may call on state and national data banks to track down criminals. The FBI has a data bank that contains information about criminals and another that contains data about specific crimes. Information about new crimes can be matched with information in these banks to help identify suspects. When arrested, suspects can be tried under either state or federal law, depending on the laws that were broken.

Software piracy is the illegal copying of programs to give or sell to others. It is obviously unfair to the people who have spent valuable time and money preparing the program. Still, piracy is extremely common.

A program belongs to the programmer who wrote it or to the publisher or computer manufacturer who paid to have it written. The owner of a published program can copyright it. (A copyright registers the name of the program and its owner with the government.) A revision of the Copyright Law, which originally protected only material such as books, took effect in 1978. This law makes it a criminal offense to reproduce or copy any work that is "fixed in any tangible medium." A computer disk is a "tangible" medium—it can be touched. The law, therefore, protects the owners of software copyrights. Programs cannot be copied by anyone without permission of the owner of the copyright. People who break this law can be fined, jailed, and ordered to pay damages, money to the copyright owner to make up for lost sales.

Many software publishers use copy-protection schemes in an attempt to stop piracy. These schemes make it very difficult to copy disks. It is not impossible, however, because other publishers sell programs and computer devices designed to defeat the protection. The publishers of the copy programs say that users should be able to make copies of the expensive programs they buy. They know disks can be damaged. They believe users should be able to make backups so that the work they do with their software will not be interrupted.

Misuse and abuse of computers is a human problem. It is growing every day, as more people learn about and use computers. The Privacy Act of 1974, an amendment to the Freedom of Information Act, is an attempt to solve part of the problem. Other laws will no doubt be written as new technology appears. But legislation alone cannot provide the final answer. Only human understanding can do that.

What Do You Know?
1. Can you look at files that contain information about yourself?
2. Can you have errors corrected in that information?
3. What are some of the security measures used to protect data?

What Can You Find Out?
1. What laws has your state passed to protect computer data banks?
2. What data banks might contain information about you?

What Do You Think?
1. What kinds of legislation should the federal government enact to control the use of data?
2. Can computers solve the problems of computer security?

KEEPING IT TOGETHER

Subscripted Variables

Collections of numbers and sets of strings can be stored
and manipulated by a computer. Subscripted variables
are used to store lists and arrays of data.

Lots of Lists

Look at the following programs. Each program and its associated experiment are computer programs which do similar tasks. Do not try to guess the output of an experiment until you RUN the program. Write your guesses on a sheet of paper. Check your answers by entering the experiments and RUNning them.

COMPUTER DISPLAYS

1. PROGRAM

```
NEW
10   READ A, B, C, D, E
20   PRINT E, D, C, B, A
30   DATA 14, 19, 7, 12, 23
40   END
```

EXPERIMENT

```
NEW
5  DIM X(5)
10   READ X(1), X(2), X(3), X(4), X(5)
20   PRINT X(5), X(4), X(3), X(2), X(1)
30   DATA 14, 19, 7, 12, 23
40   END
```

2. PROGRAM

```
NEW
10   READ A, B, C, D, E
20   PRINT A, C, E
30   DATA 14, 19, 7, 12, 23
40   END
```

EXPERIMENT

```
NEW
5  DIM X(5)
10  READ X(1),X(2),X(3),X(4),X(5)
20  PRINT X(1),X(3),X(5)
30  DATA 14,19,7,12,23
40  END
```

3. PROGRAM

```
NEW
10  READ A,B,C,D,E
20  PRINT D,B
30  DATA 14,19,7,12,23
40  END
```

EXPERIMENT

```
NEW
5  DIM X(5)
10  READ X(1),X(4),X(2),X(5),X(3)
20  PRINT X(5),X(4)
30  DATA 14,19,7,12,23
40  END
```

WHAT DID YOU LEARN?

The programs and experiments in *Discover for Yourself* illustrate ways to select and manipulate numbers in a list. In both instances, however, the numbers of the list first had to be stored in the computer. In the programs in *Discover for Yourself*, the letters of the alphabet were used to store the numbers. The first number, 14, was assigned to the variable A; the second number, 19, was assigned to the variable B; and so on, until the fifth number, 23, was assigned to the variable E. This method you already understand.

In the experiments in *Discover for Yourself*, another variable, called a **numeric subscripted variable**, was used to store numbers. The numbers listed in the **DATA** statement were assigned to the numeric subscripted variables in the **READ** statement. The first number was assigned to the first variable, the second number to the second variable, and so on, until the fifth number was assigned to the fifth variable.

All the computer programs in *Discover for Yourself* read in a list **(array)** of five numbers and assigned each number to a specific variable.

Sometimes it is convenient to assign a large set of numbers, called a **list** or an array, using any BASIC variable and numeric subscripted variables.

1. Name the list of numbers using any BASIC variable. Each list of numbers in the experiments in *Discover for Yourself* was called X.

Name	List of Numbers
X	14, 19, 7, 12, 23

Memory Bank

The **DIM** statement is written:

5 DIM X(5)

Line number. / Keyword. / List name. / Maximum number of values in list.

2. Use a **DIM**ension statement to tell the computer the maximum number of values it can expect in a list of numbers. This was done in the experiments by using the **DIM** statement,

5 DIM X(5)

Note: In some instances, with some systems, a **DIM** statement is not necessary. However, it is a good practice to include a **DIM** statement with all subscripted variables.

3. Identify the number in the list using a subscripted variable.

Example:

List Name	List	Position	Identification
X	14	1	X(1)
	19	2	X(2)
	7	3	X(3)
	12	4	X(4)
	23	5	X(5)

A number in a list or array is identified by its position in the list. The position of the number is given in parentheses following the list name. The process of assigning a list of numbers to one

Memory Bank

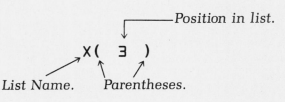

A numeric subscripted variable is written:

X(3)

List Name. / Parentheses. / Position in list.

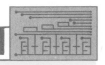
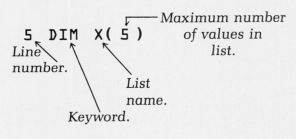

variable, and identifying each number in the list by its position, is called **subscripting**. The subscripted variable, $X(3)$, is read X **sub** 3.

The `DIM` statement must be placed in the program before any subscripted variable is used. In the table below, several examples of the `DIM` statement are shown.

DIM Statement	List Name	Maximum Number of Values
10 DIM X(9)	X	9
12 DIM A(35)	A	35
12 DIM G(7), F(23)	G	7
	F	23
15 DIM R(100)	R	100

Note: Most BASIC systems permit subscripts to begin at zero. For example, $X(0)$ is a valid variable name. Therefore, in a `DIM` statement such as `10  DIM X(15)` the maximum number of values would be 16; $X(0)$, $X(1)$, $X(2)$, ..., $X(15)$.

1. The number of values in a list <u>may be less</u> than the number shown in the `DIM` statement, but may <u>never be more</u> than that number.

2. More than one list may be specified by a `DIM` statement. The list specifications must be separated by commas. See the third example above.

3. In `DIM` statements, only positive integers may appear within the parentheses following the list name.

CHIP SAYS:
HERE ARE SOME
DIM STATEMENT
FACTS TO
REMEMBER.

USE WHAT YOU HAVE LEARNED

Study the subscripted variable program at the top of the next page and answer the following questions. Write your answers on a sheet of paper.

1. What is the name of the list of numbers to be read?

2. What is the maximum number of values in the list?

3. What is the output of the subscripted variable program?

PROGRAM

```
NEW
10 REM SUBSCRIPTED VARIABLE PROGRAM
15 DIM Y(4)
20 READ Y(1),Y(2),Y(3),Y(4)
30 PRINT "LIST "; Y(1),Y(2),Y(3),Y(4)
40 PRINT "REVERSE "; Y(4),Y(3),Y(2),Y(1)
50 PRINT "SECOND NUMBER "; Y(2)
60 DATA 59,32,61,14
70 END
```

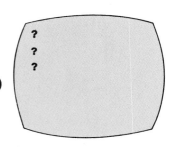

Enter the program and check your answers. This program illustrates the use of numeric subscripted variables. The computer reads in four values and places them in the Y-list. The maximum number of values allowed in the Y-list is four. The numbers are then displayed, first in the order in which they were read in, then in reverse order. Finally, only the second value in the list is printed.

E x e r c i s e s

1. Consider the following list of numbers, called list B:
13, 17, 42, 19, 83, 84
   a. What is the value of B(4)?   **b.** What is the value of
   c. What is the value of B(1)?   B(2)?
                                      d. What is the
                                         value of B(3)?

2. What is the maximum number of values in each list identified by the following DIM statements?
   a. 10 DIM A(29)   **b.** 13 DIM X(11)
   c. 14 DIM K(56)   **d.** 15 DIM B(75)

3. Consider the partial program below.
```
5  DIM R(5)
10  READ R(1),R(2),R(3),R(4),R(5)
20  _____ Missing statement.
30  DATA 6,8,10,12,14
```
What would be printed if each of the following lines were inserted as line 20?
   a. 20 PRINT R(2)
   b. 20 PRINT R(5),R(4),R(3),R(2),R(1)
   c. 20 PRINT R(3),R(2),R(5)
   d. 20 PRINT R(6)

4. Complete the following program to read the five numbers listed in the DATA statement, assign the values to the

B-list, and print the first, third, and fifth values in the list.

```
NEW
10  DIM_____
15  READ B(1), B(2), _____, B(4), _____
20  PRINT _____, _____, _____
25  DATA 35, 45, 55, 65, 75
30  END
```

5. Enter and **RUN** the program of Exercise 4 to check your answer and to verify the required computer output.

6. Determine the output of this program. Enter and **RUN** the program to check your answer.

```
NEW
5  DIM D(6)
10  READ D(1), D(2), D(3), D(4), D(5), D(6)
15  X = D(1) + D(2) + D(3)
20  Y = D(6) - D(5)
25  A = X/Y
30  IF A = D(3) THEN GOTO 50
40  PRINT D(5), D(3), D(1)
45  GOTO 60
50  PRINT D(6), D(4), D(2)
55  DATA 2, 4, 6, 8, 10, 12
60  END
```

Chip's Challenges

7. Using numeric subscripted variables, write a computer program to read in lists A and B. Then:
   a. Print the numbers in each list in reverse order.
   b. Print the sum of the numbers in each list.

List A	List B
8	18
14	32
19	23
30	42

8. Study this program and determine its output. Enter and **RUN** the program to check your answer.

```
NEW
5  DIM G(5)
10  READ G(1), G(2), G(3), G(4), G(5)
15  S = 0
20  FOR I = 1 TO 5
25  S = S + G(I)
30  PRINT G(I)
35  NEXT I
40  PRINT S
45  DATA 10, 20, 30, 40, 50
```

16.2

Playing with Arrays

DISCOVER FOR YOURSELF

Study the programs below. For each program, guess the computer's output. Write your guesses on a sheet of paper. Check your answers by entering and RUNning the programs.

PROGRAM

COMPUTER DISPLAYS

1. NEW
```
5  DIM K(4)
15  READ K(1),K(2),K(3),K(4)
20  PRINT K(1),K(2),K(3),K(4)
30  DATA 10,20,30,40
35  END
```

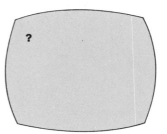

2. NEW
```
5  DIM K(4)
10  FOR I = 1 TO 4
15  READ K(I)
20  PRINT K(I),
25  NEXT I
30  DATA 10,20,30,40
35  END
```

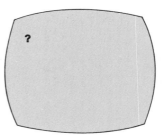

WHAT DID YOU LEARN?

The data entry procedure of Program 1 of *Discover for Yourself* is not an improvement over entering data using letters of the alphabet, such as:

```
10  READ A,B,C,D
```

In fact, it takes more time and space to write

```
10  READ K(1), K(2), K(3), K(4)
```

than

```
10  READ A, B, C, D
```

Why subscripted variables then? Look at Program 2 of *Discover for Yourself*. This disadvantage was eliminated. The subscripted variables K(1), K(2), K(3), and K(4) were written as K(I), where I was assigned the values 1, 2, 3, and 4. The values of I supply the position of each number in the K list or array.

The program analysis explains the use of the numeric subscripted variable K(I) to read in and print the numbers of the K-list of Program 2 of *Discover for Yourself*.

CHIP SAYS:
STUDY THE ANALYSIS
OF PROGRAM 2
BELOW.

Program Analysis

Statement	Explanation
5 DIM K(4)	This statement identifies K as the list name. The maximum number of values in the K-list, 4, is identified.
10 FOR I = 1 TO 4	The execution of the FOR-NEXT loop begins with I = 1.
15 READ K(I)	The value of I is 1. The <u>first</u> entry from the K-list is read in and assigned the variable name K(1). Thus, K(1) = 10.
20 PRINT K(I),	The value of I is still 1. The number 10 is printed since K(1) = 10. What does the comma make the computer do?
25 NEXT I	The value of I is incremented, or increased, by 1 at this point. Therefore, I = 2.
15 READ K(I)	The <u>second</u> entry from the K-list is read in and assigned the variable name K(2). So, K(2) = 20.
20 PRINT K(I),	The value of I is 2 at this point. The number 20 is printed since K(2) = 20.

The computer will continue to execute the three steps of the FOR-NEXT loop,

```
15  READ K(I)
20  PRINT K(I),
25  NEXT I
```

until the index, I, reaches a value of 4. Then the

fourth value of the K-list will be entered, $K(4)$ = 40, and printed by the computer. $I = 4$ is the final value of the index of FOR statement. The computer then terminates or ends the execution of the program.

USE WHAT YOU HAVE LEARNED

There are occasions when it is desirable to enter a list—or several lists—of numbers and then perform certain tasks with them. Dr. Marcella Yerman, Chief Manager of the Chemical Division of the Glacial Products Corporation, was given the March report. It showed the number of hours each employee in her division worked each week of the month.

Dr. Yerman needs a report that indicates the total number of hours each of these employees worked during March. She also needs the total number of hours worked by all the employees in her division during March.

GLACIAL PRODUCTS CORPORATION

Chemical Division

March Weekly Report

Employee	First	Second	Third	Fourth
1	38	42	31	55
2	45	39	40	22
3	33	23	18	34
4	54	45	43	37
5	52	51	48	44
6	18	21	34	46

Dr. Yerman wrote a computer program to do this task for her. She considered the three main parts of any computer program:

INITIALIZE   **PROCESS**   **OUTPUT**

INITIALIZE ————————————————————→

```
15  FOR E = 1 TO 6
20  READ F(E), S(E), T(E), H(E)

40  NEXT E
45  DATA statement with
    data listed in proper
    order.
```

Dr. Yerman decided to use a $READ$ statement and a $FOR-NEXT$ loop with numeric subscripted variables to input the data. The hours worked each week were given list names:

First week: F-list.
Second week: S-list.
Third week: T-list.
Fourth week: H-list.

PROCESS
```
15  FOR E = 1 TO 6
25  A = F(E)+S(E)+T(E)+H(E)

10  B = 0
35  B = B + A
40  NEXT E
```

Once the data was entered from each list, Dr. Yerman needed to calculate the sum of the numbers whose position was the same in each list. She also needed to accumulate each of these sums, **A**, in order to report the total number of hours worked by all the employees in her division.

OUTPUT

Dr. Yerman decided to display the total number of hours worked by each employee in the form, EMPLOYEE "number" TOTAL HOURS "sum", using the statement,

```
30  PRINT "EMPLOYEE "; E; " TOTAL HOURS "; A
```

The total number of hours worked by all employees was written

```
50  PRINT "TOTAL HOURS ALL EMPLOYEES "; B
```

Dr. Yerman's program is shown below. Study the program to determine the output. Check your answer by entering the program. Note the order of the numbers listed in the **DATA** statements. The first four numbers are in Position 1 in each list, the next four numbers are in Position 2 in each list, and so on, until the last four numbers are in Position 6 in each list.

```
NEW
5   DIM F(6), S(6), T(6), H(6)
10    B = 0
15    FOR E = 1 TO 6
20    READ F(E), S(E), T(E), H(E)
25    A = F(E) + S(E) + T(E) + H(E)
30    PRINT "EMPLOYEE "; E; " TOTAL HOURS"; A
35    B = B + A
40    NEXT E
45    DATA 38, 42, 31, 55, 45, 39, 40, 22
46    DATA 33, 23, 18, 34, 54, 45, 43, 37
47    DATA 52, 51, 48, 44, 18, 21, 34, 46
50    PRINT "TOTAL HOURS ALL EMPLOYEES "; B
55    END
```

CHIP SAYS:
COMPARE YOUR OUTPUT WITH DR. YERMAN'S BOARD OF DIRECTOR'S REPORT SHOWN ON THE SCREEN.

```
EMPLOYEE 1 TOTAL HOURS 166
EMPLOYEE 2 TOTAL HOURS 146
EMPLOYEE 3 TOTAL HOURS 108
EMPLOYEE 4 TOTAL HOURS 179
EMPLOYEE 5 TOTAL HOURS 195
EMPLOYEE 6 TOTAL HOURS 119
TOTAL HOURS ALL EMPLOYEES 913
```

Dr. Yerman's Report

E x e r c i s e s

1. Consider the partial program below.
   ```
   10  DIM X(10)
   20  FOR I = 1 TO 5
   30  X(I) = 2 * I
   40  NEXT I
   ```
   a. What is the value of X(2)?
   b. What is the value of X(4)?

2. Lee Lyter wished to write a program to enter ten numbers. However, Lee wanted to print only the second, fourth, sixth, eighth, and tenth values of the numbers entered. Help Lee by supplying the missing expressions in her program.
   ```
   10  REM LEE LYTER LIST
   15  DIM X(10)
   20  FOR I = 1 TO 10
   30  READ _____
   40  NEXT I
   50  FOR I = 2 TO 10 _____
   60  PRINT _____
   70  NEXT I
   80  DATA 13, 17, 19, 8, 42
   85  DATA 51, 32, 29, 18, 35
   90  END
   ```

3. What statements, if any, of Lee Lyter's program in Exercise 2 must be changed if there are fifty numbers in the X-array?

4. Do the indices of the FOR—NEXT loops of Lee Lyter's program of Exercise 2 have to be identical?

5. Change only one statement of Lee Lyter's program to have the computer print only the numbers of the X-array which are in odd-numbered positions in the array.

Chip's Challenges

6. Consider the partial program below.

```
10  DIM R(10),M(10)
20  FOR I = 2 TO 10 STEP 2
30  R(I) = I/2
40  M(I) = R(I) * R(I)
50  NEXT I
```

a. What values are assigned to `I`?

b. Copy the table below and fill in the missing values.
Note: A subscript may be an expression.

Value of I	Value of R(I)	Value of M(I)
2	_____	1
_____	2	_____
6	3	_____
_____	_____	16
_____	5	_____

7. Study the program below. What value will be assigned to `S` when the program is executed? Enter and `RUN` the program to check your answer.

```
10  DIM Y(5)
20  FOR I = 1 TO 5
30  READ Y(I)
40  NEXT I
50  S = 0
60  FOR I = 1 TO 5 STEP 2
70  S = S + Y(I)
80  NEXT I
85  DATA 10, 20, 30, 40, 50
90  PRINT S
95  END
```

8. Write a computer program that will produce the sequence of numbers described as follows:

The first two numbers, `A(1)` and `A(2)`, are both equal to 1. The third number, `A(3)`, and each number thereafter, is produced by adding together the two preceding numbers.

That is, $A(3) = A(1) + A(2) = 1 + 1 = 2$
$A(4) = A(2) + A(3) = 1 + 2 = 3$
$A(5) = A(3) + A(4) = 2 + 3 = 5$
and so on.

Enter your program to generate and print the first twenty numbers in the sequence.

Sets of Strings

Study the programs below. **String subscripted variables** are used in the programs to process data. Guess the output of the programs. Write your guesses on a sheet of paper, then enter and RUN the programs to check your answers.

PROGRAM

COMPUTER DISPLAYS

1.
```
5   DIM N$(4)
15   READ N$(1), N$(2), N$(3), N$(4)
20   PRINT N$(1), N$(2), N$(3), N$(4)
30   DATA MARIE, MARCY, ANNA, JOE
40   END
```

2.
```
5   DIM N$(4)
10   FOR I = 1 TO 4
15   READ N$(I)
20   PRINT N$(I),
25   NEXT I
30   DATA MARIE, MARCY, ANNA, JOE
40   END
```

Both programs in *Discover for Yourself* show that string data can be processed using string subscripted variables. The procedure for subscripting strings is similar to the procedure used when subscripting numeric data.

1. A list or array of strings is given a name, using any BASIC string variable. Each list of strings in the programs in *Discover for Yourself* was called N$.

Name	List of Strings
N$	MARIE, MARCY, ANNA, JOE

2. A DIMension statement is used to tell the computer the maximum number of strings in the list or array. This was done in both programs in *Discover for Yourself*, using the DIM statement,

5 DIM N$(4)

3. A subscripted variable is used to identify a string in the list.

In both programs, the strings of the DATA statement were given string subscripted variable names,

N$(1) = MARIE
N$(2) = MARCY
N$(3) = ANNA
N$(4) = JOE

Memory Bank

The DIM statement is written:

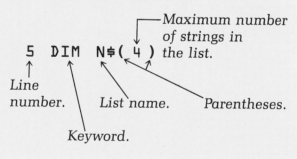

Maximum number of strings in the list.

5   DIM   N$(4)

Line number.

List name.

Parentheses.

Keyword.

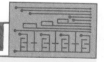

Memory Bank

A string subscripted variable is written:

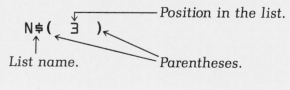

Position in the list.

N$(3)

List name.

Parentheses.

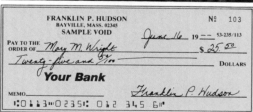

Chip's Bits

FRANKLIN P. HUDSON
BAYVILLE, MASS. 02345
SAMPLE VOID   Nº 103

PAY TO THE ORDER OF *Mary M. Wright*   *June 16* 19 _ _   53-235/113

$ *25.50*

Twenty-five and 50/100 ———————— DOLLARS

Your Bank

MEMO_____   *Franklin P. Hudson*

⑈0⑈⑈3⑈0235⑈: 0⑈2 345 6⑈

Have you ever noticed the strange-looking characters on the bottom of a check? These are MICR letters and numerals. They are printed with magnetic ink. They can be read by a Magnetic Ink Character Reader, which sends their information into the bank's computers.

Example:

List Name	List	Position	Identification
X$	JOHN	1	X$(1)
	MARY	2	X$(2)
	BILL	3	X$(3)
	ANDREA	4	X$(4)
	JAMES	5	X$(5)
	HELEN	6	X$(6)

A string in a list or array is identified by its position in the list. The position of the string is given in parentheses, following the list name. The process of assigning a list of strings to one variable is called subscripting. The subscripted variable, X$(2), is read X string sub 2.

USE WHAT YOU HAVE LEARNED

The monthly report of hours worked by each employee of the Chemical Division was well received by the Board of Directors. However, it was recommended by the President of the Glacial Products Corporation, Dr. Marie Schiller, that the names of the employees ought to be listed, rather than their employee numbers. The Board agreed. All monthly reports were sent back to the Personnel Department so the Department could put employees' names on the forms. Shown below is the monthly report sent to the Chemical Division by the Personnel Department.

GLACIAL PRODUCTS CORPORATION

Chemical Division

March Weekly Report

Employee	First	Second	Third	Fourth
Matt Diggins	38	42	31	55
Bea Rodriguez	45	39	40	22
Marge Leone	33	23	18	34
Joseph Sansky	54	45	43	37
George Abel	52	51	48	44
Sam Lucas	18	21	34	46

When Dr. Marcella Yerman received the report, she knew that a string subscripted variable was needed in her program to read in and print the names of the employees. However, this time she and her staff decided to output the data processed in a different form. Dr. Yerman and her staff wrote a program to print out data in columns, using the headings shown below.

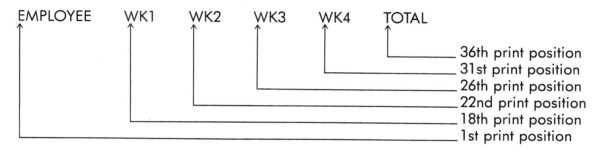

| EMPLOYEE | WK1 | WK2 | WK3 | WK4 | TOTAL |

36th print position
31st print position
26th print position
22nd print position
18th print position
1st print position

Using **TAB** functions to print data as noted above, and subscripted variables to process data, Dr. Yerman's original program was changed to print the names of the employees in the Chemical Division.

Chemical Division Program—Prepared by Dr. Yerman and staff.

```
5   DIM N$(6), F(6), S(6), T(6), H(6)
10  B = 0
13  PRINT "EMPLOYEE"; TAB(17); "WK1"; TAB(21); "WK2";
TAB(25); "WK3"; TAB(30); "WK4"; TAB(34); "TOTAL"
15  FOR E = 1 TO 6
20  READ N$(E), F(E), S(E), T(E), H(E)
25  A = F(E) + S(E) + T(E) + H(E)
30  PRINT N$(E); TAB(17); F(E); TAB(21); S(E); TAB(25);
T(E); TAB(30); H(E); TAB(35); A
35  B = B + A
40  NEXT E
45  PRINT "TOTAL HOURS ALL EMPLOYEES"; TAB(35); B
50  DATA · · · · · · · · · · · · · · · · · Supply data here.
55  END
```

Study the Chemical Division program carefully. List, in proper order, the necessary data in the **DATA** statement which would produce the output shown to the left. Enter the program, using your **DATA** statement. **RUN** the program to check your output with that shown on the screen to the left.

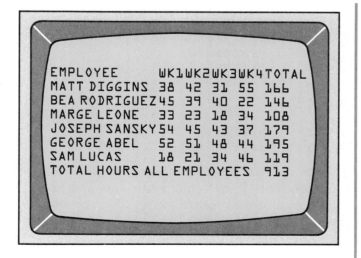

```
EMPLOYEE      WK1WK2WK3WK4TOTAL
MATT DIGGINS  38 42 31 55 166
BEA RODRIGUEZ 45 39 40 22 146
MARGE LEONE   33 23 18 34 108
JOSEPH SANSKY 54 45 43 37 179
GEORGE ABEL   52 51 48 44 195
SAM LUCAS     18 21 34 46 119
TOTAL HOURS ALL EMPLOYEES   913
```

RANDOM SILLY MESSAGES

Look at another example of the use of string subscripted variables. Most people are familiar with the statement,

APPLE A DAY KEEPS THE DOCTOR AWAY

Fruit   Time   Verb   Person   Condition

Suppose you randomly select words from several lists and substitute the selected words for those in the statements.

Fruit	Time	Verb	Person	Condition
APPLE	DAY	KEEPS	DOCTOR	AWAY
ORANGE	WEEK	HELPS	LAWYER	THERE
BANANA	MONTH	SENDS	CHIEF	HERE
LEMON	YEAR	CALLS	MINISTER	NOW

For example, select the words BANANA, WEEK, CALLS, CHIEF, and THERE from the lists above. The message then becomes:

BANANA A WEEK CALLS THE CHIEF THERE

James and Beth thought it would be a clever idea to have the computer randomly select the words from each list and then print the message. James decided to name each list in the following manner:

    FRUIT as the F-list.
    TIME as the T-list.
    VERB as the V-list.
    PERSON as the P-list.
    CONDITION as the W-list.

He then used string subscripted variables, F\$, T\$, V\$, P\$, and W\$, to process the data. Beth created the expression,

INT(4 * RND(1) + 1)

TRS-80 users substitute RND(4)

This will make the computer randomly select an integer from 1 to 4, inclusive. The expression was used in their program to select one word from each list. Together, they wrote the Random Silly Message Program shown.

Random Silly Message Program

```
5   DIM F$(4),T$(4),V$(4),P$(4),W$(4)
10  FOR I = 1 TO 4
15  READ F$(I),T$(I),V$(I),P$(I),W$(I)
20  NEXT I
25  FOR J = 1 TO 10
26  A = INT(4 * RND(1) + 1)
27  B = INT(4 * RND(1) + 1)
28  C = INT(4 * RND(1) + 1)
29  D = INT(4 * RND(1) + 1)
30  E = INT(4 * RND(1) + 1)
35  PRINT F$(A);" A ";T$(B);" ";V$(C);" THE ";P$(D);
" ";W$(E)
40  NEXT J
45  DATA...........Supply data here.
50  END
```

Study the Random Silly Message Program carefully. James and Beth used numeric variables as arguments in the string subscripted variables of the PRINT statement. Why? That is correct. This is the way a word is selected from each list. The numeric variables, A, B, C, D, and E, are the names of the randomly-selected integers 1 to 4, inclusive. The values of A, B, C, D, and E determine which of the words is selected from each list. For example, if the words were listed as shown in the lists on page 296, then:

F$(3) = BANANA V$(4) = CALLS W$(3) = HERE
T$(1) = DAY   P$(2) = LAWYER

The output of one RUN of the program by James and Beth is shown to the left.

```
ORANGE A YEAR HELPS THE MINISTER AWAY
APPLE A DAY SENDS THE MINISTER HERE
BANANA A DAY SENDS THE CHIEF THERE
APPLE A DAY HELPS THE CHIEF NOW
LEMON A MONTH KEEPS THE DOCTOR AWAY
LEMON A DAY SENDS THE CHIEF NOW
BANANA A MONTH CALLS THE CHIEF THERE
BANANA A WEEK HELPS THE LAWYER NOW
LEMON A MONTH HELPS THE MINISTER AWAY
APPLE A WEEK KEEPS THE CHIEF THERE
```

Write the information in the DATA statements in the order shown in the lists on page 324. Enter and RUN the program. Compare your results with the output shown. Should the messages be the same? The chance that all messages are the same is very, very slim. Do you know how many different messages could be printed? The answer is:

FRUIT	TIME	VERB	PERSON	CONDITION	TOTAL MESSAGES
↓	↓	↓	↓	↓	↓
4 ×	4 ×	4 ×	4 ×	4 =	1024

N-list	E-list
people	love
animals	peace
cars	beauty
towers	warm
caves	cold
mountains	signals

1. Using N$ and E$ as string subscripted variables for the N-list and E-list on the left, respectively, what is the value of each of the following variables?
   a. N$(6)   **b.** E$(1)   **c.** E$(4)
   d. N$(2)   **e.** N$(5)   **f.** E$(3)

2. Two more employees were hired by the Glacial Products Corporation. They were sent to the Chemical Division by Dr. Marie Schiller. What changes, if any, are necessary in the Chemical Division Program to process eight names rather than six?

3. Alter the Chemical Division Program to process any number of employees in the division.

4. What changes, if any, must be made by James and Beth in their Random Silly Message Program if each list of words contains eight rather than four words?

5. Alter the Random Silly Message Program to process any number of words in each list, where all lists have the same number of words.

N-list	V-list	E-list
people	sent	love
animals	are	peace
cars	went	beauty
towers	will	warm
caves	ran	cold
mountains	swam	signals

6. Write a Random Silly Message Program to select the words from the lists shown on the left and to print messages in the forms:

N-list V-list E-list
      and
E-list V-list N-list

Enter and **RUN** your program.

7. Change Dr. Yerman's Chemical Division Program on page 323 to print each employee's name, last name first. Enter your program and **RUN** it, using the March Weekly Report on page 322. Hint: See Sally's Program on page 280.

8. Alter James' and Beth's Random Silly Message Program to print a message where any word from any list can be used in the **PRINT** statement, to produce a message such as:

DOCTOR A KEEPS DAY THE AWAY APPLE
                    Any Word.

Enter your program and **RUN** it, using the words in the lists on page 324.

CHAPTER SUMMARY

1. A list of numbers or strings can be stored in a computer by means of subscripted variables where:
   a. The entire list of numbers or strings is given a variable name.
   b. Each number or string in the list is identified by its position in the list.

2. The form of a subscripted variable is:

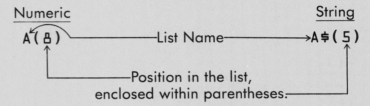

Numeric   String

A(8) ──────────List Name────────→A$(5)

──────────Position in the list,
enclosed within parentheses.

3. A DIMension statement is used to identify the maximum number of values in a list of numbers and/or strings.

4. The form of a DIMension statement is:

Maximum number of positions in each list.

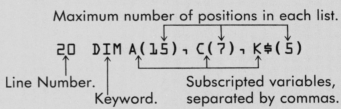

20   DIM A(15), C(7), K$(5)

Line Number.   Subscripted variables,
         Keyword.   separated by commas.

5. A DIM statement must be present before any subscripted variable is used in the program.

6. The number of values in a list may be less than the number shown in the DIM statement, but never more.

7. More than one list may be specified by a DIM statement. The list specifications must be separated by commas.

8. The position of a number or string in a list may be indicated by a variable, such as T(A) or K$(I).

9. The position of a number or string in a list may be indicated by an expression, such as X(I + 5), B$(2 * K), or R(INT(6*RND(1))).

10. Subscripted variables are often used because they:
    a. Provide a larger supply of variable names.
    b. Offer a simple technique for selecting numbers or strings from a list.
    c. Provide an improvement in the manipulation of data.

11. The process of assigning a list of numbers or strings to one variable, and identifying each number or string in the list by its position, is called subscripting.

Example:

Identification	Q-list	Position	D$-list	Identification
Q(1)	1984	1	WOW	D$(1)
Q(2)	1492	2	HOHO	D$(2)
Q(3)	1776	3	GEE	D$(3)
Q(4)	1863	4	BYE	D$(4)

PROBLEM SET 16

1. The numbers in the DATA statement

   50 DATA 19, 18, 6, 45, 38, 92, 38, 47, 53, 62

   are to be entered into a B-list in the order listed. What number will be assigned to each of the following variables?

   a. B(2)   b. B(9)
   c. B(5)   d. B(10)
   e. B(1)   f. B(7)

2. Identify each of the following numeric subscripted variables as valid or invalid. If invalid, describe the error.

   a. A(3)   b. R13
   c. X(-5)   d. 25(J)
   e. G(114)   f. J(3.7)

Position	N$-list
1	TIGER
2	GIRAFFE
3	MONKEY
4	ELEPHANT
5	LION
6	PARROT

3. The strings listed in the N$-list to the left are to be entered in the order shown. What string will be assigned to each of the following variables?

   a. N$(3)   b. N$(2)
   c. N$(6)   d. N$(1)
   e. N$(5)   f. N$(4)

4. Identify each of the following string subscripted variables as valid or invalid. If invalid, describe the error.

   a. J$(3)   b. D$55
   c. (15)N$ d. M$(33.4)
   e. V$(17)   f. N(34)$

5. What is the maximum number of values in each list identified by the following DIM statements?

a. ⌶0 DIM J(⌶4) **b.** ⌶5 DIM H$(L0)

c. ⌶5 DIM F$(35) **d.** ⌶0 DIM G(⌶00)

6. The numbers in the DATA statement

⅁0 DATA 34, 47, L3, 82, 75, 3⅁, 23, ⌶7, ⅁4, 40

are to be entered into a K-list in the order listed. What variable name will be assigned to each of the numbers below?

a. 23 **b.** 34
c. 82 **d.** 17
e. 94 **f.** 63

7. Indicate whether each of the following **DIM** statements is valid or invalid. If invalid, indicate the error.

a. DIM X(⌶7) **b.** ⌶0 DIM A$(⌶5)
c. ⌶0 DIM $(30) **d.** 5 DIM R(⌶5)
e. ⌶0 DIM(50) **f.** ⌶5 DIM G(3) X$(5)

8. Consider the partial program below.

```
5  DIM N(L)
10  READ N(1), N(2), N(3), N(4), N(5), N(L)
20  _____ Missing statement.
30  DATA 5, 10, 15, 20, 25, 30
```

What will be printed if each of the following lines is inserted as line 20?

a. PRINT N(L)
b. PRINT N(5), N(3), N(1)
c. PRINT N(2) + N(4)
d. PRINT N(2), N(4), N(L)
e. PRINT N(1) + N(2) + N(3), N(4) + N(5) + N(L)

9. Complete the program below to read the numbers listed in the **DATA** statement, assign the values to the G-list, and print the numbers in reverse order.

```
NEW
10  DIM__
15  READ G(1), __, G(3), __, G(5), __
20  PRINT __, __, __, __, __, __
25  DATA 17, 34, 42, 1⅁, 27, L1
30  END
```

Enter and RUN the program to check your answer.

10. Determine the output of this program. Enter the program and RUN it to check your answer.

```
NEW
5  DIM T$(4)
10  FOR I = 1 TO 4
```

```
15   READ T$(I)
20   DATA MY, DOG, HAS, FLEAS
25   NEXT I
30   FOR J = 4 TO 1 STEP -1
35   PRINT T$(J);
40   NEXT J
45   END
```

11. Write a sequence of program steps that would permit 1000 numbers to be entered and printed, as entered. Assume that the necessary **DATA** statements are present.

12. Determine the output of the following program sequence. Enter and **RUN** it.
```
10   DIM X(10)
20   FOR I = 1 TO 5
30   X(I) = I
40   X(11-I) = X(I)
50   NEXT I
60   FOR I = 1 TO 10
70   PRINT X(I),
80   NEXT I
```

13. Write a computer program that will enter 30 numbers, using a **FOR-NEXT** loop. Using another **FOR-NEXT** loop, have every third number printed by the computer. Enter your program, using the following data:
1, 2, 3, 2, 3, 4, 3, 4, 5, 4, 5, 6, 5, 6, 7, 6, 7, 8, 7, 8, 9, 8, 9, 10, 9, 10, 11, 10, 11, 12
RUN your program.

14. The Square Wheel Used Car Company is reducing the price of its cars by 15 percent. Write and process a computer program, using subscripted variables, which will calculate the average reduction in price of the cars. The Square Wheel cars originally sold for 2143, 1875, 3544, 1975, 3200, 2550, 3657, and 4441 dollars.

15. Consider this program:
```
10   DIM G$(12)
20   FOR I = 1 TO 12
30   READ G$(I)
40   NEXT I
50   FOR J = 2 TO 12 STEP 2
60   PRINT G$(J);
70   NEXT J
80   DATA A, S, E, T, X, R, K
81   DATA I, L, N, Q, G
90   END
```
a. What letter is assigned to **G$(4)**?

    b. What letter is assigned to G$(9)?

    c. What would be printed as a result of executing the program? Enter and RUN the program to check your answer.

16. Consider this program:

```
10   DIM B$(12)
20   INPUT A$
30   FOR J = 1 TO 12
40   READ B$(J)
50   NEXT J
60   IF A$ = "YES" THEN GOTO 90
70   PRINT B$(1), B$(11), B$(5), B$(3), B$(7), B$(9)
80   GOTO 110
90   PRINT B$(10), B$(6), B$(12), B$(2), B$(8), B$(4)
100   DATA JACK, SEVEN, EAT, AGO, COULD
101   DATA SCORE, NO, YEARS, FAT
102   DATA FOUR, SPRAT, AND
110   END
```

    a. What word is assigned to B$(10)?

    b. What word is assigned to B$(3)?

    c. What message would be printed if the word YES were entered after RUN?

    d. Rewrite line 60 so that the message of Part c will be printed as a result of entering NO.

    e. What message would be printed as a result of entering the word OK after RUN?

17. Write and process—enter and RUN—a computer program to read in the four words HOW, NOW, BROWN, and COW into an array and print the words randomly, in ten sentences of four words each.

Chip's Challenges

18. Write a computer program that will assign an A-list of twenty variables as follows:
Read two numbers A(1) and A(2) from a DATA statement.
Have each variable with an odd subscript set equal to A(1).
Have each variable with an even subscript set equal to A(2).
Enter and RUN your program, using A(1) = 2.5 and A(2) = 7.1.

19. State College conducted a survey to determine the most popular cartoon character among Snoopy, Garfield,

Pogo, and Krazy Kat. Write a computer program to count the number of votes cast for each character, if the data numbers 1, 2, 3, and 4 correspond to votes, as follows:

1 — Vote for Snoopy.
2 — Vote for Garfield.
3 — Vote for Pogo.
4 — Vote for Krazy Kat.

Forty-eight people participated in the survey and cast votes as follows:

2, 3, 4, 3, 1, 1, 4, 1, 2, 2, 2, 1, 3, 4, 3, 4, 1, 4, 4, 1, 1, 2, 1, 3, 1, 1, 3, 4, 4, 2, 3, 4, 3, 4, 1, 2, 4, 1, 3, 4, 1, 2, 1, 4, 4, 2, 2, 1

Process your program using the above entries. Which cartoon character was most popular? Surprised?

20. The Glacial Products Button Department received a three-day contract to produce buttons. There are five employees in the Button Department. The list below shows how much time each employee spent producing buttons on each of the days.

Name	Day 1	Day 2	Day 3
Jacobson	5 h	6 h	3 h
Fitzgerald	3 h	2 h	5 h
Jackson	5 h	2 h	4 h
Garcia	7 h	3 h	5 h
Homa	5 h	4 h	2 h

Write and process a computer program to enter the data above. Have the program print the total number of hours worked by each employee and the total number of hours worked by all employees. Output the data in column form, using the headings:

NAME	DAY1	DAY2	DAY3	TOTAL

21. Write and process a computer program to read the twenty-six letters of the alphabet into an array. Print ten five-letter words, with each letter of each word randomly selected.

22. Determine the output of the program sequence below. Enter the sequence and RUN it.

```
10  DIM X(6)
20  FOR I = 1 TO 6
30  READ X(I)
40  NEXT I
50  FOR I = 1 TO 6
60  PRINT X(INT(I/2) + 1)
70  NEXT I
80  DATA 1, 2, 3, 4, 5, 6
```

Computers of the Future

No one can predict the future—but it is sure to be full of computers.

Each day, the lives of more and more people are touched by computers. In this chapter, you are going to look at some of the new developments. There is a problem, however. These developments are new as this book is being <u>written</u>. But by the time you <u>read</u> this, they will no longer be new. Some will be commonplace. Others may still be under development, but much further along. And there will be a whole group of new developments that are only ideas in someone's mind as this is being written. Keep this in mind as you read.

The world may be developing a cashless, paperless society, where people can work, shop, and play without ever leaving their homes. Some of the developments that will make this possible are:

Telecommuting, working at home at a terminal connected to computers in the business headquarters.

Teleconferencing with associates anywhere in the country, eliminating expensive, time-consuming business trips.

Information Networks providing access to research data stored in electronic "books."

Electronic Mail, transferring letters and memos without paper or postage.

Robotics, performing jobs in industry and in the home.

Computerized appliances, making housework easier.

Computerized teaching, drilling, testing, and recording progress, in the school or at home.

Electronic bank tellers, accepting deposits, cashing checks, and even making loans.

On the technical side, scientists and engineers are working to make computers smaller, faster, cheaper, and easier to use. They are designing memories and peripheral devices to hold more information.

Videodisks are being developed for data storage. Each disk can hold more than ten **gigabytes** of information on each side. (A gigabyte is one billion bytes or one thousand megabytes.) That is more than five thousand floppy disks can store!

Manufacturers are developing **bubble memory storage** that does not depend on electricity to retain information. Devices incorporating this will probably be used as peripheral memory or for information storage.

Other scientists are working on **transphasors**, or optical switches.

These can go from on to off in **picoseconds** (trillionths of a second) instead of **nanoseconds** (billionths of a second) as transistors do.

Scientists all over the world are racing to produce the first fifth generation computers. These computers, they say, will possess artificial intelligence and be capable of "learning" as they operate. They will obey oral instructions, spoken in ordinary language. They will probably use **Very Large Scale Integrated Circuits** (VLSI), capable of doing the work of thousands of the chips now in use. They may include more than one processor, with each assigned a part of a very large program. Working together, the processors could execute the program as quickly as today's microcomputers run your programs!

Charles Kettering, automotive engineer, inventor, and one of the founders of General Motors, once said, "We should all be concerned about the future because we will have to spend the rest of our lives there." No one knows just what the future holds. But one thing is certain: the computer is going to be part of it.

What Do You Know?
1. How is the "Computer Revolution" affecting our society?
2. Why may the world of the future be cashless and paperless?

What Can You Find Out?
1. What new storage devices are available for your computer?
2. Do banks in your community use electronic bank tellers?
3. Do any manufacturers in your community use robotics?

What Do You Think?
1. Will computers make life easier or more difficult in the future?
2. What remarkable things might a fifth generation computer do?

MAKING IT RUN
Debugging and Editing

Programming mistakes are called bugs. Some bugs are marked for extermination by the computer. Others must be tracked by the programmer and eliminated before the program can be run successfully.

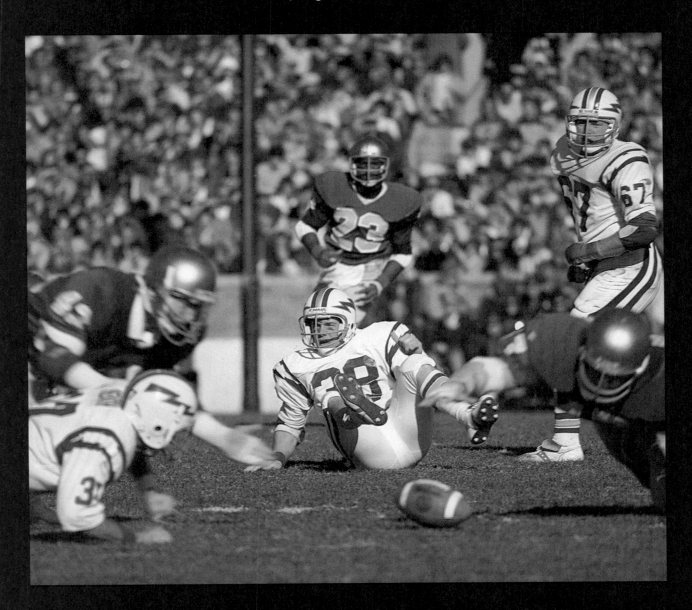

17.1

Trapping Bugs

In this chapter, you will discover the most frequent causes of program errors. You will learn some ways to avoid errors. You will also learn some methods of finding and correcting those errors that do creep into your programs.

A <u>bug</u> is a mistake in a computer program. Anything that keeps your program from running, or from giving the correct answer, is called a **program bug**. If you have tried writing your own programs, you have certainly met several program bugs.

Two types of program bugs are:

1. Errors which the computer detects. These are errors in vocabulary, spelling, punctuation, and form. They are called **syntax errors**. While these errors are the most frequently made, they are often the easiest to find since the computer lets you know when you make them.
2. Errors which the computer does not detect. These are **logic errors** and are often more difficult to find and trace down. This is when your program produces an answer, but you find it is the wrong answer. Errors in logic will be covered in the next section of this chapter.

You have many opportunities to make errors when you write BASIC programs. It is very important that you know where these errors may be made. If you can avoid making them,

Chip's Bits

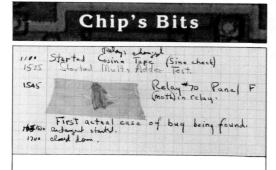

The Navy log book that records the operation of the Mark I computer contains a record of the first computer bug. Taped to a page in the book is a dead moth, with the note "first actual case of bug being found." The moth was killed by a relay in the computer, and made the computer stop. Grace Hopper found it and entered the record in the log book.

you may save a great deal of time and trouble looking for them later. (Finding and eliminating bugs is called **debugging** a program.)

Syntax errors cause the computer to print messages indicating the kinds of error and the numbers of the lines in which they occur.

Some of the most frequently made errors, even though detected by the computer, are difficult to find. A few of these errors are shown below.

1. **INPUT** statement errors:
    If the **INPUT** statement has a numeric variable, an error will occur when alphanumeric data is entered. This error can usually be avoided if you **INPUT** only one variable at a time and prompt the user for all input.

2. **READ** and **DATA** errors:
    There are several ways to make errors using **READ** and **DATA** statements. Usually, they are one of three types:
    a. Not enough data in the **DATA** statement. The computer will inform you that you are <u>out</u> of <u>data</u>. Your program stops and you are very unhappy.
    b. Your **DATA** statement contains string data where numeric data is expected. Look <u>very</u> carefully at the data and how it is separated. If you use a period or a semicolon when you should have used a comma, you will cause an error. Some of these errors are <u>very</u> difficult to find and leave the programmer quite sad.
    c. You end a line of data in a **DATA** statement with a comma. This makes the computer think that there is an extra item in the line. It reads the extra item as a blank or a zero.

3. Mixing letters and digits:
    The letter O and the digit 0 are easily mixed. So are the letter L and the digit 1. These errors can often be very hard to find.

4. **RETURN** without a **GOSUB** statement:
    This is an easy error to make! The best way to avoid it is to place a **STOP** or **END** statement before the first line of every subroutine.

5. Numbers Out of Range Errors:
This kind of error occurs when using functions or subscripted variables. If the subscript of a variable is negative, or if it is greater than allowed in the DIM statement, a BAD SUBSCRIPT (BS) ERROR will occur.

6. Division by Zero Error:
This error occurs if you attempt to divide a number by zero.

The examples below illustrate some types of errors and how they can be corrected. See if you can detect and correct the errors before reading the solutions.

Example 1: Mitzi wrote the program on the left to read and print the names of four of her friends. As you can see by the output, it did not quite work. Can you find the error?

The computer's output is given below:

```
FOUR OF MY FRIENDS ARE
LISA
ZENEY


MARCIA
```

What happened to REGGIE?

When Mitzi asked Mr. Pierce for help, he told her to look at line 100. That was when she saw the nasty comma after ZENEY. This comma made the computer think there was another item in that line. So it read a blank as the third name. To correct this error, Mitzi only had to remove the last comma in line 100. Did you notice the nasty comma?

Example 2: It took both Angelo and Mr. Pierce a long time to catch this one. See if you can do better.

The program to the left is supposed to add the numbers from 1 to 10.

```
5   Clearscreen
10    READ A$, B$, C$, D$
20    PRINT "FOUR OF MY FRIENDS ARE"
30    PRINT A$
40    PRINT B$
50    PRINT C$
60    PRINT D$
100   DATA LISA, ZENEY,
110   DATA MARCIA, REGGIE
```

```
5   Clearscreen
10   S = 0
20   FOR J = 1 TO 10
30   S = S + J
40   NEXT J
50   PRINT "THE SUM OF THE 1ST 10 NUMBERS IS";S
```

Here is what the computer said when they ran it:

?SYNTAX ERROR IN LINE 20

Do you give up? Look at the very last character in line 20. Does it look like the digit zero? It is not. It is the letter O. Simply change this character to a zero and the program will work.

E x e r c i s e s

1. Find and correct the error in the program below. If you try it on your computer, enter it exactly as it appears. Do not change anything, even if it appears wrong.

```
5   Clearscreen
10   PRINT "PICK A NUMBER FROM 1 TO 10";
20   INPUT K
30   GOSUB 100
40   PRINT K; " IS MY FAVORITE NUMBER!"
100   IF K < 1 THEN 130
110   IF K > 10 THEN 130
120   RETURN
130   PRINT "I CAN'T HANDLE THAT NUMBER"
140   STOP
```

2. The program below should print the numbers from 1 to 20. See if you can find the error in it. If you try it on your computer, enter it in exactly as it appears. Do not change anything, even if it appears wrong.

```
5   Clearscreen
10   FOR I = 1 TO 20
20   PRINT I
30   NEXT 1
```

Chip's Challenges

3. The program below should read and print a name, an address, and a ZIP code. It does not work. See if you can find out why. If you try it on your computer, enter it in exactly as it appears. Do not change anything, even if it appears wrong.

```
5   Clearscreen
10   READ N$, A$, Z
20   PRINT N$
30   PRINT A$
40   PRINT "BALTIMORE, MD "; Z
50   DATA YEX, EDITH E, 4342 LOG ST, 27182
```

17.2

Preparing for the Worst— Programs that Flop

If your program is free of syntax errors but still does not work, you have probably made an error in logic. This is a thinking error. It could be that you have written an incorrect formula or arithmetic expression. Perhaps some program steps are out of order. Worse still, perhaps your whole solution to a problem is incorrect. In any case, you must find and correct the errors.

Sometimes logical errors are very hard to find. One way to help ease the task of finding these errors is to plan carefully. A few minutes of advance planning can save hours of debugging time later.

Using Rule No. 1, means to:

1. Place many **REM** statements in your programs. Be sure that they identify and explain each part of the program.
2. Do much of the programming in subroutines. Test your subroutines as you write them. Use **REM** statements to describe the subroutines.
3. Draw a flow chart for any routine or subroutine which has more than two branching steps.
4. Enter only one item in each **INPUT** statement, and prompt every **INPUT** statement.
5. Place all **DATA** statements in order at the very end of the program. This makes them easy to find and keeps them out of the way of the rest of the program.
6. Label all output data.

> **Rule No. 1**
>
> Plan, organize, and document your program.

Rule No. 2

Test your subroutines and final program using data for which you know the answer.

Sometimes, even when you follow both of these rules, your program will still give you the wrong answer. If this happens, place **PRINT** statements in every part of your program which might cause trouble. These may be after every calculation, after **FOR-NEXT** loops, or after random numbers have been picked. For example, the values of variables which have just been calculated can be printed to see if they are what you expected. The index of an outer loop can be printed each time it is about to change (just before the **NEXT** statement). Or data which has just been entered can be printed, to see that it has been done correctly.

Sometimes, the information displayed by these **PRINT** statements is placed on the screen so rapidly that you cannot read it. If this happens, you can add the instruction **INPUT Q$** immediately after each **PRINT**. This will make the program come to a complete stop until you press the (RETURN) or (ENTER) key. Meanwhile, you can take your time reading the information on the screen.

After you have discovered and corrected the errors, you can remove all helpful **PRINT** and **INPUT** statements.

Finally, the last Rule is given to help you when you are tired of looking for errors and confused by the computer's stubbornness.

The examples that follow will illustrate some kinds of errors and the way they can be corrected. In the next section of this chapter, you will see how an entire program can be planned to help prevent errors in logic. See if you can detect and correct the errors before you read the solutions.

Example 1: Jake wrote the following program to read in his three test grades and print their average. The output follows the program. What is wrong with the program?

Chip's Bits

The computer science department at Yale has an artificial intelligence project that has written a program called MAGPIE. MAGPIE is a natural language program that can "learn" word definitions, spelling, and grammar, and can start a conversation with human beings.

Rule No. 3

Resist the temptation to blame the computer. It does not do what you want it to do. It only does what you tell it to do.

```
5  Clearscreen
10   READ A, B, C, N$
20   PRINT N$;" 'S AVERAGE IS "; A+B+C/3
30   DATA 87, 74.5, 93, JAKE
```

The output for this program is below:

`JAKE'S AVERAGE IS 192.5`

Jake looked at his program for a long time. He knew that the answer was incorrect but he was not sure why. He finally realized that he could use smaller numbers to test the program. He changed line 30 to

`30   DATA 10, 10, 10, JAKE`

Now the output was

`JAKE'S AVERAGE IS 23.33333`

This made him realize that only the last number entered was divided by three. He wanted the sum to be divided by three. He changed line 20 as shown below. He was very pleased that his program worked this time.

`20   PRINT N$;"'S AVERAGE IS "; (A+B+C)/3`

Example 2: Tahia earned money mowing lawns. She wrote the program below to find her total earnings for four weeks. The amount she earned each week is given in the DATA statement in line 100.

```
5  Clearscreen
10   S = 0
20   FOR J = 1 TO 4
30   READ X
40   S = S + X
50   NEXT J
60   READ N$
70   PRINT N$;"'S TOTAL IS $"; S
100   DATA 7.50,8.25, 10.50, 8.75.TAHIA
```

When she ran the program her computer gave her this strange message:

`? SYNTAX ERROR IN LINE 30`

Needless to say, she was very puzzled. Line 30 clearly did not have an error. Had her computer been overloaded with many impulses? She added the PRINT statement below and ran the program again. See if you can find the problem.

`35   PRINT X`

Here is the computer's output:

```
7.5
8.25
10.5
?SYNTAX ERROR IN LINE 30
```

When Tahia noticed that the first three numbers were entered correctly, she looked at the fourth number in the **DATA** statement. She spotted the error immediately. Did you? She had typed a period where she meant to type a comma. This had left her computer very confused. Happily, the error was easy to correct.

E x e r c i s e s

1. Jeffrey bought 5 gum balls for 10 cents each and 15 Toothie Rolls for 20 cents each. He wrote the program below to calculate the cost of the candy. His total came out wrong. Find and correct the error. (Hint: Place a **PRINT** statement after line 10 to see if all of the numbers are read correctly.)
```
10   READ A, B, C, D
20   S = A*B + C*D
30   PRINT "THE COST IS ";S;" CENTS"
40   DATA 5, 10,
50   DATA 15, 20
```

2. Linda bought two bags of Clearwater Taffy. One bag cost $2.45 and weighed 1.3 pounds. The other bag cost $3.18 and weighed 2.1 pounds. To get the average cost per pound, she had to divide the sum of the costs by the sum of the weights. Her program to do this has an error. Find and correct the error. (Hint: Try a new **DATA** statement with very simple numbers in it.)
```
10   READ A, B, X, Y
20   C = A + X / B + Y
30   PRINT "COST PER POUND IS $"; C
40   DATA 2.45, 1.3, 3.18, 2.1
```

Chip's Challenges

3. The program below simply reads some numbers and places them in a list. When **RUN** it gives the message:
```
SUBSCRIPT OUT OF RANGE IN LINE 30
```
Find and correct the error.
```
10   DIM A(3)
20   FOR K = 1 TO 4
30   READ A(K)
40   NEXT K
100   DATA 5.4, 6.2, 7.1, 8.5
```

WHITNEY'S SPECIAL OF THE DAY

Whitney had a good idea for a fun program. He would let the computer make up some silly foods. First, he made up four lists of words:

List A	List B	List C	List D
FRIED	BANANA	BEAN	LOAF
CREAMED	LEMON	EGGPLANT	CASSEROLE
BOILED	HAMBURGER	LETTUCE	STEW
ROASTED	HOT DOG	CABBAGE	SOUP
JELLIED	FISH	PARSNIP	SALAD
MASHED	SPAGHETTI	RHUBARB	SANDWICH
CHOPPED			

Next, he planned to let the computer pick one word from each list and print the four words together. He would call the result "Whitney's Special of the Day".

Whitney realized that his program would probably have some errors in it. He planned it so that any errors would be easy to find.

Before Whitney wrote any BASIC program steps, he outlined his program like this:

1. First, the four lists will have to be entered. This will be done in a subroutine which will begin at line 1000.
   After the entry of the lists, they must be PRINTed to be sure that they are correct. These PRINT statements will not be in the final program.
2. Second, one word from each list will be randomly picked. This will be done in a subroutine which will begin at line 2000.
3. Third, the four words picked in the second part will be placed in a PRINT statement. This will be done in a subroutine which begins at line 3000.
4. The lists will be placed in DATA statements. These will begin at line 4000.

Now Whitney did some clever thinking. He figured that he should write the DATA statements first because he could not test any other part of the program without them. He also realized that he needed only a few words from each list to test his program. After he had his program tested he could add the rest of the data. Here are his first DATA statements:

```
4000    REM THE FOUR LISTS OF WORDS
4010    DATA FRIED, CREAMED, BOILED
4020    DATA BANANA, LEMON
4030    DATA BEAN, EGGPLANT
4040    DATA LOAF, CASSEROLE
```

Next, he wrote these BASIC statements to READ and PRINT the DATA above:

```
1000    REM DATA ENTRY ROUTINE
1010    FOR K = 1 TO 3
1020    READ A$(K)
1030    NEXT K
1040    FOR K = 1 TO 2
1050    READ B$(K)
1060    NEXT K
1070    FOR K = 1 TO 2
1080    READ C$(K)
1090    NEXT K
1100    FOR K = 1 TO 2
1110    READ D$(K)
1120    NEXT K
1130    REM THE ROUTINE BELOW WILL BE DELETED
1131    REM AFTER THE PROGRAM IS FINISHED
1140    FOR K = 1 TO 2
1150    PRINT A$(K); B$(K); C$(K); D$(K)
1160    NEXT K
1170    PRINT A$(3)
1180    RETURN
```

Now Whitney could test his subroutine by writing this drive program (see Chapter 13). Notice that he placed a DIM statement at the beginning of his drive program and an END statement at the end.

TRS-80 users need this to free additional space for string variables.

```
5   CLEAR 500
10    DIM A$(7), B$(6), C$(6), D$(6)
20    REM READ THE DATA
30    GOSUB 1000
900    END
```

This part of the program worked! The output looked a little strange because there were no spaces between the words of the lists. All of the words were read in however, and they were in the proper order.

The second part of Whitney's program picked the random numbers to select words from the lists. For the first list, he needed a number from 1 to 3. For each of the other lists, he needed a number from 1 to 2. A very simple subroutine let him do this:

```
2000   REM ROUTINE TO PICK A RANDOM NUMBER
2010   R = INT( N * RND( 1 ) + 1 )
2020   RETURN
```

TRS-80 users can use
```
2010   R = RND( N )
```
here.

```
40    REM GET THE RANDOM NUMBERS
50    N = 3
60    GOSUB 2000
70    A = R
80    N = 2
90    GOSUB 2000
100   B = R
110   GOSUB 2000
120   C = R
130   GOSUB 2000
140   D = R
```

By calling this routine four times, and storing the results in the variables A, B, C, and D, Whitney was able to pick the four random numbers he needed. To do this, he added the statements on the left to the drive routine.

He knew that the easiest way to test this routine was to write the third and final routine. This subroutine writes the four words. This is the routine:

```
3000   REM OUTPUT ROUTINE
3010   PRINT "WHITNEY'S SPECIAL OF THE DAY"
3020   PRINT A$( A );" ";B$( B );" ";C$( C );" ";D$( D )
3030   RETURN
```

Note: It is necessary for Whitney to supply blank spaces between the words.

And here is the single statement in the drive program which calls this routine:

```
150   REM FINAL OUTPUT
160   GOSUB 3000
```

Whitney tested his program by running it several times. Here are two of the results he got.

```
WHITNEY'S SPECIAL OF THE DAY
CREAMED LEMON BEAN LOAF
```

```
WHITNEY'S SPECIAL OF THE DAY
BOILED BANANA BEAN CASSEROLE
```

Whitney was overjoyed with his program. He was very anxious to add the rest of the words to the lists and see what kinds of Specials he could create. You may wish to add some words of your own to the list. If you do, please try not to be too disgusting!

E x e r c i s e s

1. If the random number subroutine in Whitney's program had picked the following set of numbers, what output would be printed?

   A = 1   B = 1   C = 2   D = 2

2. What random numbers would have to be picked for the following output to be printed?

   BOILED BANANA EGGPLANT LOAF

3. Rewrite each of the following lines in Whitney's program on a sheet of paper so that all of the 25 words in his original lists can be added.

   50_____   1100_____
   80_____   4010_____
   1010_____   4020_____
   1040_____   4030_____
   1070_____   4040_____

Chip's Challenges

4. How many different Specials can be picked in Whitney's program as it is written above? How many Specials could be picked if Whitney added all 25 of the words in his original lists?

C H A P T E R   S U M M A R Y

1. There are two kinds of programming errors:
   a. Those which are detected by the computer. These include syntax errors, input/output errors, missing keywords, and other errors in form. There is always a message given by the computer for these errors.
   b. Errors which are not detected by the computer. These are called errors in logic. There is no error message for this kind of error.
2. Careful planning and detailed documentation can help prevent many programming errors.
3. Long programs should be planned as sets of subroutines. Each subroutine should be tested as it is written.
4. Always test a program or routine using simple data for which you know the expected answers.
5. Insert temporary PRINT statements to help track down program errors. These will be erased from the final program.

PROBLEM SET 17

In Problems 1 through 15, each of the BASIC statements would give an error message, if entered and RUN. For each, find and correct the error.

```
1.   10    COMPUTE C = A + B
2.   14    PINT "THE SUM IS "; A+B
3.   25    FROM I = 1 TO 10
4.   18    ENTER A
5.   25    PLEASE READ X
6.   50    IS C = 0 THEN GOTO 37
7.   65    MY NAME IS LOIS
8.   48    HOW MUCH IS 88 TIMES 64?
9.   62    READ, A, B
10.  80    THIS ROUTINE FINDS THE SUM
11.  55    D + E = B
12.  20    Z$ = HELLO
13.  35    DATA 23; 54; 66
14.  100   X = "A + B"
15.  RETURN
```

In Problems 16 through 20, find and correct the errors in each program segment.

```
16.  10    FOR K = 1 TO 5
     20    READ X
     30    NEXT K
     40    DATA 16, 72.1, 38.2
17.  10    DIM A$(3)
     20    FOR M = 1 TO 3
     30    READ A$(M)
     40    NEXT M
     50    DATA JAMES MARY , BETTY
18.  5   DIM C(4)
     10    FOR X = 1 TO 4
     20    READ C(X)
     30    NEXT X
     40    DATA HI, 62, 18, 29
19.  10    FOR K = 3 TO 7
     20    PRINT K
     30    NEXT L
20.  10    PRINT "STEP 1"
     20    GOSUB 30
     30    PRINT"STEP 2"
     40    RETURN
```

21. This program is supposed to print the names of three people. It does not work. Find and correct the error.

```
     10   DIM X$(3)
     20   FOR I = 1 TO 3
```

```
30   READ X$(1)
40   PRINT X$(I)
50   NEXT I
60   DATA SYLVIA, LEONARD, SLIM
```

Find and correct the error in each of the following programs.

22.
```
10   S = 0
20   FOR K = 1 TO 5
30   READ Z
40   S = S + Z
50   NEXT K
60   PRINT "THE SUM IS ";S
70   DATA 22, 33, 44,
80   DATA 18, 43
```

23.
```
10   DIM N$(4)
20   FOR J = 1 TO 4
30   READ N$(J)
40   PRINT N$(J)
50   NEXT J
60   DATA HEWEY, LOUEY
70   DEWEY, SAM
```

24.
```
10   DIM A(3)
20   FOR I = 1 TO 4
30   READ A(I)
40   NEXT I
50   DATA 3.3, 4.4, 5.5, 6.6
```

Chip's Challenges

Find the error in each of the following program lines.

25.
```
25   FOR I = 1 TO 10
```
26.
```
10   READ H,1,J,K
20   DATA 75, 89, 36, 54
```
27. The program below should print the following:
LINE NO. 1
LINE NO. 2
LINE NO. 3
Find out why it does not work and make corrections.
```
10   PRINT "LINE NO. 1"
20   GOSUB 50
30   GOSUB 60
40   END
50   PRINT "LINE NO. 2"
60   PRINT "LINE NO. 3"
70   RETURN
```

COMPUTER AWARENESS

Careers and You

A computer programmer on the job.

Will you be one of the people who finds a career in the world of computers? Whether you are or not, the more you can learn about them, the more likely you are to succeed in whatever occupation you choose. Remember, whatever you do, there's a strong probability that there's a computer in your future.

Computers are everywhere! No matter what career you choose, it is almost certain to involve some sort of contact with a computer. Whether you choose business, engineering, science, journalism, publishing, education, or social science, you will probably find yourself using a computer in your job.

You may even choose the field of computers itself for your career. There are many opportunities! Peo-

ple are needed to design, build, and service computers. They are needed to program and operate them. And people are needed to sell them, teach others how to use them, and write user manuals and other materials about computers.

Computer workers are needed by government agencies, service industries, financial institutions such as banks, manufacturers of almost every product imaginable, wholesale and retail businesses, transportation companies, public utilities, communications systems, farm bureaus, fisheries, mining and drilling operations, and construction companies.

Scientists, especially chemists and physicists, develop new chips and circuitry. Scientists need college degrees. Most companies prefer to hire people who have earned advanced, or graduate, degrees in their special field. Mathematicians with advanced degrees and computer knowledge also help design new computers.

Electronics, mechanical, and industrial engineers work to produce new circuits, systems, and peripheral devices for computers. Electronics engineers research new products and develop plans for them. Mechanical engineers further the product development and industrial engineers design methods to make the new products. All of these people need college degrees and graduate work in their specialties. They need a strong background in mathematics and science.

Computer technicians test and maintain equipment. Some assemble computers. Others may assist in the design of new equipment. Technicians control the chemical processes used in making printed circuit boards and chips. Some are photographic technicians who reproduce circuit designs on boards and chips. Still others are engineering aides who make drawings of new designs and test them. Technicians are usually graduates of vocational or technical schools where they have studied computers. Some are veterans who were trained in the armed forces.

Assemblers put parts together to make computers. Machinists make cases for computers and their peripherals. Inspectors test finished equipment to be sure it works the way it should. All of these computer workers need some training after high school, in addition to the on-the-job training computer manufacturers supply.

Computer operators run the computers in offices, hospitals, schools, and factories. There are data-entry clerks, who use keypunch equipment, optical-character-recognition-machines, or other input devices. There are computer operators who specialize in printers or data-storage devices. Some operators work at terminals and never see the computer. There are others who work with the **console,** the computer itself. They follow the instructions of programmers and managers, keep necessary supplies on hand, and do routine maintenance tasks. All of these jobs usually need only high school or vocational or technical school training. Some companies train computer operators on the job. (If you plan a long-term career as a computer operator, you may find yourself being retrained, on the job, as new and different computer devices appear.)

Computer programmers are usually college graduates. They need to know several computer languages and often have other specialized knowledge. **Systems programmers,** who develop computer operating programs, are often engineers. **Applications programmers** may sometimes have a business, legal, or medical background.

The work of programmers is often directed by a **systems analyst.** Systems analysts are planners who determine the kinds of equipment, both hardware and software, that companies need. They decide where computers should be installed, how they should be used, and who should use them. Systems analysts need both computer science and business training. They usually have more than one college degree.

Computer consultants also advise businesses about computer use. They need to understand hardware and software. They need training or experience in business management.

Electronic Data Processing is a new job field made possible by computers. In addition to computer operators, EDP companies hire managers who are usually programmers. They need to understand computer hardware and software and be able to supervise many workers. EDP auditors need a college degree in accounting. Data base administrators and project leaders are usually programmers or systems analysts. Computer security specialists are often experts in data processing.

Technical writers, who prepare hardware and software documentation or manuals, need language skills together with technical training. Documentation specialists usually need college degrees.

The name **word processor** is used both for a computer function or operation and for the person who makes use of that function. This person requires secretarial skills. Training is usually on the job, using the company's own word-processing equipment, although special courses are also given in vocational, technical, or business schools.

Many companies hire software librarians to keep track of program and data tapes, cards, and disks. Sometimes these people are also responsible for the filing of the printed output of computer operations. The main requirement for the job is excellent filing skills. Some companies hire only librarians with a college degree in library science.

Computer instructors train employees and customers in the use of computer hardware and software. They may work for a computer company, a software publisher, or a company that uses computers. Some instructors are certified teachers. Others have only technical training. EDP training specialists need a college background in data processing.

College instructors need a masters degree in computer science or a related subject.

Computer salespeople usually have both sales experience and some technical training. They must be able to demonstrate computers and answer questions about them. Computer manufacturers' sales representatives usually have college degrees.

The computer industry continues to grow, and the job market grows with it. The United States Department of Labor predicts that well-trained people in most computer-related fields will be in demand well into the 21st century. There will be many new developments in this area. Robotics, for example, will grow and will provide many jobs.

What Do You Know?
1. Do all computer careers require a college degree?
2. What do computer operators do?
3. What is a systems analyst?

What Can You Find Out?
1. Do all areas of the nation offer the same opportunities for computer careers?
2. How are computers involved, or how are they likely to be involved in the future, in the career you are considering?
3. What kinds of computer education will you need?

What Do You Think?
1. How will the continuing development of robotics affect other kinds of work?
2. Are there any computer careers with limited job opportunites?

SOFTWARE APPLICATIONS
Evaluating and Using Software

Many computer users purchase software packages. What are some common software applications? How do you decide if a program is the right one for you?

18.1

Working with Words

Stephen was interested in computers. When he was assigned an English composition to write, he decided to write about hardware. Part of the first draft that Stephen typed is shown below:

> computer Hardware
>
> Computer programing has developed itw onw vocabulary. one common word is hardwere Hardware is the word that refers to the actual equipment wsed in computer programming. examples ofhardware are printers, monitors, joysticks diskdrives, and central processing untis.

Identify the corrections Stephen had to make in each of these categories:

1. Misspelled words

2. Capitalization

3. Punctuation

4. Run-together words

Stephen reviewed his draft and penciled in the corrections shown on the next page.

```
                    C
                    ≡
              ¢omputer Hardware

        Computer programing has developed
                            m
      S   wn                O
    its own  vocabulary.  ∅ne common word is
                 ≡
              a
    hardw∉re⊙ Hardware is the word that refers
                              u
    to the actual equipment √sed in computer
                      E
    programming.  ∉xamples of hardware are printers,

    monitors, joysticks, disk drives, and central
                        i +
    processing unⴱs.
```

WHAT DID YOU LEARN?

Stephen knew that the report could not be submitted unless the errors were corrected. He had to retype the report several times before it was correct.

Clean, error-free reports can be produced easily and quickly. Some writers use their computers to help them work. When a software package called a **word processing** program is used, the computer becomes a valuable writing tool. Word processing includes the operations to create, revise, print, and store the text for written material. Using a word processing program would have made Stephen's task easier. Although he would still have had to type his essay on the keyboard, the word processing program would have made all the correcting an easy job.

All word processing programs are not the same. They are written for specific computer systems and make use of special keys on the computer. One program may provide a feature or operation that another does not. The commands and instructions vary from program to program. You will need to consult the program manual or the command summary sheet that your teacher gives you to fully understand your word processing program.

USE WHAT YOU HAVE LEARNED

When you load a word processing program into a computer, the video screen displays the **main menu**. The main menu is a list of the tasks the program can perform. Your program's menu may look similar to the one shown on the next page.

```
 ┌─────────────────────────────────┐
 │  ╲                           ╱   │
 │                                  │
 │     WELCOME TO THE WORLD         │
 │            OF                    │
 │      WORD PROCESSING             │
 │                                  │
 │     SELECT NUMBER OF             │
 │     OPTION DESIRED               │
 │                                  │
 │   1.  TYPE     5.  SAVE          │
 │   2.  EDIT     6.  RETRIEVE      │
 │   3.  FORMAT   7.  REMOVE        │
 │   4.  PRINT                      │
 │                                  │
 │  ╱                           ╲   │
 └─────────────────────────────────┘
```

The main menu shown has several options:

TYPE allows you to type, or enter, new material.
EDIT allows you to make changes in a document.
FORMAT allows you to instruct the computer how to print a document.
PRINT allows you to print a paper copy of a document.
SAVE allows you to store a document on a cassette or disk.
RETRIEVE allows you to reload a previously saved document into your computer's memory.
REMOVE allows you to delete a document from a cassette or disk.

Memory Bank

The main menu of a program lists the tasks the program can perform. It is similar to a menu in a restaurant.

If you choose the TYPE option, you can use the keyboard as a typewriter. The **document,** or material you type, will appear on the video screen and will also be stored in the computer's memory. The cursor, a flashing pointer, shows where the next typed character will appear. The cursor can be moved throughout the document when corrections, deletions, or additions are necessary. Usually the keyboard's arrow keys are used to move the cursor. Some possible movements of the cursor are:

1. Right or left one space
2. Up or down one line
3. To the beginning or end of a line
4. To the beginning or end of the document

On the typewriter it is necessary to strike the carriage return key before writing on the next line. Most word processing programs avoid this by providing a function called **word wrap.** As you reach the end of a line, the computer automatically takes the first letters of the last word and moves them to the beginning of the next line. For example, if you typed

WHEN YOU COME TO THE END OF THE LI

and the "i" was the last space on the line, the computer would move the "li" to the next line. When you struck the "n" key, you would see

WHEN YOU COME TO THE END OF THE
LIN

and you would continue typing without a break.

If you are entering a long document, some of it may disappear from the screen as you type. This does not mean that the material is lost; all the typed text is still stored in the computer's memory. The video screen is simply not large enough to contain all the writing at once. The unseen part can be brought back from the memory by a function called **scrolling.** Scrolling, shown on the three screens to the left and below, can move the text vertically or horizontally on the screen.

COMPUTER HARDWARE

COMPUTER PROGRAMMING HAS DEVELOPED ITS OWN VOCABULARY. ONE COMMON WORD IS HARDWARE. HARDWARE IS THE WORD THAT REFERS TO THE ACTUAL EQUIPMENT USED IN

WORD IS HARDWARE. HARDWARE IS THE WORD THAT REFERS TO THE ACTUAL EQUIPMENT USED IN COMPUTER PROGRAMMING. EXAMPLES OF HARDWARE ARE PRINTERS, MONITORS, JOYSTICKS, DISK DRIVES, AND CENTRAL PROCESSING UNITS.

PRINTERS, MONITORS, JOYSTICKS, DISK DRIVES, AND CENTRAL PROCESSING UNITS. SOFTWARE IS THE WORD THAT REFERS TO THE COMPUTER PROGRAMS THAT INSTRUCT

PUT YOUR PROGRAM TO WORK

Once the text has been typed into the computer, the editing begins. **Editing** includes all changes to the document, from correcting spelling errors to inserting sentences or deleting paragraphs. Almost all word processing programs provide the following editing features:

1. Correcting typing errors by inserting characters or by overtyping.

2. Deleting characters, words, sentences, or paragraphs.

3. Exchanging blocks or sections of text.

4. Searching for and replacing specific words in the document.

After the editing has been completed, the document can be saved on cassette or disk. Every word processing program requires that file names be given to any saved material. The rules for proper file names vary from program to program. If changes are needed later, the saved document can be reloaded and the corrections made.

When Stephen's report was edited and saved, he wanted to print it on paper. A paper copy of a document is called a **hard copy.** Before the printing can be done, the format commands are used to tell the computer how to print the report. Stephen was able to instruct his computer to center the title of his report, to set the space between the lines, and to determine how wide the margins should be.

Some programs require that the format commands be given before you begin typing. Others provide **on-screen formatting,** which permits you to see how the document looks on the screen before it is printed. Most word processing programs have some or all of these formatting options:

1. Change the spacing of the lines.

2. Adjust the width of the margins.

3. Place page numbers, supplied by the program, anywhere on the page.

4. Right-justify (make the edges even on the right side).

5. Set tabs for typing in columns.

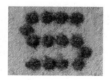

Word processing users must choose letter-quality printing (left) or dot-matrix printing (right).

6. Vary the size and style of the print.

7. Underline words or sentences.

Consult your program manual for the editing commands, the guidelines for file names, and the formatting features available with your program.

Memory Bank

Formatting instructions tell the computer how the hard copy should look. Before you can use formatting commands, you must know what operations your printer can perform.

Exercises

1. Explain the following terms.
   a. word processing program
   b. menu
   c. on-screen formatting
   d. cursor
   e. scrolling
   f. hardware
   g. document
   h. hard copy
   i. word wrap
   j. editing
2. Each sentence below contains an error. Identify the editing command needed to correct the error.
   a. SOME PEOPLE LIKE TO TIPE.
   b. MY SISTER TYPES VERRY FAST.
   c. MAKE UP YOUR YOUR MIND NOW.
   d. BRING BACK THE   WORD.
   e. WHAT'S FORLUNCHTODAY?
3. Identify and describe the purpose of each of the options on the main menu of your word processing program.
4. List the special keys on your keyboard that control scrolling, and describe how each of them works.
5. List the editing commands of your word processing program and explain when each would be used.
6. What are the rules for file names on your system?
7. List the formatting options available on your program.

Chip's Challenges

8. Prepare and print a document that summarizes the features of your word processing program. Use paragraph form.

18.2

Working with Data

Lorrie was president of her computer **users group.** (A users group has members who usually own the same kind of computer. They meet to share what they have learned about their machines and software.) Lorrie's group has a large collection, or library, of software programs.

As each new program was purchased, the owner wrote a short description of it, using a word processing program, for the group's catalog. Soon there was a large stack of computer printouts, too many for a single notebook. Lorrie decided to store the program summaries in file folders. First she identified each printout with one or two **key words** that described the program.

How might Lorrie arrange the programs in folders for filing?

Lorrie discovered that the key words could be organized into groups, such as games, education, or writing. She wrote the names of the categories on file folders and collected the similar types together. Then she placed the summaries within each group in alphabetical order according to the name of the program.

Lorrie organized the user group's collection of software summaries the same way data is organized for computer use. A complete collection of data is called a file. Each individual item is called a record. The records can be arranged in any manner that is useful and convenient. A software package that helps organize data is called a **data base management system.** A **data base** is a collection of related information. With data base management programs, the file that contains all the data is created first. The computer stores this information under a file name. In some cases, the information can be used by other programs. Some advantages of data base systems are:

1. Accuracy of the records is increased and maintained more easily.

2. Repetition of data entry is reduced.

3. Records can be arranged in any order the user wishes.

USE WHAT YOU HAVE LEARNED

Part of the user group's collection is shown here:

Title	Purpose	Owner	Cost
Wordworx	word processing	Lorrie Mont	$49.98
Starwrek	action game	John Yin	$29.95
Nuscript	word processing	user group	$99.00
Arithfax	math practice	user group	$39.75
Filefast	data base management	user group	$97.95
Goforit	adventure game	Wilson Poindexter	$39.99

Lorrie decided to use the data base management program to keep track of the user group's software. She first had to determine the format for each record in the file. What information did she want? Did she need the titles or the purpose in alphabetical order? Did she want the software owners' full names or last names only?

Once she determined what information was needed, she could begin using the software program. Every data base management program consists of one or more disks or cassettes, and the program manual. It is important to read the manual carefully before starting to use the system.

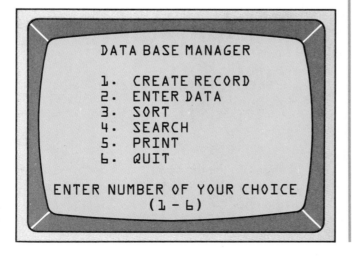

```
DATA BASE MANAGER

  1.  CREATE RECORD
  2.  ENTER DATA
  3.  SORT
  4.  SEARCH
  5.  PRINT
  6.  QUIT

ENTER NUMBER OF YOUR CHOICE
        (1 - 6)
```

Most systems display a main menu similar to the screen shown at the left.

PUT YOUR PROGRAM TO WORK I

The main menu shown has several options:

CREATE RECORD allows you to design the record form.
ENTER DATA allows you to look at the record and add or change information.
SORT allows you to arrange records in almost any order you wish.
SEARCH allows you to find any individual record.
PRINT allows you to make a copy of one or more records on a page.
QUIT allows you to leave the program without doing anything.

Lorrie began using her data base system by choosing option 1. A blank screen appeared, with the cursor in the upper left corner. Lorrie needed to complete the following steps:

1. Decide how to arrange her information.
2. Choose names that best describe each piece of data.
3. Decide how much space to allow for each entry.

Each entry in the record is called a field. The most important information should be listed first in the **key fields.** The data base system uses the key fields when it sorts or searches for records in the data base. As a rule, the first data entry should be the one used most often.

Memory Bank

A collection of data is a file. Each individual item within a file is a record. Each entry in the record is a field. A data base management program helps to organize all this data.

Lorrie chose to list the software's purpose in her first field, since this was of the most interest to her group. Her completed record form is shown on the next page.

It is necessary to leave enough space in each field for the longest entry that will be made. Lorrie was ready to enter data after saving the record she had designed.

PUT YOUR PROGRAM TO WORK II

To enter the information, Lorrie returned to the main menu and chose option 2, **ENTER DATA.** The form she had created was displayed on the screen and she recorded the data. Her first record is shown here:

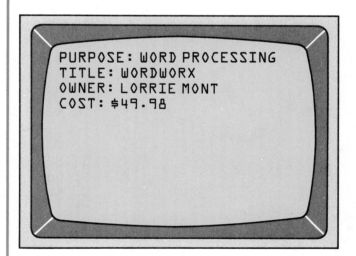

Lorrie continued to enter the data for each program. As she worked, Lorrie checked each record for accuracy. Making accurate entries when creating the data base simplifies all future use.

When all the information in a file is entered, the user can do many useful things. For instance, in this example Lorrie could:

1. Print a list of all software, in alphabetical order by purpose.
2. Print a list of all software, in alphabetical order by title.
3. Print a list of all software owned by a particular member.
4. Print a list of all software purchased for more than $40.00.
5. Update the file by adding information every time the group or a member buys a new program.

Exercises

1. Match the menu items with the function.

   a. PRINT   **1.** Find a form
   b. SEARCH   **2.** End program
   c. SORT   **3.** Make a copy
   d. CREATE RECORD   **4.** Design form
   e. ENTER DATA   **5.** Add information
   f. QUIT   **6.** Arrange records

2. Write the word or words that best complete each statement.
   a. A data base management system can help to _____ data.
   b. Each entry in a record is called a _____.
   c. As a rule, make the _____ field the one you will use most often.
   d. A collection of related information is a _____.

3. Suppose Lorrie decided to print the records of her collection according to alphabetical order of owner's names. Make a list in that order, using the data on page 361.

Chip's Challenges

4. Using your data base management program, create the data base for the user group's catalog of software.
5. Find the record for Goforit. Change the name to Goferit and the owner to user group.
6. Delete the record for Nuscript and print a new listing of the group's programs, alphabetizing them by title.

18.3

Working with Numbers and Formulas

DISCOVER FOR YOURSELF

Salvadore kept the record of ticket sales for his class play. He listed the number of tickets sold and the money collected by each of his classmates. Each ticket sold for $2.50. On the fourth day of sales, his record looked like this:

Name	Number sold	Money Collected
Marie	5	$12.50
Angie	2	5.00
Lou	6	15.00
Stan	3	7.50
Val	3	7.50
Marge	4	10.00
TOTALS	23	$57.50

On the fifth day, Marie sold two more tickets and Val sold three.

1. How many numbers in Sal's record must be changed?

2. What are the new values for these places in the record?

3. How many numbers on the chart are affected by the sale of a single ticket?

WHAT DID YOU LEARN?

Keeping an accurate record of numerical data that can change often is difficult. Each change in a chart like Sal's affects other numbers. To record the additional sales, Sal would have to change six numbers on his chart. If everyone sold a ticket on the sixth day, Sal would have to change 14 numbers—and do a lot of arithmetic!

Sal decided to use a computer to help him keep his records. His chart is a **spreadsheet,** a table

365

of numerical data, with the rows and columns related by mathematical formulas. A spreadsheet is like a large sheet of paper spread out on a tabletop. The sheet is divided into rows and columns. Each position on the spreadsheet is called a **cell.** The information in that cell is an entry.

The computer screen is a window that shows all or part of the spreadsheet. The user can move to any cell in any part of the spreadsheet and make a new entry or change an old one. The computer will then quickly calculate any other resulting changes.

USE WHAT YOU HAVE LEARNED

When you begin using a spreadsheet program, the window displays the upper left corner of the sheet. Keys, usually the arrow keys, are used to move the window to other parts of the sheet. The columns in most spreadsheets are identified by letters and the rows by numbers. The cells are named by their column-row position. This identification of a cell is its **coordinate,** or location in the spreadsheet.

The cursor highlights a cell of the spreadsheet. Pressing one of the cursor movement keys makes the cursor jump to a neighboring cell. (On some computers, pressing RETURN or ENTER also makes the cursor jump to a neighboring cell.) Data can be entered or changed in the cell highlighted by the cursor.

	A	B	C	D	E	F
1	NAME		SOLD		MONEY	
2	MARIE		5		12.5	
3	ANGIE		2		5	
4	LOU		6		15	
5	STAN		3		7.5	
6	VAL		3		7.5	
7	MARGE		4		10	
8						
9	TOTALS		23		57.5	
10						
11						
12						

Sal entered his original sales data in the spreadsheet above. In this example, the entry in column A, row 2 (A2) is the name Marie. To move the cursor from cell A2 to cell B2, you would use the cursor movement key that moves the cursor to the right. Of course, the cursor cannot move up if it is on the top row or to the left if it is in the first column. One key (the > key on some computers) allows the user to enter a cell coordinate, such as D3. This entry causes the cursor and window to move directly to the cell named.

PUT YOUR PROGRAM TO WORK I

One of the computer's keys is used as a **control key.** If this key is the first one pressed in a cell, it tells the computer that the next keystroke is a command. While the actual keys used may vary from program to program, we will study the most common of these commands.

Clearing: The clear command means that you wish to clear, or empty, the entire spreadsheet. Before you can perform this command, the computer asks you to verify it. The computer asks you whether you really want to erase all the data. If you respond Yes, the spreadsheet is cleared and made ready for new entries.

Entering labels: The first line of Sal's report consists of labels, or headings. Most spreadsheets have a specific number of spaces in each cell. To enter string data, move the cursor to the cell where you want the label to appear and type the words. When you have filled a cell with characters, move the cursor to the next cell and continue typing the heading. Some computers do not permit the first space in a cell to be a blank. In that case, the label should be placed in quotation marks. The quotation marks will not appear in print, either on the screen or on paper.

Entering numbers: The only numbers that Sal entered as data in his chart are those in cells C2 through C7. (The values in the E column are calculated by a formula.) If the first keystroke of a cell entry is a digit, a decimal point, or one of the symbols **+**, **−**, **(**, or **@**, the entry will be a number or a formula with a numeric value. To enter a numeric value, move the cursor to the proper cell and type the number. After a number is entered, it moves to the right side of the cell. It is said to be **right-justified.** (All string entries are **left-justified,** or moved to the left side of the cell.)

Memory Bank

Text or copy that has a smooth right margin is <u>right-justified</u>. Copy that has a smooth left margin is <u>left-justified</u>. Copy can be both right-justified and left-justified at the same time.

Storing on disk: Each spreadsheet program has a $STORE$ or $SAVE$ command. You must give the data a file name, following the rules for your system.

Error handling: One method of handling an incorrect entry is to erase the entry in the cell by striking the RETURN or ENTER key and re-entering the data. Most computers also allow the user to backspace and type over incorrect characters.

Entering formulas: In Sal's chart, the amount collected (column E) is found by multiplying the number of tickets sold by $2.50. You can direct the computer to do this work by entering the proper formula in cell E2. The formula is +C2*2.5. The asterisk (*) stands for multiplication, as it does in BASIC. The + symbol tells the computer that C2 is the value currently stored in cell C2. The multiplication will be done automatically and the result placed in E2.

Replicating entries: The spreadsheet program can **replicate,** or repeat, an entry or formula throughout a row or column. This can save the user a great deal of time. Since Sal's formula for calculating the amount collected is the same for each person in his chart, the use of a replicating entry is very convenient.

As Sal's formula is repeated through column E, however, a slight change has to be made. For row 2 the formula is +C2*2.5, while for row 3 it should be +C3*2.5, and so on. The spreadsheet can make this change easily. The formula entered in cell E2 becomes the **source** of the replication. The cells E3 through E7, where the formula is to be copied, are the **targets** of the replication.

In the formula in cell E2, C2 is a variable. The computer will ask if you wish the variable to be relative to its position, that is, use C4 in row 4, C5 in row 5, etc. If you wish the variable to be relative to its position, the computer will replicate the formula into each cell, calculate the answer, and display the results.

Built-in functions: Several mathematical functions are built into most spreadsheet programs. For a complete list for your system, check the program manual.

One special function can calculate the sums of numbers in a column. In Sal's chart, this function is used to find the values for the TOTALS row. To calculate the totals, move the cursor to the proper cell and call the SUM function. Most spreadsheets use a special symbol (perhaps the @) to notify the computer that a built-in function is being used.

Chip's Bits

One of the newest peripherals for computers is a mouse! The mouse is pointed at the video screen in order to input information. It is about the size of a bar of soap, with switches to begin the computer's actions. Its tail is the wire that connects it to the computer.

PUT YOUR PROGRAM TO WORK II

When spreadsheets had to be done by hand, forecasting was extremely time-consuming.

The spreadsheet program stores labels, numbers, and formulas in its memory. It displays the labels and numbers, and calculates and displays the results of each formula. Each time a new number is entered or an existing number is changed, the computer recalculates all the values affected by the change and displays the new information.

The speed with which the computer can re-evaluate the entire spreadsheet is one of the most important advantages of spreadsheets. Many companies use spreadsheet programs to **forecast,** or predict, their business activities. The spreadsheet provides an excellent "What if?" situation. The company can change one variable and project the effect this change will have on all other items in the sheet.

Sal can easily update the information in his spreadsheet shown on page 367. The first change is to record the additional two tickets that Marie sold. When he moves the cursor to cell C2 and types a 7, the computer immediately recalculates the chart. The new values appear in E2 (17.5), C9 (25), and E9 (62.5).

Sal also changed the value in C6 to 6, since Val had sold three more tickets. He watched the new values seem to "ripple" through the spreadsheet. All the calculations are automatic and rapid. His final spreadsheet is shown below.

	A	B	C	D	E	F
1	NAME		SOLD		MONEY	
2	MARIE		7		17.5	
3	ANGIE		2		5	
4	LOU		6		15	
5	STAN		3		7.5	
6	VAL		6		15	
7	MARGE		4		10	
8						
9	TOTALS		28		70	

Exercises

In problems 1 through 7, fill in the blanks with the best answer.

1. A spreadsheet is like a large sheet of _____ .
2. A position on the spreadsheet is called a _____ .
3. The computer screen is like a _____ that shows a portion of the spreadsheet.
4. If an entry begins with a digit, a decimal point, or one of the symbols +, −, (, or @, it is a _____ .
5. One of the keys, called a _____ key, is used to indicate that the keystroke that follows is to be a command.
6. Labels are always _____-justified, while numbers are _____-justified.
7. The spreadsheet has several built-in _____ , such as ΣUM, which allow certain mathematical operations to be completed.
8. How is a spreadsheet similar to a data base management system?
9. Name three advantages of making a spreadsheet on a computer over doing one with paper and pencil.
10. Sal's class had a goal of selling 100 tickets. Describe how the number of tickets remaining to be sold could be calculated and placed in cell C12.

Chip's Challenges

11. Two students in Sal's class, Bess and Len, sold some tickets to the class play. If these names and the corresponding numbers of tickets sold were added after Marge's row, how would this affect the last rows of the chart? Show how these last two rows would look and how they would affect the row of totals.

18.4

Working with Integrated Software

DISCOVER FOR YOURSELF

Lorrie wanted to send a letter to each member of the user group listing all the recent additions to their software library. She also wanted to give a brief description of each program and to include a form for members to return if they had other new programs to add. The letter should be personalized, that is, addressed to each person by name. Lorrie did not want to have to retype the letter for each person in the group.

Which applications programs will Lorrie have to use?

WHAT DID YOU LEARN?

Lorrie knew that the data base management system she had used, Filefast, was part of an integrated package, Workfast. **Integrated software** packages are groups of programs that can work together for greater speed and ease for the computer user. They usually include word processing, spreadsheets, and data base management. Some include graphics software and other components as well. Lorrie bought another part of the package, Typefast, a word processing program.

Every application program saves data to a disk in a slightly different way. Some files can only be read by the program that saved them. To integrate data files, the program must use the same save and load codes. Although Lorrie had another word processing program, she needed Typefast to be able to use the files of Filefast in preparing her letter.

USE WHAT YOU HAVE LEARNED

Lorrie discovered that she could **build,** or create, a data file of member names and addresses with Filefast. This file would include the information needed to address letters to each member of the group.

```
LAST NAME: BELL
FIRST NAME: TOMMY
LAST NAME: BELL
ADDRESS: 1614 BELVEDERE AVE.
CITY: COLUMBIA STATE: MD
ZIP: 21131
PHONE: 555-2327
```

Lorrie built a file, **MEMBERS**, with fields to store first names, last names, addresses, and phone numbers of the group members. The record in that data base file for one member is shown at the left.

Notice that the last name appears twice, before and after the field for first name. This permits the user to print the individual's name either LAST NAME, FIRST NAME or FIRST NAME, LAST NAME.

PUT YOUR PROGRAM TO WORK

Using the Typefast part of the integrated system, Lorrie created her letter. It is shown here, as she typed it:

```
DEAR *FIRST NAME*,

  I AM ENCLOSING THE LATEST
UPDATE OF OUR SOFTWARE LI-
BRARY. PLEASE USE THE AT-
TACHED FORM IF YOU WOULD LIKE
TO MAKE ANY OTHER ADDITIONS
TO OUR COLLECTION. IF YOU
WISH TO TRY ANY OF THE PRO-
GRAMS LISTED, PLEASE CALL
ME.

     YOUR PRESIDENT,

     LORRIE MONT
```

One item in the letter stands out. The notation ***FIRST NAME*** identifies a field in one of Lorrie's records in the **MEMBER** file. When using one part of an integrated software system, Lorrie can call upon the files of another part. The word processing program will use the MEMBER file of the data base management program to find the different first names for each copy of the letter. Letters prepared this way are called form letters.

For the greeting of the letter, Lorrie selected the field FIRST NAME. This field is indicated by the asterisk (*) symbol around the field name. (Different computer systems require different **identifiers,** or markers. Check your manual for the correct symbol to use.) Lorrie's letter to Tommy Bell, when printed, will begin:

Dear Tommy,
↑___ Name selected from the data base by the computer.

The computer system is now ready to print personalized copies of the letter to each group member.

PUT YOUR PROGRAM TO WORK II

When she is ready to address the envelopes, Lorrie can use the MEMBER file to prepare the mailing labels. She would create the form:

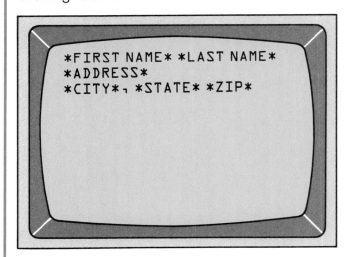

```
*FIRST NAME* *LAST NAME*
*ADDRESS*
*CITY*, *STATE* *ZIP*
```

The printed label for Tommy's letter would look like this:

Tommy Bell
1614 Belvedere Ave.
Columbia, MD 21131

Lorrie also used the word processing program to create the list of software additions. She called upon the file SOFTWARE, which she had previously created when she organized the catalog. She was easily able to print the list with descriptions using this integrated package.

Lorrie began saving to buy other parts of the Workfast package. She planned to use Drawfast to create artistic covers for future catalogs. She wanted to have another member of the group design an emblem that could be printed on their letters. Lorrie also recommended that the group buy Compfast, to keep a record of the treasury.

By using integrated software systems, computer users can save time and take full advantage of the power of the computer.

E x e r c i s e s

1. What is an integrated software package?
2. What are the usual programs included in an integrated system?

Answer the following questions if you are using an integrated software package. Consult the manuals included with the package.

3. What programs are included in your package?
4. What special symbol(s) are used to include names from the data base program in letters prepared with the word processor?
5. What special command is used by the word processor to prepare mailing labels?

Chip's Challenges

6. Use your data base program to build a file of five names and addresses.
7. Use your word processing program to write a letter that could be sent to each person recorded in the data base.
8. Using the integrated system, print a personalized letter to each of your friends.

18.5

Looking at Software

Penny was running an arithmetic program when she was asked this question:

HOW MUCH IS SEVEN PLUS NINE?

She type in this answer:

SIXTEEN

The computer gave this response:

?REENTER

Following directions, Penny retyped:

SIXTEEN

Again the computer gave the response:

?REENTER

The computer is in an infinite loop. How can Penny get the program out of this loop? What can a good programmer do to avoid this problem?

The program Penny used probably had an **INPUT** statement that required a numeric answer. The answer SIXTEEN is a string, and does not satisfy the computer's requirement. The ?REENTER message was the computer's way of telling the user to enter a number instead of a word. Penny's trouble could have been avoided if the program had displayed a message telling her what kind of response was expected.

Good programs are written so that they trap, or catch, any error made by the user. They should also prompt the user to reply correctly. This is called **error handling**. Testing a program's

376

error handling can help you decide if the software is good or bad.

There are five major questions to ask when evaluating new software.

1. Is the software easy to use?
2. Does the software perform well?
3. Does the software handle errors well?
4. Does the software have good documentation?
5. Do you like the software?

We will look at each of these questions in more detail.

USE WHAT YOU HAVE LEARNED

Is the software easy to use? Good software does not require the user to know any programming or special commands. It is written so that it is **self-booting,** or loaded as the system is turned on. (Some computer systems require that the disks be inserted after the computer is turned on. With these systems, you push the reset button and the program boots.)

After the program is loaded, a menu should appear that shows everything the program can do. If input is needed, the user should be clearly prompted. After selecting an option from the menu, you should be able to continue with the program or return to the menu to make another selection. There should always be an option to quit, or **exit,** the program.

Finally, a program that needs many commands or instructions should offer help to the user. At the stroke of a certain key, a **help screen** should appear with the needed information. This option should be available throughout the program.

Does the software perform well? A program should do everything its advertisements claim it can do. Try to test it in many ways. If it is a mathematical program, try using very large or very small numbers to test input. Test the program with negative numbers. Use a set of data for which you already know the answer. Make sure that the answer given is correct.

Businesses that use computers need to be sure that their software will perform well.

Chip's Bits

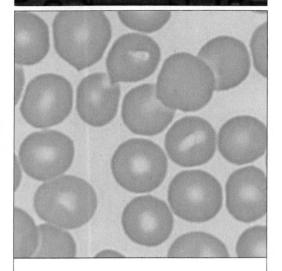

A human blood cell is very tiny. It is about eight microns in diameter. (A micron is a thousandth of a millimeter.) Some computer scientists are experimenting with mini-mini computer parts. They have already made some that are only two microns in diameter. Now they are trying to make some with diameters of half a micron or less.

Try complicated examples. Is the program too slow? A good program performs its tasks quickly, particularly arithmetic calculations and the sorting of lists. If the process is a long one, does the computer display a message telling the user that it is still working? Or is the user left wondering if the program has **crashed** (stopped running)?

Does the software handle errors well? The program itself should contain *no* errors! If the user makes an error in entering information, the computer should display an error message. This message should help the user to correct the mistake and to re-enter the required information. Some programs automatically display a help screen when an error is repeated.

You should test a program by entering every error you can think of. Make incorrect data entries repeatedly to see how the program handles them. Give numeric answers when strings are expected and see what happens. Press keys at random to create long string entries. This should not make the program crash. The program should catch every error. It should never be necessary for the user to know any programming to correct an error or to make the program run smoothly.

Does the software have good documentation? Every program should come with a clearly written, easily understood manual. The manual should contain good explanations of the program and many examples. Every option offered by the program should be explained in detail.

It should not be necessary to read the complete manual before beginning to use the program. The manual should provide quick and easy reference with a complete, extensive index. This can help the user answer questions about the program quickly. Many programs also offer a card or sheet with a summary of the program's commands and operations. These cards, along with help screens within the program, will make the program easier to use.

Do you like the software? Perhaps the most important test of a software program is how you feel about it. Was it interesting to run, or boring? Did it use colorful pictures and action where appropriate? Did it use sound effects appropriately? Did it do what you wanted it to do quickly, efficiently, and effectively? Do you think your friends would enjoy using this software?

PUT YOUR PROGRAM TO WORK

All the questions discussed here are shown in this Software Evaluation Form. You should use this form, or one like it, whenever you evaluate a software program.

SOFTWARE EVALUATION FORM

Name of Program: _____

Name of User: _____

I.   Is the software easy to use?

____ **1.** Is it self-booting?
____ **2.** Does it display a menu right after booting?
____ **3.** Does it prompt all input?
____ **4.** Does it allow you to correct your mistakes?
____ **5.** Can you always return to the menu?
____ **6.** Is there always a way to exit the program?
____ **7.** Does it let you call for help?

II. Does the software perform well?

____ **1.** Does the program perform all the tasks listed in the menu?
____ **2.** Are all of the calculations accurate and are all answers correct?
____ **3.** Does the program complete its tasks quickly?
____ **4.** When you must wait while the program completes long tasks, does it explain what is happening?

III. Does the software handle errors well?

_____ **1.** Is the program free of errors?
_____ **2.** If you enter data incorrectly, does the program give you a chance to re-enter?
_____ **3.** Can you press keys randomly without causing the program to crash?
_____ **4.** Does the program run smoothly even when you give it wrong answers and bad data?

IV. Does the software have good documentation?

_____ **1.** Is the manual easy to read?
_____ **2.** Are all the directions clear and easy to follow?
_____ **3.** Are all of the program's operations explained clearly?
_____ **4.** Is there a complete index and/or a quick reference sheet?

V. Do you like the software?
_____ **1.** Was it fun to use?
_____ **2.** Did it do what you wanted it to do?
_____ **3.** Would you recommend it to your friends?

Summary of the Software

```
21 - 22 Yes answers . . . . . . .Excellent
18 - 20 Yes answers . . . . . . .Good
15 - 17 Yes answers . . . . . . .Fair
Under 15 Yes answers . . . . .Poor
```

Exercises

In problems 1 through 5, fill in the blanks with the word or phrase that makes the statement true.

1. A program that loads itself upon startup is called _____.
2. After booting, a good program displays all of the user's options in a _____.
3. If a user is lost or confused, a good program will provide a _____ screen to guide the user through the difficulty.
4. A program's documentation should have clear explanations and many _____.
5. Every user error should be _____ by the computer.
6. Explain how you can test a program to see if it does its calculations quickly and accurately.

7. How can you test a program to see if you can make it crash?

8. Imagine that you were testing a piece of software and the following message appeared on the screen:
SYNTAX ERROR IN 1075
Explain why you might think this is a poor program.

9. Why is a user's help screen useful?

 Chip's Challenges

10. Look at the program Penny was using on page 376. Write two program statements that would cause the display she saw on her screen. Then rewrite this section of the program so that Penny would be prompted to answer correctly.

CHAPTER SUMMARY

1. Word processing programs allow text to be typed, edited, stored, retrieved, and printed.

2. Editing a document involves changing all or any part of it.

3. A data base management program is a program that allows information to be organized, stored, and retrieved. Records can be sorted in any order or by any field, and reports can be printed.

4. A *file* is an entire collection of related information stored in a data base system. A *record* is a single unit of information in a file. A *field* is an individual entry in a record. Fields are used to organize the information.

5. A spreadsheet is a program that allows many rows and columns of information to be stored and organized in a computer.

6. Whenever any number in a spreadsheet is changed or the spreadsheet is displayed, all numeric values in the spreadsheet are recalculated. The rapid spreadsheet calculation allows the user to investigate the effects of small changes in numeric entries.

7. Integrated software programs allow the user to use word processing, data base management, and spreadsheet programs together.

8. A software evaluation form helps a user determine whether a piece of software is good or poor.

9. Good software is easy to use, has good documentation, performs accurately and rapidly, and handles users' errors well.

PROBLEM SET 18

In problems 1 through 17, fill in the blanks with the word or phrase that makes the statement true.

1. The cursor in a word processor can usually be moved about the screen by means of the _____ keys.

2. When text is forced off the top of the screen because of new text added at the bottom of the screen, the text is said to _____ off the screen.

3. Editing text involves making _____ in text that already exists.

4. The most important field of information in a record should be listed _____.

5. The _____ _____ option of a data base management system allows the user to design a record form.

6. _____ entry of data simplifies future use of a data base.

7. The spreadsheet is divided into many _____ and _____.

8. Spreadsheets are useful because of their ability to do _____ automatically and rapidly.

9. The _____ highlights one cell of a spreadsheet at a time.

10. When a value or formula is repeated throughout several cells in a spreadsheet, it is said to be _____.

11. If an entry in a spreadsheet begins with a letter or quotation marks, it is called a _____.

12. The data in a spreadsheet can be stored on a _____.

13. The three main components of an integrated software package are _____, _____, and _____.

14. If input is needed from a program's user, it should be clearly _____.

15. One user option that should be present from any point in the program is the option to _____ the program.

16. Good documentation for a program means a clearly written user's _____.

17. If the user makes an error in entering data, the program should allow the chance to make _____.

18. How is a word processing program different from a data base management system?

19. How is a spreadsheet similar to a data base management system?

20. How is a spreadsheet different from a data base management system?

21. Name four options that should be present in the menu of a data base system.

22. In the spreadsheet on page 367, suppose that Sal wanted to find the *average* number of tickets sold by the six people in his spreadsheet. Describe how the average could be calculated and placed in cell C12. Place the label "Average" in B12.

23. Sal's class had a goal of selling 100 tickets. Describe how the number of tickets remaining to be sold could be calculated and placed in cell C13.

In problems 24 through 28, use your word processing system and type in the sentences exactly as they appear here. Then find and correct the error(s) in each sentence, using commands from your word processing program.

24. NOW IS THETIME TO USE THE WORD PROCESSOR.

25. A WORD PROCESSOR IS FAST, EASY, AND AND FUN TO USE.

26. ALL WORD PROCESSING PROGRAMS HAVE SOME INSTRUKTIONS THAT ARE SIMILAR.

27. MS HINTON SAID COME HERE JOHN.

28. JEAN AND I WENT TO SEA A MOVIE CALLED RETURN OF THE THUNDER DOGS.

In problems 29 and 30, type the short, choppy sentences into your word processor. Using word processing commands, combine each set into one complete sentence.

29. THE SUN SHINES TODAY.
THE SUN SHINES BRIGHTLY.
THE SKY IS CLEAR.
THE SKY IS CLOUDLESS.
THE DAY IS HOT.

30. MARIE IS A STUDENT.
MARIE GOES TO CENTRAL SCHOOL.
MARIE IS A MEMBER OF A SCHOOL CLUB.
THE CLUB IS CALLED THE CENTRAL COMPUTER USER'S GROUP.
MARIE IS PRESIDENT OF THE CLUB.

 Chip's Challenges

Use the restaurant menu below to help you answer problems 31 through 33.

POTTS DINER - DINNER MENU

Day	Special	Price
Sunday	Beef and Noodles	$4.75
Monday	Closed	
Tuesday	Fish and Chips	$3.15
Wednesday	Hamburger, French Fries, and Hot Dog	$3.95
Thursday	Steak and Potatoes	$5.25
Friday	Pork and Cabbage	$2.95
Saturday	Fried Chicken and Potato Salad	$3.55

31. Enter this menu in your word processor, data base system, and spreadsheet.

32. On your spreadsheet, add a column called *Number Sold*. In this column enter the numbers 35, 0, 41, 58, 42, 25, 37. Add a fifth column called *$ Received*. Calculate each entry in this column by multiplying the number sold by the price. Find totals for the last two columns.

33. On both your data base and word processor, add mushrooms to Wednesday's steak dinner. Remove hot dogs from Thursday's special. Move Saturday's dinner to Sunday and Sunday's dinner to Saturday.

34. In the school store, ball point pens sell for $.59 each. Prepare a spreadsheet that contains two columns labeled *Number Sold* and *Cost*. In the first column, place the numbers from 1 to 10. In the second column, have the computer calculate the corresponding cost of that number of pens.

35. Eloise sells magazines after school. She can be paid under one of two plans. Under Plan 1 she receives a salary of $5 per week plus $.15 for each magazine sold. Under Plan 2 she receives no salary, but gets $.50 for each magazine sold. Prepare a spreadsheet with four columns to show:

Number Sold   Plan 1   Plan 2   Difference

In the column labeled *Number Sold*, place the numbers from 1 to 20. In the columns *Plan 1* and *Plan 2*, calculate Eloise's income under each plan. In the column labeled *Difference*, calculate the difference between the incomes under each of the plans.

36. In problem 35, how many magazines must Eloise sell before she would receive more income from Plan 2 than from Plan 1?

37. Using a data base system, enter the ten largest cities in the United States. For each city, enter as separate fields its name, population, and area. Print the data in two ways: first, in alphabetical order, and second, by order of population, with the largest first. Use an encyclopedia, atlas, or almanac to collect your information.

Before and After BASIC

Programmers must become familiar with a variety of programming languages.

The earliest computers were instructed, or programmed, by turning switches on and off. Next, programs were entered in patterns of ones and zeros. These binary digit patterns are a code for ons and offs. Programs written this way are said to be in **machine language**. They can be "understood" by the computer.

Machine language requires the programmer to know where every bit, every one and zero, is stored. The programmer has to understand what all the gates and registers of the computer are doing. It is very easy to make mistakes writing machine language programs. It is also easy to make mistakes entering all those ones and zeros.

Some computers allow use of another number system to enter programs. This system is based on the number 16, instead of the number 2, as the binary system is. This **hexadecimal** system (**hex** for short) uses the digits 0-9 and the letters A-F. A in base sixteen equals 10 in base 10, the common number system. F in base 16 is 15 in base 10. (Remember that 0 is one of the 16 digits.) Each byte of information, represented by eight binary digits, can be shown in two hex digits.

Programs that use numerals are said to be written in **low level languages**. They look very different from those written in **high level** languages such as BASIC.

One low level language is known as **assembly language**. It is made up of codes called **mnemonics**, which are abbreviations for primitive operations. Assembly languages cannot be understood by the computer. They must be translated by other programs, called **assemblers**, into machine language.

Each kind of computer has its own special low level languages. They depend on the set of primitive instructions built into the CPU. Programs written in a low level language for one computer will not work on any other computer.

Low level programs work very fast. However, they are quite difficult to write and to enter. Very early in the history of modern computers, manufacturers realized that many people wanted to use computers but did not want to become computer experts. They wanted more "user friendly" languages.

The earliest effort to make a computer language that was easier to use began about thirty years ago. In the 1950s, John Backus and Irving Ziller designed a language called FORTRAN for IBM computers. (FORTRAN is named for FORmula TRANslation, and it was designed for mathematical programming.) It is a **compiled** language. That is, a program called a **compiler** changes FORTRAN programs to machine language. The compiler translates the entire program, then lets the machine run it.

FORTRAN is still widely used, especially by scientists and engineers. It has been revised and rewritten several times.

In its early version, FORTRAN could not work with strings. But businesses need to use strings to keep records of products, customers, and equipment. So in 1959 the COmmon Business Oriented Language, COBOL, was written. Two of its authors were Jean Sammet and Commodore Grace Hopper of the United States Navy. (Commodore Hopper wrote the very first computer language, even before FORTRAN was designed.) Like FORTRAN, COBOL is a compiled language and is still in use.

In 1963, a language was invented by two mathematicians at Dartmouth College. John Kemeny (later to become Dartmouth's president) and Thomas Kurtz wrote BASIC. BASIC was intended to be easy to learn and simple to use. It does not usually use a compiler. A program called an **interpreter** changes each line of a BASIC program to machine language as the program is running.

There are many dialects, or versions of BASIC, and some parts of BASIC programs are hard to change from one computer to another.

A Swiss mathematician, Nicklaus Wirth, wrote a language called PASCAL, named after Blaise Pascal. PASCAL was designed to work as well with numbers as FOR-TRAN does, to handle strings as well as COBOL does, and to be as easy to learn as BASIC. PASCAL is a **structured** language. This means that certain patterns must be followed exactly in writing programs. It is a compiled language, and PASCAL programs that work on one computer will work on any other. PASCAL is popular with many microcomputer users. The newest version of BASIC, called TRUE BASIC, has many of the features of PASCAL.

In 1975, the United States Department of Defense announced a contest to find a new programming language. The winner was a French company called CII-Honeywell-Bull. Their language, adopted by the Defense Department, is called ADA. It was named in honor of Charles Babbage's assistant, Ada Lovelace.

There are many other special purpose high level languages. Two of these are often found in schools.

PILOT (Programmed Inquiry Learning Or Teaching) is used to develop teaching and testing programs. LOGO is often used to teach programming language ideas to young children. Using LOGO, children can easily produce interesting displays of geometric shapes and designs.

What Do You Know?
1. What is the most visible difference between high level and low level languages?
2. What is the difference between an interpreter and a compiler?

What Can You Find Out?
1. What are the names of some other high level languages?
2. For what purposes are these languages used?

What Do You Think?
1. What are the characteristics of a good computer language?

APPENDIX

Graphics for the Apple II

Graphics on the Apple II microcomputer come in three varieties—low resolution, high resolution, and super high resolution (only on the IIe)—and in color. A fourth variety—using only text characters—does not have color capabilities and does not make full use of the Apple's graphic potential.

LOW RESOLUTION GRAPHICS

Think of the Apple screen as a page of graph paper—40 columns wide and 40 rows high. To make a graphic (or a picture), you have to "color in" the squares on the graph paper. By the way, the columns and rows are numbered 0 to 39. The upper left corner of the screen is column 0 and row 0.

To place a light blue square at column 20 and row 25 on the screen, type in the following:

```
Tells the Apple ────────→ GR
you want low            COLOR=7 ←──── You have to
resolution              PLOT 20,25      tell the Apple
graphics.                    ↗     ↑     what color
                        Column.   Row.   you want. 7
                                         is light blue.
```

The following program will draw an orange line across the screen at row 10:

```
5  GR
10  COLOR=9
20  FOR I=0 TO 39
30  PLOT I,10
40  NEXT I
```

To see the line "move," add `50  GOTO 5`.

Try this program:

```
5  GR
6  COLOR=8
10  FOR I=1 TO 24
20  READ X,Y
30  PLOT X,Y
40  NEXT I
50  DATA 0,0,0,2,0,5,0,7
51  DATA 1,1,1,6
52  DATA 2,0,2,2,2,5,2,7
53  DATA 3,3,3,4
54  DATA 4,3,4,4
55  DATA 5,0,5,2,5,5,5,7
56  DATA 6,1,6,6
57  DATA 7,0,7,2,7,5,7,7
```

This program plots 24 sets of points to produce a snowflake.

Crayons, graph paper, and your imagination are all you need to draw pictures on the low resolution screen.

388

HIGH RESOLUTION

In low resolution you draw pictures using small squares on the screen. In high resolution, you draw using "dots." Each row on the high resolution screen is 280 dots wide and each column is 192 dots high. The columns are numbered from 0 to 279 and the rows are numbered from 0 to 191.

Compare the appearance of low resolution and high resolution computer graphics in these photographs.

To display a blue dot on the screen, type in the following:

```
Tells the Apple ────────→HGR
you want high      HCOLOR=6←───You have to tell
resolution     HPLOT 100,100  the Apple what
graphics.            ↗     ↖  color you want.
                Column.   Row.  6 is blue.
```

Type in this program to draw a rectangle and RUN it. Note the use of the word "to" to draw a line from one dot to the next.

```
10   HGR
20   HCOLOR=3←─white
30   HPLOT 30,20 TO 150,20 TO 150,150
TO 30,150
TO   30,20
```

Now let us add the diagonals.

```
40   HPLOT 30,20 TO 150,150
50   HPLOT 30,150 TO 150,20
```

Perhaps the most difficult geometric shape to draw on the high resolution Apple II screen is a circle. A graphics or arcade programmer almost always relies on tricks or aids to draw a circle. The program that follows is an example of a circle-drawing aid and will draw a circle on the high resolution screen if you input the RADIUS and the CENTER. The program uses principles learned in a high school trigonometry course to plot the dots in a circular pattern.

```
10   TEXT
20   HOME
30   HCOLOR=3
40   INPUT "WHAT IS THE RADIUS? ";R
50   PRINT
60   PRINT "WHERE IS THE CENTER?"
70   INPUT "HOW MANY UNITS DOWN? (0 TO
191)? ";Y
80   INPUT "HOW MANY UNITS ACROSS? (0
TO 279) ";X
90   HGR
100  VTAB 22
110  PRINT "CENTER (";X;",",Y;")";"
RADIUS ";R
120  FOR I = 1 TO 100
130  IF (X + R * COS(I)    0 OR X + R *
COS(I)    279) GOTO 160
140  IF (Y + R * SIN(I)    0 OR Y + R *
SIN(I)    191) GOTO 160
150  HPLOT X + R * COS(I),Y + R *
SIN(I)
160  NEXT I
170  VTAB 23
180  INPUT "DO YOU WANT TO DRAW
ANOTHER? ";N$
190  IF LEFT$(N$,1) = "Y" THEN GOTO
10
```

Try the program using different values for the radius and center. Experiment with changing some of the values within the program.

While higher level mathematics skills are not necessary to become a good programmer, a thorough knowledge of geometry is helpful in becoming a good graphics programmer.

By using the high resolution screen creatively, you can draw just about any 'shape' that you can imagine. High resolution graphics are used in arcade games and in the new area of computer aided design.

Visit your library to find books that give advice on how to design high resolution APPLE graphics. You will find that graphics are worth the programming effort.

Graphics for the TRS-80

The screen of TRS-80 Model III computers has 6144 pixel locations. There are 48 lines (numbered from 0 TO 47). Each line has 128 graphic locations (numbered from 0 TO 127). The pixels are lit with the SET command:

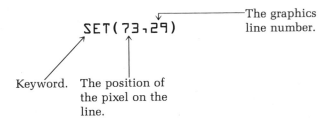

The first number of the argument cannot be greater than 127 and the second cannot be greater than 47. A pixel is turned off by the RESET command.

```
RESET(73,29)
```

To draw a line across the screen use a FOR-NEXT loop. The loop index represents the changing value of the position of the pixel in the line.

```
10  CLS
20  FOR H = 0 TO 127
30  SET (H,20)
40  NEXT H
```

To draw a vertical line use a similar loop. This time, the index represents the screen line.

```
10  CLS
20  FOR V = 0 TO 47
30  SET (90,V)
40  NEXT V
```

To prevent the break in the vertical lines, caused by the READY message and prompt, add this line:

```
50  GOTO 50
```

This program will draw a rectangle:

```
10  CLS
20  FOR H = 50 TO 75
30  SET(H, 20)
```

```
40  SET(H, 30)
50  NEXT H
60  FOR V = 20 TO 30
70  SET(50, V)
80  SET(75, V)
90  NEXT V
100  GOTO 100
```

Each set of six pixels forms a screen location. By adding the @ symbol, read "at", to a PRINT statement, you can use these locations. Add these lines:

```
100  PRINT @ 540, "your name";
110  GOTO 110
```

(Be very careful of the punctuation in line 100. The PRINT @ statement requires a comma after the number. The semicolon at the end of the line is needed to prevent a break in the vertical lines.)
You may have to adjust some of the numbers in the program to center your name in the rectangle.

There are 1024 PRINT @ locations on the screen. They are arranged in 16 lines, each three pixels high. Each line has 64 locations, each two pixels wide. The first position in the top line is 0 and the last is 63. The first position of the second line is 64 and its last is 127, and so on. The position in the lower right corner of the screen is 1023.

Sets of six pixels in a location can be used to create low resolution animated graphics. The pixels can be turned on in 64 different ways! To use these graphics characters, study this code.

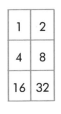
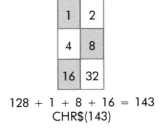

128 + 1 + 8 + 16 = 143
CHR$(143)

390

Each small rectangle is a pixel. If you add the numbers of the pixels you want lit to 128, you have the graphic character's code number.

128 + 2 + 4 + 32 = 166
CHR$(166)

128 + 4 + 8 = 140
CHR$(140)

The code numbers range from 128 (no pixels lit) to 191 (all pixels lit). Use the string function CHR$, read, "character string" to PRINT these graphics on the screen.

Use graph paper to create a design. Shade the pixels you want lit and find the code number for each. Try this program to see how it works. (Notice how the character strings are connected and assigned to a variable to make the picture.)

```
10  CLS
20  P$ = CHR$(138) + CHR$(140) +
CHR$(140) + CHR$(191) + CHR$(132)
30  PRINT @ 475, P$
```

To make the figure move across the screen, add:

```
30  FOR P = 448 TO 506
40  PRINT @ P, P$
50  IF P = 506 THEN 70
60  PRINT @ P, " "  ←One space here.
70  NEXT P
80  GOTO 80
```

Experiment with your own pictures. If you are very creative, you can use more than one line of graphic characters!

Fast action graphics can be created using this technique. Begin by defining a string variable:

A$ = "a space for each character code"

Then direct the computer to find the string's location in its memory. This is done with two functions, PEEK and VARPTR, read "variable pointer." The VARPTR function uses the string as its argument and returns the memory location of the string. The PEEK function looks into the VARPTR function to find the string address. You then direct the computer to POKE, or put, code numbers into the string instead of spaces.

Be sure you check carefully and correct all errors before running this program!

```
10  CLS
20  A$ = "12345"  ←Use spaces if you wish.
30  DATA 138, 140, 140, 191, 132
40  V = PEEK( VARPTR( A$ ) + 2 ) * 256
+ PEEK( VARPTR( A$ ) + 1
50  FOR N = 0 TO 4
60  READ C
70  POKE V + N, C
80  NEXT N
90  FOR P = 448 TO 506
100  PRINT @ P, A$
110  IF P = 506 THEN 130
120  PRINT @ P, " "  ←One space here.
130  NEXT P
140  GOTO 140
```

(Line 40 will always be almost the same. Only the string variable changes to match the variable you choose.)

After you run the program, list it and be prepared for a surprise. You can delete lines 30 to 80 and the program will still run!

Graphics for the Commodore 64

Graphics on the Commodore 64 can use color, keyboard characters, and sprites. Sprites are high resolution images that can be stored in memory, used in programs, and animated.

The front of each key of the Commodore 64 shows two graphic characters. To display these characters, you will have to use a second key. Hold the shift key down to type characters on the right side of the keys. Press the Commodore key ⌫ to type characters on the left side of the keys. The Commodore 64's screen has 25 lines of 40 characters each, in low resolution. Try this program for a low resolution drawing.

```
10   PRINT"♡"
20   FOR L = 1 TO 5
30   PRINT
40   NEXT L
50   PRINT TAB(9); " ↑"; No spaces here.
60   FOR HL = 1 TO 18
70   PRINT "⌫/@";
80   NEXT HL
90   PRINT
100  FOR VL = 1 TO 18
110  PRINT TAB(9); "⌫/H"; TAB (26);
"⌫/N"
120  NEXT VL
130  PRINT TAB(9); ""; ← No spaces here.
140  FOR HL = 1 TO 18
150  PRINT "⌫/T"
160  NEXT HL
170  GOTO 170
```

Before you can do more with Commodore 64 graphics, you need to know about its screen and color memories. The computer reserves memory locations 1024 TO 2023 to store display information. Memory locations 55296 to 56295 store color information for the display. To display something on the screen, you must put its code in the memory location. The keyword POKE will do this.

POKE 1482, 83

stores the code for the heart character in the memory location for a position near the middle of the screen. Try it. If nothing happened, you have a newer model Commodore 64. You will have to POKE a value into the color memory location for the screen display. The number for that location is the display memory number plus 54272. Try this:

POKE 1482 + 54272, 254

Add these lines to the program above to see a familiar word in the screen frame.

```
170  D = 1479
180  POKE D, 19: GOSUB 500
190  POKE D, 3: GOSUB 500
200  POKE D, 8: GOSUB 500
210  POKE D, 15: GOSUB 500
220  POKE D, 15: GOSUB 500
230  POKE D, 12: GOSUB 500
300  GOTO 300
500  REM IF YOU ARE USING AN OLDER
COMMODORE 64, OMIT LINE 510
510  POKE D + 54272, 254
520  D = D + 1
530  RETURN
```

To find the POKE code for any character, enter

PRINT ASC ("character")

and subtract 32 from the number given.

To create sprite graphics, you will need graph paper, marked this way:

Line	Byte 1								Byte 2								Byte 3							
	128	64	32	16	8	4	2	1	128	64	32	16	8	4	2	1	128	64	32	16	8	4	2	1
1																								
2																								
3																								
4																								
5																								
6																								
7																								
8																								
9																								
10																								
11																								
12																								
13																								
14																								
15																								
16																								
17																								
18																								
19																								
20																								
21																								

392

Draw a picture, shading the pixels to be lit. Add the numbers of the shaded pixels in each byte. (You should have three for each line.)

Byte 1								Byte 2								Byte 3							
128	64	32	16	8	4	2	1	128	64	32	16	8	4	2	1	128	64	32	16	8	4	2	1

Byte 1 Number	Byte 2 Number	Byte 3 Number
3	192	0
1	248	0
0	126	0
96	63	254

Now, study this table:

Sprite Number	Sprite Value	Pointer Address	Horizontal Value	Vertical Value	Color Value
S0	1	2040	0	1	39
S1	2	2041	2	3	40
S2	4	2042	4	5	41
S3	8	2043	6	7	42
S4	16	2044	8	9	43
S5	32	2045	10	11	44
S6	64	2046	12	13	45
S7	128	2047	14	15	46

This program will show you a sprite in action.

```
10   CH = 53248        Display chip address.
20   S0 = CH + 21      Always add 21 here.
30   S0 = 1            Sprite 0's value.
40   POKE S0, S0       This turns sprite 0 on.
50   POKE 2040, 13     Memory block number 13.
60   FOR B = 0 TO 38   Sprite 0 has 39 bytes.
```

```
70   READ BN
80   POKE B + 832, BN   Stores byte number.
90   NEXT B
100  DATA 3, 192, 0, 1, 248, 0, 0,
126, 0
110  DATA 96, 63, 254, 96, 63, 254,
255, 255, 255
120  DATA 255, 255, 255, 0, 63, 192,
0, 127, 0
130  DATA 0, 252, 0, 1, 240, 0, 3,
192, 0, 7, 0, 0
140  PRINT"♡"
150  FOR H = 1 TO 255
160  POKE CH + 0, H     Horizontal position.
170  POKE CH + 1, 90    Vertical position.
180  NEXT H
190  GOTO 140
```

Experiment with your own sprites. You will find help in your manual and in books in your library.

Comparison Chart

BASIC Language Statements and Features for Major Microcomputer Systems

BASIC Statement	Ap	At	TR	TI	Vc	Cm	IB	Pt	Sn
Variables									
Integer	*		*		*	*	*	*	
Single Precision	*	*	*	*	*	*	*	*	*
Double Precision			*				*		
String Variable Type									
Microsoft	*		*	*	*	*	*	*	*
Hewlett Packard		*							
Arrays									
DIM	*	*	*	*	*	*	*	*	*
Numeric Arrays	*	*	*	*	*	*	*	*	*
String Arrays	*	*	*	*	*	*	*	*	*
Arithmetic									
LET	*	*	*	*	*	*	*	*	*
Optional LET	*	*	*	*	*	*	*	*	
Operators									
+ − * /	*	*	*	*	*	*	*	*	*
Exponentiation	*	*	*	*	*	*	*	*	*
Logical (AND, OR, NOT)	*	*	*		*	*	*	*	*
Relations (=, <, >)	*	*	*	*	*	*	*	*	*
Arithmetic Functions									
ABS	*	*	*	*	*	*	*	*	*
INT	*	*	*	*	*	*	*	*	*
RND	*	*	*	*	*	*	*	*	*
SQR	*	*	*	*	*	*	*	*	*
String Functions									
ASC	*	*	*	*	*	*	*	*	*
CHR$	*	*	*	*	*	*	*	*	*
LEN	*	*	*	*	*	*	*	*	*
LEFT$	*		*		*	*	*	*	
RIGHT$	*		*		*	*	*	*	
MID$	*		*		*	*	*	*	
VAL	*	*	*	*	*	*	*	*	*
STR$	*	*	*	*	*	*	*	*	*
STRING$			*				*		

BASIC Statement	Ap	At	TR	TI	Vc	Cm	IB	Pt	Sn
Control of Program Flow									
Branches									
GOTO	*	*	*	*	*	*	*	*	*
IF . . .THEN	*	*	*	*	*	*	*	*	*
ELSE			*	*			*		
ON – GOTO	*	*	*	*	*	*	*	*	*
Subroutines									
GOSUB	*	*	*	*	*	*	*	*	*
RETURN	*	*	*	*	*	*	*	*	*
POP	*	*							
ON – GOSUB	*	*	*	*	*	*	*	*	*
Loops									
FOR	*	*	*	*	*	*	*	*	*
NEXT	*	*	*	*	*	*	*	*	*
STEP	*	*	*	*	*	*	*	*	*
Other									
REM	*	*	*	*	*	*	*	*	*
STOP	*	*	*	*	*	*	*	*	*
END	*	*	*	*	*	*	*	*	*
Input/									
READ	*	*	*		*	*	*	*	
DATA	*	*	*		*	*	*	*	
RESTORE	*	*	*		*	*	*	*	
INPUT	*	*	*	*	*	*	*	*	*
GET	*				*	*	*	*	
INKEY$			*				*		*
Output									
PRINT	*	*	*	*	*	*	*	*	*
PRINT AT			*						*
PRINT USING			*				*		
TAB	*	*	*	*	*	*	*	*	*
HTAB	*								
VTAB	*								
Clearscreen	*	*	*	*	*	*	*	*	*

Legend:
Ap	Apple II Plus Applesoft	TI	Texas Instrument TI99/4 Standard BASIC	IB	IBM Personal Computer
At	Atari	Vc	Commodore VIC-20	Pt	Commodore Pet
TR	TRS-80 Radio Shack Level II BASIC	Cm	Commodore 64	Sn	Timex 1000/Sinclair ZX/81

BASIC Statements and Commands for Major Microcomputer Systems

An example is given for each statement, or command for each computer. If a statement or command is not available for a certain computer, it is so designated.

Command or Statement	Apple II+/e	Atari 400/800	TRS-80 Mod III/IV	Texas Instrument
DIM	DIM A(25)	DIM A(25)	DIM A(25)	DIM A(25)
INT	INT(3*X+Y)	INT(3*X+Y)	INT(3*X+Y)	INT(3*X+Y)
RND	5*RND(1)	5*RND(1)	RND(5)	5*RND(1)
LEN	LEN(X$)+1	LEN(X$)+1	LEN(X$)+1	LEN(X$)+1
LEFT$	LEFT$(S$,4)	Not Available	LEFT$(S$,4)	Not Available
RIGHT$	RIGHT$(A$,6)	Not Available	RIGHT$(A$,6)	Not Available
MID$	MID$(W$,3,2)	Not Available	MID$(W$,3,2)	Not Available
GOTO	GOTO 120	GOTO 120	GOTO 120	GOTO 120
IF..THEN	IF A<B THEN 25	IF A<B THEN 25	IF A<B THEN 25	IF A<B THEN 25
GOSUB	GOSUB 1000	GOSUB 1000	GOSUB 1000	GOSUB 1000
RETURN	RETURN	RETURN	RETURN	RETURN
FOR/STEP	FOR K=1 TO 5 STEP 2	FOR K = 1 TO 5 STEP 2	FOR K = 1 TO 5 STEP 2	FOR K =1 TO 5 STEP 2
NEXT	NEXT K	NEXT K	NEXT K	NEXT K
REM	REM COMMENT	REM COMMENT	REM COMMENT	REM COMMENT
END	END	END	END	END
READ	READ A,B$	READ A,B$	READ A,B$	READ A,B$
DATA	DATA 3,TERRI	DATA 3,TERRI	DATA 3,TERRI	DATA 3, TERRI
RESTORE	RESTORE	RESTORE	RESTORE	RESTORE
INPUT	INPUT X, R$	INPUT X, R$	INPUT X,R$	INPUT X, R$
PRINT	PRINT A, B; C	PRINT A, B; C	PRINT A, B; C	PRINT A, B; C
TAB	PRINT TAB(3);A	PRINT TAB(3);A	PRINT TAB(3);A	PRINT TAB(3);A
Clearscreen	HOME	GR. 0	CLS	CALL CLEAR

Commodore VIC 20	Commodore 64	IBM Personal Computer	Commodore Pet	Timex 1000/ Sinclair ZX/81
DIM A(25)	DIM A(25)	DIM A(25)	DIM A(25)	DIM A(25)
INT(3*X+Y)	INT(3*X+Y)	INT(3*X+Y)	INT(3*X+Y)	INT(3*X+Y)
5*RND(1)	5*RND(1)	RND(5)	5*RND(1)	5*RND(1)
LEN(X$) + 1	LEN(X$) + 1	LEN(X$)+1	LEN(X$)+1	LEN(X$) + 1
LEFT$(S$,4)	LEFT$(Z$,4)	LEFT$(S$,4)	LEFT$(Z$,4)	Not Available
RIGHT$(A$,6)	RIGHT$(A$,6)	RIGHT$(A$,6)	RIGHT$(A$,6)	Not Available
MID$(W$,3,2)	MID$(W$,3,2)	MID$(W$,3,2)	MID$(W$,3,2)	Not Available
GOTO 120	GOTO 120	GOTO 120	GOTO 120	GOTO 120
IF A<B THEN 25	IF A<B THEN 25	IF A<B THEN 25	IF A<B THEN 25	IF A<B THEN 25
GOSUB 1000	GOSUB 1000	GOSUB 1000	GOSUB 1000	GOSUB 1000
RETURN	RETURN	RETURN	RETURN	RETURN
FOR K=1 TO 5 STEP 2	FOR K = 1 TO 5 STEP 2	FOR K = 1 TO 5 STEP 2	FOR K =1 TO 5 STEP 2	FOR K=1 TO 5 STEP 2
NEXT K	NEXT K	NEXT K	NEXT K	NEXT K
REM COMMENT	REM COMMENT	REM COMMENT	REM COMMENT	REM COMMENT
END	END	END	END	END
READ A,B$	READ A,B$	READ A,B$	READ A,B$	Not Available
DATA 3,TERRI	DATA 3,TERRI	DATA 3,TERRI	DATA 3,TERRI	Not Available
RESTORE	RESTORE	RESTORE	RESTORE	Not Available
INPUT X, R$	INPUT X, R$	INPUT X,R$	INPUT X, R$	INPUT X,R$
PRINT A, B; C	PRINT A, B; C	PRINT A, B; C	PRINT A, B; C	PRINT A, B; C
PRINT TAB(3);A	PRINT TAB(3);A	PRINT TAB(3);A	PRINT TAB(3);A	PRINT TAB(3);A
PRINT "hold SHIFT , press CLR"	PRINT "hold SHIFT , press CLR"	CLS	PRINT "hold SHIFT , press CLR"	CLS

GLOSSARY

Abacus (20)   an aid to calculation, using markers, strung on wires, cords, or rods to record results of arithmetic operations.

Accumulating (291)   adding, each time a number is read or entered, using a variable called the accumulator to store the sum.

Accumulator (160)   a special register, or storage space, in the Central Processing Unit. Results of the work of the Arithmetic Logic Unit are stored in the accumulator.

Address (127)   the number of a memory location.

Address buffer (160)   a storage space in the Central Processing Unit. It keeps track of the addresses of locations of instructions and data.

Address bus (160)   a special track which carries information about data·locations.

Algorithm (287)   a set of steps to relate data collected to solve a particular problem.

Amplifier (240)   a device that magnifies, or strengthens, signals.

Analog computer (108)   a computer using continuous and changing information. Analog computers can also simulate, or represent, changing events.

Analogy (109)   a relationship.

Applications programmer (351)   writes programs for special purposes or applications.

Argument (267)   the number variable to be acted on by a function.

Arithmetic Logic Unit (127)   the component that performs computations and comparisons.

Arithmetic Register (127)   the part of the Arithmetic Logic Unit that holds a number being used in an arithmetic operation. The result of the operation is then stored in the arithmetic register.

Arithmetic statements (73)   use an = symbol, even when no arithmetic is to be done, to assign values to variables.

Array (310)   a list or a set of numbers or strings.

Arrow (190)   indicates the direction or flow of the process shown in a flow chart.

Artificial intelligence (9)   a branch of computer science.

Assembler (386)   a program which translates an assembly language program into machine language.

Assembly language (386)   a low level language made up of codes called mnemonics. The codes are abbreviations for the computer's primitive operations. They must be translated by other programs, called assemblers, into machine language.

Backup (67)   copy a disk.

Bar code (2)   computer coded number used for labeling things.

Bar code readers (2, 144)   peripheral that reads the marks on packages.

Base two system (88)   See binary system.

BASIC (26)   stands for, and is made up of, the first letter in each of the words, Beginners All-purpose Symbolic Instruction Code. It is the most popular conversational computer language and the one understood by most microcomputers.

Binary system (88)   groups numbers by twos and uses two digits, zero and one, to write any number. Also called the base two system.

Bit (160)   a signal to a computer, usually represented by a binary digit.

Block (185)   a group of program statements.

Block diagram (185)   an illustration used in designing a program.

Branching instruction (128)   sends a new number to a computer's instruction pointer. The computer skips to the instruction indicated instead of following instructions in numerical order.

Branching to Repeat (196)   uses a decision statement to repeat an instruction. The program flow continues when the computer's question is answered YES.

Branching to Select (196)   uses a decision to test a value. If the answer to the computer question is YES, one set of steps, or branch, is completed. If the answer to the question is NO, another branch is completed.

BREAK (91)   pressed to stop an infinite loop.

Bronze box (109)   a model of part of the solar system. The models of the sun, planets, and moon could be moved to represent the movement of the real things. The box was used to help sailors find their course, or direction. It was an analog computer.

Bubble memory (334)   a memory that does not depend on electricity to retain information.

Buffer (160)   a storage space in the Central Processing Unit.

Build (373)   create a data file.

Bus (160)   a track which connects the Central Processing Unit to a printed circuit board and to the rest of the computer. Plural form: busses.

Byte (144)   usually a set of eight binary digits, or bits.

Calculate (20)   compute or perform arithmetic operations.

Carriage Return (24)   the movement of the cursor to the next line on the video screen, caused by pressing RETURN or ENTER

Cassette (143)   See magnetic tape.

Catalog (68)   a record of the names of all the programs and collections of information stored and the place where they are written on a disk. (See directory)

CATALOG (68)   a command used by Apple computers to display a disk catalog.

Cell (366)   each position on the spreadsheet.

Central Processing Unit (128)   the Control Unit and the Arithmetic Logic Unit. It may also be called the CPU or processor.

Character Generator (143)   the part of the computer that contains patterns of dots to match the codes of the keyboard.

Chip (22)   a small piece of silicon engraved with electrical circuits and parts.

Circuit (22, 126)   an unbroken path which electricity takes from its source, through the devices it runs, back to the place it started.

CLEAR (345)   reserves extra space for strings in TRS 80s.

Clearscreen (25)   NOT a BASIC statement. Each computer has its own special command for clearing the screen.

CMD (68)   a command used by TRS-80 computers to execute a DOS command from BASIC.

Compact disks (240)   digital disks to record music to be played by lasers.

Compiled language (386)   a high level language which is translated to machine language by a compiler.

Compiler (386)   a program to translate an entire program to machine language, before it is run.

Component (127)   a part of a computer. The major components are: Input Unit, Output Unit, Memory, Arithmetic Logic Unit, and Control Unit.

Computation (38)   an arithmetic operation.

Computer Assisted Instruction (CAI) (4)   computer programs designed to teach.

Computer network (109)   a system to connect computers, usually using telephone wires, so users can share information. Some networks connect microcomputers to minicomputers and mainframes.

Computer programmers (59)   people who write programs.

Computer science (9)   the study of computers.

Computer terminal (3)   equipment that looks like a keyboard and TV screen.

Computerized appliances (334)   household appliances directed or controlled by a computer to drill, test, and record progress.

Console (351)   the input unit of a mainframe or a minicomputer.

Contents (127)   the number stored in a memory location.

Control Bus (160)   a special track, connecting the Central Processing Unit with the rest of the computer, to carry directions for data entry.

Control key (367)   one of a computer's keys which, when pressed first, tells the computer that the next keystroke is a command.

Control Unit (127)   a computer component that directs all of the computer's operations.

Coordinates (239)   the numbers that tell how far over and how far down a point is located.

Coordinate (366)   the column-row position of a cell in a spreadsheet.

Counting (109)   the process of assigning numbers, beginning with one, and continuing in order until each item being counted has a number. The last number matched tells the count—how many there are.

CPU (128)   See Central Processing Unit.

Crashed (378)   stopped running.

Cursor (24, 160)   a small, perhaps blinking, square of light on the video screen. It tells where the next character typed will appear.

Daisy wheel printer (144)   a peripheral named for its print head, a hub with 96 or more arms arranged around it like the petals of a daisy. The characters on the end of the arms press against an inked ribbon.

Data (127)   information to be computed or stored.

Data bank (304)   a store of information in data files.

Data base (206, 361)   a collection of information in files.

Data base management system (361)   a software package that helps organize data.

Data bus (160) a special track that carries information from the Central Processing Unit to the computer's memory.

Data file (206) See file.

Data processing (205) entering, filing, sorting, arranging, combining, finding, and displaying data.

Demodulation (144) the changing of signals that come over telephone lines into computer pulses.

Diamond (192) the flow chart symbol for decisions. It has only one arrow pointing into it and two arrows pointing out.

Difference (39) the result of subtraction.

Digital computer (108) a computer using digits, or separate pieces of information. Digital computers work with numeric instructions.

Digital data (12) numbers representing every part of a picture.

Digital plotter (239) See plotter.

Digitization (12) a process whereby high-speed pictures are used to produce computer graphics.

Digitizer (144) a peripheral that converts visual images to digital information.

Digitizing tablet (239) an input device. A stylus can be moved over the shape to be drawn. When the stylus is stopped, a button is used to send the computer the coordinates of the point the stylus is touching.

DIM (310) tells the maximum number of values to be expected in a list or array.

Directory (68) See catalog.

Disk (144) See magnetic disk.

Disk drive (144) a peripheral used to read from and store data on a magnetic disk.

Disk operating system (66) (DOS) a special set of commands to direct the actions of a disk drive.

Display chip (239) determines the smallest amount of screen space the user can control.

Document (356) text typed into a word processor.

Documentation (217) directions, instructions, remarks, or comments to help a person read or run a program.

Dot matrix printer (144) a printer that uses a rectangle of pins, which can be directed to form character images. The pins press against an inked ribbon.

Drive program (243) the part of a program that calls a subroutine. After the subroutine is executed, the drive program continues.

Editing (358) adding a line, dropping a line, or making changes in a line of a program.

Electrodes (51) used in transistors to do the work of the wires and plates of vacuum tubes.

Electronic (50) using vacuum tubes, special conductors, or semiconductors, such as transistors, to control the movement of electrons. Electrical devices use metal conductors.

Electronic bank tellers (334) computerized devices to take deposits, cash checks, and make loans.

Electronic Data Processing (351) a job field made possible by computers.

Electronic mail (334) communications sent by one computer to another.

ENIAC (51) the first electronic computer. Its name is an acronym for its title, Electronic Numerical Integrator and Calculator.

END (90) used to mark the last step in a computer program.

ENTER (24) sends information into the computer.

Error handling (376) the way a program traps or catches errors made by the user.

Error Trapping (179) includes using IF-THEN statements to prevent the entry of numbers that are obviously wrong.

Exit (377) quit a program.

Field (data) (205, 362) a unit of data.

Fields (24) evenly-spaced areas, across the video screen. Commas in PRINT statements tell the computer to display data in fields.

File (data) (205, 360) a collection of data records.

File names (358) required by word processing programs for saved material.

First generation (51) usually dated from the invention of UNIVAC 1, in 1951.

Flag (176) a value used in an IF-THEN statement to tell the computer to stop reading data when the flag is read.

Floppy disk (144) See magnetic disk.

Flow chart (189) an illustration that indicates program steps in order. It can be a useful tool to help understand or plan programs.

Forecast (370) predict.

FORMAT (66) a command used by TRS-80 computers to prepare a disk for use.

FOR-NEXT (95) used together they, and all statements between them, form a loop. The FOR statement labels a variable, and gives it a beginning and an ending value. All program steps, to the NEXT statement, are done as many times as the ending value of the index directs.

FOSDIC (14) stands for Film Optical Sensory Device for Input to the Computer; it stores information on magnetic tape.

Fourth generation (52) began with the invention of the monolithic integrated circuit, used as a microcomputer to produce microcomputers.

Gate (160) a combination of switches in a computer.

Gigabyte (334) one billion bytes.

`GOSUB` (244) calls a subroutine. `GOSUB` is followed by the number of the line that begins the subroutine.

`GOTO` (91) tells the computer to skip to the line named after `GOTO`.

Graphic display (238) a picture of information, prepared by special software from user data.

Graphics (6) computer pictures.

Graphics pad (144) a peripheral to translate visual symbols to instructions the computer can understand.

Great Brass Brain (110) the name of an early analog computer, built to help predict tides.

Hard copy (358) a paper copy of a document.

Hard disk (144) See magnetic disk.

Hardware (354) the computer and any devices connected to it.

Help screen (377) display of needed information.

Hex (382) See Hexidecimal system.

Hexidecimal system (386) a number system that is based on 16. It uses 16 digits and groups numbers by sixteens.

High level language (386) one that uses words instead of numbers or mnemonics to instruct the computer. It must be translated, by a compiler or an interpreter, into machine language.

High resolution graphics (239) graphics which use as many as 50,000 pixels to create illustrations.

Home keys (26) the keys on which a typist's fingers rest in a standard hand position.

Identifiers (374) markers.

`IF-THEN` (168) changes the path through a program. The `IF` part of the statement asks a computer question. The `THEN` part directs the computer to change the program path if the answer is `YES`.

Index (95) the variable of a `FOR-NEXT` loop. Plural form: indices.

Industrial robots (8) computers that can perform physical tasks.

Infinite (91) a mathematician's word for unending. An infinite loop is one that continues until stopped by pressing the `BREAK` key.

Information network (334) See computer network.

Information processing (16) using computers to remember and organize information.

`INIT` (67) a command used by Apple computers to prepare a disk for use.

Initialize (209, 287) the part of a program that gets data ready. Variables are named and their beginning values given.

Inner loop (116) a loop that lies inside another loop.

Input (23) anything entered through the keyboard (or other devices).

Input/Output buffer (160) a storage space in the Central Processing Unit that regulates the input and output of data.

Input/Output (symbol) (190) the parallelogram used in flow charts to indicate `READ`, `INPUT`, and `PRINT` instructions.

`INPUT` (131) stops the program, displays a ?, and waits for data (information) to be entered, or input.

Input unit (127) usually a keyboard. Other devices can be used to input, or enter, information.

Instruction (127) information used to direct a computer's actions.

Instruction pointer (127) the part of the Control Unit that holds the memory address of the computer's next instruction.

Instruction register (127) a storage space to hold the instruction indicated by the instruction pointer, when that instruction is brought to the Control Unit.

`INT` (266) changes a number, called the argument, into the largest integer which is less than or equal to the argument.

Integrated Circuit (51) a chip that does the work of wires, tubes, and transistors.

Integrated software (372) groups of programs that can work together.

Interpreter (386, 160) a program that changes a language such as BASIC into machine language, line by line, as the program runs.

Intervention (258) a change in an environment.

Jet ink printer (239) shoots tiny dots of colored ink onto paper. Jet ink printers can make the dots overlap, to create different shades of colors.

Joy stick (144) a peripheral. Its movement sends coded electronic signals to the computer.

Jumping instruction (128) sends a new number to the instruction pointer. The computer skips to that instruction instead of continuing to follow instructions in numerical order.

Keyboard (23) an input device that lets the user type numbers and other characters and send them into the computer.

Key fields (362) the fields the computer searches when it sorts the data base.

Key words (360) headings that identify types of programs.

Label (213) a statement to explain output displayed by a program.

Left-justified (368) moved to the left side of the cell.

LEFT$ (278) selects certain characters of a string, beginning the choice at the left of the string.

LEN (279) calculates the length of a string, to find the number of characters it contains.

Letter (71) used to store information in the computer's memory. The letter is called a variable and it names a storage area in memory.

Light pen (5, 144) a device that enables a computer to locate a spot at which it is pointed.

Line number (54) tells the computer to store, or save, the instruction that follows.

LIST (55) directs the computer to display the stored program lines. They are LISTed in order of line numbers.

LOAD (66) a command that directs a computer to copy what is read by the disk drive into its internal, temporary memory.

Locations (127) storage spaces in a computer's memory.

Logic errors (336) errors which produce incorrect answers when a program is run. They are not detected by the computer.

Looping (95) one or more statements, being repeated as a program runs.

Lower character (24) the character on the bottom of a key.

Low level language (383) one which uses numerals or mnemonics to direct the computer's primitive operations.

Low resolution graphics (239) graphics using as few as two or three thousand pixels.

Machine language (385) programs written in patterns of ones and zeroes. These patterns of binary digits are a code for ons and offs. They can be "understood" by the computer.

Magnetic disk (127) can be used to store computer data and instructions. Information recorded on the disk by a special input/output device called a disk drive. The surface of the disk records data as magnetic marks.

Magnetic tape (127) may be on a reel or a cassette. Instructions or data for a computer are stored as magnetic marks on the tape by a tape or cassette player. The information can be reentered by playing the tape.

Mainframe (108) a large computer, or computer system. Usually, mainframes are accessed by terminals.

Main menu (355) a list of the tasks a program can perform.

Main program (243) the part of a program that calls a subroutine. After the subroutine is executed, the main program continues.

Measure (109) match an item to a standard unit, such as a meter, a quart, or a pound.

Megabyte (144) one million bytes.

Memory (127) See memory unit.

Memory unit (127) the component that stores information and instructions.

Microcomputer (109) a computer which uses a microprocessor and which is small in size.

Microprocessor (51) a complete computer, containing all of the important components, on a single chip of silicon.

MID (278) selects certain characters, beginning the selection at a particular character of a string.

Minicomputer (109) a smaller version of a mainframe. It may be accessed by terminals.

Mini floppy disk (144) See magnetic disk.

Mnemonics (386) abbreviations for a computer's primitive operations.

Modem (144) an input/output peripheral device that can change the computer's pattern of electric pulses into signals that can be sent over telephone wires. It can also change the signals that come over the telephone lines back into computer pulses.

Modulation (144) changing the computer's patterned electric pulses into signals that can be sent over telephone wires.

Modulator (143) translates patterns of dots contained in the character generator to signals that the video tube can interpret.

Module (185) a piece of a program or a block of program statements.

Monolithic integrated circuit (52) a combination of integrated circuits, on one chip. Some of these are called microprocessors, and are complete computers.

Nanosecond (334)   one billionth of a second.

Napier's rods (20)   rods marked with numerals, which can be used as an aid in multiplying.

Nested loops (116)   two (or more) loops, made up of an outer loop and inner loop(s). The inner loop must lie entirely within the outer loop.

NEW (25, 55)   tells the computer to clear out, or empty, everything. This command is used before entering a new program.

Numeric (206)   in number form.

Numeric constant (38)   a number.

Numeric subscripted variable (309)   used to store numeric values in a list or an array. The variable identifies the list and the subscript gives the position of the value in the list or array.

Numeric variable (71)   a letter used to label or name a storage area for a number.

On-screen formatting (358)   provided by some word processing programs to permit the user to see how a document looks on the screen before it is printed.

OPEN (67)   a command used by Commodore 64 computers in preparing a disk for use.

Optical mark readers (144)   input devices which can read certain kinds of type.

Outer loop (116)   a loop that lies outside another loop.

Output (23)   anything that is displayed on the video screen (or sent to a peripheral).

Output (209, 287)   the part of a program that displays the answers or information calculated in the program.

Output unit (127)   a computer component. It is often a video screen but may be any device that can store, display, or make a record of the computer's work.

Peripheral (143, 3)   device attached to a computer.

Picosecond (334)   one trillionth of a second.

Pixel (239)   the smallest amount of screen space the user can control.

Plotter (144, 239)   an output device which is directed by number (digital) codes. The digital plotter used for graphics has a robot arm that can select pens of different colors to draw graphs and charts. Plotters can also produce transparencies of graphics. Plotters are directed by special software.

Pointer (data) (226)   keeps track of DATA items READ.

Primitive computer operations (88)   the simple operations a computer is able to perform.

PRINT (38)   tells the computer to display information on the screen.

Printed circuit boards (52)   (PC boards) plastic boards, coated with metal to serve as wires, used for connecting chips.

Printer (127, 144)   a peripheral which is used to produce paper copies of a computer's output or program listing.

Printout (3)   output of a computer, printed on paper.

Process (209, 287)   the part of a program that makes the computer do the calculating or other work needed for the desired output.

Process (symbol) (190)   the rectangle used in flow charts to indicate arithmetic operations. It is also used to indicate the assignment of values to variables.

Processor (128)   the Central Processing Unit.

Product (39)   the result of multiplication.

PROFS (15)   (Program for Regional Observing and Forecasting Services) a computerized weather system.

Program (4, 55, 87)   any set of instructions stored in a computer's memory, using line numbers.

Program bug (336)   error that keeps a program from running, or from giving correct answers.

Programmers (87)   See computer programmers.

Prompt (160, 24)   a signal on the video screen that the computer is ready for the user to do something.

Prompt (138, 213)   a message for a program user. It tells what kind of information to enter.

Punched cards (127)   used to store or to enter computer information. A special device called a card punch or a key punch is used to prepare the cards. A card reader sends information from the cards into the computer. Electrical current can pass through the card's holes and an on signal is sent to the computer. Where there is no hole, no signal—an off—is sent to the computer's switches.

Quotient (39)   the result of division.

RAM (160)   See Random Access Memory.

Random Access Memory (160)   user memory. Programs and data are stored in random access memory, called RAM. RAM is temporary and is emptied when the computer is turned off.

READ-DATA (147)   a READ statement tells the computer to search for a DATA statement and assign the information listed there to the variables of the READ statement.

Read light (60)   a small red light on the front of a disk drive.

Read/Only Memory (160)   permanent memory. Instructions to direct the operations of the computer and an interpreter, to translate the programming language, BASIC, into machine language are stored there. A user cannot store anything in the read-only memory, or ROM.

Read/write head (66)   a part of a disk drive which "reads" information from a disk and "writes" information on a disk.

Record (data) (205)   a set of related fields.

Record (360)   each individual item in a file.

Reel to reel tape (144)   See magnetic tape.

Register (160)   a special memory location in the Central Processing Unit. It holds information the CPU needs to use often.

Relay (35)   an electrically-operated switch to control and direct electrical current.

REM (216)   allows the programmer to include messages or remarks in a program. When the program is run, the computer ignores REM statements. When a program is listed, the statements are shown.

Replicate (369)   repeat an entry or formula throughout a row or column of a spreadsheet.

RESTORE (227)   moves the data pointer back to the first item in the first DATA statement in a program. This permits all of the data to be READ again.

(RETURN)   (24)   sends information into the computer.

(RETURN)   (statement) (244)   sends a program back to the drive, or main, program statement immediately following a GOSUB statement. RETURN is the last statement of a subroutine.

Right-justified (368)   moved to the right side of the cell.

RIGHT$ (278)   selects characters from a string, beginning the selection at the right of the string.

RND (272)   instructs the computer to produce a random number between 0 and 1.

Robotics (334, 351)   the science of machines that can be directed by computers to do some of the things done by people or animals.

ROM (160)   See Read-Only Memory.

RUN (55)   makes the computer complete or execute the program stored in memory. It begins with the statement having the lowest line number and takes each statement in order.

SAVE (66)   a command to "write" information on a disk.

Scaling factor (223)   a number that tells how many items a symbol represents.

Scanner (8)   a code reading device.

Scrolling (357)   a function of a word processing program that moves the text vertically or horizontally on the screen.

Second generation (51)   computers that began in the early 1960s, when transistors replaced vacuum tubes.

Self-booting (377)   loaded as the system is turned on.

(SHIFT LOCK) (25)   allows the use of upper characters.

Silicon (57, 159)   a common, non-metallic element used in making integrated circuits.

Simulation (4, 257)   a program that allows a user to experience a special situation and make decisions that affect what happens.

Simulators (10)   devices used to test a product or to train people to use it.

Software (4, 206)   programs.

Source (369)   the cell containing the entry to be replicated on a spreadsheet.

Spacebar (25)   allows spaces to be included, when typing.

Spreadsheet (365)   a table of numerical data, with the rows and columns related by mathematical formulas.

String (42)   See string constant.

String constant (42)   anything inside quotation marks, in a PRINT statement.

String subscripted variable (320)   used to name a list of strings. Subscripts identify each item in the list.

String variables (77)   a variable name, including a $ sign (read "string"), which is used to store letters and other characters.

Structure (185)   the organization of a program's parts.

Subprogram (210)   a small, separate part of a larger program.

Subroutine (243)   a set of computer statements which can be executed from any place in the program. After execution of the subroutine, the program flow continues from the point at which the subroutine was called.

Subscripting (311)   assigning values of a list or array to one variable, and identifying each value in the list by its position.

Sum (39)   the result of addition.

Syntax error (60, 336)   error in spelling, punctuation, vocabulary, and form. It is detected by the computer.

Synthesizers (240)   special chips that permit a computer to be programmed to make sounds or to produce music.

System command (55)   a special instruction that tells the computer what to do with a stored program. System commands should not have line numbers.

System analyst (351)   a planner who determines the kinds of hardware and software that is needed. The Systems analyst decides where computers should be installed, how they should be used, and who should use them.

Systems programmer (351)   produces operating programs for computer systems.

T A B (261)   instructs the computer to indent, counting from the first print position on the left.

Target (369)   the cells where an entry is to be copied.

Telecommuting (333)   using a computer at home to communicate with a business or office computer, through telephone lines, instead of travelling to work.

Teleconferencing (333)   conducting meetings using computers and a network. People who teleconference do not meet physically.

Terminal (109)   a station connected to a mainframe or minicomputer for the input and output of data.

Terminal (symbol) (190)   the flow chart symbol that marks the beginning and the end of a program.

Thermal printer (144)   a printer that shoots sparks at heat sensitive paper to produce images of characters.

Third generation (51)   began with the invention of the integrated circuit, and its use in computers to replace vacuum tubes and transistors.

Timing loop (113)   used to slow the computer's output.

Top-down (186)   a kind of block diagram used to plan a program's structure.

Trailer record (198)   used to test a value to end the reading or entry of data.

Transistors (51)   non-metallic material, imprinted with electrodes, to act as switches. The material is sealed in a small container and connected to other electrical devices using fine wires.

Transphasors (334)   optical switches.

UNIVAC I (51)   the first computer to be mass produced. Its invention is usually considered the beginning of the first generation of computers.

Universal Product Code (UPC) (8)   special labels on supermarket goods that can be read by a computer.

Upper character (24)   the character appearing on the top of some of the keys.

Users group (360)   a group of people who usually own the same kind of computer.

Vacuum tube (50)   a glass or metal device, somewhat like a light bulb. Electrons are given off by the tube's wire when it is heated by electrical current coming into the tube. A metal plate catches the electrons. The tube can regulate the amount of electricity flowing through it, as a switch does.

Value (70)   the information stored in a memory location named by a variable.

Variable (70)   used by the computer to store information. The variable names the storage place in the computer's memory.

VERIFY (68)   a command used by Commodore 64 computers to verify a program SAVE.

Very Large Scale Integrated Circuits (334) (VLSI)   chips capable of doing the work of thousands of integrated circuits.

Video digitizer (239)   an input device that translates pictures into data that records shades and tones of colors in the form of numbers that the computer can understand.

Video disk (334)   can be used for data storage.

Video screen (23)   like a television screen. It allows a computer user to see what is typed. It displays the computer's work.

Wand (7)   device attached to a computerized cash register that reads information from merchandise tags.

Word processor (352)   a person who uses a computer to prepare and print letters and other written materials.

Word processors (16)   computer programs used to type, edit, and revise written material.

Word wrap (357)   a function of a word processing program that automatically, as you reach the end of a line, takes the first letters of the last word and moves them to the beginning of the next line.

Write-enable notch (66)   a rectangular notch in a disk jacket. When it is not covered, a disk drive can write information on the disk.

Write-protect tab (66)   a tab used to cover a disk's write-enable notch to prevent the disk drive from writing information on the disk.

INDEX

A

abacus, 20
accumulating, 291
accumulator, 160, 291
ADA, 186
adding machine, 20, 34
address, 127, 160
address buffers, 160
address bus, 160
Aiken, Howard, 35
algorithm, 287
analog computer, 108, 109
analog device, 287
analogy, 109
Analytical Engine, 34
animated graphics, 239
Applications:
  Mixing Variables, 80
  Nested Loops, 116, 118
  Problem Solving, 176
  Whitney's Special, 344
argument, 267
arithmetic, 39, 73, 127
Arithmetic Logic
  Unit, 127, 128, 160, 205
arithmetic register, 127
arithmetic statement, 73, 74, 75, 78
arithmetic symbols, 39
array, 310
arrow symbol, 190
artificial intelligence, 9
assembler, 383
assembly language, 383
average, 138, 290, 295
average time, 104

B

Babbage, Charles, 34, 384
Backus, John, 383
bar code reader, 144, 205
bar graph, 220, 222, 262
base sixteen, 382
base ten, 88, 382
base two, 88
BASIC, 26, 383
  arithmetic symbols, 39
  commands:
    LIST, 55
    NEW, 25, 55
    RUN, 55
    system, 55

decision symbols, 173
functions:
  argument, 267
  LEFT$, 277
  LEN, 279
  MID$, 277
  RIGHT$, 277
  RND, 272
  TAB, 261
instructions, 38
statements:
  CLEAR, 345
  DIM, 308, 310
  END, 90, 91, 191, 245
  FOR-NEXT, 95, 100, 103,
    113
  GOSUB, 244
  GOTO, 91, 168
  IF-THEN, 168
  INPUT, 131
  PRINT, 38
  READ-DATA, 146
  REM, 216
  RESTORE, 227
  RETURN, 244
  STEP, 100
Bell Laboratories, 51
binary digit, 382
binary system, 88, 382
bit, 160, 382
Boole, George, 35
Boolean Algebra, 35
branching instructions, 128
branching to repeat, 196
branching to select, 196
BREAK key, 91, 93, 99, 172
bronze box, 109
bubble memory, 334
buffer:
  address, 160
  input/output, 160
bug, program, 336
built-in functions, 369
Burroughs, William, 35
bus:
  address, 160
  control, 160
  data, 160
Bush, Dr. Vannevar, 110
byte, 144, 382

C

calculations, 99
call, 243
careers, 350
carriage return, 24
cassette, 143
cell, 366
census bureau, 14
Central Processing
  Unit, 127, 128, 160
Challenger, 288
character, 24
character generator, 143
chip, 22, 51, 128
Chip Circuitry, 22
chip manufacture, 159
C11-Honeywell-Bull, 383
circuit, 22, 51, 126, 159
  integrated, 22, 51
  monolithic integrated, 52
CLEAR, 345
clear accumulator, 291
Clearscreen, 25
clock, 160
CLS, 25
COBOL, 383
code, 127, 382, 206, 239
COLUMBIA, 288
columns, 220
comma, 39, 40, 147, 148, 220,
  337
compiled language, 383
compiler, 383
components:
  Arithmetic Logic
    Unit, 127, 128, 160, 205
  Control Unit, 127, 128
  Input Unit, 127
  Memory Unit, 127
  Output unit, 127
computation, 38
compute, 46
computer:
  -aided design, 10
  analog, 108, 109
  animation, 13
  arithmetic, 73
  careers, 350
  components, 127, 160
  digital, 108
  electro-mechanical, 35

electronic, 50
future, 334
generations, 51
history, 20, 35, 50
kinds, 51, 108
languages, 383
literacy, 4
microcomputer, 52, 109
minicomputer, 51, 109
networks, 109
operations, 126, 160
peripherals, 143
prehistoric, 20
primitive operations, 88, 383
programmers, 87, 206, 351
programs, 59
questions, 164
uses, 205, 238, 257, 288, 304
Computerized:
    appliances, 334
    teaching, 334
confidential, 304
console, 351
constant:
    numeric, 38
    string, 42
contents, 127
control bus, 160
Control Unit, 127, 128
coordinates, 239, 366
counting, 20, 91, 102, 103, 104
CPU, 127, 160, 383
credit rating, 305
cursor, 24, 130, 133, 160

D

daisy wheel printer, 144
Dartmouth College, 383
DATA, 247, 340
data, 127, 147, 205
data bank, 304
data base, 206, 258, 361
data bus, 160
data entry clerks, 351
data processing, 35, 160, 205
data security, 305
debugging, 337
decimal system, 88
decision, 192
decision symbols, 173
Department of Defense, 383
diamond symbol, 173
difference, 39
Difference Engine, 34
digit, 20
digital, 239
digital computer, 109
digital plotter, 239
digital signal, 288
digitizer, 144

digitizing tablet, 239
DIM, 310
disk, 144, 205
disk drive, 144
display chip, 239
division by zero, 338
documentation, 217
dollar sign, 77
dot matrix printer, 144
draftspersons, 351
drive program, 243, 248

E

Eckert, J. Presper, 51
Edison, Thomas A., 50
editing, 59
electrical current, 35, 126
Electrical impulses, 127
Electron, 50
electronic bank tellers, 334
electronic mail, 334
electronic parts, 159
END, 90, 153, 176, 191, 245
engineer, 350
ENIAC, 51
ENTER key, 24
equal symbol, 73
error handling, 376
error messages, 60, 137, 177,
    225, 251
    error trapping, 178
    errors:
    division by zero, 338
    editing, 59
    human, 206
    INPUT, 137
    logic, 336, 340
    numbers out of range, 343
    out of data, 337
    out of memory, 252
    READ-DATA, 337
    subscript out of range, 343
    syntax, 60, 336, 337
    trapping, 178

F

FBI, 305
Felt, D.E., 35
field (data), 205
fields, 40, 43
file, 205, 360
Fisher, E.G., 110
flag, 176
flow chart, 189, 290, 340
flow chart symbols, 190
form letters, 373
force platform, 12
FOR-NEXT, 95, 100, 103, 113
FORTRAN, 383

G

gate, 160, 382
General Motors, 334
generating data, 296
gigabyte, 334
GOSUB, 244
GOTO, 91, 168
GR.O, 25
graphics:
    display, 238
    input, 239
    pad, 144
    resolution, 239
    pixels, 239
    uses, 239
Great Brass Brain, 110

H

hard copy, 358
hard disk, 144
hardware, 206, 239, 305, 354
Harris, Rollin A., 110
hex digit, 382
hexidecimal system, 382
high level language, 383
high resolution, 239
Hollerith, Herman, 35
HOME, 25
Hopper, Commodore Grace, 383

I

IBM, 383
IC, 51
IF-THEN, 168, 176
ident, 261
index, 95, 116
infinite, 91
infinite loop, 91, 93
information, 19, 304
initial value, 291
initialize, 209, 263, 273
Initialize, Output,
    Process, 209, 263, 273, 287, 317
inner loop, 116
input, 23, 35, 291
INPUT, 131, 340
input devices, 143, 205
INPUT errors, 337
Input Unit, 127
input/output buffer, 160
input/output symbol, 190
instruction, 55, 87, 127
instruction pointer, 127
instruction register, 127
instructor, 351
INT function, 267
integrated circuit, 22, 51
interpreter, 160, 383

J

Jacquard, Joseph M., 35
jet ink printer, 239
joystick, 144, 239
jump, 92, 99, 245

K

Kemeny, John, 383
Kettering, Charles, 334
keyboard, 23, 88, 126, 143, 205
keys:
   BREAK, 91, 93, 99
   ENTER, 24
   lower character, 24
   RETURN, 24
   SHIFT, 25
   similar, 26
   spacebar, 25
   upper character, 24
Kurtz, Thomas, 383

L

label, 214, 340
languages, 383
left-justified, 368
LEFT$, 277
Leibnitz, Gottfried, 34
LEN, 279
letter, 70
librarian, 351
light pen, 144
line number, 54, 152, 167
line, skip, 139
list, 310
LIST, 55
locations, 127
logic error, 336, 340
logical sequence, 189
LOGO, 384
loom, 34
loop:
   FOR-NEXT, 95
   GOTO, 91
   infinite, 91
   inner, 116
   nested, 116
   outer, 116
   timing, 113
looping, 95
Lovelace, Lady Ada, 34, 384
lower character, 24
low level language, 383
low resolution, 239

M

machine language, 382
machinists, 351
magnetic disk, 127
magnetic tape, 127
mailboxes, 71, 127

mainframe, 108
main program, 243
marked card reader, 205
MARK 1, 35, 51
Mauchly, John M., 51
measure, 109
megabyte, 144, 334
memory:
   address, 127, 160
   bubble, 334
   contents, 127
   RAM, 160
   Random Access, 160
   Read Only, 160
   ROM, 160
Memory Bank Deposits:
   Accumulating a Sum, 292
   Accumulating loops, 294
   Arithmetic symbols, 39
   Blocking subroutine entry, 251
   Branching, 196
   Columns of output, 220
   Computer Programmers, 59
   DATA, 153
   Decision symbols, 173
   DIM statement form, 310
   DIM, 321
   Documentation, 217
   Editing Tips, 59
   Subroutines, entry, 251
   Flow Charts, 189
   FOR-NEXT form, 95
   FOR-NEXT index, 95
   GOTO form, 93
   $1 = 1 + 1$, 100
   IF-THEN, 169
   Input errors, 138
   INPUT Prompts, 213
   INPUT, 131
   INPUTting strings, 134
   INT Function, 267
   Labels, 214
   LEFT$, 278
   Letters, Variables, and Numeric
      Variables, 71
   Line Number, 54, 59
   MID$, 279
   Nested Loops, 116
   Numeric Variables, 71
   Numeric Subscripted Variables,
      310, 311
   PRINT, 45
   PRINT and INPUT, 232
   Program Planning, 209
   Questions, 164
   READ-DATA Form, 160
   RESTORE, 227
   RIGHT$, 278
   RND, 272
   Strings, 43, 131

String Variables, 77
   Subprograms, 210
   Subroutines, 243
   TAB, 262
   Timing Loops, 113
Memory Unit, 127
microcomputer, 109, 383
microprocessor, 52, 109, 124, 159
MID$, 277
minicomputer, 51, 109
mini floppy, 144
mixing letters and digits, 337
mixing and combining, 121
mnemonics, 383
modem, 144
modulator, 143
monolithic integrated circuit, 52
Mount Saint Helens, 287
mouse, 369
multiplier, 34

N

nanosecond, 334
Napier, Robert, 20
Napier's bones, 20
NASA, 104, 258
nested loops, 116, 118
networks:
   computer, 109
   information, 334
NEW, 25, 55
NOAA, 15
number:
   line, 54, 59
   random, 272
   store in variable, 70
numbers, 88
numbers out of range, 338
numeric:
   code, 206
   constant, 38
   subscripted variable, 309
   variable, 70

O

odometer, 34
operators, 351
optical mark reader, 144
out of data, 163, 177, 337
out of memory, 252
outer loop, 116
output, 23, 121, 209, 35, 274
output device, 127, 143
Output Unit, 127

P

PASCAL, 383
Pascal, Blaise, 34, 383
path, program, 168
peripheral, 143, 334

picosecond, 334
PILOT, 384
piracy, software, 306
pixel, 239
planning, 247
planning around subroutines, 247
plotter, 144, 239
plus sign, 131
pointer:
    data, 226
    instruction, 127
prehistoric, 19
primitive computer
    operations, 88, 383
PRINT, 38
PRINT "♡", 25
printers, 127, 144, 239, 351
privacy, 304
Privacy Act of 1974, 306
problem solving, 176
process symbol, 190
processor, 128
product, 39
product testing, 258
program, 55, 87
    bug, 336
    jump, 90
    line number, 54, 59
    outline, 247
    planning, 209, 247
    writing, 247
Programs:
    Accumulating, 295
    Average, 138, 296, 298
    Average Salary, 290, 293
    Bar Graph, 222
    Billboard, 245
    Birthstone, 170
    Bonus, 174
    Bowling Average, 81
    Clock, 118
    Flipping a Coin, 274
    Garden, 80
    Hours Worked, 317
    Lemonade, 212, 213, 268
    Mixture, 121
    Number Guess, 178
    Psychologist, 179
    Raise the Flag, 215
    Random Messages, 325
    Reversing Names, 280
    Rocket Launch, 103
    Sales Graph, 263
    Sales Report, 178
    Sevens Table, 99
    Slogan Generator, 230, 248
    Song, 176
    Whitney's Special, 345
program outline, 247
programmers, 59, 87, 382, 206, 351

prompt (screen), 160
prompt (user), 138, 213
Problem Sets:
    26, 48, 62, 84, 106, 123, 141,
    156, 180, 201, 234, 254, 282,
    300, 328, 348
punctuation:
    commas, 39, 337
    quotation marks, 42, 43
    semicolons, 39, 40, 43
punched cards, 35, 127, 205

Q
quartz clock, 160
question, 164
quotation marks, 42, 43
quotient, 39

R
RAM, 160
Random Access Memory, 160
random number, 272
READ-DATA, 147
READ-DATA errors, 337
READing data, 147
Read-Only Memory, 160
record keeping, 20, 205, 206
record, data, 205
Redo?, 137
reel-to-reel tape, 144
register:
    accumulator, 160
    arithmetic, 127
    instruction, 127
relays, 35
REM, 216, 244, 247, 340
RESTORE, 227
RETURN key, 24
RETURN, 226, 244
RETURN without GOSUB, 244
right-justified, 368
RIGHT$, 277
RND, 272
robotics, 334, 351
robots, 8, 9
ROM, 160
rounding, 269
RUN, 55

S
salespeople, 351
Sammet, Jean, 383
scaling factor, 223
security, 305
semicolon, 39, 40, 43, 222
sensor, 287
SHIFT, 25
silicon, 51, 128, 159
simulate, 109, 257

simulation, 257
skip, 91, 99
software, 206, 238, 306
    integrated, 372
    self-booting, 377
software piracy, 306
soroban, 20
sort, 35, 206
space, 25, 132, 134, 139, 221
spacebar, 25
spreadsheet program, 365
STEP, 100
storage, 70
storage devices, 351
string, 42, 77
string constant, 42
string sign ($), 77
string subscripted variable, 320
string variable, 77, 133
strings, 131
structured language, 383
suan pan, 20
sub, 311, 322
subprogram, 210
subroutine, 243, 247, 340
    planning around, 247
    writing, 247
Subscript out of Range, 343
subscripting, 311
subscripted variables, 309, 320
sum, 39, 291
summaries:
    26, 48, 61, 83, 105, 122, 140, 155,
    180, 201, 233, 253, 281, 300, 327,
    347
switch, 35, 50, 126, 160, 382
syntax error, 60, 336
system command, 55
systems analyst, 351
systems programmers, 351

T
TAB, 260
tapes, 205
technicians, 355
telecommuting, 333
teleconferencing, 333
terminal, 109
terminal symbol, 190
test value, 198
Texas Instruments, 51
THEN, see IF
thermal printer, 144
thinking error, 340
timing, 104
timing loop, 113, 119
traffic control, 288
trailer record, 198, 297
transistor, 51, 160, 334
transphasors, 334

U

UNIVAC 1, 51
upper character, 24
US Coast and Geodetic Survey, 110
US Department of Labor, 351
US Geological Survey, 287

V

vacuum tube, 22, 50, 51
value, 70

variable:
  name, 70, 77
  numeric, 71
  numeric subscripted, 309
  string, 77
  string subscripted, 320
video digitizer, 239
video disk, 334
video graphics, 239
video screen, 23, 143, 238

W

Wang, Dr. An, 51
Wirth, Nicklaus, 383
word processing, 355
word processors, 351
writers, 351
writing subroutines, 247

Z

Ziller, Irving, 383
zones, 43, 139

Photo Credits